CAMBRIDGE STUDIES IN
MEDIEVAL LIFE AND THOUGHT

Edited by M. D. Knowles, Litt. D., F.B.A.
*Emeritus Regius Professor of Modern History in the
University of Cambridge*

NEW SERIES VOL. XII

THE JUSTICIARSHIP
IN ENGLAND
1066-1232

THE JUSTICIARSHIP
IN ENGLAND
1066-1232

BY

FRANCIS WEST

Professorial Fellow, Institute of Advanced Studies,
Australian National University

CAMBRIDGE
AT THE UNIVERSITY PRESS
1966

PUBLISHED BY
THE SYNDICS OF THE CAMBRIDGE UNIVERSITY PRESS
Bentley House, 200 Euston Road, London, N.W. 1
American Branch: 32 East 57th Street, New York, N.Y. 10022
West African Office: P.M.B. 5181, Ibadan, Nigeria

©

CAMBRIDGE UNIVERSITY PRESS
1966

Printed in Great Britain at the University Printing House, Cambridge
(Brooke Crutchley, University Printer)
LIBRARY OF CONGRESS CATALOGUE
CARD NUMBER: 66-14511

CONTENTS

LIST OF ABBREVIATIONS

Other than contractions of titles which are obvious, the following are the common abbreviations used in this work:

BM	British Museum
CChR	*Calendar of Charter Rolls*
CClR	*Calendar of Close Rolls*
CMH	*Cambridge Medieval History*
CPR	*Calendar of Patent Rolls*
CP 25 (1)	Feet of Fines
EHR	*English Historical Review*
KR	King's Remembrancer Rolls
LTR	Lord Treasurer's Remembrancer Rolls
PRO	Public Record Office
Sc I	Ancient Correspondence
TRHS	*Transactions of the Royal Historical Society*
VHC	*Victoria History of the Counties of England*

INTRODUCTION

Unlike the sheriff and the chancellor, the justiciar has had no historian, although his person, his office, and his duties have inevitably figured in many mediaeval administrative studies. The chief reason for the lack of any major work dealing with the justiciarship is undoubtedly the width and scope of the office. Because he was the king's *alter ego*, any study of his office is of almost the same magnitude as a history of the kingship itself. As soldier and politician, feudal magnate or great bishop, judge and financier, the justiciar had so many and varied aspects that to draw them within the covers of one book is a formidable and difficult task, but it is one of decided value and usefulness, because a study of the justiciarship is an examination of the centre of power in Angevin England, of the heart of English mediaeval government.

The breadth and complications of the justiciarship lead one to an approach which is suggested on other grounds. It is almost a cliché to say that the man was always more important than the office in the early Middle Ages, and that therefore the importance of an office varied with closeness of its holder's relations with the king and perhaps with his feudal significance. This alone would prompt an examination of the justiciarship through its individual tenants, but when the complexity of its duties is so great unity of theme is to be found only in the men who carried them out. This book is therefore as much a history of the justiciars as it is a history of the justiciarship, although such was the utility of the office to the king that it assumed what would later be called a 'constitutional' position within the legal and financial apparatus of government. Both Richard fitz Nigel and Glanville assume in their treatises a formal position, quite apart from any individual holder, around which the exchequer and the legal system revolved. Still, if there is such a 'constitutional' aspect of the justiciarship, the main emphasis must fall upon the individual justiciars.

The scope and complexity of the justiciarship are not the sole difficulties which face its historian; he must also contend with the uneven nature of his material. The political actions of a justiciar were likely enough to attract the attention of chroniclers, but his administrative activity, his control of the technical instruments of power, hardly ever did. Thus it is only when the record evidence survives that a full account of the justiciarship can begin to be offered and, although this begins under Henry II, only with King John does it reach the dimensions required for such a study. This is particularly unfortunate because the reign of Richard I, when the continuous absence of the king afforded great scope to the justiciar, saw the high-water mark of his power and influence, but it cannot be traced in the same detail as under John. Inevitably the evidence tends to distort a history of the justiciarship by the emphasis it places upon Geoffrey fitz Peter's tenure of office which can be examined in greater detail than that of any of his predecessors, although it seems beyond doubt that the justiciar's power and influence reached its greatest height with Hubert Walter. Nevertheless, such detailed examination of Geoffrey fitz Peter's work provides both a definition of the office and a standard of reference.

Notwithstanding these difficulties, the justiciarship deserves an attempt to describe it because of the place it occupied in the development of English government. It was a transient feature which existed for less than a hundred years, but it was an experiment in the delegation of royal power at the highest level which left its mark on the organization of English mediaeval government.

This book took its origin from a suggestion of Professor J. H. Le Patourel who first guided my research, and it owes much to the encouragement of Sir Goronwy Edwards, Professor V. H. Galbraith, and Mr Edward Miller, who continued this guidance. I must also thank Lady Stenton who, in examining my first doctoral dissertation, gave me much valuable criticism and advice, and Professor R. F. Treharne who read the manuscript with such care. One of my greatest debts is to the Master and Fellows of Trinity College, Cambridge, who elected me to a College Research Studentship and gave me the time and leisure to do the bulk of the research upon which the book is based. It need hardly be said that without the patience and courtesy of the officers of the Public Record Office and the British Museum I could scarcely have written the book.

F. W.

Institute of Advanced Studies,
Australian National University

CHAPTER I

THE ORIGINS OF THE JUSTICIARSHIP

The justiciar was the king's *alter ego* whose office met the need for an extension of the king's person and power, a need which came from two cardinal facts of English mediaeval history. The first was that the king personally ruled: he was himself the mainspring of government and his household or court the centre of power. The second was that the king was regularly and frequently abroad because England was part of a continental empire whose other dominions required the royal presence for their government in the same way that England did. Royal power had to be delegated at the highest level if government was to operate smoothly and not in fits and starts. Still, these two facts alone do not explain the justiciarship; they are necessary and not sufficient conditions. If the office be defined as a viceroyalty when the king was abroad, and a superintendence of the machinery of government whether he was abroad or not, then its creation was dependent on three other conditions: the evolution of a regular system of regency, the development of royal administration to the point at which a permanent superintendent was a great convenience or even a necessity, and the fusion of these two positions in a single office.

Such a definition, which is based on Angevin practice, can be used to answer the question: how and when did the justiciarship evolve? The emphasis placed on these different conditions has led historians to offer different answers. If regency be stressed as the essential characteristic, then the Norman Conquest, which linked England to a continental dominion, has an obvious significance as the occasion upon which the need for a regency was introduced; if administrative development be stressed, then the reign of Henry I, that formative but tantalizing period in administrative history, and even more the reign of Henry II, which decisively shaped the pattern of mediaeval government, assume an obvious importance. This definition, therefore, has its dangers, especially those of retrospective judgement, but it is a useful one for purposes of analysis if its drawbacks are borne in mind. It is not difficult to conceive a viceregal position divorced from a chief administrative one (as was William Marshal's from 1216 to 1219), nor is it difficult to conceive not one but a group of great ministers responsible to the king or his regent (as under Henry III from 1234 to 1258 and under Edward I). The needs which led, as it seems naturally, to the justiciarship admitted more than one solution, and they were not constant but varied at particular times. Sufficient conditions have sometimes been sought in outside influences, in the models provided for English practice by the Norman and Angevin offices of seneschal, or the work of the Norman curial bishops: foreign influences which were not the result of natural English growth but of transplanting. Then, too, within England, the needs which the justiciarship satisfied, or, more precisely, the degree to which those needs were actually felt at any particular time, depended upon the political, social, and economic situation, upon the extent of royal power within that situation and the instruments available for its expression, upon the personalities of the king, his family, his great barons and his ministers. All of these factors affected the creation of the justiciarship and they are not comprehended in a smooth, natural process of development, whether of regency or of administration; and some of them, although they were undoubtedly important, cannot be accurately measured. Nevertheless, they must all be considered in tracing the development of the king's *alter ego*.

I. THE REIGN OF WILLIAM I

The Norman Conquest introduced the necessity for delegating royal power, but the precise details are obscure for lack of evidence; nor is the evidence that survives altogether reliable. The names of a number of great barons are mentioned by chroniclers as royal deputies: Archbishop Lanfranc of Canterbury, a close friend of the king, Bishop Odo of Bayeux, William's half-brother, and Bishop Geoffrey of Coutances among the ecclesiastical magnates, and Count Robert of Mortain, another half-brother, Earl William fitz Osbern of Hereford, the seneschal who was also a close friend, Count Robert of Eu, Richard fitz Gilbert, Hugh de Montfort, and William de Warenne among the lay barons. Not all of this group were employed by the king in the same ways or with the same frequency, but they represent a group which was distinguished from the hundred and seventy tenants-in-chief whom William established upon the land of England, and which was called by name when the king, for example, ordered the sheriffs to be summoned to listen to royal instructions; Lanfranc, Geoffrey, Robert of Eu, Hugh de Montfort, and all the nobles of England were entrusted with this task.[1] Before, however, we examine this royal delegation in more detail, one misunderstanding must be cleared away. The belief that Queen Matilda and William the king's eldest son acted as royal deputies is based on misinterpreted evidence, supported by the fact that Matilda certainly acted as regent in Normandy, assisted by the advice and counsel of one or two great barons.[2] A member of the king's immediate family with the advice of great feudatories seems a natural solution to the problem of regency, but there is no evidence that the Norman precedent was followed in England, and the evidence of the deputies who were employed suggests very strongly that it was not. William's representatives in England came from a small circle of great magnates.

None of them was called *justitiarius* by any contemporary or near contemporary writer, and the descriptions they bear suggest a search for a descriptive phrase rather than a title of precise application. There was, indeed, little need for the king to attempt any permanent solution to the problem of regency because there was little idea that the Anglo-Norman dominion was permanent; on the Conqueror's death the lands were to be divided among his sons. Nor were William's absences so long or so regular as to

[1] *Regesta*, I, no. 50.
[2] In the *Handbook of British Chronology*, p. 34, Matilda and William the king's son are listed as regents. The mistake comes from H. W. C. Davis and M. M. Bigelow, both of whom assumed that writs of Henry I's queen, Matilda, and his son William belonged to the wife and son of the Conqueror; see below, pp. 14–15.

point to the need for a permanent arrangement.[1] His sole absence of length was from 1077 to 1080, and only with reference to that absence has the suggestion plausibly been made that a regular vice-royalty developed which was exercised by Bishop Odo of Bayeux.[2]

Among the royal representatives, Odo stands out by reason of his kinship with the king, his great landed position as earl of Kent, and his ecclesiastical dignity. In the first provision William made for the care of England, Odo was one of the two men described as the king's 'vicars'.[3] The other was Earl William fitz Osbern who, with the bishop, was left in 1067 to maintain the Norman position in a still largely unconquered land; the steward was left holding the frontier facing the unconquered north, the bishop in charge of communications with Normandy through Dover and Kent. Earl William had the senior position, but the evidence that has been used to show him acting as justiciar has been misinterpreted.[4] There is no suggestion that he issued writs in the king's name, and all the evidence points to an essentially military command. He was an old and trusted friend of the king who had been given the earldom of Hereford, and this, together with his office of steward, accounts for his pre-eminence. It was only after the earl's death that Odo was described as *totius Angliae vicedominus sub rege*, and that by a twelfth-century writer.[5] More nearly contemporary descriptions, however, justify the phrase, for the Anglo-Saxon chronicler portrayed him as 'the mightiest man in this land' when the king was abroad, and a Norman writer as 'a second king'.[6] This tradition of Bishop Odo's pre-eminence is certainly genuine and, combined with the evidence for his place in the great Norman land pleas, it provides the basis for the view that from 1077 to 1080 he exercised a regular and formal viceroyalty.

The impression made by Odo on his contemporaries or near contemporaries should not be allowed to colour interpretation of his viceregal activity, especially when the latter is of doubtful

---

[1] *Handbook of British Chronology*, p. 34.
[2] F. M. Stenton, *Anglo-Saxon England*, pp. 601–2.
[3] Orderic, II, 168.
[4] See West, 'An Early Justiciar's Writ', *Speculum*, XXXIV, 631–5.
[5] Malmesbury, *De Gestis Regum*, p. 334.
[6] *Chronicle*, 1087; Orderic, II, 222.

significance. The bishop sat in judgement in the king's place in some of the confused Evesham litigation, perhaps in 1077, and he was then occupying a viceregal position because the complaint of Abbot Walter's men that their lord had refused to receive homage was made to Odo, *qui tunc temporis sub rege quasi quidam tyrannus praefuit huic patriae*, who then convened a meeting of five shires at 'Gildenebeorge' in which he compelled Abbot Walter to give him some of the towns concerned.[1] Both Odo and the king confirmed the judgement, the former to the local sheriffs, the latter to all the barons of England. This story must be treated with some reserve. It may be accepted that it enshrines a tradition of Odo's viceroyalty, but the narrative in the Evesham chronicle is certainly garbled, as an anachronistic reference to Domesday Book shows, and the two documents may be questioned on the ground that the lands they refer to were certainly in the possession of the abbey of Evesham before the Conquest so that the narrative's assertion that Abbot Walter's predecessor had bought them after the Conquest is false.[2] The confusion of this litigation lies beyond the present discussion, but it serves to cast some doubt upon the evidence of a formal viceroyalty at a particular date. In another case of Odo's authority there is a similar ambiguity. A royal order for the Kentford inquest of 1080 into the Ely disputes was sent *per Baiocensem episcopum*.[3] Since Bishop Odo is not known to have had any other connexion with the Ely series of trials, the meaning of this phrase is obscure; it could mean that a royal order was transmitted through Bishop Odo who was then regent, as the story of his punishing the murderers of Bishop Walcher of Durham suggests, or it could mean that Odo brought the order back from Normandy with him, because he was certainly abroad in 1080 and with the king at St Georges de Boscherville.[4] Yet a third case in which he acted *vice regis* is of little help in establishing

---

[1] *Chron. Abb. Evesham*, pp. 96–7.

[2] Round, *VHC Worcestershire*, I, 254; *Regesta*, I, nos. 185, 186.

[3] *Regesta*, I, no. 122.

[4] Odo's presence in England in 1080 depends upon Simeon of Durham's local knowledge that he came north to avenge Walcher; *Opera Omnia*, I, 118; II, 211; other accounts mention only the king. Odo's presence in Normandy is shown by his witness to a charter; *Regesta*, I, no. 121.

his formal viceroyalty in these particular years, for the date at which he judged between the bishop of Rochester and Picot the sheriff in a dispute which concerned royal lands and which had begun before the king himself is uncertain.[1] Bishop Odo certainly acted in the king's place and left a tradition of viceroyalty, but it looks rather an *ad hoc* arrangement than a formal or regular one. Odo was himself frequently abroad, even within the three years of William's long absence, and although fixed points and dates are hard to come by they are sufficient to establish that he can never have exercised a formal viceroyalty for any considerable part of the reign;[2] an impression borne out when the position of other royal deputies is considered.

Archbishop Lanfranc, although not a relation of the king, was probably more trusted by him than the ambitious and turbulent Odo. A Norman tradition described Lanfranc as *princeps et custos* of England, and a Canterbury historian asserted that so great was his influence that on the Conqueror's death no one could have succeeded to the kingdom without the archbishop's assent.[3] As a great feudal baron and head of the church, Lanfranc naturally played a prominent part in the king's counsels, but he also had close personal ties with William. If the tradition of his pre-eminence is less marked than Odo's in many chronicles, this is no doubt due to his less dramatic, less political, less military exploits. Nor did he figure as judge in the great land pleas. Nevertheless, it is clear that during the crisis of 1075 he was acting on the king's behalf, even though Odo was in England,[4] and there are indications that he exercised a general oversight of the land pleas themselves. In the doubtful royal confirmation of the Evesham trial, he was addressed by name with Bishop Odo when both were

---

[1] *Placita Anglo-Normannica*, pp. 34–6.

[2] Fixed points in his itinerary in Normandy are 1074, 1077 (Bayeux), 14 July 1080 (Caen), 1080 (St Georges de Boscherville), 1082. He was there at less certain dates between 1071–7 and 1077–9; *Regesta*, I, nos. 75, 98, 105, 117, 118, 121, 150, 168.

[3] *Vita B. Lanfranci*, in Migne, *Patrologia Latina*, vol. CL, col. 55; Eadmer, *Hist. Nov.* p. 13.

[4] Lanfranc's correspondence throughout the crisis is printed in Migne, *ibid.*, and calendared in *Regesta*, I, nos. 78–83.

distinguished in the royal greeting from the generality of the baronage. Similarly, when Bishop Geoffrey of Coutances was sent by the king to hear the dispute between Evesham and the bishop of Worcester, the royal order was sent to Lanfranc and Geoffrey even though it instructed the latter alone to do justice.[1] As archbishop, Lanfranc had an obvious interest in the disputes of his bishops and abbots, but the evidence from 1075, his close association with the king, and his relatively infrequent visits to Normandy[2] make it probable that he held a special if not precisely definable position on the king's behalf, even if others might carry out specific duties; a position which is reflected in the Norman tradition of his guardianship of England.

If Odo's position must thus be qualified by Lanfranc's, both must be qualified by that of Bishop Geoffrey of Coutances. Not having so close a relationship with the king to all appearances, he was nevertheless less frequently abroad than Odo and more frequently employed as royal deputy in land pleas than any other baron.[3] His feudal position made him the seventh richest baron in England and he had a great reputation as a soldier, but it is also evident that he was treated as something of an expert on legal questions. He, with Bishop Remigius of Lincoln, Earl Waltheof, and the sheriffs Picot and Ilbert made an inquiry into the lands lost by the church of Ely, and thereafter he was treated as an expert in the legal affairs of the abbey; together with Lanfranc and Count Robert of Eu, he was involved in the difficulties over the consecration of Abbot Simeon.[4] He was associated with Lanfranc in giving seisin of the lands of the murdered Countess Mabel of Shrewsbury to the abbey of St Martin de Troarn, with the archbishop, the local bishop, and sheriff, when King William gave his chaplain the church of St Mary of Wolverhampton; with the archbishop, Robert of Eu, and Hugh de Montfort, when the king ordered

[1] *Regesta*, I, no. 84.
[2] The only certain dates of his presence in Normandy are 1077, 1080, and 1082; *Regesta*, I, nos. 98, 125, 150.
[3] See Le Patourel, 'Geoffrey de Montbray, Bishop of Coutances', *EHR*, LIX, 145 ff.
[4] *Regesta*, I, nos. 151–7; *Inq. Com. Cant.* pp. 192–5; see also Miller, 'Ely Land Pleas in the Reign of William I', *EHR*, LXII, 448.

St Augustine's, Canterbury, to be reseised with the borough of Fordwich and certain other lands which the house had lost.[1] It is always difficult to distinguish an administrative from a feudal significance in Geoffrey's place in such writs, but he had no obvious local connexion with Canterbury or Wolverhampton, his own lands being principally in the south-west. His employment as a Domesday commissioner strengthens the suggestion that he was selected by the king because of his administrative capacity, and, so far as the evidence goes, he was selected more frequently than any other of the group of prominent barons.

The lay magnates did not occupy so prominent a place in the delegation of royal power as these three bishops, although the ecclesiastical origin of the narrative sources must be allowed for. In at least one of the Ely inquests the *legati regis* were Richard fitz Gilbert, Haimo the steward, and Tihel of Helion.[2] At the crises of the Norman monarchy, in 1067 before the kingdom was secure, in 1075 when it was threatened by rebellion, the lay barons acted on the king's behalf. In 1067, Hugh de Montfort, Hugh de Grantmesnil, and William de Warenne were left in charge of fortifications; in 1075, the attack on Norwich castle was commanded by Bishop Geoffrey, William de Warenne and Robert Malet, while William de Warenne and Richard fitz Gilbert summoned the traitors to answer in the king's court. If the part these great barons played seems less active or less prominent than that of their ecclesiastical colleagues, they were nevertheless always in the background, as Lanfranc implied when he wrote in the first person plural to the king, and in the singular to other barons, and they were relied upon by the king, equally with the bishops, for giving effect to royal orders settling some difficult piece of litigation.

Absence of any precise title, even where, as in the land pleas,

---

[1] *Regesta*, I, nos. 97, 98, 210. Both the writs in favour of Troarn and St Augustine's were dated 1077 by Davis; the latter *in dedicatione Baiocensi* certainly belongs to this year, but the former is probably 1080, because a grant to the abbey of Lessay which can be precisely dated 14 July 1080 has a very similar witness list to a confirmation by the king of a private grant to Troarn which speaks of the countess as recently dead; *Regesta*, I, nos. 125, 172.

[2] *Liber Eliensis*, p. 251; *Monasticon*, I, 482; Miller, *loc. cit.* p. 445.

justitiarius would have been a literal description, and variation in
the delegation of royal power, either as a general oversight or for a
particular task, both argue for the absence of any settled system of
regency or formal office. Earlier it was suggested that there can
have been no pressing need for a definitive solution, but, even had
there been, two considerations would have produced the situation
which actually seems to have existed. The first, and in a sense
accidental, factor was that all of the great barons were affected by
the same necessity as the king: holding lands on both sides of the
Channel they too had to spend some time in each dominion. The
exception to this was Archbishop Lanfranc, but the other two
bishops both held Norman sees, and, with the apparent exception
of Richard fitz Gilbert, all of the other prominent members of the
king's circle were abroad at intervals in King William's company;[1]
quite apart from the demands of their own estates, a feudal king's
stature was determined by the presence of his great feudatories in
his retinue. Delegation of royal power therefore had to be flexible
and *ad hoc*, but it was also conditioned by the nature of feudal
society. The second and more important consideration was partly
the general need for co-operation between the king and his
baronage, and partly the particular dangers of the Norman position in England that made that co-operation urgent. The king had
to rely on the baronage as a whole, as the address of William's
writs suggests, and especially upon the really great barons, who
were therefore distinguished from the generality of the baronage
in royal orders. It is true that William inherited from his Anglo-
Saxon predecessor a financial system which was competent to
assess and collect the danegeld, a chancery which used a great seal
unknown to Norman practice, and a system of sheriffs and
shire courts which held the pleas of the Crown, but this royal

---

[1] Count Robert of Mortain was with the king on most of his journeys abroad;
Regesta, I, nos. 66, 75, 105, 117, 145, 150, 168, 182; Hugh de Montfort was there
in 1077, and between 1071–7 and 1072–82; *ibid.* nos. 98, 105, 168; William de
Warenne was with the king only once, in 1082; *ibid.* no. 150; Richard fitz
Gilbert does not appear as a witness in any of the king's Norman charters.
Attendance on the king does not, however, exhaust the possibility of great
barons being abroad on their own account but evidence is not available unless
their journey brought them into contact with the king's court.

administration operated in a feudal context, and its leading figures were feudal ones. Royal intervention was the exception rather than the rule, the great land pleas were unusual rather than common, and the delegation of royal power was therefore not urgent. The need for a formal office like the justiciarship was not really present in the first Norman reign.

2. THE REIGN OF WILLIAM II

Under William II there was no greater need to organize the delegation of royal power. Until 1091 the new king never left England, the duchy having passed to his elder brother, and after he had embarked upon the conquest of Normandy his only lengthy absence occurred in the last two years of his reign. Since Rufus had neither wife nor children, inevitably he had to use as his deputies one or more of the barons he especially trusted. Bishop William de St Calais of Durham was reputedly 'grand justiciar' until his rebellion in 1088,[1] but no precise significance can be attached to the title, unless it be a confusion with his palatine authority. Bishop Walkelin of Winchester was more important in the king's counsels. He had had some connexion with one of the Ely trials under the Conqueror, and he served Rufus in a number of ways: by carrying a summons to the rebellious bishop of Durham in 1088, by going with Bishop Gundulf of Rochester to punish the monks of St Augustine of Canterbury in 1090.[2] He was also prominent among the witnesses to the increasing number of royal administrative writs. As bishop of Winchester he was one of the great barons of England, his connexion with the royal circle was certainly close and, although he was never called justiciar or by any other title, the local Winchester tradition asserted that he was left as regent in England in 1097 at the beginning of the king's long absence.[3] For the first half of William II's reign he was the only great magnate close to the king, for others in that circle of royal advisers, although two of them were given bishoprics in the second half of the reign, were of much less feudal significance.

[1] Orderic, IV, 10.   [2] *DNB* under Walkelin.   [3] *Annales Monastici*, II, 39.

The most famous of this group of ministers was Ranulf Flambard, a clerk who was *custos* of the royal seal in the chancery of William I, who made his way in the world by devoted service as a royal minister, finding his material rewards in ecclesiastical benefices and finally the bishopric of Durham at the very end of Rufus's reign.[1] Of the small group round the king, Flambard was the one who principally attracted the unfavourable attention of nearly contemporary writers, but their descriptions of him reveal the same search for a phrase to describe his position and his work, the same inability to describe what he did with a precise title, as do the accounts of William I's delegates. Ranulf was *maximum executor voluntatis regiae* to the Canterbury historian; *summus justiciarius* to Orderic Vitalis; and the king's clerk or chaplain to other writers.[2] The odium attaching to his name suggests that his work as the exactor of money and the exploiter of judicial rights on the king's behalf was novel; certainly the employment of a minor feudal figure as the chief of the king's ministers was new, especially so ubiquitous a figure. Ranulf's arrival in Canterbury on the day of Anselm's enthronement, his commissions at Ely, at Bury St Edmunds, and in Devon and Cornwall emphasized his place as the king's chief *exactor*.[3] Two points, nevertheless, qualify any suggestion that he was a prototype justiciar. The first is that he was never alone in his pre-eminence; the second is that the basis of his activity was the treasury at Winchester, which had already been capable of organizing the Domesday survey, and the shire courts, which had a long history behind them.

Other men were associated with Ranulf in his administrative work. Haimo the steward, Urse de Abetot, and the chancellor Robert Bloet, who had crossed to England with the Conqueror's deathbed letter to Lanfranc about the succession, were members of the group of close royal counsellors. All of them witnessed the king's administrative writs, and they were singled out as addressees when the king was abroad. A judgement, for example, between the abbey of Holy Trinity, Fécamp, and the monks of Saumur, in

---

[1] Southern, 'Flambard and the Anglo-Norman Administration', *TRHS*, 4th series, XVI, 113.
[2] Eadmer, p. 41; Orderic, x, 18.   [3] Eadmer, p. 41; *Monasticon*, II, 497.

the king's court held at Fourcamont in Normandy between 1094 and 1099 was to be enforced by Bishop Ralph of Chichester, Ranulf the chaplain, Haimo the steward, and Urse de Abetot.[1] The bishop's inclusion is explained by the fact that the benefice involved lay within his diocese at Steyning in Sussex, but the king plainly relied on his group of ministers to give effect to his will. A second royal writ which ordered that the monks of Holy Trinity should have their rights in Steyning castle and in Beeding was sent from Lillebonne in 1099 to Flambard, by then bishop of Durham, Haimo, and Urse, who were told to send Hugh of Buckland to enforce the judgement. Similarly, the famous writ which ordered the assessment of Thorney abbey for gelds and services was sent to the same group of men and Bishop Robert Bloet.[2] All of these writs came from the absent king, and they treated this group of ministers as royal deputies who had charge of the king's government. Bishop Walkelin of Winchester may have been joined to them in the regency of England, but the backbone of royal government was clearly this group of trusted officials whose careers were bound up with administration rather than feudal eminence. William Rufus followed his father's example of delegating his power to a group of men, but the character of the group changed from the great magnates to the 'professional' administrators, among whom Flambard was perhaps the most prominent and most active.

This change, which is paralleled in the changes in the ranks of sheriff,[3] may have owed something to Rufus's relations with the baronage—he marred the image of a feudal king in a generation which did not know the insecurities and mutual interdependence of the barons of the Conquest—but it also owed something to Rufus's exploitation of royal rights. Whatever is meant by the phrase 'the hardening of feudal custom', employed by a number of historians, it is clear that the king's attention to his resources was close, and in their exploitation Flambard and his colleagues played a major role. The basis of their activity was the shire organization, but it rested also upon the treasury at Winchester

[1] *Regesta*, I, nos. 423, 424.   [2] *Ibid.* nos. 416, 422.
[3] Morris, *The Mediaeval Sheriff to 1300*, p. 52.

with which Flambard was closely connected and which had developed functions not exhausted by treasurership.[1] What is important about Rufus's arrangements for regency is that they drew upon the same group of men, not being great feudal magnates, who were the driving force in this royal administration when the king was in England. Thus Walkelin, Ranulf, and Roger Bigot viewed the lands which the king proposed to give to Bishop Herbert to build his church at Norwich; Walkelin and Ranulf delivered seisin of a manor to Eudo *dapifer*; and Ranulf, Haimo, and Urse bore witness to royal administrative orders.[2] These last three men had no such eminence in the great feudal meetings of tenants-in-chief, but in the day-to-day work of government they formed a small circle round the king, who relied upon them for that exploitation of royal rights and resources which, with regency, produced the two major needs which the justiciarship satisfied. The feudal insignificance of Flambard until the end of his administrative career and of his colleagues precludes their being regarded as the first of a line of justiciars.

3. THE REIGN OF HENRY I

William Rufus had faced the necessity of re-conquering and then of governing the duchy of Normandy, and of coping with some of the consequences that the alienation of royal demesne occurring under all the Conqueror's sons brought about; both required the services of men like Flambard. Both, too, confronted Henry I in a perhaps intensified form. Like Rufus, Henry encountered no serious breakdown of co-operation with the baronage, although the external threats which had originally enforced it were weakening. Unlike Rufus, Henry had a family whom he could use as regents, and an administrative system which began to acquire, as all bureaucracies do, a logic of development of its own. Thus if the

---

[1] Liebermann, *EHR*, xxviii, 153.
[2] *Regesta*, I, nos. 385, 399. Southern, *loc. cit.* p. 103, assumes that if Ranulf attested a writ, he issued it, and he cites as an example the writ which demanded reliefs from the tenants of the bishop of Worcester. The assumption is unwarranted, but his witness and those of Urse and Haimo certainly establish their close connexion with the actions taken.

royal needs which seem to be leading to the creation of the justiciarship were intensified, their satisfaction in such an office was complicated by the alternatives available to the king.

The most obvious of these alternatives was the delegation of viceregal authority to his wife and later to his son. Queen Matilda exercised the regency during Henry I's first absence in 1104, when she was travelling about England while the king was abroad,[1] and on other occasions until her death in 1118. She presided over a royal court sitting in the treasury at Winchester in 1111 to hear the abbot of Abingdon establish his rights in the manor of Lewknor, a court which was described in her charter as her lord's and her own, and whose judgement was sealed with the queen's seal; *regina quae tunc praesens aderat, taliter hoc sigillo suo confirmavit.*[2] Four years later, a man who had been brought to trial before Ralph Basset, one of the king's justices, was released by Matilda's order.[3] From 1104 until the queen's death, Henry I spent two periods of almost a year and two periods of two years abroad (the last being one terminated by his wife's death), and in these six years the government of England operated in Matilda's name. The Abingdon account of the Lewknor litigation shows that she employed her seal to authenticate royal acts, both charters and writs. Two of Matilda's orders to royal officials survive in copies, the first examples of a regent treating the administration as his or her own.[4] At some unknown date, Matilda ordered Viel Engaine and William de Lusors to ensure that Mauger the monk and his servants should have those possessions given to them by the king, and that they should prevent any injury to them. Between 1116 and 1118, she issued the first of the writs concerned with the ship of the abbot of St Augustine's, ordering Haimo the steward to restore the vessel to the abbot and to take pledges from the men who had detained it that they would stand to right in the king's

[1] *Chron. Mon. Abing.* II, 97.

[2] *Ibid.* II, 116; *Regesta*, II, 104.

[3] Orderic, III, 125; *Placita Anglo-Normannica*, pp. 111–12. Bigelow omits the part of the story dealing with the man's release.

[4] *Regesta*, I, no. 189; Davis and Bigelow both wrongly ascribe the writ, the former to the reign of William the Conqueror, the latter to William Rufus; *Monasticon*, IV, 348.

court whenever he should wish. Both orders are plainly dependent upon Henry's pleasure, but the queen treated the officials as owing her obedience. The same assumption was made by William the king's son in his writs issued after he had succeeded to his mother's position. William ordered the sheriff of Kent to hear the truth about Abbot Guy's ship through Haimo son of Viel and the good men of Sandwich to determine what the position was when King Henry last crossed the sea; meanwhile the abbot was to be reseised.[1] A second writ followed upon the verdict of the men of Sandwich, for the regent ordered the sheriff of Kent to give the abbot seisin as they had declared that he ought to have it. On two other occasions writs of the king's son ordered royal officials to take action; he told Bishop John of Bath to convey the seisin of land to one Modbert and he ordered the sheriff of Kent to hold an inquisition by the men of Middleton about customs which the abbot of St Augustine's ought to have.[2] All of these writs exhibit three features of regency. The first is that the regent had power to treat the administrative system as the king would. The second is that, although the regent could command obedience, it was usually with specific reference to the king's will, past, present, or future. The third is that the continuity of the St Augustine's writs and the attestation of the regent's orders make it clear that behind the regent there stood a small group of great royal ministers.

They were not the same group as that which had served William Rufus. Flambard may not have been so severely punished as some have believed but he disappeared from England;[3] Walter Giffard, the chancellor, was promoted to a bishopric. Of Rufus's ministers only Bishop Robert Bloet of Lincoln played an important part in the circle round Henry I, and his colleagues were new men brought in by the king from Normandy, like Bishop

---

[1] *Regesta*, I, nos. 188, 190. Davis also ascribes these to the reign of William I, but both the style and the name of the sheriff make it evident that they really belong to that of Henry I; Bigelow ascribed them to William Rufus because he misread *Willelmus filius regis Willelmi vicecomiti de Kent* for *Willelmus filius regis Willelmo vicecomiti*.

[2] *Regesta*, I, no. 191, similarly misdated by Davis; *Two Bath Cartularies*, I, 49.

[3] Southern, *loc. cit.* pp. 117 ff.

Roger of Salisbury, or promoted, like the Bassets. These were the men who stood behind the regent and who, like Flambard and his colleagues, were the backbone of royal government whether the king was in England or not. A glance at the regent's writs makes this clear. Bishop Roger witnessed one of Matilda's writs, the bishop of Lincoln the other; Roger witnessed two of William's writs alone, and one with the chancellor, who witnessed the remaining one by himself. One or more of these ministers were in the regents' company when they travelled, for example, to Oxford, Woodstock, and Windsor, but it is equally clear that the real centre of their authority was Winchester: where the treasury was located and where the rolls and charters were kept; where the queen sat with Bishop Roger, Bishop Robert, the bishop of London, William de Curci, Adam de Port and others who included Turstin the chaplain and Herbert the chamberlain to do justice to the abbot of Abingdon; where Bishop Roger could consult the treasury records and issue a decision on the basis of them.[1] Like Flambard before him, Roger of Salisbury's authority rested upon the treasury organization but, unlike Flambard, Roger was a man of considerable feudal importance from almost the beginning of his career in royal government.

Roger was described in phraseology which has affinities with descriptions rather of Bishop Odo than of Ranulf Flambard; 'he was strong and wielded all England'; he was 'second to the king'.[2] When Henry I sailed from Portsmouth in 1123, his wife and son then being dead, he committed all England to the guidance and

[1] *Monasticon*, VI, 33. This document is a writ of Henry I addressed to Richard fitz Baldwin and G. de Furnellis, ordering quittance of the land of the canons of Plympton of gelds and assizes, *quia episcopus Saresberiensis recognovit per cartam de thesauro meo* that they ought to be quit and that this land of Wembury and Colebrook *non in numerum hidarum mearum est. Et hoc idem testatur episcopus per breve suum.* Round (*Commune of London*, p. 88) thought that *carta de thesauro* meant the *Cartae Antiquae* rolls; Richardson (*Memoranda Roll 1 John*, p. LIV n. 6) thought not, on the grounds that *carta* no more meant a charter than *breve de firmis* meant a writ, and the context shows that the words cannot refer to a charter of Henry I. It is clear however that Roger consulted Domesday Book and then issued a writ in his own name which he gave to the canons. The king later ordered the local officers to observe it.

[2] *Chronicle*, 1122; William of Newburgh, I, 36; Henry of Huntingdon, *Historia Anglorum*, p. 245.

governance of Bishop Roger, and the careful William of Malmesbury adds that the king delegated to the bishop the doing of justice in England whether he himself was abroad or not. [1] There is eloquent testimony to Bishop Roger's pre-eminence and power, not only in direct descriptions of him but indirectly in such events as his influence in the Canterbury election of 1123 when, notwithstanding the objections of the papal legate, his influence and that of Bishop Robert Bloet of Lincoln secured the appointment of William of Corbeil, so great was King Henry's love for Roger, and his action in the following year when he sent over England to have false coiners brought to Winchester for punishment.[2] His power is further emphasized by the castles he built, of Devizes which was reputed to be the finest in Europe, of Sherborne, and additions to Salisbury and Malmesbury, all strongholds lying within his diocese.[3] Until 1126 he had custody of Duke Robert of Normandy, the most important political prisoner of the reign.[4] He was also in a position of power sufficient to establish his family in important offices and bishoprics and so to found an administrative dynasty lasting into the thirteenth century. Beyond question, the bishop of Salisbury achieved a position unmatched in earlier reigns and for which the only analogy was that of Odo at the height of his power, a position which in terms of power and influence can only be compared with that of later justiciars. Can he be regarded as the first holder of the office?

William of Malmesbury called Roger justiciar, but it is not clear that this is a description of an office rather than a description of one who did justice. Roger's career, which began when he was taken into Henry I's service as a chaplain before the latter's succession to the Crown of England, shows that he held a succession of offices, first as steward of Henry's pre-kingly household, then as chancellor of the king, an office he resigned when, in 1104, he was promoted to the bishopric of Salisbury.[5] Thereafter there is no evidence that he held a formal office, and it is obvious that his power and influence were of gradual growth. Even the family

[1] Malmesbury, II, 483; Chronicle, 1123.   [2] Chronicle, 1125.
[3] Newburgh, I, 36; Huntingdon, p. 265.   [4] Chronicle, 1126.
[5] Newburgh, I, 36.

tradition of Roger's importance makes this clear.[1] 'He grew in favour with the king, the clergy, and the people, was made bishop of Salisbury and held the most important and honourable posts in the kingdom, and had the profoundest knowledge of the exchequer. . . . Later by the king's command he took the seat at the exchequer.' His descendant nowhere calls him justiciar, and when Roger himself sought for a title it was *procurator*, while for others it might be *provisor*.[2] The existence of the royal regents up to 1120, as well as this gradual growth of Roger's power, suggests that there was no formal office of justiciar but rather a personal authority or influence based on his relationship with the king, his feudal position, and his great knowledge and ability in administration.

Roger's career may indicate that it is unlikely that he held a formal office, but his position certainly bore two strong resemblances to the justiciarship. The first is that government, after the disappearance of the royal regents, operated in his name while Henry I was abroad. There are surviving copies of his writs and one charter which has been claimed as an original.[3] An argument based upon cartulary copies is obviously to some degree doubtful, but it happens that certain features are common to all of them; and they have an important bearing on his viceregal authority. Except in the formal charter, Roger used no title other than bishop of Salisbury, which suggests that his authority was well known

---

[1] *Dialogus*, I, vii. Notwithstanding the assertion of Richardson and Sayles, *Governance of Mediaeval England*, p. 159, where they assign the precise date 1109 for the creation of the office of chief justiciar. This is inference both from a letter of Henry I to Anselm which refers to *justitiarii*, not to the justiciar, and to the subsequent occasion when Roger presided at the exchequer and also from the absence of previous evidence. An argument *e silentio* is not the kind of proof these learned writers so often demand of others.

[2] *Regesta*, II, nos. 1418, 1471, 1472. The solemn charter for Reading may be a forgery based on an actual writ, but the style is repeated in a genuine document. Abbot Roger of Mont St Michel who resigned in 1123 addressed Roger as *provisor Anglie;* Harl. MS 1708, fo. 198. Bishop Herbert of Norwich, asking for Roger's influence to protect his church in the first half of Henry's reign, uses *procuratio*, a term Richardson and Sayles translate as 'justiciarship', *op. cit.* pp. 160–1, although its usual meaning of regent or viceroy suggests it was, in view of Matilda's place, a piece of flattery.

[3] D. M. Stenton, *EHR*, XXXIX, 75. It is, however, described as spurious by the editors (*Regesta*, II, no. 1471), because of the term *hutfangenetheof*.

by reference to some other instrument, perhaps royal letters patent which have not survived; in this following late practice. More significant, however, is the substitution for the name of a witness of the phrase *per breve regis*; none of his writs bears an attestation, and four of them, including the charter, replace it by this phrase. The usage suggests that Bishop Roger's position was novel, that it was useful to cite the king's authority rather than a witness to the non-royal regent's orders. And one curious error seems to show that the system of writs *de ultra mare* ordering the regent to take some action was still developing. Roger told Robert son of Walter that the abbot and monks of St Edmundsbury were to have their *warpeni* of eight and a half hundreds in Glemesford, Hartest, and Nedging, *sicut melius habuerunt tempore patris et fratris mei et meo tempore. Et si quid inde retentum est postquam novissime mari transivi reddatur.* This phraseology is obviously appropriate to the king, not to Roger, a fact no doubt giving rise to the forgery of an identical writ in the king's name which, however, still retained the words replacing the witness clause, *per breve regis*,[1] The probable explanation is that Roger's scribe, writing an order in the bishop's name on the king's instructions, simply copied the wording of the royal writ from beyond the sea, substituting only the regent's name for Henry's. Bishop Roger was at Wilton at the time, away from the centre of government growing up round the treasury and the exchequer, and doubtless the scribe was unaccustomed to the practice which had evolved in dealing with writs *de ultra mare.* Whatever the explanation, the impression is that Roger's position as regent was still being treated tentatively.

Certainly the king did not work exclusively through his regent. There are many examples of royal orders sent directly to the local officials concerned, by-passing the regent.[2] Henry was usually

---

[1] Douglas, *Feudal Documents from the Abbey of Bury St Edmunds*, p. 75.

[2] For example, *Regesta*, II, nos. 1419, 1429, 1430, 1432, 1550, 1551. Examples of writs sent to Bishop Roger as regent are nos. 1417, 1573, 1682. The last two of these order Roger, the king's justiciars, and all his sheriffs or barons and officials of the sea ports to acquit the men and goods of St Ouen of Rouen and the monks of Montebourg of all tolls and passage dues. They are not different from no. 1419 sent to all officials and sheriffs and the sea ports that the monks of Bec shall similarly be quit, and which omitted Bishop Roger's name.

accompanied by the chancellor when he was abroad, and there is no evidence that he ever left his seal behind him in England. He possessed, therefore, the technical instruments for giving direct orders to local officials, and he was certainly sought out on the continent by suitors from England who wanted a royal order or charter. There is no easy answer to the question of which method the king used in any given instance: whether he would work through the regent or directly through the local officials. The nature and difficulty of any particular case probably determined his action, but one factor may easily have been the power, influence, or recalcitrance of the people involved, and another the need for a series of writs to officials in a number of shires which could more conveniently be prepared and despatched by the regent's administration in England. Whatever the reason, it is plain that regency had not been formalized to the extent that the king invariably, or even usually, worked through it.

The ways in which the king and the regent worked, or could work, depended upon the machinery available for carrying out their orders and enforcing their will. The second resemblance that the position of Roger bore to the justiciarship is therefore his position in the machinery of government, as its controller whether the king was in England or not. There can be no doubt that the central organ of government was the exchequer, and that Roger was its dominant figure. The earliest writ which refers to the exchequer by name comes from 1110.[1] The king told the barons of the exchequer that the church of St Mary of Lincoln was quit of the aid *pour fille marier*, witness Bishop Roger and the chancellor. When Richard fitz Nigel wrote his treatise, the justiciar and the chancellor were the men who should witness a royal writ issued at the exchequer, and while one cannot argue that this was already the established practice under Henry I, the association of the bishop and the chancellor is significant. In the following year Roger was at the head of those who sat with Queen Matilda to do justice to Abingdon. His long association with the exchequer continued into the period of his regency, for in 1133 Henry I acquitted the monks of Rievaulx of two shillings danegeld, sending his writ to

[1] *Registrum Antiquissimum*, I, no. 32.

Bishop Roger, the chancellor, and the barons of the exchequer.[1] Moreover, the exchequer was not merely a financial institution but a convenient meeting at which all kinds of business could be transacted. For example, when armed men came by night and damaged the church of Wennington in Essex belonging to the abbot of Westminster, the king told the bishop of London to do full right to the abbot or the barons of the exchequer would do so.[2] The exchequer would, in fact, act as the king's court if a feudal lord failed to do justice. It was a sedentary part of the *curia* which, although the audit session might occasionally be held elsewhere than at Winchester or Westminster, was the centre of royal administration and the basis of Roger's control over government: it was there that he recognized that the canons of Plympton ought to be quit of gelds and to it that he referred to establish an annual gift to St Peter's, Westminster.[3] Like Flambard before him, the bishop was not regularly with the court that travelled with the king,[4] but close to the sedentary one. The exchequer was a centre of government whether the king was abroad or not, and in his absence Roger, as its chief minister, no doubt used it as the heart of government.

Nevertheless, the bishop of Salisbury necessarily moved about England as any feudal lord did. In two pieces of Abingdon litigation he was present in Berkshire with Bishop Robert of Lincoln, the chancellor, and Ralph Basset, as one of the king's justices.[5] As bishop of Salisbury, he certainly visited his diocese: two of his *acta* show him at Wilton and Kidwelly, and it is particularly recorded of him that he devoted his mornings to his ecclesiastical duties, both organizing the administration of his diocese and carrying some of his episcopal *familia* with him to attend to its needs.[6] It is equally certain that, while he presided

[1] *Cartulary of Rievaulx*, no. 196.
[2] Armitage-Robinson, *Gilbert Crispin*, p. 148; R. L. Poole, *Exchequer in the Twelfth Century*, pp. 39–40 n. 4.
[3] *Gilbert Crispin*, p. 149.
[4] A glance at the king's charters calendared in *Regesta*, II, reveals his absence from the majority of those issued on the continent, but he is also absent on a surprising number of occasions in England.
[5] *Chron. Mon. Abing.* II, 133, 160.
[6] Foss, *Judges of England*, p. 564. His household appears in an unpublished charter given *in domo castelli de Cadwelli*; BM Add. MS 46487, fo. 14.

over the central administration, the major part of the work of
taking the king's justice to the counties fell on others. Both Ralph
and Richard Basset were described as *capitales justiciarii* in Roger's
time. Ralph was a judge in the county court of Berkshire with
Bishop Roger in trying the case of Abingdon *versus* the king's
collectors, perhaps in 1119, and in 1116 he had sat as a royal judge
at Huntingdon. In 1123 he conducted a great moot in Leicestershire and hanged many more thieves than was ever known before.[1]
This judicial activity occurred when Roger was at the height of
his power, but he had been doing similar work from the early
years of the reign. In 1106 he was one of the justices who inquired
into the customs of the church of St Peter of York.[2] Ralph was
generally in the king's company in England as the court travelled,
and he was as ubiquitous as Flambard had seemed. When the pipe
roll of 1130 was made, Ralph was dead, but he had been a justice
of the forest and an itinerant justice in ten counties.[3] His son
Richard succeeded him in this circuit, and with Aubrey de Vere
held eleven counties as sheriff.[4] One of Henry I's writs demonstrates Richard's function, for, when the king ordered William,
constable of Chester, to allow the monks of Westminster to enjoy
the land which William's own father had given them, failure in
justice would be remedied by Richard Basset.[5] He represented
royal intervention in a failure of feudal justice. The judicial activity
of the Bassets took them over the whole of England, and no doubt
this ubiquitousness was what the Abingdon chronicler had in
mind when he said of Ralph *in omni Angliae regno justitiae habens
dignatatem*, and Henry of Huntingdon when describing him as
justiciar of all England.[6] Richard, too, was, called by another
reliable chronicler, *utpote capitalis justicia.*[7] The confidence with

[1] *Chronicle*, 1124.   [2] Farrer, *Itinerary*, no. 34.
[3] Richardson and Sayles, *op. cit.* p. 177, suggest that this is not the full tale
of his work. They think he retired in 1127.
[4] Richardson and Sayles, *op. cit.* pp. 175–6.
[5] Madox, *History of the Exchequer*, p. 435.
[6] Huntingdon, p. 318; *Chron. Mon. Abing.* II, 170.
[7] Richardson and Sayles, *op. cit.* p. 165, n. 1, find this description hard to
understand in view of Roger's chief justiciarship: it is only hard if one attaches
too precise a significance to the words and ignores their analogy with *capitalis
curia.*

which the chroniclers use the title has sometimes been used to argue that Roger cannot have been *capitalis justiciarius* himself, with any precise office, but such a view depends on a precise translation of the phrase to mean ' chief justice '. This interpretation is unlikely. Besides the Bassets, Geoffrey Ridel was also called *capitalis justiciarius*,[1] and it is therefore probable that the term was used to distinguish a judge of the *capitalis curia* from local officials; and to this description the Bassets, Ridel, and Roger were all entitled. Nevertheless, the work and the place of the Bassets do qualify the notion that Roger had a formal office like the justiciarship, for it seems quite clear that they acted as heads of the itinerant royal justices whom the king increasingly employed, while Bishop Roger tended to remain at the centre of administration. Roger's pre-eminence cannot be doubted, but it seems to have been a personal and a feudal one in a circle of men upon whom Henry I relied. When Roger was himself abroad with the king, probably in 1130,[2] the government was no doubt carried on by a group of men like Richard Basset, Geoffrey Ridel, Geoffrey de Clinton (who heard pleas in eighteen counties in 1129–30), and Aubrey de Vere, who, when Roger was present, sat beside him in the central royal court at the exchequer. Their work, and the titles given to them by the chronicles, like the limitations upon Roger's authority as regent, qualify the resemblances that his position bears to the justiciarship. He was rather a precedent and an example quoted by a later generation than the first of the holders of a formal office; and the general impression of Henry I's government is of a period of experimentation, of working towards the solution of difficulties, rather than of their final resolution.

4. THE REIGN OF STEPHEN

Henry I could afford to experiment with powerful ministers to whom he delegated his authority because he was a strong king

[1] Huntingdon, p. 318.

[2] *Monasticon*, vi, 1071; *CChR*, iv, 434. The probable date of these charters is 1129, and Roger's presence with Henry I may explain the absence of reference to his authority in the Pipe Roll of 1130. Richardson and Sayles, *op. cit.* pp. 176–80, work out the pattern of the eyres the other justices conducted in 1129.

who could also enforce the limitations he wished for. His successor's reign shows clearly enough how great those ministers could become under a weak king, and how strong the administrative machinery they had been creating. When Stephen came to the crown, Roger of Salisbury was still presiding over the centre of government, his nephew or son was chancellor, another nephew treasurer and bishop of Ely, and yet another relation bishop of Lincoln. One of the bases of Roger's power was not so much a formal office as a family control of the important offices of royal government, quite apart from the feudal importance of the great bishoprics they held. Where Henry I was master of his servants, Stephen was not. Roger had referred to himself as *sub domino nostro rege Henrico procurator* but under Stephen he said *precipio tibi ex parte regis et mea*, a command to Sybil, widow of Pain fitz John to restore the property of the late husband given to the son of Miles of Gloucester, which was witnessed by the royal chancellor.[1] From another writ it appears that Miles of Gloucester had approached Bishop Roger over the property of the late Pain fitz John, for another order was sent to the sheriff of Hereford to pay the alms he had given to the monks of Gloucester, and if the sheriff failed to do so, Miles of Gloucester would.[2] The arrogance of Roger's language is surprising in itself, but it becomes even more startling when it is remembered that the order to Sybil was issued while King Stephen was in England. Not surprisingly, the king was irked by this pride and arrogance, which his own weakness permitted, and he took a weak man's action: the violent overthrow of the family's power, which involved a siege of the bishop of Lincoln's castles, and which, while it removed the great minister, damaged the efficiency of royal government and fatally

---

[1] Round, *Ancient Charters*, p. 38. Round dated the writ 1138, but H. G. Richardson has ascribed it to 1137 on the grounds that Pain fitz John was killed in July of that year, that the writ was issued shortly after his death, and that it is altogether improbable that Roger should issue a writ in his own name while the king was in England. In fact, the writ must be subsequent to a charter of Stephen's (Round, *op. cit.* no. 21) which can be dated precisely December 1137–May 1138, and it was therefore issued after the king's return from Normandy in December and while the king was in England.
[2] Balliol Coll. MS 271, fo. 101.

impaired relations with the church. The family tradition held that the exchequer system collapsed until it was restored by the treasurer Nigel of Ely under Henry II, but this probably overstates the effects of the king's action.[1] He had other loyal ministers who, although perhaps not so expert as Roger, could maintain the government, and some who, like the earl of Leicester, disliked the family of Salisbury as much as did the king. In any case, Roger's control was essentially over central government, and the local organs—the sheriffs and the shire courts—can have been affected only by a certain slackening in central control. The violence of the king's solution reinforces the idea that Roger had no formal office from which he could be dismissed and therefore excluded from the royal administration, but rather a position which was personal and feudal, making his influence and prestige independent of any formal position.

After Stephen's action in the Oxford council of 1139, when he required a regent—as he did during his captivity—it was his queen, Matilda, in whose name the royal government operated. It was to Matilda that the bishop of Winchester complained in 1141 when his lands were infringed, as the queen said *apud regem et apud me*, and who ordered the constable Baldwin of Whitsand and the knights and men under his control to leave the bishop in peace.[2] It was Matilda who, after the Londoners had expelled the empress, addressed the local justiciar and the sheriff of London *ex parte regis domini mei et mea*, and told them to let the canons of St Martin of London hold their soke of Cripplegate as the king her lord had ordered her by his writ (presumably from prison).[3] Neither of these orders, in the copies in which they survive, bears the name of a witness, but they still imply a functioning administrative system. No doubt the disappearance of the Salisbury family impaired its efficiency—it is impossible to know whether the queen's orders were actually enforced—but there were ministers like Richard de Luci, the future justiciar, in the king's service and it is inconceivable that the Salisbury family could have controlled the apparatus of government without a trained staff of ministers and clerks who survived their fall. While no pipe rolls are extant from Stephen's

[1] *Dialogus*, I, viii.   [2] *Memoranda Roll 1 John*, p. lxvii.   [3] *Ibid.*

reign, the prompt appearance of the admittedly thin rolls of the beginning of Henry II's shows that the government machine was not in chaos or chronic destruction. The royal deputy could still rely on royal ministers, and hope to be obeyed by local officials.

After his experience with Bishop Roger and his relations, Stephen had no more great ministers, although the foundations of Richard de Luci's career were laid in his time: he was sufficiently important to be given custody of the Tower of London under the terms of the treaty of Winchester. Nevertheless, there was no office or formal position which the king had to fill on Roger's fall, and he reverted to the kind of arrangements which Henry I had used in the first half of his reign: a royal regent assisted by royal ministers. Yet one of these royal deputies occupied a position which may have had some influence upon the development of the justiciarship. This was Henry II himself. Under the treaty, Henry was recognized as Stephen's heir, and associated with him in the government of England: they stood together *in regimine regni*. The writer who described the arrangement was one of Henry II's justices and he asserted that Stephen made Henry justiciar of England under himself *et omnia regni negotia per eum terminabantur*.[1] The arrangement did not last long because Duke Henry grew impatient with what was being done, but for some months he stood beside the king. Howden's ascription of the title 'justiciar' can be easily enough explained: in the second half of Henry II's reign the office was a formal one which was well known to royal justices, and if he wished to describe what he thought was an analogous position it is a title which he would naturally apply. It could hardly be a precise formal description of Duke Henry's position, but it probably represents its reality. Stephen certainly consulted Henry, but the latter's departure suggests that his advice was not necessarily taken. Henry also exercised some administrative control. Styling himself duke of Normandy and Aquitaine

---

[1] Howden, I, 212. Richardson and Sayles, *op. cit.* pp. 251-8, discuss Henry's position which they ascribe not to the treaty of Winchester but to his constant claim to be sovereign and therefore to control royal government. The treaty did, nevertheless, regularize the position, and the difficulty of dating Henry's documents makes it hard to establish his earlier control.

and count of Anjou, he told Earl Roger of Hereford, the sheriff and all his men, and the faithful burgesses of Gloucester that Roger of Tockenham should hold his land *iuxta portam de Nord'* free and quit of shire and hundred pleas and aids as he did when 'my grandfather King Henry gave him the land'; witness William the chancellor at Gloucester.[1] Another writ with a similar style was issued in favour of the monks of Gloucester between 1153 and April 1154.[2] Both of them were issued by Duke Henry in his position beside Stephen. They treat the local royal official as owing Henry obedience; they show that Henry travelled about England. Henry in fact treated the royal administration as his own, but William the chancellor was a ducal official, not a royal one; he was Henry's chancellor before his accession to the crown, but not afterwards, and it seems that Henry used his ducal household to control royal government. His position was exceptional, however much it may have resembled the justiciarship, but it has been said that it gave him some idea of the usefulness of such an office.[3] It seems unlikely. Henry's practice as king was determined by particular circumstances, and the evolution of the justiciarship depended less upon a brief royal experience as Stephen's coadjutor than upon political and administrative needs. Moreover, Henry was aware of the value of some office such as the justiciarship from his continental experience, of the value of having responsibility for government concentrated in one man when political and administrative circumstances permitted it.

5. FOREIGN INFLUENCES

This continental experience came from two sources: Normandy and Anjou; but before any argument can be accepted that the practice of either dominion influenced English development it is necessary to glance at their evolution towards an office equivalent to the justiciarship. It was once suggested that the Norman office

---

[1] Llanthony Cartulary A 5, fo. lxxxiiir; fo. cxviiv.
[2] Delisle, *Recueil des Actes de Henri II*, i, 67.
[3] D. M. Stenton, *CMH*, v, 554; Chrimes, *Administrative History of Mediaeval England*, p. 38.

of seneschal was the origin of the justiciarship because William fitz Osbern, the steward, was left in England in 1067, but enough has been said about the Conqueror's arrangements to show that this is erroneous.[1] It has also been suggested that the origins of the office are to be sought among the bishops of the Norman *curia*, among men like John of Lisieux, Arnulf of Lisieux, and Rotrou of Evreux.[2] Bishop John was certainly prominent in Norman administration under Henry I, but the title justiciar was never applied to him, and the seneschal Robert de la Haie was always at his side.[3] So far as Stephen's Norman ministers are known at all, they were Roger the *vicomte* and William de Roumare.[4] Thus in Normandy, as in England, such evidence as there is points to a group of royal ministers, and not to one man so pre-eminent as, for example, Roger of Salisbury. Normandy was then taken by Duke Geoffrey of Anjou on his son's behalf, and Henry's own rule in Normandy found Bishop Arnulf at the head of the justices of the curia but, like John of Lisieux, with the seneschal Robert de Neufbourg at his side.[5] Rotrou of Evreux, under Henry II, was certainly called justiciar and exercised justice through Normandy on the king's order,[6] but his power, too, may have been wielded conjointly with the seneschal, who gradually became head of the judicial system of the duchy. When Henry II sent Richard of Ilchester into Normandy in 1186, the seneschal was a layman, William de Curci, who was, said a chronicler, nominally succeeded by William fitz Ralph although the actual successor was Richard of Ilchester.[7] Fitz Ralph's office was in fact that of seneschal, and Richard was sent there for a particular and limited purpose, so that it is clear that the seneschal was at that time head of the Norman government. There is a parallel between the office of seneschal and the *comes palatii* of the French kings, a title which the Norman officer sometimes used, and like the *comes* the seneschal acted as his sovereign's vicar: King John was to insist upon the steward's

---

[1] Stubbs, *Constitutional History*, I, 374–80; see above n. 4, p. 4.
[2] Haskins, *Norman Institutions*, p. 58.   [3] *Ibid.* p. 88.
[4] *Ibid.* p. 91.   [5] *Ibid.* pp. 165–7.
[6] Delisle, *op. cit.* I, 286. Rotrou himself referred to his office with the words *quando . . . totam Normanniam justiciam secularem exercebamus.*
[7] Benedict of Peterborough, I, 124; Howden, II, 100.

viceregal power,[1] and when King Richard was away upon crusade it was the seneschal who was regent in Normandy. Whatever development, therefore, there had been in Normandy towards a justiciarship, it seems beyond doubt that Angevin influence was decisive in making the seneschal the ducal *alter ego*.

Angevin practice never produced an officer called justiciar but always employed the seneschal; and if this was a major determining factor in Norman development, it may seem likely that it also had some influence upon English practice. Yet it is difficult to establish that it was so. It was Henry II himself who defined the functions of the seneschal in Anjou and who made it not simply a domestic office but that of a true *vice-comte* with clearly defined functions.[2] These functions were mainly judicial, although at first the seneschal only judged on an express mandate of the count and had no permanent delegated power of doing justice. Goslin, for example, who was seneschal from 1151 to 1162, did justice between the monks of St Serge and one Becket only on a precise order, and when the monks of Ronceray wanted justice they applied first of all to Henry himself.[3] In Goslin's sealed charter setting out a judgement between the nuns of Fontevrault and the men of Angers he explained that the judgement was made by the express order of the king, and it was confirmed by the latter between 1162 and 1166.[4] The same dependence of the seneschal's authority upon a royal order appears in the stewardship of Stephen de Marçay who succeeded Goslin and who, having entrusted to him a suit between the monks of Marmoutier and Hamelin de Authenaise, could not compel Hamelin to appear; and so the monks appealed to the king who ordered the seneschal to proceed.[5] In 1168 it was still necessary for the king to order the seneschal to do justice in a particular case.[6] Nevertheless, between 1175 and 1180, the seneschal was gaining a general and regular mandate to act on the king's behalf, and litigants began to address themselves to him as the sovereign's representative. From 1180 he

---

[1] *Rot. Chart.* p. 102 b; *manifestum est quod qui senescallum non obediunt mandatum domini contempnunt.*
[2] Boussard, *Histoire du Comté d'Anjou*, pp. 113–28.
[3] *Ibid.* p. 118; Delisle, *Pièces Justicatives*, no. 3.
[4] Delisle, *Recueil*, I, 361–2.   [5] *Ibid.* I, 335.   [6] *Ibid.* I, 431.

needed a bureau of clerks to help him and, by the early thirteenth century, his office was regularly organized and almost an autonomous institution.[1]

Both Norman and Angevin practice, in using the office of seneschal, bear striking resemblances to the employment of the justiciar in England, and it is tempting to suppose connexions. It is clear, however, that whatever the interplay of these different practices on the king's experience and inclinations Norman and Angevin development towards an *alter ego* was not ahead of English practice but rather, as will appear in succeeding chapters, behind it. There is no reason to suppose that Henry II disregarded his father's advice to keep the administration of his dominions separate, nor any reason to suppose connexions other than the king's own person. There is no sign of conscious imitation, which, in the context of different dominions, might have been difficult. Resemblances, of course, can be found, but they seem to illustrate the principle that similar problems tend to produce similar solutions.

In England the needs which led to the creation of the justiciarship had all been felt acutely in the period from the Norman Conquest to 1154: the need for a regent, the need for a deputy to do justice on the king's behalf, the need for the exploitation of royal resources and their administration. Tentative solutions were tried, each dictated by the political and economic situation in which a king found himself. In the person of Roger of Salisbury, something very like the justiciarship had emerged, a figure for whom there is no real parallel in Normandy or Anjou. But whatever tradition Roger established was broken under Stephen, and something of the diversity of experiment of earlier reigns reappeared. The justiciar had a number of forerunners, but no lineal ancestors.

[1] Boussard, *op. cit.* pp. 123–4; Beautemps-Beaupré, *Coutumes et Institutions de l'Anjou et du Maine*, part II, p. 1.

31

CHAPTER II

THE JUSTICIARSHIP UNDER
HENRY II

Henry II, upon his succession to the Crown, was faced with all of the problems with which his predecessor had grappled. Since his empire was so much larger than the original Anglo-Norman dominion his absences were likely to be longer and more frequent and the need for a viceroy correspondingly greater. Because of the anarchy, he had to re-establish royal authority and restore royal resources, which meant employing efficient administrative machinery. And he must do both of these things in circumstances in which loyalties had been strained by the civil war and baronial independence asserted; he needed to re-establish that co-operation between king and baronage upon which society rested. There was an urgent need for the delegation of royal power, but the circumstances were not favourable to the creation of the justiciarship. The new king had to rely upon ministers who, with the exception of Bishop Nigel of Ely, had served Stephen. So far as they were professional royal servants their loyalty could perhaps be taken for granted, since their careers were bound up with the prestige and development of royal power and government, but, so far as they were feudal magnates as well, relations of confidence and trust between them and the king were plainly of gradual growth. Henry's action in applying to Archbishop Theobald for his chancellor is scarcely the action of a man who had a wide choice open to him. Hence the delegation of royal authority was, as it had been in earlier reigns, diffused, and for his regent the king turned, as his predecessor had, to members of his own family.

I. ROYAL REGENTS AND MINISTERS

Queen Eleanor and Henry the king's son both acted as regents, and the Empress Matilda intervened at least once in English affairs. In the early pipe rolls of Henry II many writs of Eleanor are cited as the authority for the payment, and copies of a good number of them survive. Many of the queen's writs were concerned with her own domestic affairs: provisions for her household, food and wine, and her robes.[1] Others deal with matters of the same kind as a royal writ might have done. For example, in 1156 or 1157 she ordered John fitz Ralph, sheriff of London, to compel John Bucointe to warrant 40 shillings' worth of land to the monks of Reading which his father had given them or the equivalent; if the sheriff failed to do so the royal justice of London would.[2] Like her predecessors, she treated royal officials as her own, and in another of her writs ordered the sheriff of Gloucester to give the canons of Llanthony half a virgate of land, the farm of which they rendered to Walter 'my sheriff', while yet a third writ ordering the knights and men of the abbot of Abingdon to render their services fully told them that if they did not *iusticia regis et mea* would do so.[3] Both of these writs were issued *per breve regis de ultra mare* from Winchester. They show that suitors might seek out the king rather than his royal regent, and although Eleanor might describe officials as her own as well as the king's, it is obvious that her authority, like that of Henry I's regents, waited upon the king's will. Pleading was postponed until the king's return, lands were measured by reference to the king's last crossing of the Channel. A regent must necessarily have had some discretionary authority as the writ to John fitz Ralph shows, but essentially the chief duty was to ensure that the king's will was done, and that implied an administration which could give effect to royal commands when the king was abroad.

That the government was unaffected by the absence of the royal regent is obvious from Queen Eleanor's own presence on the continent in 1159. She had ruled in Henry's name in England during his first absence of a year from June 1156 to April 1157 but, in his long absence from August 1158 to 25 June 1163, she herself left England in 1159 and again in 1160.[4] No doubt the first of

---

[1] *Pipe Rolls 2, 3, and 4 Henry II*, pp. 53, 157, 175; *Pipe Roll 5 Henry II*, p. 45; *Pipe Roll 6 Henry II*, pp. 13, 20.

[2] Harl. MS 1708, fo. 113v; Richardson, *Memoranda Roll 1 John*, p. lxviii.

[3] Llanthony Cartulary A i, fo. liiii; Richardson, *op. cit.* p. lxviii n. 4.

[4] Richardson, *op. cit.* p. lxviii n. 1.

these absences explains the empress's intervention in 1159, when, styling herself empress and daughter of King Henry, she ordered Maurice of Hereford *ex parte mea et filii mei Henrici regis* that the monks of Reading were not to be impleaded for their chattels and other lands of Bradford of which they were seised when the king last crossed to Normandy, until he returned to England; *quod nisi feceris iusticia Anglie fieri faciat.*[1] Her order was sent from Le Pré in Normandy. What probably happened is that a monk of Reading sought out the absent king who proved to be in Aquitaine, and the Reading suitor thereupon approached Matilda who exercised a regency on her son's behalf in Normandy to obtain a writ. From the phraseology it seems clear that the justiciar was then regent in England in Eleanor's absence, but the order itself was sent not to him but to the local official, and the Reading mission itself had by-passed the regent to go abroad to the king. Obviously the government could function without the presence of a royal regent; equally obviously, the royal regents had a prestige and authority which the justiciar had not.

Queen Eleanor no doubt continued to act as regent when she was in England in the short royal absence in 1163 and the long one from 1166 until the young Henry was crowned co-king in 1170, but the bulk of the evidence for her regency is confined to the years before 1160, after which her writs were no longer cited on the pipe rolls as the authority for payment. That the justiciar only acted in the absence of a member of the royal family is clear from the viceroyalty of the king's son who, as a crowned consort, took precedence over the queen as well. From 1170 to 1172 the government ran in the name of Henry *Court Mantel* who, in his writs which dealt in October and November 1172 with the election to the vacant see of Ely, styled himself *Henricus rex*.[2] In the first he ordered the prior and convent to elect six monks who would cross the Channel to Henry II with a writ from the chapter to make the election before him, 'for the lord king my father and I wish that the church be provided for to the honour of God'. His second writ ordered that the elected monks should be at

---

[1] Egerton MS 3031, fo. 94v; Richardson, *op. cit.* pp. lxviii–lxix.
[2] Cotton MS Titus A i, fo. 54v; Richardson, *op. cit.* pp. lxx–lxxi.

Winchester on 7 December prepared to cross, and the young king wished them to do so from Southampton. Perhaps because Henry *Court Mantel* left for France shortly after its issue the writ seems to have had no effect, and others of the justiciar who succeeded him became necessary.[1] Whatever the prestige of the royal regent, however, the writs show that the king himself decided and handled important affairs, that the regent was an intermediary whose authority was used to enable the king to decide policy and control the affairs of his kingdom.

With the revolt of 1173, young Henry and Queen Eleanor were both removed from positions of regency, and when need arose the justiciar took their place. He had already done so exceptionally on earlier occasions, and he and his ministerial colleagues were the effective government even when it ran in the name of members of the royal family. Nevertheless, it is clear that the apparatus of government itself developed while the royal regents exercised power, and the evolution of the justiciarship to the point at which its holder succeeded these regents was closely connected with administrative development. In the years immediately following Henry II's accession, there were a number of ministers who discharged functions or exercised influence which were later peculiar to the justiciar. Bishop Nigel of Ely was called in to overhaul the exchequer and he and the barons of the exchequer, both separately and as a group, authorized payments in their own names. The original writ survives in which Nigel and the barons order the sheriff of Gloucester to let the monks of Bordesley have their land in peace, and to take *ad opus regis* only what was right according to royal writs; witness William Cumin and John Marshal at Westminster.[2] The pipe rolls refer to payments made by order of Nigel and by writ of the barons.[3] The chancellor, Becket, whose relations with the king were closer than those of any other minister, and who had, as a chronicler said, no equal in the kingdom, also authorized payments from royal moneys, and as late as 1162

[1] Richardson, *op. cit.* pp. lxx–lxxi.
[2] Cotton MS Nero C iii, fo. 188. On another occasion Bishop Nigel told the abbot of Ramsey that Richard the clerk had rendered account of scutage and was quit by a private letter form; *Cartulary of Ramsey*, I, 255.
[3] *Pipe Rolls 2, 3, and 4 Henry II*, pp. 53, 65.

Becket's writs, described as *brevia archiepiscopi*, appear on the rolls.[1] When the treasurer wrote his Dialogue such authority was confined to the justiciar, and it is evident that in the six years after Henry's succession exchequer practice was still not rigidly organized. Such writs, appearing side by side with those of the queen and the justiciar, show that the king relied on a group of ministers, of whom Becket was the most trusted. By 1159 the empress could refer to the justiciar of England, a title which evidently had a precise meaning, but the importance of the justiciar was qualified by the activity of the king's other ministers, by the presence of the royal regents, and by the fact that the justiciarship was held not by one man but by two: Earl Robert of Leicester and Richard de Luci.

2. ROBERT, EARL OF LEICESTER

The first of these men, Earl Robert, was the greatest of the earls when Henry II became king, for his great rival the earl of Chester was dead and his heir a minor. He was a member of the Beaumont family whose father had accompanied the Conqueror. In Domesday Book the Beaumont estates consisted of large holdings in Warwickshire, lesser holdings in Leicestershire, and other lands in Northamptonshire and Wiltshire, with a total income of about £220 a year; it was a barony of the third rank in England,[2] but the father was also count of Meulan in Normandy. Robert's inheritance was complicated by a number of factors. His twin brother Waleran succeeded to the Meulan estates in Normandy, and at some time after the Domesday survey his father's brother Henry was created earl of Warwick and endowed with the Warwickshire lands of the count of Meulan and the fee of Turchil of Warwick, the father being compensated with lands of unknown extent and value elsewhere.[3] But in Rufus's reign the count of Mortain rebelled, losing his Northamptonshire estates which had made him the principal lay tenant in that county, although they

---

[1] Howden, I, 220; *Pipe Rolls 2, 3, and 4 Henry II*, pp. 83, 89, 112, 140; *Pipe Roll 8 Henry II*, pp. 1, 53, 64, 67.
[2] Corbett, *CMH*, v, 511.
[3] *VHC Warwickshire*, I, 277; *Complete Peerage*, VII, 528 ff.

were restored to his son William. The latter took sides against Henry I in 1106, and the count of Meulan, who had become earl of Leicester in 1101, obtained a good part of them. Robert succeeded his father in these English estates, and added to them by his marriage in 1128 to Amice, daughter of Robert, *seigneur* of Gael and Montfort, who was the son of Earl Ralph of Norfolk by Emma, daughter of William fitz Osbern. In the right of his wife Earl Robert acquired the fitz Osbern inheritance in Normandy (which made him Lord of Breteuil) and in England (the earldom of Hereford), and probably based his claim to the stewardship of England upon this match.[1] By 1130 he had acquired the one important borough to pass into the hands of a subject, for he possessed all the dues of the town of Leicester, the greater part of its land and houses belonging to him directly.[2] From King Stephen, he obtained a grant of the castle and town of Hereford *et totum comitatum*, except those lands held of the Crown by the bishop, the abbot of Reading, and certain lay tenants: a confirmation of the fitz Osbern inheritance.[3] Henry confirmed all his lands, and granted him the stewardship of England and Normandy.

By Henry II's reign, the earldom of Leicester was much larger and more powerful than the Beaumont barony of the Conquest, although its precise extent is difficult to discover because the earl's *carta* is missing from those of 1166. From the danegeld payments of 1162, it is clear that the bulk of his lands lay in Leicestershire, where he paid £35. 8s. 5d., Warwickshire (£15. 14s. 3d.), Gloucestershire (£8. 11s. 6d.), Northamptonshire (£11. 2s. 8d.), Sussex (£8. 6s.), Hampshire (£6), Norfolk and Suffolk (£4. 8s.), Dorset (£2. 15s.); he also paid (under £1) in Rutland, Lincolnshire, Oxfordshire, Nottinghamshire, Derbyshire, Kent, Cambridge, and Huntingdonshire.[4] Robert was thus one of the most powerful and wealthy of the barons, with the centre of his power in the Midlands but extending both west to the Welsh border and east to East Anglia, with some lands in the south-west and south-

---

[1] *Complete Peerage*, VII, pp. 529, 530; Orderic, IV, 339, 410.

[2] *VHC Leicestershire*, I, 301; Orderic, IV, 168.

[3] Duchy of Lancaster, Royal Charter no. 14.

[4] *Pipe Roll 8 Henry II*, pp. 2, 8, 10, 24, 30, 36, 43, 60, 64. Curiously enough, the earl was not mentioned in the Herefordshire account.

east. Feudally speaking, the earl of Leicester was the most important of the new king's vassals.

Any magnate of Robert's stature played an important part in the king's counsels, but something more than feudal standing was required to place him in the inner circle. The king needed the co-operation of his great barons, but he did not necessarily have to take them into the royal administration. Earl Robert's employment is perhaps indicative of Henry's need to establish loyalty and co-operation with the magnates after the stresses of the anarchy, but there were probably other reasons for his choice of the earl as justiciar.

Robert and his brother Waleran were brought up with great care at the court of Henry I, in a circle, that is to say, which was concerned with government and administration as well as feudal virtues.[1] Very probably it was in this time that he conceived a dislike for Roger of Salisbury and his family which would explain the leading part he took in their arrest in 1139. That he was himself a man of some education and reputation is clear from the cardinals' astonishment at his learning when he accompanied the king to Gisors for his meeting with the pope in 1119, and from the fact that he was quoted by John of Salisbury for his view of treason against the king in a context which emphasized royal authority.[2] It is not accidental that he exercised restraint during the anarchy, supporting the king while concluding a private agreement with his great neighbour, Earl Ranulf of Chester.[3] He served Stephen loyally, which cannot have meant that his relations with the new king were at once close or intimate, but his career and his reputation, as well as his feudal importance, must have made him a candidate for high office. In Robert, Henry II gained both feudal support and a minister who knew and accepted royal administrative procedures.

3. RICHARD DE LUCI

The colleague in the justiciarship, Richard de Luci, was a horse from a different stable. Not of great family, he was born into the

[1] Malmesbury, *Gesta Regum*, II, 482.   [2] *Policraticus*, II, 74.
[3] Round, *Geoffrey de Mandeville*, p. 380.

knightly class, his ancestors holding land in Kent, Norfolk, and Suffolk, for which they did castle guard at Dover.[1] In 1166 these lands comprised half a knight's fee at Newton, Kent, which was in demesne, and another half fee which was held of him by Richard Pereforde; in Norfolk and Suffolk, Robert de Monteni held five knights' fees of Richard de Luci, and Hugh fitz Hamlin one in Stow hundred.[2] By inheritance Richard was a person of minor consequence, but his loyal service to Stephen, and then to Henry II, substantially increased his feudal significance. Under Stephen he had been royal justiciar in Essex, and governor of Falaise, and eventually became constable of the Tower and of the castle of Windsor under the terms of the treaty of Winchester.[3] It was in this last year of the king's reign that he laid the foundations of his barony. William, the king's son, at some date between December 1153 and October 1154, gave him Stamford Rivers, Chipping Ongar, Chreshall, and Roothing, and the manors of Laughton and Chinting held of the rape of Pevensey, a grant confirmed by Henry II.[4] The new king continued to show Richard substantial marks of royal favour: £80 worth of land in Hatfield, Essex, £20 in Diss, Norfolk, and a similar grant at Bloxam in Oxfordshire, a blanch farm of £60 at Bray in Berkshire, and 25s. worth of land at Ongar.[5] Stephen's son also continued his grants, giving Richard Greensted at some time between 1167 and 1174 for the service of ten knights.[6] By 1166, when the *cartae baronum* were compiled, de Luci was a powerful baron. He then held ten knights' fees of Earl Reginald of Cornwall, nine of the fee of Adam Malherbe, in

[1] *Red Book*, p. 352.   [2] *Ibid.* p. 351.

[3] Madox, *History of the Exchequer*, p. 23, prints a writ addressed by Stephen to Richard *justiciario* and the sheriff of Essex. His association with a local royal official strongly suggests that he was addressed in his capacity of local royal justiciar in Essex. Richardson and Sayles, *Governance of Mediaeval England*, p. 166 n. 2, admit the ambiguity of the addresses of Stephen's writs to de Luci, but claim one as unambiguous, although he was given no title and addressed with the ministers of London and Middlesex, a position perhaps explained by the castles he held.

[4] Round, *Essex Archaeological Soc. Trans.*, new series, VII, part II, 144–6, prints Henry II's charter of confirmation from the *Cartae Antiquae* rolls.

[5] *Pipe Roll 5 Henry II*, pp. 4, 8, 34, 36; *Pipe Roll 7 Henry II*, pp. 36, 64.

[6] Round, *loc. cit.* p. 148. This charter too was enrolled on the *Cartae Antiquae* rolls.

addition to his fee of William the king's son, and a thirtieth knight of the *honor* of Clare.[1] Thus he was a lord of thirty knights and, together with his ancestral holdings and a knight he had newly enfeoffed in Devonshire, he had carved out a powerful barony, chiefly made up of lands held of mesne lords, of which the *caput* was Ongar, probably the head of the Essex fief of Eustace of Boulogne, an *honor* which was completed by a grant from Henry II of the hundred of Ongar.[2] In addition he held the farms of the towns of Windsor and Colchester throughout Henry's reign.

Richard de Luci was a man of steadily growing feudal importance, although never comparable to the earl of Leicester; when he witnessed royal charters, he did so after the constables in these early years. Unlike Robert's, Richard's feudal position derived from his devoted service to the king; he served Stephen loyally to the end and then Henry II with equal fidelity, earning the epithet 'the loyal',[3] but it is also clear that he could count on the favour of other great barons as his land holdings show. This feudal status, however, was the result of his administrative position. He was never quoted by John of Salisbury, but there can be no doubt that his views on royal authority were those of a *curialis* who had a vested interest in the advance and the efficiency of royal government. The tradition that he drafted the Constitutions of Clarendon is significant, and it is confirmed by his excommunication as one of the men responsible for the king's deeds.[4] No doubt relations of trust between the king and Richard were also of gradual growth but Henry II had found a useful minister, of feudal standing and administrative experience, whose career depended upon his professional services and whose fortunes were, more closely than the earl of Leicester's, bound up with his own.

[1] *Red Book*, p. 261.
[2] Cotton Charters, XI. The date is probably 1172–4; and Eyton suggested the latter, thinking the grant a reward for service during the revolt. Since Henry II took Ongar castle from Richard at this time, it seems unlikely.
[3] Benedict, p. 124.
[4] *Becket Materials*, v, 390; Gervase of Canterbury, pp. 200, 241.

4. THE DEVELOPMENT OF THE JUSTICIARSHIP

From the position of the royal regents and the activity of other ministers like Becket, it is clear that the co-justiciars' importance only developed gradually. It is also clear that between the two of them, the earl took precedence. Where Robert, at the beginning of the reign, authorized payments of royal money by his writ, Richard did not: payments were made *per Ricardum de Luci* as they were made *per cancellarium* or by other officials,[1] but his writ was not cited until after Becket's elevation to the archbishopric. Only towards the end of Earl Robert's life did his colleague's writs begin to rival his own in number. Whereas Robert had very early authorized with Becket the entertainment of the king of the Scots, supplied provisions for the household of the young king, bought horses for Henry II himself, arranged for the transport of treasure from Winchester to Carlisle, paid knights in the king's service in Wales, and authorized repairs to the castle of Colchester or the gaol of London,[2] it was only in 1163 that Richard's writs paid for the king's horses, and not until 1167 that his control over payments from royal revenue became marked. In that year he paid for work done on the Tower, the transport of treasure to Dover, the purchase of tents for the king, and the repairs of royal residences, and in the following year he was much concerned with the castles of the Marches and the men in service there.[3] It is, of course, impossible to be certain that work done or paid for by writs of the justiciars reveals the whole of their activity; since writs might be issued in the king's name on their authority, a good deal of their work may be concealed behind the phrase *per breve regis*. Nevertheless, it seems evident that there was no real difference between the kinds of responsibility they had, although there can be no doubt that, while Earl Robert lived, he overshadowed Richard de Luci, for in 1163 his court, not Richard's, took the plea of Richard of Anstey from the king's, and in 1165 or

[1] *Pipe Rolls 2, 3, and 4 Henry II*, pp. 13, 66, 185; *Pipe Roll 8 Henry II*, p. 67.
[2] *Pipe Rolls 2, 3, and 4 Henry II*, pp. 83, 115, 175; *Pipe Roll 5 Henry II*, p. 18; *Pipe Roll 7 Henry II*, p. 2; *Pipe Roll 9 Henry II*, p. 68.
[3] *Pipe Roll 13 Henry II*, pp. 1, 2, 4, 114; *Pipe Roll 14 Henry II*, pp. 1, 2, 110, 169.

early 1166 the king addressed the earl and the barons of the exchequer, not Richard de Luci.[1]

Nor can it be doubted that, as in the reign of Henry I, the centre of the justiciars' power lay in the exchequer. Both of them presided over the barons, and Earl Robert left an impression of greatness which the treasurer recorded. Richard fitz Nigel explains that he had looked upon the earl of Leicester as *virum discretum, litteris eruditum et in negotiis forensibus exercitatum*, who by the king's mandate was not merely president of the exchequer but of the whole kingdom.[2] The treasurer nowhere mentions Richard de Luci, but part of the Becket story relates that, while it was the earl of Leicester who was sent to inspect the archbishop's illness and to pronounce the judgement of the *curia regis* and who, with the agreement of the other magnates, refused in 1165 to treat with the schismatic Reginald of Cologne, it was to Richard de Luci and the barons of the exchequer that Becket appealed for quittance of those sums he had handled as chancellor.[3] Both Robert and Richard presided over the exchequer sessions, but it was the earl who left a tradition of greatness.

The sharing of the justiciarship, in spite of Earl Robert's obvious precedence, suggests that the office was still in a formative stage, and this belief is strengthened if the lack of clear definition in exchequer custom during the earl's lifetime be considered. The connexion of the two justiciars with the exchequer means that if exchequer practice had not reached the precision with which Richard fitz Nigel describes it, then the justiciarship itself was still in a formative stage, still affected by those circumstances which, it has been argued earlier, militated against such an office in the early years of King Henry II. The occasion upon which the treasurer described the earl of Leicester's greatness is itself evidence of this. Richard fitz Nigel was discussing the right of the barons of the exchequer to be quit of the reguard, and he explains that the earl of Leicester obtained a writ from the king giving him such quittance. Nigel, the treasurer, rebuked Robert. Quittance of the

---

[1] Egerton MS 3031, fo. 24v; Palgrave, *Rise and Progress of the English Commonwealth*, II, 116; D. M. Stenton, *CMH*, v, 576–8.
[2] *Dialogus*, I, xi. [3] Diceto, p. 318; Howden, I, 220.

reguard, he said, was by right of sitting at the board, not by royal favour in particular cases; whereupon the earl acknowledged his error and abandoned the writ. Since Nigel retired into private life in 1164 or 1165, one may believe that, for the greater part of the earl of Leicester's justiciarship, a process of definition was still going on in royal government to which his office was as subject as any other.

The earl's justiciarship also reveals a similar process of definition going on in judicial practice. Reference has already been made to the Reading monks who by-passed the justiciar to go to the king or a member of his family in 1159. The famous case of Richard of Anstey which began in 1158 also shows a litigant seeking his writs from the king who was abroad, although he also obtained a covering writ actually to begin the action from Queen Eleanor in England.[1] The only part played by the justiciar was the setting down of a day for the hearing, for, having a royal writ and a regent's writ, he took them both to Richard de Luci. In 1158 the abbot of Abingdon also sent a monk to France to obtain a royal writ in a case of disseisin, and, perhaps in the following year, Henry II at the suit of the men of Wallingford prohibited the abbot from holding a market until he himself could return to hear the case.[2] Violence occurred, however, and the men of Wallingford got another writ from Henry ordering the earl of Leicester to inquire through the full county what the position was in Henry I's time. The case dragged on through accusations of perjury, and the earl did not presume to judge, going instead to the king whom he informed that he had seen the church of Abingdon in enjoyment of the market; Henry II thereupon gave a judgement in favour of the abbey. A St Albans case shows the same features.[3] Robert de Valoines wanted a wood from the abbot of St Albans who refused, and, having obtained a royal writ, Robert went to the earl of Leicester, who was then hearing pleas, bearing this order which provided that if there was failure in justice the earl should remedy the default. The justiciar awarded the wood to Robert

---

[1] Palgrave, *op. cit.* II, 116; Richardson, *op. cit.* p. lxxviii ff.
[2] *Chron. Mon. Abing.* II, 225, 227; *Placita Anglo-Normannica*, pp. 197–8.
[3] *Gesta Abb. St Alb.* p. 161.

who subsequently wasted it, and the abbot, having approached the earl with no result, applied to Queen Eleanor, who gave him a writ ordering Robert to cease his depredations. A final hearing in this case was only obtained when a new order from the king to the earl of Leicester was issued after the abbot had sent gifts to the king, and when the justiciar heard the case Robert lost the wood by default.

This litigation hardly differs in character from the land pleas of the early Norman reigns, and the procedure is not much different. There was apparently no notion that an 'original' writ could be obtained from the regent or justiciar, and some reason to believe that the justiciar's order might be ineffective, as it was when the earl of Leicester summoned the earl of Arundel to appear before him at Northampton to answer the abbot of St Albans over the cell of Wymondham.[1] There is little indication of any idea that the justiciar represented the king in doing justice except on an express royal order, and therefore little notion of a defined chief judicial office. But there was, nevertheless, some conception that the justiciar had a definite place in the administration of justice.

Two writs of Earl Robert survive, one of them an original which, when Madox saw it, bore the earl's seal.[2] Both of them contain the precise and terse phraseology of royal writs, and they were both issued *per breve regis de ultra mare*. In the one, the earl ordered Reginald de Warenne to do full right to Robert de Mandeville over the land which had been his brother's at Diganeswell which Robert claimed to hold of Reginald. In the other, the earl ordered the barons of Hastings to let the abbot of St Benet of Holme hold his lands in Yarmouth in peace. In each case, failure to do so would be remedied by the local royal official or, if he failed, by the earl of Leicester himself: *nisi fecerit ego faciam*. This phraseology is the same as that of the Empress Matilda's writ, and

[1] *Ibid.* p. 172.
[2] Madox, *History of the Exchequer*, p. 23. Madox printed this from the original in the archives of St Peter of Westminster, and there was then attached to it a seal, 'upon a canton cut from the bottom of this writ . . . of yellow wax, circular near three inches large (now a little diminished). It shows a knight mounted in war-like equipage, his face to the left hand; on the reverse, a small round counter seal.'

it assumes that the justiciar would remedy the failures of feudal justice and local royal officers. The assumption was clearly made that the king's deputy, if he could not originate suits, could ensure that justice was done, and the regular use of the justiciar's position to remedy failures of justice seems well established. Henry's legal reforms lay in the future, but the justiciarship of the earl of Leicester shows an advance on earlier practice. An illustration is Robert's charter which set out to all the earls and barons and French and English of all England that Gervase of Cornhill had made a quit claim before the justiciar in favour of the abbot and convent of St Peter of Ghent of his claim to the towns of Lewisham and Greenwich.[1] Such an agreement would later have taken the precise form of a final concord, but that the earl issued it at all is an indication of growth of a judicial office which played a regular part in royal government.

Both exchequer and judicial practice reveal a development towards the office of justiciar rather than a defined office during the earl of Leicester's tenure, although there can be little doubt that the exchequer was achieving a precision of organization before Henry II undertook his legal reforms. The justiciarship of the earl of Leicester shows the beginnings of the later office, and it may have been more important than the evidence suggests, because in the years between 1163 and 1166 the king was in England and government ran in his name, thus concealing the place of his justiciars. When Henry left again for the continent, Earl Robert and Richard de Luci were in control of the exchequer and the queen accompanied the king. Becket and Bishop Nigel had vanished from government, and so the justiciars had no rivals. When the earl died in April 1168, Richard de Luci was left as sole justiciar.

He was still not alone in his pre-eminence. Henry *Court Mantel* became regent in his father's absence, but the series of Ely writs in

---

[1] Round, *Calendar of Documents Preserved in France*, no. 1380, describes this document as a letter of *R. comes de Luci*. He took it from PRO Transcripts vol. VIII. The following document in these transcripts, which Round did not calendar, is an identical letter in the name of Robert earl of Leicester, and there can be no doubt that this, and not Round's version, is the original. Nevertheless, the confusion of names is suggestive.

his name and Richard's shows that his position was largely honorary: the justiciar could replace him and maintain the continuity of government.[1] If young Henry had remained faithful to his father and had continued as co-king, his power and influence would certainly have grown. For this reason, Henry II's intentions with the justiciarship were probably that it should be a chief executive office with no viceregal quality except as emergency dictated. But the revolt of the young king with encouragement from Queen Eleanor left Richard de Luci as chief executive officer with no royal regents, and his loyal action against the king's enemies must have strengthened his position. After 1173 Richard took the place of the royal regents as the king's *alter ego*, and the prestige of the justiciarship was enhanced at a time when its functions were being much more precisely defined.

5. DEFINITION OF THE JUSTICIARSHIP

When Richard retired from office in 1178, the exchequer could be described in dogmatic terms by the treasurer, as if its custom was fixed, clear, and of long standing. In the earl of Leicester's time, the exchequer was still being reorganized and its practices were not rigid, but by the end of de Luci's justiciarship, Richard fitz Nigel described a bureaucracy which in his eyes permitted no such deviations. It was primarily during Richard de Luci's term of office that this definition occurred, and at the end of his life the treasurer could lay down the duties of the justiciar at the exchequer in a precise fashion. He was the king's representative who sat there *ex officio* to supervise everything that was done in either the upper or the lower exchequer, and his control extended to the disposition of the inferior offices, like knight silversmith or melter, who fulfilled their duties at his command.[2] The justiciar had jurisdiction over the barons of the exchequer if dissension arose among them, with the right to fine them for bad behaviour. He controlled the internal organization of the exchequer, but the more obvious signs of his greatness were external. He set the exchequer in motion by his order, by his summons to the sheriff to render

[1] Richardson, *op. cit.* p. lxxi.   [2] *Dialogus*, I, v and vi.

account, controlling for the purpose a duplicate of the great seal which was kept in the treasury.[1] The justiciar's control of this exchequer seal—for it was only brought out on his order and for exchequer business—and his right to issue writs under its authority in the king's name under his own witness, or in his own name under the witness of others, was the real test of his greatness in the treasurer's eyes.[2] *Magnus est hic, cujus fidei totius regni cura, immo et cor regis committitur;* 'where the treasure is, there will the heart be also'.

The justiciar's work was not the technical business of accounting, nor the supervising of the writing of the pipe rolls, although he had a general oversight of all that was done, but the solving of the difficulties which arose out of the accounts. The greater science of the exchequer consisted in its judgements, and the justiciar with his colleagues, the barons, deliberated and decided upon these matters in a separate room: the matters which later appear upon the memoranda rolls. None of the latter survives before the reign of King John, although they undoubtedly existed earlier,[3] and in their absence it is impossible to examine the justiciar's work or personal influence, but the problems which arose cannot have been substantially different from those which faced the justiciar in 1199. The justiciar presided over the exchequer, as the treasurer said, to dispose of business so that it turned out to the king's advantage, and the precision of the exchequer organization the Dialogue describes gave a precise meaning to the justiciar's office as the king's *alter ego*. Over the *curia regis* sitting for financial purposes the justiciar represented the king.

Nevertheless, the definition of the justiciarship which is implied in the exchequer organization does not mean that the office was fully developed. So far as legal administration is concerned, the justiciar's position was still undefined, but the justiciarship of Richard de Luci saw the beginning of the legal reforms of Henry II. The Assize of Clarendon of 1166 was enforced by Earl Geoffrey de Mandeville and Richard de Luci, who undertook a general eyre through seventeen shires, with the justiciar enforcing the assize

[1] *Dialogus*, I, xv.   [2] *Ibid.* I, v.
[3] Richardson, *op. cit.* pp. xvi ff.

alone in an eighteenth.[1] Such judicial work in a county was not new to Richard, for he had three years earlier held pleas at Carlisle which were intended to pacify Cumberland as the later Assize of Clarendon was intended to establish peace and good order throughout England.[2] His extensive work in 1166, however, marked the beginning of regular visitations, and it is clear that he was the chief agent of the king in establishing royal authority. Thereafter, Richard never undertook a general visitation, but between 1174 and 1177 he heard at least one case in the north at Pontefract, in the earlier year he assessed the tallage with the sheriff in Nottinghamshire and Derbyshire, and in the later year he heard pleas and assessed the tallage in Hampshire and in Middlesex with Roger fitz Renfrey and Gervase of Cornhill.[3] Richard de Luci was plainly a man of great experience in judicial and financial affairs, but the years of his justiciarship were ones of experiment.

In his Dialogue, the treasurer relates that

when the kingdom was saved from shipwreck and peace restored, the king once more essayed to renew 'the golden days' of his grandfather, and making choice of prudent men he divided the kingdom into six parts so that the justices chosen whom we may call 'justices in eyre' might go on circuit through them and restore the rights which had lapsed. They, giving audience in each county and doing full justice to those who considered themselves wronged, gave the poor both labour and money.[4]

Richard fitz Nigel was describing the Assize of Northampton of 1176 and the aftermath of the young king's revolt, but the justiciar took no part in the work of these itinerant justices, most of whom were exchequer officials. The subsequent rearrangements

---

[1] *Pipe Roll 12 Henry II*, pp. 7, 14, 18, 57, 70, 87, 108, 116.

[2] *Pipe Roll 9 Henry II*, p. 10. Richardson and Sayles, *op. cit.* p. 200, make the point that the justiciars supervised the work of local officials in carrying out the Assize, but did not hear pleas themselves.

[3] Farrer, *Early Yorkshire Charters*, III, 1774; *Pipe Roll 20 Henry II*, p. 60; Richardson and Sayles, *op. cit.* p. 203 think that de Luci visited Yorkshire and Staffordshire and perhaps Cumberland in the general eyre of 1170 which perhaps began in 1167 or 1168. The entries look more like isolated visits or survivals from earlier work.

[4] *Dialogus*, II, ii.

show that Henry II was still experimenting with methods of making royal justice popular and accessible in the shires, but Richard de Luci remained at the centre of administration and did not repeat his extensive tour of 1166. In 1174, in the first final concord which was drafted in the later normal form, he was presiding at the exchequer over Richard, bishop elect of Winchester, Geoffrey, elect of Ely, Humphrey de Bohun, the constable, Hugh de Gundeville, Thomas Basset, Ranulf de Glanville, and Bertram de Verdun.[1] The justiciar's part in this legal activity of the period after the great revolt is obscure, but the evidence suggests that his place was at the centre of government and that he played no great part in carrying it into the shires. This does not mean that he played no part at all. When the justices of 1176 returned to Westminster, they completed their unfinished pleas at the exchequer, and they were men like Bertram de Verdun and Hugh de Gundeville who normally sat there under the justiciar.[2] The identity of personnel between the barons of the exchequer and the itinerant justices shows that the exchequer was the central organ of government,[3] a convenient place for the doing of justice as well as financial business, and the justiciar's presidency meant in fact his control over much judicial work as well as finance.

Two, at least, of the possessory assizes, and perhaps more, were available to litigants during the justiciarship of Richard de Luci,[4] and the king's legal measures undoubtedly began to prove popular. Payments began to appear in the royal accounts for the transfer of a suit into the king's court. After the great revolt, the foundations were laid for the enormous influx of judicial business which began to tax the strength of the royal justices, but it cannot be said that these effects were really apparent in the time of Richard de Luci. In the Assizes of Clarendon and Northampton Henry was making the benefits compulsory before putting them up for sale, and their increasing popularity is really a phenomenon of Richard's reign. Still, one of the necessities of this legal revolution was the equation

[1] Lansdowne MS 415, fo. 22v; West, 'The Curia Regis in the Late Twelfth and Early Thirteenth Centuries', *Historical Studies*, vi, no. 22, p. 182.
[2] *Pipe Roll 23 Henry II*, pp. 7, 31, 32, 45, 112.
[3] West, *loc. cit.* p. 174.
[4] Van Caenegem, *Royal Writs in England*, pp. 283, 319, 328, 332.

of the justiciar's authority with the king's if justice were to be speedily and readily available. The uncertainties of his early years had to be replaced by an assumption that the justiciar's writ was equally effective. It is possible that this assumption was being made soon after the Assize of Clarendon. Roger de Mylei, making a grant in free alms to the nuns of Stixwould, referred to a jury of the hundred which had declared the land in question to belong to his fee, having been empanelled by the sheriff of Lincolnshire *per preceptum justicie regis Ricardi de Luci*,[1] but lack of evidence makes it impossible to trace the growth of use of the justiciar's writ or the firmness with which it was equated with the king's. There was an obvious quickening of the legal spirit during Richard's justiciarship, but, unlike the exchequer, there is not much indication of a defined and regular exercise of judicial authority. Nevertheless his tenure of office spans a gulf between the world of the *Leges Henrici Primi* and that of Glanville's treatise.

By 1178, when Richard de Luci retired into his own monastic foundation, the office he held had come to have some precision of meaning. After the young king's revolt he had been regent when Henry II was abroad and the government operated in his name. On the king's behalf he defended the Welsh marches, fortified royal castles and residences, paid the king's servants, arranged for the king's supplies of money and provisions. His activity was scarcely less than that of Henry II himself, although his authority was always limited by the king's will; and his actions, as in the case of the suspension of the forest laws, might be disavowed.[2] To meet emergencies, like the great revolt itself, he obviously had to exercise discretionary power, but more usually his principal duty was as chief executive officer to ensure that the king's will was done. The seat of his authority was the exchequer, which was the heart of royal government, and the justiciar's presidency gave precise definition to his office and his function. As the king's *alter ego*, the justiciar was no more bound by the routine of government which the king created than the monarch himself, and like the

---

[1] BM Add. MS 46701, fo. 39v. The date of Richard de Luci's order must be 1167–70 since Philip of Kyme was sheriff of Lincolnshire only in those years.
[2] Benedict, p. 94.

king he might have his *vis et voluntas*, his *ira et malevolentia*, but the assembling of royal ministers and the control which could be exercised over royal officials at the exchequer provided an instrument by which his authority could be expressed and the technical means by which the king's will could most conveniently be done. For this reason, definition of the exchequer meant the definition of the justiciarship, and because the legal reorganization had not yet caused a further 'differentiation' of the *curia regis*, the justiciar's presidency meant control of royal government.

It has sometimes been doubted that the justiciarship was very important when Richard de Luci retired. 'He was relatively of so little consequence that, on his retirement . . . the office remained vacant for more than a year.'[1] Other scholars have maintained that Henry II thought the office a dangerous one and would have liked to let it lapse but found that he could not do so, and some that it was difficult to find a suitable person to fill it. Each of these views involves some consideration of Richard de Luci's colleagues.

After the young king's revolt, the castles of the rebel bishop of Durham were taken into the king's hand, but their custodians swore to return them to the bishop 'if anything adverse happened' *per mandatum Ricardi de Luci vel per mandatum Ricardi Wintoniensis episcopi vel per mandatum Gaufridi Elyensis episcopi.*[2] These two bishops who shared the justiciar's responsibility on this occasion were plainly important in the king's counsels. They were the men who sat beside Richard de Luci in the central court and the exchequer, and who, in the year of his death, became *archijustitiarii* of two of the circuits into which Henry divided England.[3] Bishop Richard was a *curialis* of long experience, until 1162 *scriptor curie* and in the following year archdeacon of Poitiers.[4] He was obviously a man of influence, for the abbot of St Albans sought his favour as one who had the ear of the king.[5] He was loyal to Henry during the Becket quarrel and was excommuni-

---

[1] Richardson, *op. cit.* p. lxxvii; Chrimes, *op. cit.* pp. 39–40.
[2] Benedict, p. 178.
[3] Diceto, I, 435; Howden, II, 190–1; Benedict, p. 238.
[4] *DNB*.   [5] *Gesta Abb. St Alb.* I, 151, 154.

cated in June 1166 when he was one of the envoys who recognized the anti-pope. From 1165 he sat as a judge in the central royal court, and he took his place at the exchequer by the king's special command.[1]

He was a great man [wrote the treasurer] and had many avocations of importance. Before his promotion when he held a slightly lower position in the king's court, he approved himself a trustworthy and diligent court servant, zealous and dutiful in the matter of accounts and in the writing of rolls and writs. Wherefore a place was given him beside the treasurer, so that he should, jointly with him, attend to the writing of the roll and all such matters.

The other matters were checking the copies of the summonses. He may in fact have been the treasurer's official supervisor, for the references to the *rotulus archidiaconi* suggest some such position.[2] His place at the English exchequer was apparently a recent innovation of Henry II,[3] but it was not permanent. He was sent into Normandy to overhaul the exchequer there. In addition to his financial work, he was a justice in eleven counties in 1168 and thirteen in the following year.[4] The rewards for his service increased in importance. By 1164 he was known as a great pluralist, and two years later he became custodian of the vacant bishopric of Lincoln, in 1171 of Winchester and the abbey of Glastonbury, having also held the *honor* of Montacute.[5] His great experience and proven loyalty led to his promotion to the great bishopric of Winchester in 1174, both John of Salisbury and Bartholomew of Exeter writing on his behalf to the Pope. 'He was', said Gerald of Wales, 'a man of more natural sense than scholarship; more clever in worldly business than versed in liberal arts.'[6] Exactly the qualities Henry II needed in a minister, for there can be no doubt that Richard of Ilchester was high in the king's confidence and an important colleague of the justiciar.

[1] *Dialogus*, I, v.
[2] *Pipe Roll 11 Henry II*, p. 4; *Pipe Roll 13 Henry II*, p. 34.
[3] Richard fitz Nigel described it as *novella; Dialogus*, I, v.
[4] *Pipe Roll 15 Henry II*, pp. 27, 58, 63, 164, 168, 172.
[5] *Becket Materials*, v, 150; *Pipe Roll 13 Henry II*, pp. 57–8, 149; Madox, *History of the Exchequer*, I, 366, 630, 631.
[6] John of Salisbury, *Epistolae*, cccxiii, cccxvi; Giraldus, vii, 70.

Bishop Geoffrey Ridel of Ely was a man of similar stamp. He too began his career as a clerk in the chancery under Becket, whom he succeeded as archdeacon of Canterbury in 1163.[1] He too was loyal to Henry during the famous quarrel, and was excommunicated by the archbishop in 1169. From 1165 he was a baron of the exchequer and in the following year became custodian of the Great Seal which he may have held immediately upon its withdrawal from Becket.[2] He too became custodian of a vacant bishopric, Ely, to which he succeeded as bishop at the same time as Richard got Winchester. Like Richard, he continued to sit in the royal court as a judge, and in 1176 became custodian of the *honor* of Eye.[3] His career was perhaps not so active in financial organization as Richard's, but he too was an important and trusted royal minister who stood beside the justiciar at the centre of government. The presence of these two bishops obviously provided the justiciar with colleagues of great experience whom, as being high in the king's confidence, he would naturally consult. This is not to diminish the importance of Richard de Luci. A strong king was a king who had good counsel, and a strong justiciar was one who was supported by important colleagues. And there were limits beyond which the king, after his experience with the double allegiance put to the test by Becket, could not use prominent ecclesiastics; however loyal, they were exposed to pressures which might make their utility doubtful. Their importance in the work of royal government cannot be doubted, but the justiciarship required a lay baron of greater and longer experience and as great loyalty. Richard de Luci measured up to these requirements, and he had been in the forefront of those men who reorganized royal government and asserted effective royal power. Certainly from 1172, and perhaps from 1168, he was the most important single minister of the king. As a powerful baron who was also a professional administrator he had no equal, and the office that he held was as important as he was. The man made the office, and the question of his successor cannot have been easy to answer. With the development of royal government, with the

---

[1] *Becket Materials*, III, 120; Wendover, I, 24.
[2] Madox, *Formulare*, p. xix.   [3] Eyton, *Itinerary*, p. 208.

'differentiation' within the *curia regis* proceeding but not yet extensive, and with the incapacity of the royal family and the king's repeated absences, the importance of the justiciarship as the king's *alter ego* was obvious, and the apparent delay of a year before the office was filled has another explanation.

When Richard de Luci retired, Henry II was almost certainly in England; he had returned from France in July 1178, and he remained in the country until April 1180.[1] It was, therefore, only at this later date that a regent became necessary, only then that it was necessary to give some minister authority to govern on the king's behalf in his own name. While Henry II was in England for a period of nearly two years, a justiciar might be a convenience but scarcely an urgent necessity. The trusted ministers who had stood beside Richard de Luci sat in the royal *curia*, together with others like Bishop John of Norwich,[2] another confidant of the king, and Ranulf de Glanville, a trusted baron who was also an experienced royal administrator. Such men could be set over the judicial circuits of 1179, and through them the king could control his administration. Only when he left for France in 1180 was it necessary to delegate his power to one man charged with responsibility for government. The delay may suggest that if the king had remained in England the justiciarship might have been dispensed with and a group of trusted ministers considered an adequate arrangement. It is equally possible that there was no delay before a new appointment as justiciar was made. The evidence of his authority would not appear while Henry II himself was present, for government ran in the king's name, and the viceregal authority of the justiciar would appear only in 1180 when the king departed. But delay or not, when Henry left for France the justiciarship was necessary, and from 1179 there had been an obvious candidate for the office, a man of similar feudal significance and administrative experience to Richard de Luci.

---

[1] *Handbook of British Chronology*, p. 35.
[2] *DNB* under Oxford, John of; Foss, *op. cit.* pp. 493–4. John's career was rather that of a diplomatist than an administrator, but he was closely associated with the king in the Becket quarrel, and with the justiciar and the other two bishops in the central court.

6. RANULF DE GLANVILLE

The candidate was Ranulf de Glanville who, in 1179, was *archi-justitiarius* of the northern circuit. Like Richard de Luci, Glanville came from modest feudal beginnings. He was the second son of a Suffolk baron who held his lands of the *honor* of Eye, and the grandson of one of the Conquest barons who had been the man of Robert Malet, lord of the *honor*.[1] The family holding as it appears in Domesday Book was not large, although it was sufficiently prosperous for Glanville's father, William, to bestow all the churches of his barony upon the Cluniac monks in the reign of Henry I and for his brother Bartholomew to found Bromholm as a cell of Castle Acre.[2] Ranulf succeeded to the barony on the death of this brother, but his fame and fortune never rested upon his family lands. Like de Luci, he gained power by loyal service to the king. In 1164 he became sheriff of Warwickshire and Leicestershire for one year, at the same time becoming sheriff of Yorkshire.[3] In this northern county he improved his position by a good marriage to Bertha, daughter of the Yorkshire baron Theobald de Valognes who was also lord of Parham and a neighbour of Glanville in Suffolk, with whom he obtained the lordship of Brochous.[4] Ranulf established firm connexions in the north by marrying his sister to the lord of Middleham and his niece to another important baron, William de Stuteville.[5] In 1170 he was removed from the shrievalty of Yorkshire after the Inquest of Sheriffs. At Easter 1170 Ranulf no longer accounted for the farm of the shire, and some years later he was called upon to pay the large sum of £1571. 1s. 1d. in money, together with silver plate, chargers, and palfreys taken by his officers partly from the county and partly from the lands of Everard de Ros which he had held in custody.[6] The king pardoned the whole amount. Glanville's services were valuable to Henry II, and he was made sheriff of

---

[1] Dugdale, *Baronage*, i, 423.
[2] *Ibid.*; in 1187 Glanville was pardoned 30s. of the scutage of the *honor* of Eye, *Pipe Roll 33 Henry II*, p. 62.
[3] *Pipe Roll 11 Henry II*, p. 45.   [4] Dugdale, *op. cit.* i, 424.
[5] *Rot. de Dominabus*, p. xxiv.   [6] *Pipe Roll 23 Henry II*, pp. xxvi, 81.

Lancashire and custodian of the great *honor* of Richmond which he farmed until 1183.[1] Until 1174, however, Glanville's career suggested nothing more than that of an efficient local royal officer of baronial rank, the kind of man upon whom royal administration ultimately depended. The turning-point in his career came with the young king's revolt.

In 1174 Ranulf captured William the Lion, king of the Scots, at Alnwick. Henry II's joy at the news is well known, and from that date Ranulf began to rise rapidly. In 1174 he was sitting in the royal court beside the justiciar, Richard of Ilchester, Geoffrey Ridel, and other prominent ministers.[2] Two years later he was one of the justices assigned to the northern group of shires to enforce the Assize of Northampton. At Michaelmas 1176 he and Hugh de Cressi accounted for pleas held in the East Anglian counties, Buckinghamshire and Bedfordshire, Oxfordshire, Northamptonshire, Nottinghamshire and Derbyshire, as well as those which Ranulf held in Yorkshire and Northumberland with Robert Pikenot and Robert de Wallibus.[3] In 1179 he also accounted for the judicial profits from his and Hugh de Cressi's pleas in Cumberland.[4] When Richard de Luci retired, Glanville was already a judge of some experience, and as a sheriff and custodian he had had a much longer acquaintance with exchequer procedure. He had also established himself as a northern baron, connected with some of the great families of Yorkshire. Moreover, he had rendered the king a signal service during the revolt. If Henry II wanted a layman of whose loyalty he could be sure, of some feudal standing and administrative capacity, Ranulf was plainly an obvious choice. Like de Luci, his interests were those of the king, and his fortunes tied him to the progress of royal government.

The precise date of his appointment to the justiciarship is uncertain. The chronicles describe it under the year 1180, but this is the occasion on which Glanville was left as regent. He may have

---

[1] *Pipe Roll 21 Henry II*, p. 8. The accounts he rendered for the *honor* of Richmond disappear from the roll in 1184, an account of nearly £434 p.a.; *Pipe Roll 30, Henry II*, p. xxix.

[2] Lansdowne MS 415, fo. 22v.

[3] *Pipe Roll 22 Henry II*, pp. 5, 18, 19, 30, 49, 66, 72, 80, 98, 108, 138.

[4] *Pipe Roll 25 Henry II*, p. 30.

been justiciar before this date. In 1179 he was, with Bishops Richard, Geoffrey, and John, head of one of the four circuits and, unlike his three colleagues, he actually undertook the judicial work involved. The three bishops did not serve as itinerant justices in that year, but Glanville visited Yorkshire, Shropshire, Worcestershire, Staffordshire, Oxfordshire, Herefordshire, Nottinghamshire and Derbyshire, a grouping of counties which took him through the north, west, and midlands.[1] In February 1180 he and the bishops were with Henry II at Oxford where the new coinage was decided upon. Glanville's position in 1179, if it does not clearly indicate that he was already justiciar, certainly indicates that he had succeeded to de Luci's position as the layman associated with the king's intimate counsellors.

With the king's departure and Glanville's assumption of a vice-regal position, it has been said that the heyday of the justiciarship begins. This judgement, which really rests upon an association between Glanville's justiciarship and the legal treatise bearing his name, is misleading. In terms of his relations with the king, his feudal standing, and his viceregal power, Glanville can hardly be distinguished from Richard de Luci. Like his predecessor, he conducted campaigns against the Welsh, many border castles being maintained, knights paid, and supplies furnished by his authority or by the king's direction from overseas.[2] He supplied Count John's household and provided him with the means to cross to Ireland, as, in a similar case, he paid Alan Trenchmer to take William de Braiose to Spain in the king's service.[3] From baronies or wardships in the king's hand, he made grants to the king's pensioners or servants.[4] In all of this activity, whether it was initiated by order of the king or whether it lay within the justiciar's discretion, Ranulf's work did not differ from that of Richard de Luci. In quantity it may seem more, because Henry II spent relatively little time—less than a third—in England in the

[1] *Pipe Roll 26 Henry II*, pp. 6, 10, 13, 27, 67, 78, 117, 138, 141.
[2] Benedict, p. 289, describes the Welsh campaign of 1182; *Pipe Roll 29 Henry II*, pp. 27, 108, 109; *Pipe Roll 30 Henry II*, p. 59.
[3] *Pipe Roll 27 Henry II*, p. 115; *Pipe Roll 31 Henry II*, pp. 143, 154, 173, 217; *Pipe Roll 30 Henry II*, pp. 58, 80, 87, 119.
[4] *Pipe Roll 33 Henry II*, pp. 18, 26, 27, 28, 29, 172, 187.

last ten years of his reign, and the justiciar's authority, as it can be traced in the rolls, seems the greater for his absence. The justiciar may have had more work to do, but his duties were essentially the same as any of his predecessors who had filled a viceregal position. No doubt in Glanville's time the office of justiciar was increasingly accepted as a normal part of royal government, but this acceptance had certainly begun in the justiciarship of Richard de Luci. The viceregal duties of the justiciar were, by their very nature, defined and limited by his relationship with the king; he was there to execute the king's will and so to order affairs that they turned out to the king's advantage. He did not decide policy—the attack on Wales, for example, or the refusal of the pope's envoys —but he was meant to make its execution smooth and efficient.[1] Where the nature of the justiciar's work did change was in the technical means at his disposal to carry out this duty.

The exchequer organization had, at least in the treasurer's eyes, been perfected during the justiciarship of Richard de Luci, and there is no evidence that its operation changed under Glanville. He bore witness to a routine writ in the royal name, ordering the monks of Rochester to appear before the king or his justices to make an election to the bishopric in late 1184 and following the exchequer practice described by the treasurer.[2] A writ of *liberate* in his own name also followed the form Richard fitz Nigel described.[3] Like de Luci before him, he despatched the Easter and Michaelmas summonses to the sheriffs which set the exchequer in motion,[4] and he regularly presided over the exchequer sessions, sitting beside that familiar group of barons and justices made up of Bishops Richard, Geoffrey, and John, Roger fitz Renfrey, William Basset, Michael Belet, and other ministers.[5] There was some

---

[1] Glanville was certainly summoned to the king for consultation on several occasions, no doubt to know the king's will and to offer advice, and the payment of his passage was duly recorded, e.g. *Pipe Roll 33 Henry II*, p. 205; *Pipe Roll 32 Henry II*, p. 193.

[2] Richardson, *op. cit.* pp. lxxi–lxxii.

[3] PRO E 404 1/2; the writ is an original. [4] *Pipe Roll 28 Henry II*, p. 159.

[5] Cotton MSS Vespasian E xx, fo. 45v; Nero E vii, fo. 182; Faustina A iv, fo. 49v; Claudius D xiii, fo. 126; Harl. MS 2110, fo. 108; these are all unpublished concords, calendared in West, *loc. cit.* pp. 182–3. See also *Feet of Fines Henry II and Richard*, pp. 1–3.

increase in the business handled by the exchequer as a consequence of Henry II's reforms, but there is nothing to indicate that Glanville's tenure of office altered its character.

The real difference between Glanville's justiciarship and Richard de Luci's is therefore to be sought in the judicial organization. At the end of the latter's career this was still in an experimental stage, and it was Glanville who played a large part in giving it the kind of definition which had already taken place at the exchequer. To say this is not to draw a rigid distinction between financial and judicial work; obviously pleas were heard at the exchequer and obviously the same group of officials dealt with both. Nevertheless, it is equally obvious that these ministers had had much longer practice and much more experience in dealing with financial matters than with those newly arising out of Henry II's reorganization. The Dialogue of the Exchequer is precise, definite, and authoritative; Glanville's treatise is tentative and experimental, seeming almost to anticipate difficulties which have not yet arisen. The significance of Glanville's justiciarship is that it covers the period in which these difficulties were being worked out.

The world Glanville describes is, legally speaking, very different from the early years of Henry II. The importance of the king's personal presence and the difficulty of suitors in obtaining an original writ find no place in the treatise. Glanville assumed that a writ of the king and a writ of the justiciar were equally effective: the same assumption as the exchequer had made at an earlier date. In his discussion of dower, Glanville stated that if a husband died and his widow's dower were vacant, then a writ of right should be sent to the warrantor to do full justice, and proved failure in justice should lead the case to the county court whence it might be brought to the *capitalis curia domini regis* at the pleasure of the king or his chief justice by use of the writ *pone*.[1] Discussing the case of a lord whose tenant had done something which disinherited the lord or had failed to perform his due service or render reasonable aids, the lord might try to distrain his tenant in his own court in accordance with custom, but if the latter proved difficult or impossible then the lord might have recourse to the king or the

[1] *Tractatus*, p. 90.

justiciar.[1] The sheriff's pleas covered cases in which a lord failed in justice, questions of exaction above due service, and matters of villeins born, but the treatise explains that a sheriff might hold any other pleas for which he had the writ of the king or the justiciar.[2] And when Glanville enunciated the famous principle that no one need answer for his free tenement without the king's writ, he understood that the justiciar's writ was equally effective.[3] The treatise assumes that legal writs may run in the justiciar's name as a matter of course, and that nothing is to be gained by obtaining the one rather than the other. Such an equation of royal and justiciar's writs was essential for the operation of Henry II's judicial system, but it is in contrast with the situation when Earl Robert of Leicester sat in judgement. When Abbot Hugh of Bury St Edmunds died, Glanville was informed of the death as a matter of course as well as the king, and when, during the vacancy, the custodians of the abbey wished to appoint a new reeve of the town of St Edmunds, the monks complained at once to the justiciar.[4] Glanville's justiciarship saw his office assume a routine place in judicial administration.

His own extensive judicial work was part of this process of definition. Unlike Richard de Luci, he was immensely active in the itinerant work of the judges. In 1180 he was at Northampton in the company of Richard fitz Nigel; in the following year in the south-western counties; in 1184 in Westmorland, Berkshire, Hampshire, and Essex; in 1185 in two of the same counties; in the following year in Northamptonshire; in 1187 in Yorkshire where he sat at Doncaster in September with the Archdeacon Joscelin and Godfrey de Luci, brother of his predecessor; and in the next year he was again in the north at Pontefract.[5] The justiciar's

---

[1] *Ibid.* pp. 125, 130, 131.   [2] *Ibid.* p. 152.
[3] *Ibid.* p. 157.   [4] Brakelond, I, 215, 276.
[5] Cotton MS Caligula A xii, fo. 123; *Pipe Roll 29 Henry II*, pp. xxiv, 115–16; *Pipe Roll 30 Henry II*, p. 37; *Pipe Roll 31 Henry II*, pp. 23, 108; *Pipe Roll 32 Henry II*, pp. 7–9, 46, 174; Farrer, *Early Yorkshire Charters*, I, 291, 383. It was at Pontefract in 1188 that he gave the manor of Upton to his steward, Reiner of Waxham, on whose behalf he was accused by a chronicler of having encompassed the death of Gilbert of Plumpton; *Monasticon*, VI, 380 n. 3; Benedict, p. 315.

annual travels were an important part of the increasing popularity of royal justice; he helped to make it accessible in the counties and plainly bore a large share in working out the purposes of royal assizes. As he moved over England, litigants came to him to seek writs. In 1183 Benedict, son of Josci de Quatre Buches, offered a gift to have the suit between himself and Abraham the Jew of Lincoln before the king, and in the same year many of the *oblata de curia* must have been offered to the justiciar.[1] When the *Rotulus de Dominabus* was compiled in 1185, it is evident that some custodians had gained their places by fines made with Glanville.[2] The justiciar's presence in the counties brought royal justice or favour within reach of those who wanted it and could afford it. Helias, the parson of Pickhill, took advantage of his presence at York in 1187 to obtain Glanville's witness to the charter by which he gave his churchyard and a chantry to the abbey of Swainby.[3] The justiciar was coming to be the point round which the judicial system revolved.

The extent of the justiciar's judicial work in eyre is not difficult to trace, and it shows his extensive part in the development of royal justice. The absence of plea rolls prevents any examination of his part in actual pleadings, but it is unlikely to have been much different from that occupied by his protégé Hubert Walter some ten years later. Nor can the extent of his work in the central courts be accurately measured. From surviving final concords, it is evident that Glanville sat regularly in the *curia regis* at Westminster, for he is named at the head of the justices in all of the extant concords.[4] The Treatise, and the opinions of his colleagues quoted in some recensions of it, demonstrate that in this central court the machinery of justice was being hammered into shape,

---

[1] *Pipe Roll 29 Henry II*, pp. 9, 89, 111, 115, 163. The heading *placita de curia* no doubt distinguished work done by the justiciar from the itinerant justices to which it was not applied; e.g. *ibid.* pp. 3, 73, 145. See Round, *Feudal England*, p. 513, who attaches the title to the king's own *iter*. It seems here to distinguish the justiciar's.

[2] *Rot. de Dominabus*, p. 9.

[3] Farrer, *Early Yorkshire Charters*, v, 157. Ranulf witnessed first, styled *summa justicia*, with his colleagues of the eyre.

[4] See note 5, p. 57, above.

and the attachment of Glanville's name to it, whoever may have been the actual author, symbolizes the truth that this work was done under his supervision.[1] His fellow justices make it clear that this *curia regis* was still 'undifferentiated', that the personnel of the administrative *curia* sat in both exchequer and judicial capacities.[2] Nevertheless their activity was coming to be distinct. A plaintiff might offer three marks to have his suit *in curia regis ad scaccarium*.[3] With the same men involved in each aspect of the doing of justice in the *curia*, the distinction between judicial and financial business was even more blurred than the financial consequences of any business naturally meant, but it is obvious that the intense judicial activity of Glanville's justiciarship was making the distinction necessary. The *curia* was elusive—not even Walter Map knew what it was[4]—but its activity was directed and its unity secured by the office of justiciar. In this generation of judicial experiment, Glanville's presence at Westminster, and his presiding over the same small group of colleagues, meant that the justiciarship could control the administrative system on the king's behalf. But it was also a system which, for short periods, could operate without the king or the justiciar. Glanville was on occasion summoned to Normandy to the king, but the routine business of government went on without him. Once the system was organized, the justiciar's intervention was required principally for the difficult cases or for those of political importance, and, although he was responsible for the smooth conduct of ordinary affairs, there was a group of trained ministers to attend to the details.

Part of the importance of Glanville's justiciarship lies in the group of men he gathered round him, who were no doubt responsible for that tradition which attached his name to the Treatise.

---

[1] Southern, 'Note on the Text of Glanville', *EHR*, LXV, 81.
[2] West, *loc. cit.* pp. 182–3.
[3] *Pipe Roll 34 Henry II*, p. 155; Van Caenegem, *op. cit.* p. 31, where it is shown that the *curia regis* and the exchequer were quite distinct in contemporary minds, as against Richardson's view that the exchequer was omnicompetent, *op. cit.* p. lxiv. William fitz Stephen, in Becket's time, did not distinguish so clearly (*Becket Materials*, III, 51), so that the distinction may easily be a result of Glanville's work.
[4] *De curia loquor, et nescio, Deus scit, quid sit curia*, Map, p. 1.

With his rise in the administrative world, Glanville's baronial status increased, sometimes through royal grants like the manor of Upton in Suffolk, the lordship of Beauchamp, or 500 acres of land in Braham,[1] sometimes through offices like custodian of the great Richmond *honor* and the constabulary of Richmond castle,[2] sometimes through the custody of land which had belonged to his relations, like the town of Acton of which part had belonged to his niece, or Waterbeach which another niece had held.[3] Glanville's feudal status was confirmed by Henry II's committing his favourite son John to the justiciar's household, an action with incalculable results because John obviously acquired a taste for and a knowledge of administration which no doubt came from his association with Ranulf's circle.[4] Other members of it were Hubert Walter, who was a kinsman and already rising in the world, Osbert de Glanville, the justiciar's brother who witnessed his exchequer writ and sat in the *curia* at Westminster in April 1182 and in 1189.[5] Ranulf of Gedding was another who witnessed two of the justiciar's feudal grants and who also sat beside him in the *curia* at Westminster and in eyre.[6] Gilbert of Colwell and Thomas Basset were members of the justiciar's circle in both household and court, the former's widow and heir being in Glanville's custody in 1185.[7] The husband of one of Glanville's daughters, the Yorkshire baron William de Auberville, was in court at Westminster in 1182, and Reginald de Courteney, who witnessed some of the justiciar's charters, was his colleague in the eyre at Lincoln in 1180.[8] Three important justices, Michael Belet,

[1] Dugdale, *Baronage*, p. 423; Cartae Antiquae roll N, no. 36; *Monasticon*, VI, 380 n. 3; Farrer, *Early Yorkshire Charters*, I, 291; *Records of the House of Glanville*, p. 16.

[2] BM Add. MS 40009, fo. 215. In a charter made in the earl's court at Richmond, Ranulf is called constable.

[3] *Rot. de Dominabus*, pp. 60, 83.   [4] Diceto, II, 310.

[5] *Feet of Fines Henry II and Richard*, pp. 2, 3.

[6] *Monasticon*, vi, 879; Farrer, *Early Yorkshire Charters*, I, 255–6; *Feet of Fines Henry II and Richard*, pp. 1, 2.

[7] *Rot. de Dominabus*, p. 61; Farrer, *Early Yorkshire Charters*, I, 255; *Monasticon*, VI, 383; *Feet of Fines Henry II and Richard*, p. 1; Lansdowne MS 415, fo. 22v; Gilbert had been one of Ranulf's officers when the justiciar was sheriff of Yorkshire, *Pipe Roll 23 Henry II*, p. 81.

[8] *Feet of Fines Henry II and Richard*, p. 2; Cotton MS Vespasian E xx, fo. 49.

Roger fitz Renfrey, and Robert of Whitefield, never appeared in the attestations of Glanville's grants, but they too sat regularly by his side at Westminster.[1] The justiciar was surrounded (both in his feudal and in his official functions) by the men who were making the reforms of Henry II work, and out of this group there came a future justiciar and archbishop of Canterbury, and many of the prominent justices of later reigns. It is in this sense that Glanville's tenure of office marks the beginning of the heyday of the justiciars, not so much for what it was as for its future possibilities.

[1] *Feet of Fines Henry II and Richard*, pp. 1, 2, 3; and MS references in note 5, p. 57, above.

CHAPTER III

THE JUSTICIARSHIP UNDER RICHARD I

Henry II, whether he was in England or in his continental dominions, kept a firm grip upon the administration of his kingdom. So far as one can perceive his character, with the mastery of his lands there went a close and sustained interest in the details of their government. His justiciars were men who, being of some feudal stature and devoted to royal interests, were under constant supervision by the king himself; there was never any doubt that their greatness was conditional upon royal greatness. The relationship of the king and his justiciar obviously determined the importance of the justiciarship, and whatever view be taken of Henry's personality or those of de Luci and Glanville a new king meant a different relationship and therefore a different justiciarship. Richard was a man of different calibre from his father. Of the same imperious stamp, he was nevertheless not interested in the administrative detail of government so long as his will was realized. His reputation and chief interest were warlike, and his immediate aim, upon his succession, was the crusade. The new king's preoccupations allowed greater scope to his justiciars. This lack of sustained interest in government meant that their place became the more important, especially when royal demands for money necessitated intense administrative activity. His continuous absence also offered his justiciars greater responsibility, not merely for ensuring that the machinery of government ran smoothly but also by offering them somewhat greater scope for deciding the policy which would achieve the king's desires. It is in this sense that in Richard's reign the justiciarship reached an unprecedented importance, but its development was not constant, and the influence of the justiciars varied in difficult political circumstances also taking their origin from the king's absence.

1. RICHARD'S EARLY ARRANGEMENTS
FOR GOVERNMENT

Glanville remained in office for some six months, acting under the general supervision of Queen Eleanor, released from the captivity in which she had spent the last half of her husband's reign and now representing Richard until he arrived in England. In these few months, Glanville carried out his duties on the queen's instructions, and payments were made by his writ authorized by the queen; he continued to pay attention, for example, to the security of the Welsh border.[1] His justiciarship came to an end at the council of Pipewell in September 1189, when it was arranged that he should accompany the king on crusade. In the same council, Richard made the first of his arrangements for the government of England, superficially making a break with the immediate past. He had never disguised his desire to leave for the Holy Land at the earliest moment, and some of his dealings led to the impression that he did not expect to return. His departure from England in December meant that for an unknown length of time he would be out of easy touch with England and therefore he had to provide for its government in these novel circumstances before he left, but the breaking of regular contact between king and country would only occur when he actually left western Europe. Whatever representatives he appointed, he could still exercise some control over them until he sailed from France, or perhaps from Sicily.[2] Only after that would the regency of England find itself in an unprecedented situation.

The first provision Richard made to govern England was the appointment of the co-justiciars Bishop Hugh de Puiset of Durham and Earl William de Mandeville.[3] Both of these men were

---

[1] *Magnus Rotulus Pipae Anno Primo Regni Ricardi Primi*, pp. 163, 180; Howden, III, 4.

[2] Landon, *Itinerary of Richard I*, pp. 38, 48. Richard left Marseilles for Italy on 7 August 1190, and sailed from Messina for the Holy Land on 10 April 1191. The possibility of his intervention in English affairs was therefore considerable until August and somewhat reduced between that date and April of the following year; it was scarcely more difficult than that faced by the papal *curia* at any time. [3] Benedict, II, 87; Howden, III, 16.

great magnates of distinguished ancestry and connexions, but neither was a *curialis*. They represented a balance of feudal power in England; the bishop, having bought the earldom of Northumberland and holding his palatinate, being dominant in the north, the earl in East Anglia and the south. The arrangement was essentially a political one, and it divorced the justiciarship from administration, a fact recognized by the stories of colleagues like Geoffrey fitz Peter, William Briewerre, and Hugh Bardulf being left as barons of the exchequer, or William Marshal, Geoffrey, Robert of Whitefield and Roger fitz Renfrey being associated *in regimine regni*.[1] These men were, some of them, considerable barons, and all of them, except William Marshal, were experienced administrators. Whether any formal commission was given to these associates of the two justiciars is doubtful—the chroniclers' inconsistency over their names suggests not—but the nature of the king's appointments to the justiciarship made their presence essential. They were the men, trained in Henry II's *curia* under Glanville, who actually ran the apparatus of government. The result of Richard's first provision was therefore to revert to the divided justiciarship of Henry II's early years and to divorce the office from an intimate connexion with royal administration. Such an arrangement is intelligible on the assumption that the king thought his absence in the Holy Land would produce a situation in England with which a single administrative justiciar could not cope. He may, as some have thought, simply have been feckless, desiring to sell appointments for the maximum price and being ignorant of English practice.[2] The second is no doubt true, but the first seems improbable even in the most improvident Angevin king. It is also possible, since his journey to the east was gradual and the possibility of royal intervention existed in its earlier stages, that the arrangement was experimental; certainly, in the event, Richard did not hesitate to change it.

Whatever the king's intentions, they were frustrated by Earl

---

[1] Richard of Devizes states that they were left *in fiscum*, Howden *in regimine regni*; Devizes, iii, 386; Howden, III, 16.
[2] Stubbs, *Historical Introductions to the Rolls Series*, p. 207; Powicke, *CMH*, VI, 207–8; A. L. Poole, *Domesday Book to Magna Carta*, p. 351.

William's death in Rouen in November 1189, before Richard had even left England. When he sailed in December, he simply left Bishop Hugh as justiciar, but added William de Longchamps, his own chancellor, to the colleagues, giving him control of the royal seal of absence and custody of the Tower of London.[1] Longchamps was a foreigner whose ancestors came from Beauvais where they had some but not great feudal standing.[2] He seems to have offended English magnates but not the monks of Canterbury nor the exchequer clerks. He was relatively unacquainted with English government methods, but he was well educated in canon law and continental practice.[3] He had served Richard as chancellor before his succession, and at the Pipewell council he had become an English magnate when he obtained the see of Ely. Longchamps was closer to the king than any of the other ministers or the justiciar, and he repaid royal trust with loyalty which seems neither to have been doubted nor to have swerved in subsequent events. Plainly there was something in his character—arrogance, ambition, and physical defects perhaps—which made him unpopular, but from Richard's knowledge of him and his ability, he was not an unreasonable choice as the justiciar's principal colleague. And this second arrangement, although it has been doubted, actually worked for at least two months. Of the series of writs and charters in the king's name issued by the chancery in England in January and February 1190, one was issued under the witness of the justiciar, and on 25 January 1190 he was certainly presiding over the central *curia* at the exchequer, for he sent a letter to the justices and barons of the exchequer telling them of a final concord made before himself, Longchamps, Bishop Hugh of Coventry and other justices.[4] The balance of power in the arrangement tipped in favour of the chancellor who controlled the technical

---

[1] Benedict, II, 101; Howden, III, 28. The chroniclers differ as to Longchamps's precise position when the king left, and over the justiciar's colleagues.
[2] Stubbs, *op. cit.* pp. 214–15.
[3] He had been a clerk in the chancery under the king's half-brother before he entered Richard's service in Aquitaine, and a civil law treatise is ascribed to him; A. L. Poole, *op. cit.* p. 351; Richardson, *Memoranda Roll 1 John*, p. lxii.
[4] Landon, *Itinerary*, p. 183, lists the charters granted at this time; Round, *Calendar of Documents Preserved in France*, p. 443; PRO Transcripts III, 202.

instrument of government, the seal, and enjoyed the king's confidence. There were many more writs in January 1190 issued under his witness than under the justiciar's. Part of the weakness of the latter's position was his divorce from the detailed control of administration, and there can be little doubt that Hugh de Puiset came to occupy the place of the highest dignity rather than effective power. Hugh Bardulf and William Briewerre were said to be his colleagues *in justitiis faciendis*, William Marshal and Geoffrey fitz Peter to be associates, and they were as necessary to this second arrangement as they had been to the first.[1] They were unable, however, to prevent the unbalancing of power between the justiciar and the chancellor, and in March 1190 Richard summoned his counsellors to Normandy to make yet a third provision. It had become obvious that a justiciar who had neither administrative experience nor control of the seal could not function.

The king's third scheme recognized this.[2] He made Longchamps justiciar as well as chancellor, and confined Bishop Hugh to a justiciarship from the Humber to the Scottish border, an office which could have given him little more authority than his palatine bishopric and his earldom already conferred. The justiciarship was in theory divided, but in practice recognized that the real power lay with one man who was chief justiciar and controlled the seal. Longchamps left Normandy for England before Hugh and, when the latter arrived, excluded him from the exchequer. He was supported in this by the men named as colleagues in the earlier arrangements, and his position was still further strengthened by the king's obtaining for him, in June 1190, the papal legation in the absence on crusade of Archbishop Baldwin.[3] Richard had apparently reverted to one powerful justiciar whom he could trust, no doubt expecting that government would necessarily be carried on by co-operation and consultation between Longchamps, ignorant of English practice, and the experienced *curiales* he found

---

[1] Benedict, II, 101; Howden, III, 28.   [2] Benedict, II, 105.
[3] Devizes, III, 389; Howden, III, 35. Benedict describes Longchamps's legation under March 1190, but Clement III's letter is dated 5 June; Diceto, II, 83. Both archbishoprics were vacant, the one through death, the other by the elect not having been consecrated.

in the *curia*, and perhaps making no formal provision for this co-operation. When Richard was at Bayonne in June 1190 he ordered that the chancellor was to be obeyed by all,[1] and when he left France in August, there was but one justiciar in England. It seems most improbable that he had drawn a distinction between *negotia regis* and *negotia regni*, the one to be transacted under the justiciar's seal, the other to be transacted by a council; the suggestion is based only on the wording of the chronicle stories and not on any clear difference between the two sorts of business in the records.[2] There is no need to suppose any formal distinction to explain the charges that Longchamps ignored his counsellors, and it is axiomatic that government in the late twelfth century depended upon the co-operation of the magnates. Longchamps's difficulties came not from his infringement of some hypothetical constitution Richard had set up, but from his own unprecedented power, his personality, and the political circumstances involving Count John.

2. WILLIAM DE LONGCHAMPS

Longchamps as bishop of Ely, chancellor, and papal legate, as well as justiciar, had a more powerful combination of offices than any of his predecessors. It was this combination that made him dominant in England, that removed some of the normal checks upon his authority—the chancellor had always had some such function at the exchequer,[3] and the archbishop of Canterbury in wider spheres—while the king's absence had weakened royal control. But Richard did not leave Messina until April 1191, and, although distant, could still intervene. He did so by his letters of 9 and 23 February, but these were in a sense conditional; he was not willing

---

[1] Diceto, II, 83.

[2] Wilkinson, 'The Government of England during ... the Third Crusade', *BJR*, 28, 490 ff., works out an elaborate distinction between *negotia regis* which the justiciar could deal with under his own seal, and *negotia regni* which he could only deal with in consultation with his colleagues under the royal seal of absence. The distinction rests entirely upon the wording of the chroniclers, and the implicit assumption that the use of a particular seal included or excluded colleagues. Neither basis is convincing.

[3] *Dialogus*, I, v.

to subvert Longchamps's authority because he thought it dangerous but because he suspected a difficult political situation might
require it. The root of that difficulty was only in part Longchamps's combination of offices and his personal characteristics;
the major part was the position of the king's brother John, controlling seven counties, the earldom of Gloucester, and the
honours of Lancaster, Peverel, the Peak, Tickhill, Wallingford,
Eye, Ludgershall, and Glamorgan, but yet unrecognized as his
brother's heir.[1] This political situation was not created by the
justiciar nor by the offices he held, although it was made more
difficult by them, and eventually it proved impossible for a justiciar, a single powerful minister, to cope with. It is unnecessary to
inquire deeply into the well-known story of Longchamps's downfall, but its effects on the justiciarship are important.

During his brief period of office, Longchamps discharged the
same kind of duties that had fallen to Glanville and de Luci, but
there was probably a greater urgency about them since the king's
needs were urgent, and a more intense quality as the administration Henry II created was exploited for the king's gain. Indeed, it
was the very efficiency of Longchamps's justiciarship that contributed to his unpopularity. Benedict of Peterborough compares
his passage to that of a flash of lightning because of its ruinous
quality,[2] and the point of his remark is that the justiciar was
ubiquitous, that he was efficient in gathering the money the king
needed. Longchamps's tactlessness in unfamiliar routine may have
fostered dislike, but the root of the resentment was his effectiveness. Throughout 1190 he was concerned to prepare for the
crusade, to levy the Welsh scutage, and to exact heavy fines from
those who sought the king's good will, like Reiner, Glanville's
steward, who paid 1000 marks.[3] Longchamps also fined those

---

[1] *Pipe Roll 2 Richard I*, p. xx. The question of Count John's recognition as
heir to the English Crown was plainly of vital importance, and no doubt
explains his relations with the chancellor who accepted Richard's view that
Arthur was his heir, Newburgh, IV, 14; and later with the archbishop of Rouen
and his colleagues, Howden, III, 204.
[2] Benedict, II, 143.
[3] *Pipe Roll 2 Richard I*, pp. 14, 18, 21, 25, 30, 35, 44, 48, 57, 68, 72, 90, 102,
109, 116, 122, 130, 137, 143, 151.

involved in the massacre of the Jews. In the following year, he travelled through most of the counties receiving offerings, and he dealt with the immense debts owed to Aaron the Jew and now due to the king.[1] The justiciar's activity shows that he was the driving force behind the attempt to raise for Richard as much money as possible, and that he personally took a major share in collecting it. He showed the same care for royal interests in judicial work. In 1190 there were six groups of justices at work, and all the shires, apart from those in Count John's control, were visited, with the exception of Oxford and Berkshire which saw the justices in the following year.[2] In 1191 the justiciar himself visited Northampton in January and joined a party of justices in East Anglia in September, while Leicester and Lincoln were also visited by royal judges.[3] Apart, therefore, from his own extensive travels, the whole of England was covered by a judicial visitation during the two years of Longchamps's justiciarship. He himself sat in court on occasion, but for the most part the work was undertaken by his colleagues. Each of the eyres contained one or more of the men associated with him, and they were the basis of Longchamps's effectiveness as justiciar.

The bishop of Ely was accused at his downfall of ignoring the colleagues the king had set beside him. This is certainly untrue so far as the work of government was concerned. All of them were sent out as itinerant justices, and Longchamps used them to strengthen royal administration. By Michaelmas 1191 he had removed a number of sheriffs. William Briewerre had replaced Robert de la Mara, a friend of Count John, in Oxfordshire and Buckinghamshire, Geoffrey fitz Peter took Essex and Hertford-shire from Otto fitz William, Hugh Bardulf replaced the bishop of Coventry, another friend of John's, in Warwickshire and Leicestershire, two knights of the earl of Arundel, the justiciar's friend, were substituted for Urse de Lincis and the earl of Salisbury in Sussex and Wiltshire, and another friend of the justiciar, John de Rebez, became sheriff of Hampshire in place of Oger fitz Oger.[4]

---

[1] *Pipe Rolls 3 and 4 Richard I*, pp. xiii–xiv, 135.
[2] *Ibid.* pp. xxi–xxv, where Lady Stenton works out the eyres in detail.
[3] *Ibid.* pp. xxii–xxiii. [4] *Ibid.* pp. xiv–xv.

Nine counties were thus given to sheriffs of Longchamps's choice, and in addition he replaced John Marshal with his brother Osbert de Longchamps after the Jewish massacre in Yorkshire on Palm Sunday 1190.[1] So far from excluding his colleagues from the work of government, the justiciar was using them with men who were his personal dependants to ensure the efficiency of the royal administration. It is impossible to know whether he also discussed policy with them, or took much heed of their advice, but it seems unlikely that he failed altogether to do so. They sat side by side in the *curia regis* and the exchequer at Westminster. In December 1190 and May 1191 Longchamps was presiding over them there.[2] In January 1191 he had been at Northampton accompanied by the earl of Arundel, William Marshal, Geoffrey fitz Peter, Hugh Bardulf, William Briewerre, Simon of Pattishall, and Robert of Whitefield, and two months later, at Winchester, Geoffrey fitz Peter, Hugh Bardulf, and William Briewerre (as a litigant) were with the justiciar and the bishops of Bath and Winchester.[3] The occasions for consultation and discussion existed, and, whatever Longchamps's personal arrogance or pride of office, it is almost inconceivable that his lack of knowledge of English practice should not have led him to seek his colleagues' advice. The part they played in his government suggests that he co-operated with them in the king's interests; without them his justiciarship would have been ineffective, and this it certainly was not. He was able to supply the king with money and goods for the crusade and to undertake a campaign against the Welsh. He kept the judicial and financial administration operating efficiently in the pattern Henry II had established. He was plainly an efficient superintendent of royal business. But his justiciarship was not one of innovation or experiment. He left his mark on chancery practice,[4] but in justice and in exchequer procedure he depended upon the men trained under Glanville whose knowledge and experience enabled the administration to survive unchanged the crisis of his downfall.

---

[1] *Pipe Roll 2 Richard I*, p. 59.
[2] Harl. MS 2110, fo. 108; *Feet of Fines Henry II and Richard I*, p. 7.
[3] *Monasticon*, I, 391; *Vetus Registrum Saresb.* i, 262.
[4] Richardson, *Memoranda Roll 1 John*, pp. lx ff.

If the colleagues of de Puiset and Longchamps could not hold them together in January and February 1190 when the king was near at hand in Normandy, it is unreasonable to suppose that they could impose co-operation on the justiciar and Count John when Richard was far away, even when they had a royal intermediary in the person of Walter, archbishop of Rouen.[1] The occasion of Longchamps's fall may have been the rash action of his sister in arresting Archbishop Geoffrey of York, but the real grounds for it were John's power and ambitions which were too great to be contained by a single justiciar. To restrain John, it required a united group of powerful people and, because of his mistake over Archbishop Geoffrey alone, Longchamps could never create this. The king had allowed for such a possibility when he sent Archbishop Walter of Rouen back to England as his representative, armed with at least two letters. The first, of 9 February, told William Marshal and 'the barons' that Richard was sending Walter so that by his counsel, and that of Longchamps, Hugh Bardulf, Geoffrey fitz Peter, and William Briewerre, the business of the kingdom might be done; if the chancellor did not take this counsel, William Marshal and these colleagues were to act according to Walter's disposition, especially in the matter of castles and escheats.[2] The second, of 23 February, told Longchamps, Geoffrey, William Marshal, Hugh Bardulf, and William Briewerre that they were to listen to what Walter told them of the king's wishes, especially about the election to the see of Canterbury, and that Walter should be added to their counsels.[3]

---

[1] Landon, *op. cit.* p. 192, shows that the archbishop could not have reached England in April as Diceto says, but about 27 June as Gervase implies.

[2] Diceto, ii, 90.

[3] *Ibid.* ii, 91; Giraldus, iv, 400. Wilkinson, *loc. cit.* pp. 494 ff., discusses these letters as evidence of the distinction between different kinds of business. The real difficulty, apart from reconstructing the text from two different versions, is that one cannot assess their significance in the absence of the texts of other letters which the archbishop probably had. Also it is difficult to determine their significance when both of these are dated in February but the archbishop did not leave the king until April. Can there have been any sense of urgency? Or are the letters an invention of the chroniclers to explain later events? The confusion their interpretation causes may be seen in the conflicting judgements of Stubbs, Powicke, Wilkinson, and Poole.

The genuineness of these letters is not beyond question, nor can one be sure that they were the only letters the archbishop of Rouen had. From the knowledge at his disposal in Messina, the king can have had no clear idea of what was happening in England, and the strong probability is that he issued a number of conditional orders, an impression confirmed by Walter's actions when he arrived in England.[1] He certainly joined the justiciar and his colleagues, for he may be found sitting with them in the *curia*, but he did not produce his alternative commission until October of 1191 when Count John organized a formidable opposition to Longchamps upon the occasion of Archbishop Geoffrey's arrest.[2] But the confusion of Richard's orders is not material to the justiciarship. What matters is that Longchamps fled in the face of this opposition, and the archbishop of Rouen took his place as justiciar.

3. WALTER OF COUTANCES

Unlike the bishop of Ely, Walter of Coutances had had experience in English government; in spite of his name and his archbishopric he was an Englishman from Cornwall.[3] For fifteen years he had been important in the royal chancery and in the chamber administration, bearing the king's seal and perhaps the title *vice cancellarius*.[4] His ecclesiastical promotion had been steady: the archdeaconry of Oxford in 1175, the bishopric of Lincoln 1182, the archbishopric of Rouen 1184.[5] When Richard left on crusade Walter accompanied him, but at Messina he was sent back to England, because of the reports reaching the king. One chronicle asserted that Walter was nervous and wavering at Messina and that Richard, who cared for money rather than persons, took his treasure and sent him back.[6] It is altogether probable that the archbishop paid his share towards Richard's expenses, but it is also obvious that Richard entrusted him with a delicate mission in difficult circumstances. Walter was not alone. Queen Eleanor

---

[1] Stubbs, *Constitutional History*, I, 561–3.
[2] Stubbs, *Historical Introductions*, pp. 236 ff.
[3] A. L. Poole, *op. cit.* p. 355.
[4] *Ibid.* and note 1; Tout, *Chapters*, I, 116–17.
[5] *DNB.*   [6] Devizes, III, 404.

returned to England at the same time,[1] but it was Walter who was given the alternative commission of justiciarship and who must in addition have had verbal instructions to direct his use of any or all of the royal letters. From Richard's orders reaching England after Walter's departure, Longchamps clearly had the royal confidence,[2] and the archbishop's discretion counted for much. He never used his authority to displace Longchamps until the council at St Paul's early in October 1191, when he was acclaimed justiciar under John as *rector regni*.[3] The latter, whatever his influence, can have had no position of control, his subsequent treason suggesting that he was dissatisfied with the results of his victory over Longchamps. The government of England was still in the hands of the justiciar and his colleagues, supported by the power and influence of Queen Eleanor.

Archbishop Walter was an obvious choice for the king's purposes, especially if he was, as the chronicle suggests, lukewarm in his enthusiasm for crusade. Unlike Longchamps he had had a long experience of English government, having been head of Henry II's chancery for perhaps fifteen years, and playing some part in chamber administration. His importance is indicated by his steady ecclesiastical preferment. If the confused reports Richard I received at Messina included complaints of Longchamps's tyranny and foreignness, an old and well-known official of his father's reign who was also a great ecclesiastic may have seemed the very man to lend stability to government. Later events suggest that Walter never enjoyed the king's confidence or trust in the way that Longchamps did, but Walter was not to act alone; he was associated with experienced colleagues and, more important, with the queen. The circumstances of his justiciarship were exceptional, but he was much more a man of the same kind as the barons and justices associated in the government than was Longchamps. His appointment was a reassertion of the government of Henry II.

[1] Benedict, II, 157; Howden, III, 96. William Marshal was said to have accompanied the queen from Messina to England, but Landon, *op. cit.*, shows that it was Gilbert de Vascoeuil who did so. William Marshal did not go on crusade.
[2] Stubbs, *op. cit.* p. 230 and note.
[3] Benedict, II, 213; Devizes, III, 415.

In one important respect Walter's short term of office broke a tradition. Unlike his predecessors, he did not govern in his own name but in the king's. No doubt there were good political reasons for this, but Gerald of Wales attributes it to the new justiciar's modesty.[1] The implication is that the justiciar would normally govern in his own name and under his own seal, and it seems evident that Walter did not because of the position of Count John as *rector regni* and perhaps because of the need to maintain the unity of royal counsellors in the face of challenges to royal authority. The king's name might be expected to carry more weight. Walter certainly issued orders in his own,[2] but the financial and judicial business was invariably conducted in the king's. Yet, if this practice broke the tradition of justiciarship, Walter's government, so far as it can be traced in spite of this breach, was substantially the same as his predecessor's. Like Longchamps, in 1192 the archbishop may be found receiving offerings in almost every shire from suitors who wanted the king's favour.[3] Perhaps he had not visited every county, but he must certainly have travelled widely in England on political or military business. In 1192 he was at the head of a group of justices visiting London and

[1] Richardson, *op. cit.* pp. lxxiii–lxxiv.

[2] *Rolls of the King's Court, Richard I*, p. 78. It should be noted that this is not a routine judicial writ but an order that an outlaw be handed over to Geoffrey fitz Peter.

[3] *Pipe Rolls 3 and 4 Richard I*, pp. xxv, 174, 178, 194, 203, 221, 244, 251, 267, 274, 292, 305, 317. Those shires from which offerings did not appear at Michaelmas 1192 appeared in the following year with the exception of Northampton, Berkshire, and Wiltshire. Lady Stenton explains that the new offerings are payments which would later have been entered in the roll of oblates and fines and they do not imply that the justiciar visited every shire. It may be accepted that suitors might come to the justiciar from neighbouring counties in which he did not set foot, or even from a considerable distance. Usually the accounts explain that the fines were made with the archbishop and other unnamed justices although sometimes with Walter alone. Two things need to be said. The first is that suitors had approached the justiciar, for other oblates were offered to other justices under their own names. The second is that in the following year no new accounts appear of dealings with the justiciar. Therefore the appearance of his name is not a formality but an account of an actual transaction with him, and if he did not visit all of these shires, he must certainly have travelled sufficiently widely to enable neighbouring counties' suitors to come to him.

Middlesex, Kent, Surrey, and Sussex.[1] Like his predecessors he presided over the central *curia*, and was at Westminster immediately after the council at St Paul's presiding over the exchequer session begun at Oxford.[2]

The king's needs were as great as ever, and from January 1193, when Richard was discovered to be a captive, the ransom had to be thought of. The justiciar also had to defend the Welsh borders and to restrain Count John. This supervision of royal government therefore involved the rapid assessment and collection of a large amount of money. He was himself extremely active in providing for the siege of Windsor,[3] and Gerald of Wales records the frequency of his being sent into Wales by the queen and the justiciar.[4] Obviously Walter did not take important decisions alone. Gervase of Canterbury speaks of Queen Eleanor as ruling in England, but Walter summoned a council to Oxford in February to take steps to preserve the kingdom, to take oaths of fealty, and to put castles in readiness for defence.[5] In these preparations the justiciar relied on his colleagues and on loyal barons, but the financing of them, and then the speedy collection of the ransom, must obviously have made the efficient supervision of the technical detail of government immensely important. Walter's full part in this is impossible to trace, but he certainly took an active share in the collection of money as well as in the decisions about its raising. Although the formality of government running in the king's name obscures the justiciar's part, there is nothing to suggest that Archbishop Walter did not discharge his office in exactly the same way that Glanville had, and with far more expertise than William de Longchamps. The ransom involved an unprecedented amount of money and, obscure though its details are, the government showed an awareness of new bases of taxation.[6] Whether this was

---

[1] *Pipe Roll 5 Richard I*, pp. xxv, 152, 157, 161, 171.
[2] *Feet of Fines Henry II and Richard I*, pp. 8–17; *Pipe Rolls 3 and 4 Richard I*, pp. xix; Harl. MS 1708, fo. 173.　　　[3] *Pipe Roll 5 Richard I*, p. xviii.
[4] *Ibid.* pp. xiii–xiv; he was paid £15. 4s. 2d. as his livery for two years at 7d. per day.
[5] *Pipe Roll 5 Richard I*, pp. xv–xvi. Howden preserves a letter of Walter summoning the bishop of Durham.
[6] Mitchell, *Taxation in Medieval England*, pp. 171 ff.

Walter's influence cannot be known, especially because Hubert Walter, newly elected archbishop of Canterbury, was then in England with other experienced barons of the exchequer like William de Ste Mère Eglise.[1] The most that can be said is that, whatever Walter's part in the decisions about the form of taxation, he was an efficient justiciar at the head of the administration raising the money. But with Hubert Walter in England and Richard once again in regular touch with the country, he was replaced. Having kept England for the king in co-operation with the queen and the justices, when a more normal situation was restored Walter was called to Richard in Germany, and a man much deeper in royal confidence became justiciar before the end of 1193.

4. HUBERT WALTER

Hubert Walter came of a baronial family in Norfolk, being the son of Glanville's sister-in-law who was the daughter of Theobald de Valognes.[2] He made his way in the justiciar's household with such effect that he was described as sharing the rule of the kingdom with Glanville.[3] Certainly he found his way into the *curia regis*, sitting as a baron of the exchequer in 1185, and among the justices in 1189. His ecclesiastical promotion was steady. In 1186 he became dean of York and was one of the candidates for the archbishopric when Geoffrey was elected. On Richard's accession he became bishop of Salisbury. His rise was apparently a rapid one, but he had had experience of exchequer and judicial procedure in the five years before he obtained his bishopric, and his training in the household of Glanville obviously went back still further. It was not an extensive training compared with that of his colleagues like Richard fitz Nigel or even Roger fitz Renfrey, but he was learned in government practice. Gerald of Wales describes him as a tall, handsome man, subtle of wit but not eloquent, and more interested in worldly things than those of the spirit. His connexions ensured that these qualities came to royal attention, and his usefulness during the crusade, when he acted as spiritual adviser, diplomatist, and military leader, especially com-

---

[1] Landon, *op. cit.* p. 74.　　[2] Foss, *op. cit.* p. 699.　　[3] *DNB*, under Hubert.

mended him to King Richard.[1] Hearing of the king's captivity at
Messina on his way home, Hubert was one of his first visitors in
Germany, and when he left Richard to go to England in 1193, it
was as one very much in the king's confidence, bearing a letter to
Queen Eleanor referring to the bishop's work at Rome and in
Germany and desiring that he be elected to the see of Canterbury.[2]
A similar letter was sent to Archbishop Walter, William Marshal,
Geoffrey fitz Peter, Hugh Bardulf and William Briewerre, while
William de Ste Mère Eglise, another trusted ecclesiastic and royal
administrator, was sent to England to advise the chapter of
Canterbury of the king's wishes. Hubert became archbishop of
Canterbury in May 1193, and in the following month at the
council of St Albans, he was made one of the trustees for the
money collected for the king's ransom,[3] and acted in association
with the justiciar and his colleagues, succeeding Walter in
December when the latter was called to be one of the king's hostages with the emperor.

The justiciarship of Hubert Walter lasted less than five years,
but its circumstances gave the office an unequalled importance and
prestige. The king was, with the brief exception of four months in
1194, abroad, but close enough at hand to direct and support the
justiciar as he had not been able to do in Longchamps's case.
Richard was still indifferent to the details of administration but he
still needed money in large quantities. Thus Hubert, so long as he
satisfied the king, had a much wider discretion in matters of
government than his predecessors, and he could count on support
from a not too distant master. These reasons alone would magnify
his office, but when they are combined with his position as archbishop of Canterbury, one of the greatest barons and head of the
church in England, and, from 1195, papal legate, his figure over-
shadows all his predecessors and contemporaries.[4] There was no

---

[1] Giraldus, III, 28, 38, 39. Gerald was, of course, a severe critic of the
archbishop because of his own failure to become a bishop.
[2] Landon, op. cit. pp. 74–6.   [3] Mitchell, op. cit. p. 25.
[4] The legatine commission was dated at Rome, 18 March 1195; Diceto, II,
195. The suspicion that Longchamps was intriguing for his own election to
Canterbury, which would have given him the position Hubert in fact achieved,
was one of the main reasons for action against him by his enemies.

parallel in England for his position as head of the church and head of the secular government since the time of Lanfranc. Great as he was, however, his power depended upon the king, and his greatness was conditional upon his ensuring that the king's will was done.

The overriding necessity for Hubert was to satisfy the royal need for money. He had, of course, to defend the realm as well, and like his predecessor was much concerned with the Welsh marches. Upon his becoming justiciar he had to deal with the revolt of Count John's men, consulting with other magnates in council upon the action to be taken, and himself besieging Marlborough castle.[1] One of his writs relates that in this operation the monks of Reading lent him their carts to carry a military machine.[2] In 1196 he undertook an expedition against Gwenwynwyn of Powys, and in the following year he attacked Welshpool.[3] The justiciar organized and paid for these military actions, but his principal duty was to keep Richard supplied with the money collected in England. The characteristic of Hubert's justiciarship is the innovations that he introduced to raise and handle the revenue, and the development that therefore took place in the administrative system over which he presided. None of these changes can certainly be ascribed to Hubert's own initiative. He had experienced colleagues like Geoffrey fitz Peter, William de Ste Mère Eglise, Hugh Bardulf, and William of Ely to help him, but whatever changes occurred necessarily involved his authority and support, and some of them were very probably his own work.

Since financial necessity was so pressing, it was the exchequer that was most nearly affected by the justiciar's actions. In the collection of the king's ransom, Hubert was only one of several ministers, while in the settlement of the kingdom after John's revolt the king himself took part, rearranging the shrievalties and driving financial bargains with his tenants and towns.[4] The idea of a special exchequer to cope with the ransom was probably

---

[1] *Pipe Roll 6 Richard I,* pp. xv, 251, 256.
[2] Egerton MS 3031, fo. 72.
[3] *Chancellor's Roll 8 Richard I,* p. xxiv; *Pipe Roll 10 Richard I,* p. xxxi.
[4] *Pipe Roll 6 Richard I,* pp. xvii–xxvii.

not the justiciar's, for it was perhaps set up in 1193,[1] but the appointment of two general escheators, Hugh Bardulf in the north, William de Ste Mère Eglise in the south, may well have been, because their appointment seems closely connected with the eyre of September 1194.[2] Every county was visited except Buckinghamshire and Bedfordshire. This great eyre was carried out very quickly and its results actually appeared on the pipe roll made up in 1194. Apart from its judicial aspects, it shows the justiciar's concern for the stocking of royal manors to maintain the value of the land. The justices were also instructed to tallage the cities, boroughs, and royal demesne, but Hubert Walter himself supervised this tax, sometimes intervening to assess it himself; in Hampshire and Southampton, in York, Scarborough, and Doncaster, in Northampton and Oxford, the archbishop arranged the payments.[3] The long lists of fines and amercements, their sums somewhat erratic, suggest that the justiciar was collecting as much money as he could where he could. Throughout his term of office, the justiciar's initiative can be detected in the assessment and collection of revenue. In 1195 a second scutage for the army of Normandy was taken, and the roll is full of new offerings and agreements made with the archbishop.[4] It was another busy year, for Hubert's edict for the preservation of the peace which was enforced by itinerant justices also employed the knights ordered to assist them to assess the tallage.[5] In the following year a third scutage was taken, and the justiciar's personal interest in the silver mines of Careghofa producing some of the metal for coinage reinforces the impression of his personal initiative, as does his promulgation of the Assize of Measures in November.[6] In 1197 he was arranging *oblata* with those who could pay for privileges or to avert royal displeasure, and the men of Count John were

---

[1] Mitchell, *op. cit.* p. 14; *Pipe Roll 6 Richard I*, p. xx.
[2] Howden, III, 262–7; *Pipe Roll 7 Richard I*, pp. xviii, xxiii ff.
[3] *Ibid.* pp. xxiv, 91, 105, 146, 211.
[4] *Chancellor's Roll 8 Richard I*, pp. 184, 186, 188.
[5] *Ibid.* pp. xxi, 142.
[6] *Pipe Roll 7 Richard I*, pp. 182, 246; *Pipe Roll 9 Richard I*, p. xxi; Lady Stenton corrects the accepted dating of the Assize of Measures from 1197 to November 1196.

paying to regain their lands. He was negotiating with the Jews and trying to collect long-standing debts.[1] At the Oxford council in December, he made the famous demand on the king's behalf for knight service and maintained it, although unlike the king he was prepared to take a cash equivalent.[2] The year 1198, the last of his justiciarship, is filled with financial bargainings with monastic tenants over this demand, tallages assessed by the justiciar, and the results of the great eyre which, according to Howden, reduced the whole of England to poverty by its fresh tallages and its aid of five shillings on the carucate.[3] From 1194 to 1198 England was taxed to the limit under the justiciarship of Hubert Walter, who himself took a major share in financial activity. It is altogether likely that in the calling in of royal debts the treasurer and other experienced colleagues played a great part, but the justiciar's authority was used to arrange the amounts and to coerce recalcitrant individuals.

That Hubert Walter personally supervised the financial effort made in these years is evident from his reaction to the king's proposal of 1196 to send the abbot of Caen and the bishop elect of Durham to inquire into the exactions of justices, sheriffs, and their ministers.[4] The justiciar evidently protested and was reassured by Richard, although it is said that he wished to resign, changing his mind when the king reluctantly agreed. Reviewing two years of office, the justiciar discovered that he had provided the king with eleven hundred thousand marks of silver. This represents an astonishing administrative achievement, for which Hubert took personal credit. It also represents a considerable pressure for change and innovation upon the exchequer. So far as these changes were technical and their precise authorship obscure, they are outside the scope of this book, but so far as they concern the *curia regis* they are important in the history of the justiciarship.

The broad aim of these changes was either to relieve the exchequer of work by setting up supplementary organizations to

---

[1] *Pipe Roll 9 Richard I*, pp. xx, 7, 215, 224, 232-4.

[2] Howden, IV, 40; Gervase, I, 549; Brakelond, p. 63; *Pipe Roll 10 Richard I*, pp. xix-xxiv.

[3] Howden, IV, 61-2; *Pipe Roll 10 Richard I*, pp. xxiii-xxviii, 7, 71, 91, 139, 186, 221.

[4] Howden, IV, 5, 13.

handle large sums of money like ransom, or to adjust its procedure to the pressure of business, like the appointment of general escheators and the statement of the farm. None of them are radical inventions for they introduced no rivals to the exchequer, but they introduced greater 'differentiation' into the *curia*. Some of them also involved direct payments to the king's chamber, for which accounts do not necessarily appear on the great roll of the pipe.[1] Part of the ransom and of the tallages was treated in this way, and an exchequer of the Jews was also in existence. Such devices may have assisted the working of the exchequer, but they undoubtedly complicated the task of supervising the work of the *curia*. If, whatever their interdependence, different men were appointed for special tasks, the supervision of the work they did was broader than supervision of a single and smaller group of men within an 'undifferentiated' court. The justiciarship of Hubert Walter witnessed a development within the *curia* making for complication of the justiciar's duties and the beginnings of a division of his labours.

Until Hubert's justiciarship the men who sat in the *curia regis* at Westminster had been a regular group: one or more of the curial bishops such as Richard fitz Nigel or Gilbert of Rochester, important ministers such as William Briewerre, Hugh Bardulf, and Geoffrey fitz Peter, and other well-known *curiales* like Roger fitz Renfrey, Robert of Whitefield, Thomas of Hurstbourne, and Michael Belet.[2] Occasionally they were joined by other ministers who played a part in exchequer or itinerant judicial work. In 1195, for example, the archdeacons of Ely and Hereford and William de Ste Mère Eglise sat at Westminster.[3] Whether or not the court was said to be sitting at the exchequer, its personnel remained a constant group of men who served the king as barons or justices or ministers, together with some barons whom the king particularly favoured or trusted. From 1196, however, the group was not nearly so comprehensive. In October of that year the

[1] *Pipe Roll 7 Richard I*, pp. xv–xvii; Mitchell, *op. cit.* p. 14; *Pipe Roll 10 Richard I*, pp. xxix–xxx.
[2] West, 'The *Curia Regis* in the Late Twelfth and Early Thirteenth Centuries', *Historical Studies*, p. 183; *Feet of Fines Henry II and Richard*, pp. 4–17.
[3] *Ibid.* pp. 20, 22, 23, 81.

justiciar presided over the archdeacon of Ely, Osbert fitz Hervey, Simon of Pattishall, Thomas of Hurstbourne, and Richard of Herriard; and although this group might be joined on occasion by others, it constituted a regular bench at Westminster.[1] The personnel of the *curia* before which final concords were made at Westminster had ceased to have the diffused appearance of the 'undifferentiated' court of earlier years, and had become the justiciar and those men to whom the description 'professional justice' may increasingly be given.

By Hubert's time, some of Henry II's important justices had disappeared. Roger fitz Renfrey and Robert of Whitefield had both sat in the *curia* and had been colleagues of the justiciar in the early years of Richard's reign, but they had gone. William Briewerre, Hugh Bardulf, and Geoffrey fitz Peter were alive and active in royal service but they no longer sat regularly at Westminster. The constant element of the *curia*, other than the justiciar, consisted of Osbert fitz Harvey, a judge of long experience under Henry II, Thomas of Hurstbourne who had also served Henry, and the newcomers Simon of Pattishall, Richard of Herriard, and John of Guestling.

Simon of Pattishall was probably a knight of the *honor* of Wahull, of which the Northamptonshire village from which he took his name was probably a part.[2] He must have entered royal service under Henry II, perhaps as a clerk, and by 1190 he was responsible for the escheats in his home county, and for the castle of Northampton. At the same time he began his long judicial career by hearing pleas in Kent and Surrey and in the following year in the East Anglian shires and Northampton. His employment as a judge was thereafter continuous, both in eyre and, from 1191, in the *curia* at Westminster. Richard of Herriard was a man of similar origin, his father Alfred being a modest landowner in Hampshire, Surrey, Wiltshire, and Kent, extending his holdings

---

[1] Harl. MS 2110, fo. 103 v; Cotton MS Appendix 21, fo. 17.

[2] There is a brief discussion of Simon's career by Lady Stenton in the *Northamptonshire Assize Rolls*, pp. xvii ff., and by M. S. Walker, *Feet of Fines Lincolnshire 1199–1215*, p. xxviii. A more extended discussion may be found by West, *loc. cit.* p. 177.

by purchase in Middlesex.[1] He too had served an apprenticeship in administration under Henry II, and as a knight of the earl of Salisbury he was pardoned twenty-five shillings of the scutage of Wales in 1191. In 1192 he farmed Essex and Hertfordshire with Geoffrey fitz Peter and from 1194 sat regularly in the *curia* at Westminster and as a justice in eyre. In the following year he took money across the Channel to the king. The third of the newcomers, John of Guestling, came from Sussex, where he had property at Winchelsea.[2] He had helped to fortify Dover castle against invasion during Richard I's captivity in 1193. His administrative training is unknown before his appearance as a justice at Westminster, being the last named of the judges in 1197. All three men were *curiales* of knightly rank, but not landowners of the stature of the judges of Henry II who made way for them. Under Hubert they were at the beginning of their careers, and, although all of them must have been familiar with the work of government, their introduction into court under Hubert's presidency was no doubt the immediate result of pressure of work. The experienced ministers had their hands full and, to fill their place in the doing of justice at Westminster and as the professional element in the eyres, these new men were brought in. Their later careers, especially Simon's, were distinguished, but they also represented a narrowing down of function. Justice and finance could not be easily separated when the itinerant justices had to assess the tallage and impose amercements, but their work was different from that of a baron of the exchequer sitting in judgement on the accounts. Their connexion with the exchequer is slight by comparison, and they represent the first appearance of professional justices distinct from the barons.

If the pressure of business was thus compelling the justiciar to increase the number of the prominent *curiales* and to achieve, however informally, some division of their labours into financial and judicial work, the same pressure also fell on him personally. Leaving aside his Welsh campaign and his ecclesiastical duties, the task of supervising the work of government would have been

---

[1] West, *loc. cit.* pp. 175–7; Walker, *op. cit.* p. xxxiv.
[2] West, *loc. cit.* pp. 180–1; Walker, *op. cit.* p. xxxii.

heavy enough, even if he had not himself borne an active part in administrative activity. From what has been said of the financial crisis of the reign, it is plain that the justiciar's authority was involved in the assessment of taxes, that in addition to his presidency of the exchequer he acted as one of its agents. In both central and local work, his financial activity was carried on at the same time as judicial. Justice was *magnum emolumentum*, yet in the doing of justice, as distinct from its financial results, Hubert Walter had equally extensive duties. His legal fame is reflected in the attempt to father on him the *Tractatus* bearing Glanville's name, partly because he was thought to have studied in the law schools of Bologna and therefore to have been familiar with learned treatises.[1] The relatively slight Roman influences in the treatise appear to militate against the suggestion,[2] and Hubert's experience in the courts was not so extensive as that of some of his colleagues. Nevertheless the real basis for the suggestion—that Hubert was deferred to in his own day as having great knowledge of legal custom[3]—is true. He earned the reputation by his work as justiciar.

Hubert Walter's judicial work was extensive because it produced financial profit for the king; it was part of the same financial crisis that prompted the measures already discussed. It is likely enough that Hubert shared an interest in justice for its own sake with other men who had been bred in Henry II's *curia*; good justice was also good business. The Assize of Measures was not solely or even primarily a device for earning money. But whatever the archbishop's motives, the result of his extensive judicial work was change and development in royal administration. The distinction

[1] On the problem of authorship see Southern, *EHR*, LXV, 81–9; D. M. Stenton, *Pleas Before the King or his Justices 1199–1202*, pp. 9–10. The original suggestion of Hubert's authorship was Maitland's; Southern shows that it is unlikely and Lady Stenton suggests Geoffrey fitz Peter instead.

[2] Van Caenegem, *Royal Writs in England*, pp. 373 ff., examines the influence of 'learned law' upon the Treatise and shows that it was slight. He does not go on to argue that if Hubert had had a civil training at Bologna this would seem odd in a work of his own which not only refrains from general principles of learned law but is vague at crucial practical points like the *mutuum* contract (*ibid.* pp. 380–1) and the *actio spolii* (pp. 386 ff.).

[3] *Curia Regis Rolls*, I, 279.

between exchequer and bench which has been discussed in the context of financial pressures owed something also to the increase in judicial work. The appearance of a bench at Westminster consisting of men whose work was primarily judicial not only relieved the labours of those financial officers who had previously sat in court, but it enabled the justices to become a distinct professional group. Hubert himself regularly presided over the bench. In almost every one of the final concords levied at Westminster from 1195 onwards, the archbishop of Canterbury headed the list of judges consisting of the archdeacon of either Hereford or Ely, Simon of Pattishall, Richard of Herriard, Thomas of Hurstbourne, Osbert fitz Hervey and John of Guestling.[1] Others might sit occasionally, but these men were the nucleus of the *curia*. A litigant might find it worth his while to offer a gift in order to have his suit before this court in which the archbishop sat, and the pipe rolls are full of such offerings.[2] The increasingly professional character of the *curia* certainly helped to attract litigation, and it was a valuable privilege to have a case heard before it.

Since the beginning of Richard's reign, royal charters had regularly included the grant that the beneficiary need not plead *nisi coram nobis vel coram capitali justiciario*. In September 1189 charters issued under the sole witness of Earl William de Mandeville, one of the justiciars appointed at Pipewell, contained the clause,[3] but, except for the regularity of its grant, it was not novel. The degree to which pleadings in the early years of Henry II had waited upon the king's presence shows that the privilege was valuable, and the king was always reluctant to allow judgement to be given without his presence in the matter of his own alms or those of his ancestors.[4] Such royal intervention was possible when

---

[1] *Feet of Fines, passim.*
[2] E.g. *Pipe Roll 6 Richard I*, pp. 122, 147; *Pipe Roll 7 Richard I*, pp. 188, 214, 234, 240; *Chancellor's Roll 8 Richard I*, pp. 22, 67, 117, 186.
[3] *CChR*, II, 66, 313, 335.
[4] Between May 1175 and March 1182 Henry II issued a charter for the house of St Valéry confirming its franchises and declaring that 'I may not permit judgement to be done concerning the alms of myself or my ancestors unless before me'; Delisle, *Recueil des Actes de Henri II*, II, 174. King John repeated the same reason for a grant of his own; *Curia Regis Rolls*, II, 245.

the king was frequently in England, but if he were in the Holy Land it was necessary to make regular provision for the justiciar to act on his behalf. Such suits necessarily came before the court over which the justiciar presided, and so did other cases in which an offering had been made. In Richard's second year, it cost ten marks to gain confirmation of the right not to plead unless before the king or his justiciar, but a litigant like Alfred son of Alfred gave one mark to have his case before the chief justice.[1] In 8 Richard I an offering of forty shillings was given that a case might be judged in the king's court before the archbishop of Canterbury who was then justiciar.[2] By the reign of King John two palfreys were a common offering. The precise interpretation of *coram nobis vel coram capitali justiciario* presents some difficulties—it may originally have meant the *capitalis curia* as distinct from the shire or local courts and judges[3]—but in the reign of Richard it had a precision of meaning, and very early in John's reign it was used to try to stop pleading in the bench at Westminster when neither the king nor the justiciar was present.[4] Those who held such royal grants or offered money in particular cases wanted to be heard before the king or his justiciar, and, given the circumstances of Richard's reign, this meant the justiciar. Hence Hubert Walter's regular presidency of the court at Westminster. Hence too, no doubt, the apparent presence of Hubert in court when he was certainly elsewhere. From 14 to 20 October 1197 he was named in final concords made before the central *curia*,[5] although on 5 October he was with Richard at Sées and eleven days later at Rouen where he witnessed the charter by which the king compensated Walter of Coutances for the damage suffered by his

---

[1] *Pipe Roll 7 Richard I*, p. 173.   [2] *Chancellor's Roll 8 Richard I*, p. 289.

[3] Howden's use of the words *capitalis curia* in the commission of eyre of 1194 (III, 262–7), following Glanville's usage, suggests that a justice of that court might be called *capitalis justiciarius*. If this was its original meaning, it is clear that by Richard's reign it had a more precise one, for the king's letter of July 1198, replacing Hubert Walter, used the term *justiciarius* to refer to his office, and in a plea early in John's reign a litigant was equally precise. It might also be argued that in the oblates entered upon the pipe rolls *capitalis curia* is not used; offerings are made instead to have a suit *in curia regis apud Westmonasterium*.

[4] *Curia Regis Rolls*, I, 462.

[5] *Feet of Fines 9 Richard*, pp. 25–48.

archbishopric during the building of Château Gaillard.[1] The chroniclers agree that Hubert was in Normandy at this time and that he did not return to England until November.[2] Plainly, the justiciar's presence was deemed important in this court of professional justices, and although it is likely that pressure of his other duties caused his occasional absence, there can be little doubt that he sat regularly to do justice.

Both his nominal control and his actual interest in legal proceedings appear from two of his writs. In one, styled archbishop, primate of all England, and papal legate, he ordered the sheriff of Hereford to take pledges in a case of tresspass.[3] It was issued between 1195 and 1197 under the witness of Geoffrey fitz Peter, and was one of those routine legal writs sent out in large numbers. Indeed, from the earliest *curia regis* rolls, the administration of justice depended on the ready availability of such writs issued in the name of Hubert Walter.[4] Formally the legal system revolved around the justiciar, and although its actual operation depended upon the justices and upon greater men like Geoffrey fitz Peter (sufficiently well known to be called *G. fil P.* by the scribe) who witnessed this justiciar's writ, Hubert's 'informal' activity also guided its working. In the second of his writs the archbishop ordered the sheriff of Devon to let Margaret daughter of Guy of Britwell have her rightful dower of which she had been disseised.[5] This document, which is not in a chancery hand, is not properly a writ in the form in which it survives; it has no witness and the style is simply *archiepiscopus salutem vic'*. It may be a draft of information upon which a writ in regular form might be based, but it is clearly one prepared within the justiciar's circle or household and indicative of his personal as distinct from his formal control of the legal system.[6]

Hubert's legal fame has been mentioned, and it is based upon his

---

[1] Landon, *Itinerary of Richard I*, p. 123.   [2] Diceto, II, 158; Gervase, I, 544.
[3] D. M. Stenton, *Pleas Before the King or his Justices*, I, 350–1.
[4] *Rolls of the King's Court, Richard I*, pp. 8, 20, 34, 41, 71, 122, 123.
[5] Ancient Correspondence, I, 17.
[6] Cheney, *English Bishops' Chanceries*, p. 18, points out how little distinction there was between the royal and archiepiscopal secretariates in Hubert's term of office.

knowledge of, and intervention in, judicial work. He was consulted by the justices on difficult points; he was appealed to by litigants. His office and his training made this inevitable, especially at a time when the legal reforms of Henry II were still being worked out in practice. Between 1187 or 1189, when the Treatise was written, and the end of Hubert Walter's justiciarship, new writs were introduced, and the practice or wording of others slightly changed.[1] Hubert's writ of entry suggests innovation, with its interlineations and alterations. Neither the working out of the practices implied in Glanville's treatise nor the innovations in the writs themselves can be directly ascribed to Hubert; they did not, in any case, introduce radical departures from the practice described by Glanville. But it seems altogether likely that they happened under Hubert's eye while the justices of the *curia* were becoming professionals and perhaps themselves sealing and issuing judicial writs.[2] It cannot altogether be accidental that the earliest court rolls, the depositing of the feet of fines, and the alterations in the personnel of the central *curia*, all come from Hubert's justiciarship. Nor can it be coincidental that similar evidence of a driving force behind the judicial work comes from the eyres which went out during his justiciarship.

The general eyre was not new in Hubert's time. Henry II had used it to enforce his assizes and in 1190 there were groups of justices at work in all the counties not under Count John's control. In this, as in other matters, Hubert was not an innovator, but the survival of the articles of 1194 and 1198 suggest that the king's necessities led the justiciar to a much more rigorous and comprehensive activity. An eyre might be of two kinds, either general or limited to cases of a particular type; the justices might have general competence or they might be ordered simply to take assizes and deliver gaols, or, even more limited, they might be *ad hoc constituti*. And a general eyre was concerned not merely with judicial matters but with others of wider administrative significance. The commissions of general eyre belonging to the justiciarship of Hubert Walter are the first of their kind to survive. The general eyre took place every four years; thus the first of

---

[1] D. M. Stenton, *Pleas Before the King or his Justices*, I, 25–6.　[2] *Ibid.* pp. 29 ff.

these commissions was in 1194, the second in 1198, and the next in the serics was the general eyre of 1202.[1] No doubt Hubert Walter was the motive force behind the actual commission. Although the king alone could formulate policy, the justiciar must have attended to the detail involved. The eyre of 1194 was aimed at the restoration of the country after Count John's revolt. It laid down the method of electing juries and the questions which should be put to them. These consisted of the pleas of the Crown, both old and new, and all pleas which were before the king's justices and not yet finished. Further, they were to deal with all recognitions and pleas which were summoned before the justices by the king's writ or that of the justiciar, or sent to them by the *capitalis curia*. Escheats in the king's hand were to receive attention, together with churches in the king's gift, wardships, and marriages; in fact the value of the king's feudal rights were to be investigated systematically by the justices to see that the Crown lost nothing. Criminal matters, too, came under review, and the justices were to take cognizance of those who shielded malefactors, forgers, murderers of Jews, and the debts which were owed to the latter. Of immediate concern was the amount of the king's ransom which was outstanding, and those men who had supported Count John in his treasonable doings, and also the feudal rights such as escheats and wardships which belonged to him.[2] Usurers were to receive attention; and also wine sold against the assize; and the chattels of dead crusaders were to be dealt with, side by side with a clause prescribing the holding of the grand assize for lands of less than a hundred shillings. The activity of coroners was to be supervised. It was not merely judicial matters which were covered, but the whole range of government interest. The famous principle that the sheriff was not to be a justice in his own county was asserted, nor in any county which he had held after the king's

---

[1] Howden, III, 262–7; IV, 61–2; D. M. Stenton, *Earliest Lincoln Assize Rolls*, p. xl. Several other questions, in addition to those covered by the eyre of 1198, may have been added; for example, an inquiry about the chattels of the Flemings, and about tolls and markets. Such questions were topical. The contents of the justices' commission can be deduced from the entries on their rolls of assize.

[2] The Wiltshire assize roll of 1194 had the results of this clause; *Rolls of the King's Court*, pp. 71, 92.

first coronation. And, in addition to all these, financial and economic matters were handed over to the attention of the justices; a tallage was to be levied and royal manors were to be stocked. Royal rights of all kinds were thus to be protected, and the farmers of lands in escheat or wardship were to hold them until the term of the year and then to render account, on which matter they had the letter of the justiciar, a document including the text of the king's charter which regulated prices of livestock. A separate section of the commission dealt with the Jews, the enrolment of their lands and debts, their method of payment, and the prescribed manner in which their deeds were to be kept. To round off this comprehensive investigation, an inquisition was projected into the exactions of royal officers, but this was postponed on the authority of Hubert Walter. The whole commission was plainly in his charge since the king was abroad, and his authority was invoked on points of detail. This general commission was one method of raising money and preserving royal rights that might have slipped into abeyance during the king's long absence. If it was authorized by Richard during his brief visit to England in 1194, its detail and execution seem just as plainly the work of Hubert Walter, and it reveals the far-reaching interest of the justiciar in every aspect of royal government. The justices who carried it out were equally certainly not mere judicial officers, for their work demanded financial and local knowledge, but in each group there were one or two of the men from the *capitalis curia* of Westminster. It is a striking illustration of the close connexion between the different aspects of royal administration, and of the authority of the justiciar who presided over it. The commission was exceptional in its circumstances, since the country had just witnessed the struggle with the king's brother John, but it was not different in kind from its successors; indeed it constituted a prototype.[1]

After four years there was another such general commission. Again, all unfinished pleas of the Crown were to be dealt with,

---

[1] This is not to deny that justices had earlier toured the country under a commission, for example the Assize of Northampton in 1176, but the regular four-year cycle was new, and the articles of 1194 were closely followed by the subsequent articles of eyre.

and all assizes (the grand assize so far as the land was worth up to £10 and the three possessory assizes). The election of juries to make the grand assize was to be held by command of the king or his chief justice. The churches in the king's gift formed another topic for inquiry, and escheats and wardships again received attention, together with the fines offered by widows for their remarriage. Sergeanties were to be valued, and the identity of their holders to be discovered, especially those who had not contributed to the king's ransom. The other articles ranged over userers, those who had not paid amercements, purprestures, coiners, malefactors, weights and measures, especially of wine. The conduct of officials was to be inquired into, also that of the custodians of ports, and merchants; and it was further to be discovered whether everyone had come to the summons of the jury as he should have done. In addition to these two general commissions, there was issued an edict of the peace, a commission to the justices of the forests in 1194, and the assize of weights and measures in 1196. This spate of activity which characterizes Hubert's justiciarship is not accidental. It represents a very remarkable attempt to overhaul the administration, not merely to raise money but also to satisfy the need for justice, and these great eyres initiated the policy followed by King John and Henry III. The distinction which grew up between the officials whose concern was primarily with the exchequer and those who foreshadow a group of professional justices was part of the overhauling of the administration implied in all this activity, and it marks an attempt to provide better or speedier justice.

Hubert's personal interest in judicial affairs is undoubted. In the plea between Croyland and Spalding he would not permit judgement without his consent.[1] He himself did a good deal of judicial work in eyre as well as in the central royal court, both directing the activity of the justices and hearing pleas in person. In 1195 he was on eyre in the East Anglian counties, although he was too busy to ride the whole circuit.[2] In the same year he sat at Oxford

---

[1] Fulman, *Rerum Anglic. Scriptores*, 1, 462; the case is discussed by Lady Stenton, *Pipe Roll 7 Richard I*, pp. xxii–xxiii.
[2] *Pipe Roll 7 Richard I*, pp. 73, 121.

with William de Warenne, William Briewerre and Geoffrey of Buckland.[1] The following year found him in Worcester on the Monday after the feast of St Bartholomew, his companions being the bishop of Hereford and his archdeacon, Geoffrey fitz Peter, William Briewerre and Michael Belet, a session of a court which may have taken place during his expedition to Wales against Gwenwynwyn of Powys.[2] In 1197 the justiciar visited Warwickshire and Leicestershire, but this was not an extended *iter* and a final concord was also made before him at St Benet of Holme.[3] January following saw him at Shrewsbury attended by Roger Bigot, Geoffrey fitz Peter, and Geoffrey of Buckland, the purpose of his visit being endorsed on the final concord *in itinere archiepiscopi in Walliam ad deliberandum David' regem Wallie.*[4] The justiciar was a busy man, but his control over judicial work was real enough. In 1195, newly made papal legate, Hubert arrived in York where he held a court christian, at the same time causing his ministers to hold assizes of all pleas of the Crown and assizes of novel disseisin and *mort d'ancestor*, while in the previous year he had sent a commission of judges to York to hear the dispute between Archbishop Geoffrey and his canons.[5] His concern for the tranquillity of England appears from the edict of the peace which was his handiwork, concerned with the capture and trial of malefactors, the hue and cry, and the reception by knights of the shires of the oaths of all over fifteen to keep the peace.[6] The effect of the measure was to cause many to flee, leaving home and goods, and many were imprisoned. The words of the chronicler are borne out by the pipe roll of that year, where the number of fugitives and prisoners was unusually large, but the operation of the edict took time.[7] Not until 1197 was it enforced in East Anglia.[8]

The picture of Hubert Walter's judicial administration is one of

---

[1] *Feet of Fines Henry II and Richard I*, pp. 70–1.   [2] *Ibid.* p. 188.
[3] *Pipe Roll of Richard I*, p. xvi; *Feet of Fines 7, 8 Richard I*, p. 23. The final concord was made on 1 April.
[4] *Feet of Fines 9 Richard I*, p. 79. It was received by the hand of Geoffrey of Buckland.   [5] Howden, III, 261–2, 292–4.
[6] *Ibid.* III, 299–300. The chronicler described it as the work of the archbishop and justiciar.   [7] *Pipe Roll 7 Richard I*, pp. 123, 141, 242, 250, 251.
[8] *Pipe Roll 9 Richard I*, p. xvii.

remarkable vigour and enterprise. Not only did he initiate the measures which overhauled the administration of England, but he took part in their execution, and also in the routine operation of justice, both hearing pleas and guiding the course of litigation. In the Easter term 9 Richard he gave a day for hearing litigants at the coming of the justices into the county, and in the same term he bore witness to the fact that a man was in the king's service, in order that he might not be penalized for his non-appearance in court.[1] These were ordinary judicial duties which fell to the justiciar, but when he was not in court a suit might be given a day so that it could be heard by him,[2] and another litigant was told by the justices in eyre in Dorset that he should produce his warranty at the Tower of London unless the archbishop was at Westminster.[3] In a criminal matter the king might send an order to Hubert that he was to apprehend the men who had wounded a man and killed his servant.[4] And there were constant offerings to him that he might issue a writ for some purpose.[5] The judicial system, in the absence of King Richard, revolved round the person of Hubert Walter, the justiciar; justice was done in his name, and a litigant who went over his head to the king might be punished.[6] Glanville had described the way in which the system worked; it was under Hubert Walter that the great rush of judicial business came into the king's court, and his judicial work was, no doubt, largely responsible for it. After the uncertain years earlier in the reign, he introduced his commissions of assize which settled England after conflict and disturbance. He put into operation the king's will and he shared in the labour of carrying it out. During his justiciarship there began to grow up a staff of professional judges, and with the growing complexity of administrative processes the efficiency of judicial work depended upon some such development. The day was to come when the justiciar would himself be a professional judge and nothing more, but Hubert Walter, great judge as he was, was more than a mere chief justice.

---

[1] *Curia Regis Rolls*, I, 33, 53.   [2] *Rolls of the King's Court, Richard I*, p. 14.
[3] *Ibid.* p. 52.   [4] *Ibid.* p. 19.
[5] *Ibid.* pp. 34, 71, 92.
[6] Sayles, *Select Cases in the Court of King's Bench*, p. xxix.

Hubert's power and prestige were certainly greater than those of his predecessors, partly because of his great ecclesiastical and baronial status, partly because of the prolonged absence of a king of Richard's character. The justiciar's own greatness impressed contemporaries, even the hostile Gerald of Wales, and his reputation was not seriously dimmed even by his high-handed action against William fitz Osbert.[1] As justiciar, he satisfied the king. The administration performed well enough to raise unprecedented amounts of money while at the same time securing and maintaining the safety and good order of the kingdom. None of the Angevin kings was especially noted for gratitude, but Richard's letter by which he released Hubert from the justiciarship in July 1198 reveals some appreciation of his work.[2] Hubert, says Richard, had often asked to be released from the burden he carried but for 'our welfare and yours and the peace of the kingdom' he had never agreed. At length, considering his sickness, 'the intolerable burden of labour and his weakness, we have released him at his request'. The northern chronicler Howden suggests that Hubert resigned the justiciarship because the monks of Canterbury complained of him to Pope Innocent III, who thereupon wrote to the king asking him to dismiss Hubert.[3] It is not unlikely that Innocent disliked the idea of an archbishop who also held the highest secular office, but there is no evidence to support Howden's tale. No papal letter survives, the king gives different reasons, and in the following year Hubert did not scruple to become chancellor without papal denunciation. It is certainly true from the evidence of Hubert's activity that he bore a heavy burden with all his offices, and the appointment of Geoffrey fitz Peter to succeed him, undoubtedly with his own advice, relieved him of the strain while it secured his continued influence in government. And if Richard's reasons for Hubert's replacement are true, it is evident that, at the highest point of its development, the justiciarship was becoming an unmanageable burden for any one man.

[1] Howden, IV, 6. The chronicler links this with the papal request for Hubert's resignation in 1198, but for this there is no evidence.
[2] Rymer, *Foedera*, I, 71.
[3] Howden, IV, 48.

CHAPTER IV

THE JUSTICIARSHIP UNDER JOHN: BEFORE THE LOSS OF NORMANDY

King John had much more in common with his father Henry II than with his brother Richard. He had been an English magnate and was familiar with the country and its people, and they with him; indeed this knowledge may very well have been decisive for his succession instead of Arthur's. He had the same sustained interest in government and its workings as Henry, and, unlike Richard, he actively intervened in its details. The person of the king therefore circumscribed his justiciar as Hubert Walter had not been circumscribed by Richard. Moreover, John's first justiciar probably had not the personal greatness of Archbishop Hubert and certainly not his combination of powerful offices. Hubert himself took the chancery at the beginning of John's reign, and even if that office did not give him authority beside the justiciar his other offices and his great prestige as ex-justiciar certainly complicated Geoffrey fitz Peter's own position. Apart from references to Hubert's former authority or present knowledge in the rolls of exchequer and bench, one incident alone reveals his importance. Perhaps in March 1202 Geoffrey fitz Peter was with the archbishop and the king in Normandy, and he remained abroad until early May. On 11 May Hubert Walter was sent to the justiciar and the justices in England whom John ordered to accept without question the things Hubert would tell them and to summon him to all their discussions, adding that he would 'hold firm and established that which you decree with his counsel touching the furtherance of our business'.[1] The justiciar was thus limited in deciding policy and practice, but within these limits his was the authority that moved government.

[1] *Rot. Lit. Pat.* p. 12.

I. GEOFFREY FITZ PETER

Geoffrey fitz Peter who was justiciar when King John came to the throne and whom he created earl of Essex at his coronation feast, was a man of relatively humble origin who had risen to the highest office by ability and good fortune. Geoffrey was the son of Peter, forester of Ludgershall under Henry II, and his elder brother Simon was one of that king's sheriffs. His family was one of *curiales*, royal ministers whose feudal position was of no great significance. Geoffrey's own holdings were extremely modest. In 1161 he held a fee of half a knight in Hampshire on which he paid scutage in that year.[1] The survival of the *carte baronum* of 1166 reveals that he held some land of mesne lords. Of Girard Giffard he held Cherhill in Wiltshire for the service of one knight as part of Girard's new enfeoffment; in Buckinghamshire, jointly with Hugh de Diva, he held another knight's fee of the countess of Clare; and finally Walter of Beck recorded that in the time of King Henry I he had enfeoffed Guy, father of John son of Guy,[2] of the third part of a knight's fee on his demesne, which Geoffrey fitz Peter held in 1166 together with the wife of Adam, son of John son of Guy.[2] The total of Geoffrey's holdings was far from large, but it placed him within the pale of society; he was a knight. For one in this position, the king's service was the road to advancement, and Geoffrey must have served an administrative apprenticeship before he figured as a reasonably important and certainly very active royal official. In 1184, when the king's justices toured Oxfordshire, he accounted before them for the farm of Kinver which was worth £4. 10s.[3] One year later he was himself a judge, and heard the pleas of the forests in an extensive circuit through the English counties; in addition he was an ordinary justice in Northamptonshire of which county he was sheriff.[4] In

---

[1] *Pipe Roll 7 Henry II*, p. 57; *Red Book*, p. 28. The place was Sparsholt; and for this fee he paid scutage in 1165 and 1167; *Pipe Roll 11 Henry II*, p. 43; *Pipe Roll 13 Henry II*, p. 179.

[2] *Red Book*, pp. 247, 316, 402, 407.   [3] *Pipe Roll 30 Henry II*, p. 69.

[4] *Pipe Roll 31 Henry II*, pp. 18, 23, 27, 45, 51, 54, 59, 92, 103, 108, 113, 121, 138, 170, 193, 211, 237. Two years later he heard the forest pleas in Rutland, Nottinghamshire and Derbyshire; *Pipe Roll 33 Henry II*, pp. 113, 168.

that year, too, he had custody of the land of Robert son of Bernard in Berkshire, and Herbert son of Herbert in Surrey.[1] This sudden emergence into the administrative picture betokens long training. Perhaps he had been the clerk of the royal judge Thomas son of Bernard into whose shoes he stepped as guardian of the heir of Gilbert de Monte.[2] For his service to the king there were rewards. When he heard the forest pleas, for instance, he already held several wardships; and there were others. Geoffrey had the land and heir of William de Chauz of Elton in Buckinghamshire, and in Norfolk and Suffolk, Burton, which Roger Caperon had held of Earl Hugh of Chester.[3] The grant by the king of a wardship could be extremely valuable to its holder. Apart from the profits of the land while a male heir was under age, should the minor be a girl the custodian had the right to marry her where he would, or to marry her himself. To a relatively obscure official, guardianship of a great heiress might be the making of his fortune. Thus William Marshal married the heiress of the earl of Pembroke, and thus in 1185 Geoffrey fitz Peter obtained custody of Saham in Norfolk, which had belonged to William de Say, and the wardship of his two daughters.[4] The farm itself was relatively valuable, but the daughter Beatrice whom Geoffrey fitz Peter married was even more attractive, for she was co-heiress to the Mandeville barony.

[1] *Pipe Roll 31 Henry II*, pp. 27, 239. He held the farm of Newton in Berkshire which was part of the land of Robert son of Bernard; and he accounted for the old farm of the manors in the land of Herbert son of Herbert in Surrey.
[2] *Rot. de Dominabus*, p. 29. Together with the heir, Geoffrey had in wardship his three sisters and his mother. Thomas son of Bernard had held this wardship for seven years, and had then retired into the monastery of Eynsham. The land lay in the two hundreds of Sutton in Northamptonshire.
[3] *Rot. de Dominabus*, p. 39. William de Chauz was fifteen years of age. He was the ward of the king who had given him into custody of Geoffrey fitz Peter two years before the roll was compiled i.e. in 1183; *Magnus Rotulus Pipae Anno Primo Regni Ricardi Primi*, p. 55. Earl Hugh had been dead since 1181.
[4] *Ibid.* p. 40. The farm was worth £23. 16s. 8d. annually. The king had originally given the custody to Richard Ruffus whom Geoffrey succeeded. The stock had then somewhat depreciated. The value of Saham had, however, risen since the Domesday survey when it was worth £20 *ad pensum*.

The Mandeville *honor* was created after the conquest for Geoffrey de Mandeville, and its income placed it in the top rank of baronies.[1] The *caput* of the *honor* was Pleshy in High Easter and its manors were scattered through Essex (where Geoffrey de Mandeville held Great Waltham and Saffron Walden), Middlesex (Edmonton and Enfield), Hertfordshire (Sawbridgeworth), Buckinghamshire (Guarrendon and Amersham), Berkshire (Streatley) and Warwickshire (Long Compton), in addition to lands in Surrey and the counties of Suffolk, Cambridge and Northampton.[2] Considerable as these estates were, the Mandeville fortunes were greatly increased by the activities of the notorious Geoffrey de Mandeville in the reign of King Stephen. The total of his bargains produced the title of earl of Essex, the third penny of the county, four hundred librates of land from the king, a hundred from the Empress Matilda, the service of twenty knights granted by the latter and sixty from the former, the offices of hereditary sheriff and justiciar in Essex, to say nothing of the lands which Eudo the *dapifer* held in Normandy.[3] When his son, another Geoffrey, obtained a confirmation of his father's land from King Henry II, the lands were extensive.[4] It is impossible to ascertain the income which they produced, but the rough test of knight service credits the earl with 97 and one-third knights of the old enfeoffment and 15 and five-sixths newly enfeoffed, of which the service rendered to the king was sixty. Moreover, the earls of Essex were not magnates who attended merely to honorial business; they took an active part in royal administration. The Earl Geoffrey of Henry II's time was the fellow justice of Richard de Luci the justiciar,[5] and his son, Earl William, was one of the justiciars whom Richard I proposed to appoint in 1189.[6] Before the end of the year Earl William lay dead in Rouen, leaving no children; his heir was his aunt, Beatrice de Say. This lady had two sons, William and Geoffrey, and it was the two daughters of the former whom Geoffrey fitz Peter had in wardship. The dispute over the earldom

---

[1] *CMH*, v, 511; N. Denholm-Young, *Collected Papers*, p. 159 n. 4.
[2] *Complete Peerage*, v, 113.   [3] *Ibid.* p. 115.   [4] *Ibid.* p. 117.
[5] *Pipe Roll 12 Henry II*, pp. 7, 14, 30, 46, 57, 70, 76, 87, 108, 115, 128.
[6] Benedict, II, 87; Howden, III, 15.

was between the daughter Beatrice whom Geoffrey married, and her uncle, Geoffrey de Say. Longchamps, the justiciar of Richard I, adjudged the barony to the latter at his mother's wish for seven thousand marks, and gave him seisin of the lands. There was difficulty about the payment of this relief, and for three thousand marks down Geoffrey fitz Peter received the barony in the right of his wife. In fact he paid only £200 at once, but nevertheless he held the Mandeville barony and received the third penny of the county of Essex, although he was not granted the title of earl until 1199.[1]

Geoffrey fitz Peter entered the magnate class in 1190, but his landed position did not rest solely upon the Mandeville lands either before or after that date. Henry II had already augmented his holding of Cherhill by the grant of land worth twenty-two pounds blanch and the service of one knight, and in the last year of his reign he granted him land to the value of seven and a half pounds at Sutton in Kent.[2] At some unknown period, the king gave Geoffrey the house which had belonged to Thomas Brown in Winchester and, perhaps at the same period, four knights' fees which the Justiciar Richard de Luci held of the honor of Boulogne, and four more which were fees of Earl Roger.[3] By the end of Henry's reign, Geoffrey also had two more wardships, one carucate of land in Little Barton or Barton Mills near Mildenhall,

---

[1] Howden, III, xlviii n. 6. For the payment by Geoffrey of part of the fine; *Pipe Roll 2 Richard I*, p. 104. The value of the third penny of the county was £20. 5s. 5d. for the half year in 1190; *ibid.* p. 111.

[2] *Pipe Roll 23 Henry II*, pp. 172, 174, 178; *Magnus Rotulus Pipae Anno Primo Regni Ricardi Primi*, p. 231. It was probably this land at Sutton at Hone which King John confirmed to William de Wrotham as a gift of Geoffrey fitz Peter; *Rot. Chart.* p. 29.

[3] *Book of Fees*, pp. 77, 249. The house of Thomas Brown belonged to his possessions which escheated to the king on his death and Henry II passed on the house in Winchester to Geoffrey. The fees of Richard de Luci of the *honor* of Boulogne were in Essex, being Stamford (Rivers), (Chipping) Ongar, Chreshall and Roothing, which Richard de Luci had been given between December 1153 and October 1154 by William son of King Stephen, and confirmed by Henry II; Round, *Essex Archaeological Soc. Transactions*, new series, VII, part II, pp. 144–5, 146. In addition, the four fees of Earl Roger which the justiciar held were also in Essex at Little Stanford and Little Nutley *iuxta* Ongar. Geoffrey denied the service of one of these knights.

and the fee of William Blund at Greenhow in Norfolk.[1] Geoffrey's rewards were normal ones for an industrious royal servant, and in the ordinary course of events he could have hoped for little more than this substantial but moderate wealth. The good fortune which attended his marriage was the essential accompaniment to his ability; without it he could hardly have risen so high. Previous justiciars, if they were not already great barons, tried to carve out baronies for themselves, a by no means easy process. Richard de Luci, for example, into whose shoes Geoffrey stepped in the case of the four knights' fees, had created a barony for himself comprising thirty fees held of mesne lords.[2] Geoffrey's holding of the Mandeville barony alone gave him nearly one hundred. Without ability and industry Geoffrey fitz Peter might never have been in a position to obtain so profitable a wardship; without his marriage and its potentialities, he might never have reached the eminence he did.

Geoffrey fitz Peter became justiciar in succession to Hubert Walter in 1198. When there was discussion and perhaps doubt over the rights in the matter of succession, Geoffrey was loyal to John, and at Northampton he was partly responsible for obtaining for the latter the allegiance of important members of the baronage.[3] He was rewarded with the title of earl, but also with other substantial marks of the king's favour. Thus before Normandy was lost he had received the grant of a fair at one of his manors and the gift of a new manor at Winterslow in Wiltshire to be held at fee farm by himself and his heirs for an annual rent of £20, to be paid to the keeper of the *honor* of Berkhampstead, and the service of a quarter of a knight.[4] His increase in landed power before the

---

[1] *Book of Fees*, p. 1324. The land was *in Claia*, South Greenhow. For this fee, in 1191, Geoffrey paid 70s.; the Welsh scutage of 10s. on the fee in that year credits him, therefore, with seven knights. Barton or Barton Mills was in Suffolk; Farrer, *Honors and Knights' Fees*, I, 218; *Pipe Roll 34 Henry II*, p. 85. Geoffrey had custody of this land for nine months in 1189.

[2] See above, pp. 38–9.

[3] Wendover, I, 285. With Hubert Walter and William Marshal whom John sent from Normandy; *convenientes convocavunt proceres universos de quibus magis dubitant*.

[4] *Rot. Chart.* pp. 73 *b*, 134 *b*. In addition, in 1200 Geoffrey had the reversion of 100 acres in Stradley which the king confirmed to Baldwin count of Aumale

loss of Normandy was not great. Geoffrey does not seem to have used his position to gain very much for himself, but after the continental dominions had gone there came his second great increase in territorial power. On 29 May 1205 the king granted to Geoffrey fitz Peter the castle and *honor* of Berkhampstead at fee farm, for a rent of £100 per annum and the performance of foreign service, the grant to descend to his heirs by his second wife Aveline.[1] This barony was an extremely valuable one, and in 1214, the year after the justiciar's death, its income was £400.[2] Perhaps this magnificent grant explains the relative modesty of some of the justiciar's other rewards, but the *honor* increased Geoffrey's wealth and power in a way which an accumulation of lesser gifts would not have done. The lands of the barony stretched across central England, lying in Buckinghamshire, Hertfordshire and Northamptonshire; and in the former two counties the justiciar's power was already established. It included twenty-two knights' fees of the *honor* of Mortain which John had formerly held and from which he had taken his title prior to his accession,[3] and it is not the only case of the justiciar's obtaining land previously held by the king. When the inquiry of 1211–12 was conducted Geoffrey held 10¾ fees of the *honor* of Gloucester, another of the baronies which John had possessed as count of Mortain, and these holdings lay in Essex and Hertfordshire, thus strengthening his power at its centre.[4] Such acquisitions quite overshadow such lesser grants as Queenhithe in London in 1208, and fairs and markets which he obtained at his manors at Kimbolton and Morton, the latter having been given to him by Henry son of William de Tracy and confirmed to him by the king.[5] There was one other considerable royal gift which was a direct consequence

and Hawis his wife; *ibid*. p. 53. In 1204 the king confirmed to Geoffrey the land of Gervase of Southampton which the justiciar bought from his widow and land in Southampton bought from Robert son of Roscelin; *ibid*. p. 126 b.

[1] *Ibid*. p. 151 b.
[2] Pipe Roll 16 John.
[3] *Red Book*, p. 498 states that it comprised this number of fees, and also gives the counties in which they lay.
[4] *Red Book*, p. 609.
[5] *Rot. Chart*. pp. 79 b, 166 b, 182 b. In addition to these grants, on 6 March 1205 the king gave Geoffrey 55 acres of meadow in various named places in the

of the loss of Normandy. The lands of the Norman barons were treated by John as being at his disposal after the continental dominions had gone. One such Norman was Robert son of Ernis, and his land was given to the justiciar.[1] The position was rather complicated since John did not regard the loss of Normandy as permanent, a view which was reflected in the terms of some of his grants from these lands. Some of the Norman lords could certainly be bribed with these estates, but other lands could equally be regarded as a source of reward to Englishmen. The grant of this particular Norman escheat to Geoffrey fitz Peter was, in fact, permanent, and it descended to one of his sons.[2] It was, moreover, valuable; it comprised the manor of Hatfield Peverel in Essex which was worth £30 annually, and in the same county the manor of Depden worth £50 per annum; there were two fees in Norfolk and Suffolk held of the *honor* of Gloucester, and in Great Massingham land worth £10. 13s. 6d. yearly, and six carucates of land elsewhere worth at least another £10.[3] At the lowest estimate, this Norman land added £100 to the justiciar's income, and it represented a not inconsiderable fraction of the total land which became available to the king as a consequence of the defection of

vill of Alconbury, Hunts., which had been formerly held by Eustace of Sibthorpe and Robert son of Ralph; *ibid.* p. 144 *b*. The last gift the justiciar received was of the forests between Kimbolton, his manor, and Melbourne, on 24 July 1213, very shortly before his death. The gift of Morton, where the justiciar was now granted a fair, took place in 1200. It may have been a bribe; Painter, *King John*, pp. 38–9.

[1] In the fragmentary Memoranda Roll of 10 John the barons wished to talk with the justiciar about money due from Robert son of Ernis for land which Eudo son of Patrick held in Maldon, Essex; *Memoranda Roll 10 John*, p. 52.

[2] *Rot. Lit. Claus.* I, 154 *b*. In 1213 the sheriffs of Essex, Norfolk and Lincoln were notified that the king had delivered to William de Mandeville the whole of the land late of Robert son of Ernis to hold as Geoffrey fitz Peter his father had held it of the king.

[3] *Book of Fees*, pp. 615, 619; *Red Book*, pp. 479, 610, 803. The manor of Depden in Suffolk passed to the archbishop of Canterbury, and in 1237 it was recorded that it should be held by Humphrey de Bohun, earl of Essex, the successor of Geoffrey fitz Peter. Great Massingham was divided. Ely de Chenedut held land there to the value quoted in the text, but Geoffrey le Sire and John of Helegeton held 100 shillings worth, and the rest John son of Geoffrey held. In 1237 Richard de Kauz held £10 of land in Lincolnshire which belonged to this escheat of Robert son of Ernis; *Book of Fees*, p. 617.

his Norman barons.[1] The loss of Normandy was thus a direct source of profit to Geoffrey fitz Peter; it increased his estates at the centre of his landed power; it also enabled him to provide for one of his sons; and one manor descended to a successor in the justiciarship.[2]

When Normandy was lost, the justiciar was among the greatest magnates in England, but he did not disdain lesser accumulations of land. Thus at the end of his life he held one knight's fee at South Thoresby of the earl of Chester, 1¾ fees of the *honor* of Henry of Essex, two of the *honor* of Peverel of London, one in the hundred of Sandford, Suffolk, in addition to Gersiz (?) in Dorset and one in Norfolk and Suffolk of the *honor* of Lancaster.[3] As justiciar his position was the most important within the administration. His goodwill could be invaluable to any suitor. There is no suggestion that he utilized his position to enrich himself unduly—Hubert Walter, for instance, obtained many more wardships—but there is always the possibility that some of these lesser holdings were gifts to obtain his influence, or the profits which any man in his position might reasonably expect. In one case the custody of land came to him as a consequence of the death of a relation by marriage, the daughter of Hugh of Buckland who was husband of Geoffrey's wife's sister who had married William de Lanvalei.[4]

[1] Late in 1204, or early 1205, John ordered his justices to estimate the value of these lands. An incomplete roll survives and the total value therein was £1512; *Rotuli Normanniae*, I, 122–43. But with the *honor* of Richmond it would be about £4000; Painter, *King John*, p. 150.

[2] This was the manor of Hatfield Peverel which Hubert de Burgh held; *Book of Fees*, p. 615.

[3] *Book of Fees*, pp. 92, 134, 138, 161; *Red Book*, pp. 591, 595. An entry in the Book of Fees under 1219 reveals that, at some time in John's reign, Geoffrey held the soke of Springthorpe and Stivegarth (?) in Lincolnshire. Gersiz (?) in Dorset had formerly belonged to Roland de Dinant, and Geoffrey held it in chief of the crown for a service which was unknown. The returns of 1212 also show that Geoffrey had another fee in Wiltshire besides Cherhill, at Lavington. This he had presumably acquired in 1189 when he gave sixty marks to have the daughter of Bartholomew of Lavington and the right to give her in marriage; *Magnus Rotulus Pipae Anno Primo Regni Ricardi Primi*, p. 122.

[4] *Pipe Roll 13 John*, m. 6r. The fine was actually offered that the land, which is at Lullingstone and Farningham in Kent, should be taken into the king's hand with all the chattels which were there when Alexander de Ros had seisin; *Rot. de Finibus*, pp. 523, 533. Walter of Streetly held one fee of the *honor* of Peverel

Three years later, in 1208, Geoffrey received custody of the land and heir of Werresius de Valognes. But in two cases the justiciar exerted himself to obtain such wardships. In 1211, for example, he gave the king 30 marks and two Norwegian hawks for the land of Jordan de Ros, and 20 marks and a palfrey to have the land and heir of William of Streetly. Wardships were profitable because of the income from the land involved and also for the feudal dues which accrued: the relief from the heir, or the right to give the daughter in marriage. In the building up of his barony and his attention to the possibilities of feudal incidents, Geoffrey fitz Peter was, no doubt, typical of any great magnate. He may even have been less rapacious than some; than, for example, Ranulf earl of Chester. But Geoffrey's position did not rest solely upon his feudal standing. He was justiciar, the highest officer known to men under the king, and the combination of feudal and administrative power can, in this period, never be divorced.

When Normandy was lost, Geoffrey fitz Peter was one of the greatest magnates in England. The son of the forester of Ludgers-hall had reached the top of the feudal structure; a relatively obscure official had risen to the greatest office in the country. If Geoffrey, in 1190, had ceased to take part in the administration of the kingdom, he might have remained an important yet politically limited baron, but this did not happen. When he married Beatrice de Say, he had already been an industrious royal servant, both as a justice of the forests and sheriff and justice in Northamptonshire.[1] His family and his training, as well as the reflexion that the royal gift of a wardship was the foundation of his social position, prevented his retirement from administrative duties to the task of administering his own great estates. Throughout Henry II's reign he had continued to hear the forest pleas and to act as sheriff of Northampton[2] and his importance is reflected in the accounts of

in Streetly Adbolton and Costock (in Northamptonshire) in 1212. He died before 1214 according to Farrer, *Honors and Knights' Fees*, I, 179; but since Geoffrey fitz Peter offered this fine, the date of William's death must be 1213, as the justiciar also died in that year. Geoffrey fitz Peter gave the custody of this land to Philip of Stanton who complained that Geoffrey de Mandeville had disseised him.

[1] See above p. 98.   [2] *Complete Peerage*, VII, 122.

Richard I's provision for the regency of England which associated him with the justiciar in governing the kingdom. Whether or not there was such a commission of justiciarship in those early years of that reign is not here material;[1] Geoffrey's part in the work of administration is not in doubt. King Richard was given permission by the pope to release from the vow of crusade those whom he deemed necessary for the government of England in his absence. Geoffrey fitz Peter was one; and he paid the king a fine to be so released.[2] By one version of the arrangements which the king made, Geoffrey was left to assist the justiciar as a baron of the exchequer; another asserted that Geoffrey and his colleagues were to do justice; yet a third that they were to assist *in regimine regni*.[3] Whatever the truth of the matter, Geoffrey fitz Peter sat as a baron of the exchequer, he acted as a justice in eyre, he became sheriff of Essex and Hertfordshire in 1190 and resumed Northamptonshire in 1191 which he had relinquished at the beginning of Richard's reign.[4] The shrievalty which he accepted in 1190 was part of a scheme of the justiciar's to change unreliable sheriffs for some of those men whom the chroniclers describe as his counsellors, although in Geoffrey's case the choice of county may have been determined by his feudal interests.[5] When Longchamps was driven from England, Geoffrey fitz Peter was excommunicated for his part in this affair, together with others of Longchamps's enemies, but he was one of the assistants of the new justiciar Walter of Coutances who was sent into England by Richard I with a commission of regency alternative to that of Longchamps's.[6] Part at

---

[1] See above, p. 66.   [2] Foss, *op. cit.* p. 266.   [3] See above, p. 66.

[4] *Complete Peerage*, VII, 122–3. He was sheriff of Northamptonshire 1185–9, 1191–4. King Richard replaced the sheriffs at the beginning of his reign putting the offices up for sale; Benedict, II, 90.

[5] See above, pp. 99–101. Since he already held the lands of earl of Essex, possession of the shrievalty of the county would undeniably have added to Geoffrey's power.

[6] Benedict, II, 213; Giraldus, IV, 500. In final concords made before the court at Westminster over which Walter of Coutances presided, Geoffrey fitz Peter occupied a prominent place among the lay judges, being second only to William Marshal; *Feet of Fines Henry II and Richard I*, pp. 8–12. On one occasion, 28 October 1193, Geoffrey fitz Peter presided at Westminster over a court composed of Osbert fitz Harvey, Michael Belet, and William son of Richard; Cotton MS Faustina A iv, fo. 49.

least of the reason for Geoffrey fitz Peter's presence with the justiciar's enemies in 1191 may have been his differences with the monks of Walden, a priory in the patronage of the earls of Essex, who were supported by Longchamps.[1] In spite, however, of these personal or political differences, Geoffrey did not cease to sit at the exchequer, or to serve as a justice, both in the central court at Westminster and in eyre.[2] When, in 1193, Hubert Walter, archbishop of Canterbury, replaced Walter of Coutances as justiciar, Geoffrey fitz Peter became his most important colleague. Thus he took precedence over other judges, and thus he accompanied the justiciar on his travels; to Worcester in 1196, to Shrewsbury in 1198 when Hubert Walter stopped in the town on his Welsh excursion *ad deliberandum David' regem Wallie*, and together they tallaged Northampton in King Richard's last year.[3] Geoffrey fitz Peter was then a significant figure in royal administration, and, more than all his colleagues, a significant feudal figure. He had been trained as a judge when sleepless nights were spent in King Henry's court hammering out the form of the assizes, and when Glanville was justiciar; he was the chief assistant

[1] *Monasticon*, IV, 145–8; *DNB* under Fitz Peter.

[2] In 1190 he was excused payment of several sums on the ground that he sat at the exchequer; *Pipe Roll 2 Richard I*, pp. 109, 113, 115, 258; and again in 1193; *Pipe Roll 5 Richard I*, p. 7. For his presence in the central court at Westminster see *Feet of Fines, passim*. His eyres may be collected from the pipe rolls for these years without difficulty; and unpublished copies of final concords made before him may be found as follows: at Northampton in 1190, 1192, Cotton MS Claudius D xiii, fo. 66, 88; at Warwick in 1190, Cotton MS Vespasian E xxiv, fo. 4; at Leicester on some unknown date, possibly 1191, BM MS Royal II B ix, fo. 114v.

[3] At Worcester, on the Monday after St Bartholomew, both the bishop and the archdeacon of Hereford were present, but Geoffrey took precedence of William Briewerre and Michael Belet. The archbishop was at Shrewsbury in January 1198, accompanied by Earl Roger Bigot and Geoffrey of Buckland as well as Geoffrey fitz Peter; *Feet of Fines Henry II and Richard I*, p. 188; *Feet of Fines 9 Richard I*, p. 79. At Michaelmas 1197 an account was rendered at the exchequer of amercements imposed by the justiciar, Geoffrey fitz Peter, Earl Roger Bigot, and Michael Belet in Warwickshire and Leicestershire and probably also in Norfolk and Suffolk; *Pipe Roll 9 Richard I*, pp. 178, 236. Archbishop Hubert and Geoffrey assessed the tallage of the men of Norwich which was required by the exchequer in 1198; *Pipe Roll 10 Richard I*, p. 94. Geoffrey (with William Briewerre and Hugh Bardulf) assessed the tallage in Staffordshire, and in Essex and Hertfordshire; *ibid.* pp. 123, 134.

of Hubert Walter, the pupil and relative of Glanville; as a baron of the exchequer, chief justice of the forests, and an experienced sheriff, he knew the mysteries of finance and justice. Socially, politically, technically, he was a suitable candidate for high office, and on 11 July 1198 Richard substituted Geoffrey fitz Peter for Hubert Walter as justiciar and commanded general obedience to him: *dilectum et fidelem nostrum Gaufridum filium Petri ad custodiam regni substituimus mandantes et firmiter precipientes quatenus eidem gaufrido tamquam justiciario nostro obedientes sitis de cetero et intendentes.*[1]

King John's first justiciar was thus a man of long experience in government, and if he suffers in comparison with Hubert Walter —some scholars have spoken of his 'competence' as distinct from Hubert's 'genius'[2]—it is nevertheless plain that he had some ambition or driving force that distinguished him from those ministers of similar origin who failed to profit by their opportunities. Geoffrey fitz Peter, but by a different route, attained eminence of the same order as William Marshal. Obviously there was something more in him than 'competence', and perhaps the chief contrast between Hubert and Geoffrey is one of opportunity rather than ability. That opportunity was the character and whereabouts of the king. In the first years of Geoffrey's justiciarship, a traditional situation existed. The king was more often than not on the continent and the justiciar represented him in England. But after Normandy was lost the situation changed; thereafter John was in England for all but a few months, and the justiciar was overshadowed. Geoffrey's justiciarship therefore provides a picture of two aspects of this office, the one as regent, the other as chief executive officer, and because of the greater abundance of evidence it can be examined in greater detail. The two phases of Geoffrey fitz Peter's tenure of office are separated by the loss of Normandy and the other continental dominions. There is no clear dividing line, because King John was abroad in 1206, in 1210, and in 1214, but these were absences of a few months; after the winter of 1203, the king spent nearly all of his time in England. In the

---

[1] Cotton MS Vespasian C xiv, fo. 298; Rymer, *Foedera*, I, 171.
[2] D. M. Stenton, *Pipe Roll 10 Richard I*, p. xxxiii.

second phase, therefore, the justiciarship lost much of its viceregal quality, but in the years up to 1203 the office can be seen in its most developed form. From his accession until Normandy was lost, King John spent less than eleven months out of four and a half years in England, and in those years Geoffrey fitz Peter ruled the kingdom for him.

2. THE JUSTICIAR AND THE EXCHEQUER

Leaving aside the accidental circumstances the justiciar might have to face—the disturbances consequent upon Richard's death or the Welsh attack, for example—Geoffrey's major preoccupation was the king's need for money. John, quite as much as his brother, faced the enormous financial effort of continental war and the French threat to his dominions. His justiciar had to raise the money while maintaining law and order in the country, and the chief instruments by which he performed his duties were the exchequer and the court of professional justices; it was through them that his authority was most formally expressed and exercised. Both of them were strong instruments, for they operated smoothly and with no apparent dislocation in the time between Richard's death and John's arrival.

The increasing quantity of business coming to the exchequer as a result of the king's need for money made the justiciar's intervention in the deliberation of the barons inevitable. In 1199 his authority was invoked in cases of difficulty or doubt. From Worcestershire there came a complicated case in which the bearer of a summons in the king's name had died on the way, and a second writ of summons issued by the justiciar brought forth the excuse that the sheriff was on royal business at the justiciar's order.[1] The sheriff's messenger had summoned certain knights, not all of whom appeared, to answer for their scutage which had not been paid to Master Roger of Charlcote but which they said had been rendered at the exchequer and the tallies had been delivered to the clerk of the marshal. Since Geoffrey fitz Peter was not present, the suit was postponed until the quindene of

[1] *Memoranda Roll 1 John*, p. 11.

Martinmas. Another case went back to Richard's reign. The barons of the exchequer wanted to discuss the 50 marks required from Peter de Scudemor as the increment of the counties of Dorset and Somerset for half the year.[1] Peter said that when he received the shires he had stated that he would not pay the increment since he took them unwillingly. Not only Geoffrey fitz Peter, but Hubert Walter who had been justiciar at the time, was to be consulted and the dispute placed before them. In a third case, when the citizens of Gloucester owed 200 marks of their fine of which the sheriff had paid nothing, the barons wished to discuss things with the justiciar at the octave of St Martin.[2] Such difficulties could be multiplied, and it is obvious that the justiciar's authority was frequently needed to resolve the problems facing the barons of the exchequer. It is clear that Geoffrey fitz Peter did not sit with them day by day, but the postponements to dates within the same audit period show that he was expected and that he was perhaps close at hand; certainly, after his visit to East Anglia, the midlands, and the north in the summer of 1199, he had returned to Westminster by early October.[3] His control of exchequer proceedings was obviously close, since the barons were unwilling to proceed with their deliberations until his will was known.

The justiciar's part in exchequer judgements was traditional; no doubt it simply became more necessary and more extensive as business increased. But he was also closely concerned with the actual assessment and raising of revenue. From 1200 a scutage was almost an annual event, and other forms of taxation such as tallages, carucages, the fortieth of 1202, the seventh of personal property and fifteenth of the goods of merchants of 1203, were introduced under Geoffrey's eye.[4] The fortieth was the subject of a letter from the justiciar to all the sheriffs about its levy and collection, but the personal property taxes, although Geoffrey fitz

[1] *Ibid.* p. 65.
[2] *Ibid.* p. 40.
[3] Geoffrey's itinerary has been worked out from financial writs by Richardson, *op. cit.* p. lxxxviii, and from judicial writs by D. M. Stenton, *Pleas before the King or his Justices 1198–1202*, pp. 52–3.
[4] Mitchell, *Taxation in Medieval England*, pp. 133, 134, 177.

Peter was said to have taken the seventh from the laity while Hubert Walter taxed the clergy, did not pass through the exchequer audit.[1] Some of the taxes Geoffrey assessed himself. In the year of his becoming justiciar he had tallaged Essex, Hertfordshire, and Staffordshire,[2] and in the winter of 1198/99 he had arranged the carucage in the shires he visited with other justices.[3] In 1202 he assessed the tallage in Berkshire.[4] This work of assessment was not extensive, and it was no doubt carried out incidentally with other duties, but there can be little doubt that Geoffrey fitz Peter had a keen interest in raising as much money as possible. That the proceeds of the eyres of 1202 and the tallage passed through the exchequer audit of the same year suggests that the justiciar was making a determined effort to collect as much money as he could, while at the same time trying to spread his expenditure generally over the whole of the kingdom.[5] In 1202 he moved through a great deal of country, supervising the work, and in the following year it is evident that he was trying to lighten the labour of the exchequer by getting rid of obsolete debts.[6]

Apart, however, from the general duty of supervision and the more local one of assessment, the justiciar had money under his control from which he supplied some of the king's needs. In two of the castles under his control royal treasure was stored, and some of the money raised from taxation was sent straight to the chamber.[7] This latter organization was not new, and so far as one can tell, the justiciar had little to do with its internal organization, but he certainly acted as a channel by which the exchequer was by-passed. In 1201 Geoffrey fitz Peter paid 140 marks into the chamber for John's expenses, another £10. 17s. 3d. to buy the king's robes, and £93. 5s. to pay the *balistarii* who crossed into Normandy; another £111. 18s. 8d. were paid in by the justiciar for the wages of servants and *balistarii* at Hereford.[8] In 1202 money was collected directly from debtors instead of waiting for

---

[1] Mitchell, *Taxation in Medieval England*, p. 132; Wendover, I, 318–19; *Pipe Roll 6 John*, p. x.

[2] *Pipe Roll 10 Richard I*, pp. 123, 134.

[3] *Pipe Roll 1 John*, p. xx.

[4] *Pipe Roll 4 John*, pp. 10, 11.

[5] *Ibid.* pp. xviii–xix.

[6] *Pipe Roll 5 John*, p. xvii.

[7] *Rot. Lit. Claus.* pp. 6, 22.

[8] *Rot. de Liberate*, p. 14.

its payment into the exchequer, and the justiciar despatched the money to the king. Simon of Avranches's fine of 100 marks was thus paid into the chamber, while on the Wiltshire roll Geoffrey fitz Peter accounted for £807. 10s. 4d. of which 800 marks were sent directly to the chamber overseas; in fact the justiciar spent more than he actually collected, and the account was not cleared until two years later.[1] He also received money from the treasury for despatch to John; in 1200 the sum of 200 marks from the treasurer and chamberlains.[2] The justiciar very frequently witnessed the writs of *computate* and *liberate* which directed the use of royal money.[3] He was himself ordered, when he was at the exchequer, to send money to the king and to pay royal officials and servants.[4] It is evident that the justiciar was the link between exchequer and chamber upon which the king relied for his financial needs. It was the justiciar's authority that diverted money where it was needed; it was to the justiciar that the roll of fines made with the king abroad was sent for transmission to the exchequer.[5] Other officials undertook the assessment and collection of revenue, and the barons of the exchequer audited the accounts, but the justiciar was charged with responsibility for the supervision of the machinery, which entailed both general oversight and sometimes detailed intervention.

The strength of the justiciar's position in carrying out either duty lay in his occupancy of lower ministerial offices within the administrative system. When he became justiciar in 1198 he was sheriff of Stafford, a county he held until 1204.[6] In 1199 he accounted for Yorkshire, in the following year for Westmorland and Bedford and Buckinghamshire, and in John's fourth year for Shropshire and Hampshire.[7] Thus in 1204 he was sheriff of seven

[1] *Pipe Roll 4 John*, p. xiii.   [2] *Rot. de Liberate*, p. 8.
[3] *Rot. Lit. Claus. passim*. The attestation of these writs was either that of the justiciar, or *teste meipso*. Where they concerned chamber business, however, the witness or warranty might be Peter des Roches or Peter of Stokes.
[4] *Rot. Lit. Claus.* pp. 5, 6, 22.
[5] *Pipe Roll 1 John*, pp. 68, 160, 208. These accounts all contain the heading *Nova oblata facta coram rege in partibus transmarinis et missa Galfrido filio Petri* or some similar heading.
[6] *Ibid.* p. 162.
[7] *Ibid.* p. 38; *Pipe Roll 2 John*, pp. 33, 254; *Pipe Roll 4 John*, pp. 44, 68.

counties. The coincidence of these offices with the position of other ministerial sheriffs suggests what his careful control of revenue confirms: that some reorganization was in progress. The justiciar accounted for his shires by deputy, but when he relinquished them, the men who had been his deputies, for example Thomas of Erdington in Stafford and Robert of Braybrook in Bedford and Buckingham, succeeded, rendering their accounts not as sheriffs but as custodians. Whereas a sheriff held his county at farm, a custodian accounted for all the revenue collected. It is impossible to know whether the justiciar evolved a scheme for raising the money flowing into the crown, but he certainly played a major part in its execution.

3. THE JUSTICIAR AND THE LAW COURTS

Control of the financial system when royal needs were so great in itself placed an immense burden upon the justiciar, but he had judicial duties which were equally extensive. His principal sphere of work was the bench of justices at Westminster, but during the king's brief visits he was also involved in some work in the court *coram rege*, while the responsibility fell upon him for arranging the itinerant judicial work of his colleagues. The full development of the court *coram rege* belongs to the period after the loss of Normandy, but the Hilary term of 1200 saw the king in England. The justiciar left the justices at Westminster to meet John at Portsmouth on 25 February, and thereafter he accompanied his master from 10 March onwards to Woodstock, Clipstone, Tickhill, York, and on the return journey through Worcester and Windsor to Westminster on 20 April.[1] The king's arrival cut short the pleadings at Westminster on 23 February, and thereafter pleadings went on before the court that travelled with him.[2] It is clear that neither he nor the justiciar was always present, for many entries record the justices' desire to speak with John, and on one occasion with the justiciar.[3] Geoffrey fitz Peter certainly left John's company between 10 and 15 March, although the reason is unknown,

[1] D. M. Stenton, *Pleas before the King or his Justices 1198–1202*, p. 57.
[2] *Ibid.* pp. 60, 296–320.   [3] *Ibid.* pp. 296, 297.

for he was at Quorndon by himself, probably rejoining the court at Nottingham.[1] His authority is not much referred to in the pleadings, but John's is, and although the continuity of judicial work necessarily involved the justiciar's authority, it is clear that the king's presence eclipsed him as well as the court at Westminster. A similar situation arose with the king's arrival in October 1200, when the Michaelmas term was just beginning. Geoffrey fitz Peter postponed suits from day to day to await John's arrival,[2] but the latter stayed in the capital for only a few days before moving on to the Welsh border and thence across country to Lincoln, taking the justiciar with him. Some justices continued to sit at Westminster, but others accompanied the king; both Simon of Pattishall and Eustace de Fauconberg were missing from Westminster.[3] The royal presence at Lincoln in November 1200 drew cases from Westminster as the number of postponements to the court *coram rege* shows,[4] but the justiciar's authority in the latter court was not much in evidence. Geoffrey fitz Peter may have instructed the justices at Westminster that cases of difficulty should be adjourned until they could be before the king in the following term,[5] and although he himself was with John throughout October and November, and rejoined him early in January for part of the Hilary term 1201, it does not appear that he did much work in the court *coram rege*, although he certainly told a plaintiff that his case had been transferred from the bench.[6] In the king's presence, the justiciar and the bench both faded into the background of judicial activity, but it is probable that Geoffrey organized the personnel of the court *coram rege* and the more regular keeping of its records.[7] During these early royal visits to England, the foundation was laid for the efficient organization of the court which was a regular feature of administration after the loss of Normandy.

The real burden of the justiciar's work in these years was the bench at Westminster. Even when John was in England, Geoffrey

[1] *Ibid.* p. 67.   [2] *Curia Regis Rolls*, I, 302, 303, 338, 370, 417.
[3] D. M. Stenton, *op. cit.* pp. 98–9.
[4] *Ibid.* p. 103.   [5] *Ibid.*
[6] *Curia Regis Rolls*, i, 391.
[7] D. M. Stenton, *op. cit.* p. 124.

fitz Peter had divided his time between the bench and the royal entourage. His name regularly headed the list of justices at Westminster, and his presence enhanced the prestige of the court. It is quite clear that Geoffrey was not always present, but writs were regularly issued and final concords regularly made in his name.[1] In 1199, for example, for which year many of his writs survive, he was in Westminster from 23 June to 10 August, thence moving to St Albans and Cambridge on his way to the north.[2] The justices at Westminster were completing their work of the Trinity term after he left them, but the justiciar was back in Westminster for the following Michaelmas session. Exchequer business, apart from other matters which inevitably followed him, took Geoffrey away from sittings, but his actual presence was important. Cases were adjourned for his decision and for consultation with him.[3] Equally important was his seal. In the Michaelmas term of 1202, work could not properly begin because Geoffrey fitz Peter had taken his seal with him, and a case was adjourned until it should be back in London.[4] This was an urgent matter because of the volume of work involved. In the Easter term of 1200, for example, two hundred and eighty cases had been heard up to 5 May, and five hundred before the court finally rose on 17 May.[5] Geoffrey was said to be presiding over this court day by day, but even after it had risen a litigant replevied his land before Geoffrey fitz Peter, a fact which the justiciar was called upon to warrant in the following Trinity term.[6] The pressure of business on the bench did not relax. Throughout the Michaelmas term of 1201, a large volume of business came before the justices, and the justiciar's duties required him to decide points of law, to regulate technical details of pleading, and to maintain a general supervision over the work of the bench; and all this was entirely apart from the writs coming in considerable numbers from beyond the sea, ordering him to carry out the king's instructions.

The importance of the justiciar's authority in the bench is

---

[1] D. M. Stenton, *op. cit.* pp. 51, 87–8, 351–418.   [2] *Ibid.* pp. 51–2.
[3] *Curia Regis Rolls*, I, 273, 278, 334.
[4] *Ibid.* II, 91; D. M. Stenton, *op. cit.* pp. 88–9.
[5] D. M. Stenton, *op. cit.* p. 92.   [6] *Curia Regis Rolls*, I, 172.

suggested by the regular inclusion of his name in final concords as the presiding judge. Naturally, when John was in England and Geoffrey in his company, the king's presence was what mattered, not his justiciar's, but cases were heard before the bench while the court *coram rege* was sitting,[1] and the justiciar's presidency, whether it was real or fictitious, lent prestige to the bench. The court *coram rege* automatically heard replevins even if the case had begun at Westminster by order of the justices, but if the justiciar himself were there, a litigant might replevy his land before him.[2] The importance of the justiciar's presence is also reflected in the well-known case of Henry of Rugby in the Easter term of 1201 while King John was in England.[3] Henry brought the king's writ to have his rightful record and judgement in a plea between himself and the abbot of Leicester as it was rightfully treated before the king's justices at Westminster, and that it should not be postponed because of a charter of King Richard that the abbot claimed to have which granted that the abbot should reply for nothing nor be impleaded except before the king or his chief justiciar 'since all pleas which are held before the justices of the bench are understood to be held before the king or his chief justiciar'. The words quoted are not a judgement of the court.[4] They may have been part of Henry's pleading, but it seems more likely that they were part of the royal writ. They bear a striking resemblance to the formula used later for a plaintiff whose case had got into the county court and where the county refused to give judgement.[5] Taken in conjunction with the king's order of the previous Michaelmas term that in cases which came before them the justices should take no account of charters or letters patent issued by his ancestors unless they saw his own confirmation,[6] it seems probable that the king was asserting the prestige of the bench. Whether or not he was declaring a general rule—and later circumstances suggest not—in 1201 he seems to have wished to avoid pleas of exemption. He could make the assertion of the bench's

---

[1] In the Hilary and Easter terms of 1201 there are rolls for both courts; *Curia Regis Rolls*, I, 374–91, 399–409, 417–41, 442–67.
[2] *Curia Regis Rolls*, I, 391.   [3] *Ibid.* I, 462.
[4] D. M. Stenton, *op. cit.* pp. 101–2.   [5] *Registrum Omnium Brevium*, p. 10.
[6] *Curia Regis Rolls*, I, 331.

dignity, however, because it was the place where his justiciar usually sat and where he was available for consultation with the justices when difficult points arose. The justiciar's absence from Westminster, whether he spent time with the king or himself moved about England, was usually a matter of days rather than of whole legal terms. The bench and the exchequer sat in the same building, and the justiciar, whatever his other duties, spent some time near at hand in Westminster to guide their working, and the postponements for his opinions to be sought are usually to days within the same term.[1] Attendance at Westminster was a major part of Geoffrey fitz Peter's duties.

Geoffrey's movements in 1199, combined with other casual indications, show that he was constantly moving about the country whether the king was present or not, and his judicial work certainly required him to organize and to undertake eyres. When he became justiciar, he had been involved in the great eyre of 1198, which took him to the home counties. He led the party visiting Essex, Hertfordshire, Bedfordshire, Buckinghamshire, Surrey and Kent in September, October, and November, and visited Berkshire in January 1199.[2] These labours may have prevented any regular sessions at Westminster in the Michaelmas term of 1198, but Geoffrey was close enough to London to visit it when need arose, and very probably he held a council there in November.[3] In 1199 he organized three eyres in the late summer and early autumn, one of which, through Warwick, Leicester, and Northampton, he led himself,[4] but in 1200 the king's return required the justices to be available to accompany him or to stay at Westminster. Geoffrey had planned to send out eyres at the beginning of 1201, but the king lingered on. The justiciar sat at Westminster immediately after John's departure, but he sent Simon of Pattishall, Eustace de Fauconberg, Michael Belet, and Richard Fleming to the south-west, and when their work was

[1] *Curia Regis Rolls*, I, 270–5.
[2] *Pipe Roll 1 John*, pp. 58, 67, 68, 98, 111, 258; Hunter, *Feet of Fines*, i, 6–13, 20, 100–5, 159, 163–8.
[3] *Feet of Fines 10 Richard I*, pp. 53, 92–3, 101. The bishops of Ely and Durham, who had been with the king, were then sitting with the justices.
[4] D. M. Stenton, *op. cit.* pp. 53–4.

finished in July they joined him at Northampton.[1] Geoffrey fitz
Peter was in Norfolk in early August and back at Northampton
by the middle of the month, and he had probably visited Staffordshire, Shropshire, Herefordshire, Gloucestershire, Cambridge-
shire, and Huntingdonshire at the same time.[2] It is unlikely that
his purpose was solely judicial, but the imminence of war with
France probably prompted an attempt to keep some check upon
the latent discontent revealed during the king's visit.[3]

Geoffrey's greatest activity occurred in the summer and autumn
of 1202, when he organized a general eyre as far-reaching as those
of 1194 and 1198.[4] Four parties of justices visited the whole of
England except the west and south-west which had been covered
in the previous year, and shortage of judges compelled him to use
barons of no judicial training, although some of the professionals
formed the nucleus of each party. Geoffrey himself took Richard
of Herriard, Geoffrey of Buckland, Jordan de Turribus, and
Master Ralph of Stoke to Surrey, Kent, Berkshire, Wiltshire,
Hampshire, and Sussex; they sat at Reading at the beginning of
July, at Winchester at the end of the month and into August, at
Chichester in September, and Bermondsey in October, with a
break in their work for the harvest. Geoffrey bore his part in the
work of an eyre, as well as planning and organizing it, and its
achievement resulted in a lightening of the judicial work at
Westminster in the following term. Nevertheless, it did not
lighten the burden of the justiciar. The Lincolnshire eyre of 1202,
which was led by Simon of Pattishall and Eustace de Fauconberg,
produced a number of cases which were reserved for consultation
with Geoffrey fitz Peter. One lady who was appellant in a
criminal case was said to have withdrawn before the lord Geoffrey
who was to be consulted.[5] Another case was postponed until the
justices came to Bedford because of the absence of a litigant
beyond the sea; meanwhile they would consult the justiciar.[6] In
addition to his own work in eyre, the justiciar had difficult or

---

[1] *Ibid.* pp. 125, 137.   [2] *Pipe Roll 4 John*, pp. 46, 137, 177, 185, 275.
[3] D. M. Stenton, *op. cit.* p. 139.
[4] *Ibid.* p. 143.   [5] *The Earliest Lincolnshire Assize Rolls*, no. 922.
[6] *Northampton Assize Rolls*, no. 483.

doubtful cases referred to him by his colleagues on other circuits, or even, as in the case of his own eyre at Northampton in 1203, by his colleagues in the circuit who were sitting concurrently with his own sessions.[1] In addition, the justiciar had to keep the justices informed of the appointment of attorneys before him, of the presence of litigants in France with the king, of the transference of cases to Westminster, of pardons to outlaws.[2] Such strictly judicial business kept Geoffrey fitz Peter busy, but other work followed him wherever he went, and his financial duties were also carried out at the same time.

4. THE JUSTICIAR AS CHIEF EXECUTIVE

As chief justice and president of the exchequer, Geoffrey fitz Peter's formal duties were heavy enough. The popularity of royal justice and the exigencies of the financial situation both placed a heavy burden upon his shoulders. The exchequer and the courts are simply the most formal expression of his duties, but do not exhaust them. The justiciarship could not become the office of a professional judge nor of a professional financial official without losing its original character. Geoffrey fitz Peter, at a time when he was deciding difficult cases of law or finance, was engaged in those duties which fell to him as regent and in numerous executive duties. While King John was abroad in these early years, a great many royal writs arrived in England directing the justiciar to take various actions. He was responsible, for example, for sending treasure to finance the king's activities in France, and was summoned there himself in 1202 partly to discuss ways of raising yet more money.[3] It says much for the strength of Angevin administration that it could be left to run itself while the king, the justiciar, and the chancellor took counsel on the continent. And, indeed, when the justiciar was regent in England routine writs of finance were sent directly to the barons of the exchequer, not through the

---

[1] *The Earliest Lincolnshire Assize Rolls*, no. 1301.

[2] *The Earliest Lincolnshire Assize Rolls*, nos. 2, 5, 305, 524, 980, 1213, 1331; *Northampton Assize Rolls*, nos. 66, 168, 321, 501, 527, 532, 874.

[3] *Rot. Lit. Pat.* pp. 12, 65.

justiciar.[1] It was the exceptional cases, and those involving important persons or business, which were transacted through the justiciar by writs *de ultra mare*. So he was ordered to send two justices to assist Hubert Walter, if required, in recalling to the court of the archbishopric of Canterbury what had been unjustly alienated from it;[2] and thus he was informed of the agreement which the king had reached with Berengaria, widow of Richard I and formerly queen of England, concerning her dowry.[3] Not all matters involved people so exalted as this. As a result of an inquisition which Geoffrey fitz Peter had carried out with John, bishop of Norwich, record of which had been sent to the king, a church was to be restored to the bishopric of Ely.[4] He was to permit a foreign merchant to come into England to do business;[5] he was told that the king had made a gift to Gregory, nephew of Gerard de Furnivall, of the rent of the first church to fall vacant;[6] he was to deliver to Robert fitz Walter the castle of Hertford which the king had committed to him, and to William de Braiose the lands and castles of Glamorgan;[7] or he was to send foreign prisoners kept in England to the king in Normandy.[8] These examples could be multiplied many times, but so to do would lead only to the conclusion that the justiciar, in addition to the routine work which he supervised when the king was in England, had many duties over and above them imposed upon him when the king was abroad, for the discharge of which he was ultimately responsible. The calls upon the justiciar, therefore, were many. The bench and the exchequer could proceed with their routine business without immediate or constant supervision by the

---

[1] *Rot. Lit. Pat. passim;* the same is true of routine judicial writs, for example, notifications of the appointment of an attorney, or of respite of a suit; *Curia Regis Rolls,* I, 338; II, 40, 129, 210; III, 31, 48.

[2] *Rot. Lit. Pat.* p. 6. There was a series of commands on this subject. After the first on 15 February 1202 a second on 13 March ordered the chief justice and justices of England that Hubert might recall to his court all demesne unjustly alienated by the oath of lawful men, two justices being sent to help if necessary. On 3 May Geoffrey fitz Peter and the barons of the exchequer of Westminster were instructed that Hubert was to have the amercements of all men of the fee of Canterbury as was customary; *ibid.* pp. 6*b*, 10.

[3] *Ibid.* p. 2.　　　　[4] *Ibid.* p. 6*b*.　　　　[5] *Ibid.* pp. 9, 11*b*, 14*b*.
[6] *Ibid.* p. 16.　　　　[7] *Ibid.* p. 19*b*.　　　　[8] *Ibid.* pp. 22, 28*b*.

justiciar, as his absence in France demonstrates, but he could also delegate some of this supervisory work. There is no direct evidence of this in the bench, although the position of Richard of Herriard, the high proportion of Geoffrey fitz Peter's legal writs which he witnessed, his accompanying the justiciar's eyres, the seniority which he possessed in court may all suggest that he stood in some special relationship to the justiciar. In the case of the exchequer, Geoffrey of Buckland occupied an equivalent position. He was a man of substance, an ecclesiastic who in 1200 was made archdeacon of Norfolk and before 1210 dean of St Martin le Grand; he also held the churches of Teynham and Pagham.[1] Geoffrey was probably the younger brother of William of Buckland who married the sister of Geoffrey fitz Peter's first wife, Beatrice, and as a relation of the justiciar he was mistakenly described by a chancery clerk as his brother when, after Geoffrey fitz Peter's death, he was ordered to let the king have the crops, pigs, and chattels of the justiciar's farm of Berkhampstead.[2] Geoffrey of Buckland occasionally served as a justice in the reign of Richard I. He was sitting in court, for example, at the Oxford council of 1197 when two final concords were made.[3] He accompanied Hubert Walter, then justiciar, Earl Roger Bigot and Geoffrey fitz Peter on their journey into Shropshire to deal with Welsh affairs, and one of the concords resulting from a suit tried before them was deposited in the treasury by his hand.[4] None of these appearances in court can be described as normal judicial work, for these were exceptional sittings. Only on one occasion did Geoffrey sit in court at Westminster and that is of uncertain date.[5] Moreover, of the justices named he was always last. Although he imposed amercements in Herefordshire and Gloucestershire his judicial work was inconsiderable.[6] Nevertheless, his experience and his personal relationship with the justiciar explain his witness to a number of Geoffrey fitz Peter's legal writs in 1199.[7] Geoffrey of Buckland was more concerned with

[1] Foss, op. cit. p. 103.   [2] Rot. Lit. Claus. I, 139.
[3] Feet of Fines 9 Richard I, pp. 70–1.   [4] Ibid. pp. 78–9.
[5] Ibid. p. 190.   [6] Pipe Roll 9 Richard I, p. 197.
[7] D. M. Stenton, op. cit. pp. 30–32. He witnessed more of these surviving writs than Simon of Pattishall. His personal connexion with the justiciar is

financial administration at the exchequer,[1] and he is another example of an official whose work, although not completely specialized, lay in one direction rather than another. He conveyed information to the barons from the justiciar, and he seems to have been the latter's deputy in the exchequer, taking precedence over the treasurer who was in the process of becoming its departmental head.[2] Apart from any deputies whom he may have employed, lesser officials were used by Geoffrey fitz Peter to make known his will. Thus he variously instructed the bench by his orders conveyed through Ralph of Stoke, Richard Duket, Reginald of Cornhill and Pollard the usher.[3] The justiciar's control may not have been personal or immediate, but it was effective; and it was exercised either by deputy or through messengers, expedients used to cope with an administrative situation which was outgrowing the justiciarship.

Justice, finance, and regency did not exhaust the duties laid upon exemplified in the latter's baronial charters. Geoffrey's foundation charter to Shouldham was attested by Geoffrey of Buckland together with Hubert Walter, John, bishop of Norwich (in whose diocese the foundation lay), Walter, abbot of Waltham, and Earl Roger Bigot as well as lesser men. A charter of Geoffrey fitz Peter to the hospital of St Thomas the Martyr of Acre in the city of London was witnessed by Geoffrey of Buckland, styled dean of St Martin's; and another of the justiciar's foundations, Sutton at Hone in Kent, received a charter which bore the witness of the lord Simon, abbot of Tilty, and Geoffrey of Buckland at the head of its attestations; *Monasticon*, VI, 647, 669, 974.

[1] *Rot. Lit. Claus.* I, 473; *Rot. Chart.* p. 99.

[2] In 1199 Robert de Bernières had his farm reduced by the king and the justiciar passed this information on to the barons of the exchequer through Geoffrey; (*Pipe Roll 1 John*, p. 26); for the writ in which he preceded the treasurer, *Memoranda Roll 1 John*, p. 67.

[3] Ralph of Stoke was another witness to the legal writs of Geoffrey fitz Peter at Michaelmas 1199; D. M. Stenton, *op. cit.* pp. 30–2. At that time he had never sat as a justice, although he came to do so later. He was the justiciar's messenger on several occasions; *Curia Regis Rolls*, I, 71, 204, 391; and he had accompanied the justiciar on his journey to the north in the summer of 1199; D. M. Stenton, *op. cit.* p. 32; *Memoranda Roll 1 John*, pp. 45, 50. He also acted as the justiciar's messenger to the exchequer; *Memoranda Roll 1 John*, p. 10. He was a clerk who had the church of Woodford in Northamptonshire in 4 John, and one in Staffordshire. From King John's 2nd year he sat as a judge at Westminster and in eyre. Five years later he was in disgrace for tampering with a jury in Yorkshire; Foss, *op. cit.* p. 633. Richard Duket was also on the threshold of his career at the beginning of John's reign.

Geoffrey fitz Peter. Apart from his position at the head of the administration, he occupied other lower ministerial offices within it. He had to deliver seisin of lands and castles in the bailiwicks which he held and, when the king so willed, to hand them over to others. He was ordered, for example, to give the castle and county of Northampton to Walter of Preston and two castles and the bailiwick of Westmorland to Peter of Stoke.[1] The picture of the justiciar's activity which emerges from these early years of King John's reign, while Normandy was held and John himself abroad, is one of intense activity. Geoffrey fitz Peter was regent which involved both filling the king's place in England, and acting in accordance with instructions from the continent. He was responsible for the exchequer, both as the final authority in difficult or doubtful cases, and as one who must organize and, indeed, collect taxation imposed to meet the king's needs;[2] he was the chief justice who controlled litigation in the central court and who himself went on circuit to administer justice in the counties. He was responsible for the realm, for its administration, for the means with which the king pursued his policy abroad. This was the position of the justiciar until on 6 December 1203 King John returned to England, and within a matter of months, with the exception of two fortresses which held out much longer, Normandy and the other lands had gone.[3] The duchy which had been ruled by the kings of England for nearly a century and a half was conquered by Philip Augustus, and the Anglo-Norman realm, whose needs had created the office of justiciar, came to an end.

---

[1] *Rot. Lit. Pat.* pp. 27, 30*b*.

[2] Geoffrey was thus responsible for the assessment of and collection from laymen of the seventh of movables in 1203; *Wendover*, I, 318–19; *Rot. de Liberate*, pp. 43, 47. It was not paid to the exchequer but to those in charge of its assessment and collection; *Pipe Roll 6 John*, p. 256; Mitchell, *Taxation in Mediaeval England*, p. 16.

[3] These were Loches, guarded by Gerard d'Athée, and Chinon under Hubert de Burgh (on whom see below, chapter VII). Rouen had fallen on 24 June 1204. Guienne and Gascony were all that remained of the continental dominions.

CHAPTER V

THE JUSTICIARSHIP UNDER JOHN: AFTER THE LOSS OF NORMANDY

King John's return to England in the winter of 1203 marked a new political, even, considering the *terrae Normannorum* which the king acquired, a new economic situation. Monarchy, for all practical purposes, was confined almost entirely to England,[1] and its resources had been enlarged. The political condition was permanent; the economic was not. The immediate effect of these events upon the administrative system was, as previously observed, slight. The justiciar's duties were not at once different from those which have been described. Yet the king was now confined to England, and if the consequences of the new political situation were not immediate, this factor was potentially very important because it tended to shift the centre of administrative gravity. The royal household, with its financial departments the chamber and the wardrobe, entered the sphere of government in England to a much greater extent than they had when they were half of the time abroad; the court *coram rege* was a constant factor, and ultimately in King John's reign it survived while the bench disappeared.[2] The king's return in 1203 produced exactly the same consequences as the arrival in England of any previous monarch from his continental lands, and no doubt the presence of

---

[1] For his subsequent absences, amounting in sum to about a year and a half in the remaining thirteen years of the reign, see *Handbook of British Chronology*, p. 36. This should be compared with the numerous periods of royal absence both in earlier reigns and in the first years of John's own, which are listed in the same volume.

[2] The reasons for the disappearance of the bench when its sessions came to an end with a meagre roll of pleas in 1210 are obscure. Probably they were political. It was the king's will that pleas should no longer be heard at Westminster; *Curia Regis Rolls*, v, 81; Flower, *Introduction to the Curia Regis Rolls*, p. 33. Thereafter there was only the court *coram rege*, except during the period of John's absence in 1214 which will be described below.

John in 1203 was regarded as temporary in exactly the same way as that of his ancestors. But this time it was different. John was to remain in England, except for a few months, for the rest of his reign, and whether or not his presence was at first regarded as temporary until he re-conquered his dominions, such a belief must have waned with the passing years and vanished after the disastrous battle of Bouvines in 1214. The years after 1203 slowly produced a different administrative outlook. Temporary or not, the king's presence meant that he had a closer and more sustained interest in the administration, especially, from what is known of his inclinations, in the case of King John. Consequently the importance of the justiciar tended to decline, even in his routine supervision of the administration in view of contemporary development. The justiciarship, after the loss of Normandy, must be seen against this background of John's own activity. The scope of the office must, perhaps almost imperceptibly, have narrowed as the succeeding years went by.

The most obvious difference in the justiciar's position when the king was back in England was that he was no longer regent. Even here, however, the loss of Normandy did not change the position completely. Geoffrey fitz Peter was regent for six months in 1206, and for two months in 1210. His successor, Peter des Roches, was regent for about eight months in 1214. During these periods the administration operated in the justiciar's name; legal, financial, and miscellaneous business was all transacted by his writ even if ordered by the absent king. When the latter was in England, the royal writ set government in motion, and the justiciar's writ was not recognized.[1] John's almost constant presence after 1203 meant that the amount of work done in the justiciar's name dropped sharply, and from that year the number of his writs mentioned on both plea and pipe rolls steadily decreased. So, too, did his authority in difficult cases vanish, for the king's interest was actual.

The administration of both law and finance was affected by the king's interest. From John's sixth year there began the series of final concords levied before the king in person and the justices

[1] *Curia Regis Rolls*, VI, 80–1.

coram rege.[1] This court was not a new development: there had been justices who accompanied Henry II;[2] and such a group had travelled round England with John during the time he spent in the country in the first years of his reign, their work being recorded in separate plea rolls from those of the bench.[3] It was in 1204, however, that the king was first named in the final concords made before this court. To the justices *coram rege* came those pleas which were difficult, or which involved important people, appeals for the errors of other courts to be remedied, and cases in which the king chose to take an interest.[4] If doubt arose upon any point, the final appeal was to the king himself. Thus in both 1207 and 1208 during the Michaelmas and Trinity terms, many cases were adjourned for consultation with the king: *loquendum cum rege*; and in the Hilary and Easter terms of 1210 and in the Trinity term of 1212, the justices postponed a number of cases until they could talk matters over with the king.[5] As in the court of law, so in the exchequer. During the financial year which ended at Michaelmas 1204, the king was present at the exchequer session on at least one occasion.[6] Four years later, when the barons discussed the accounts, difficulties were referred to John himself. In 1199 Geoffrey fitz Peter had been appealed to to decide points which cropped up, but in 1208 it was the king. John was to be consulted about 50 marks exacted from the abbot of Bury St Edmund's for having an inquisition, and about 100 shillings exacted from Hugh de Neville the chief justice of the forests.[7] Such personal royal interest in the details of government would tend to exclude the justiciar, but the work to be done was great, and if the king travelled ceaselessly throughout his land, the convenience of a deputy at Westminster must have remained. Geoffrey fitz Peter

---

[1] Hunter, *Feet of Fines*, I, liv.   [2] Round, *Feudal England*, p. 511.
[3] See above, pp. 114–20.
[4] Flower, *op. cit.* pp. 25, 30.
[5] *Curia Regis Rolls*, V, 53 ff., 227, 234–5; VI, 19, 54, 351.
[6] *Pipe Roll 6 John*, p. 147.
[7] *Memoranda Roll 10 John*, pp. 42, 58. There was a possibility that the king might appear at the exchequer on the feast of St John Baptist, for a *loquela* between the order of the hospital of St John of Jerusalem and Philip of Oldcoates was postponed until then *coram rege si venerit*.

frequently accompanied the king on his journeys, but often, for considerable periods, he was not to be found in the royal train; he was, instead, at Westminster or elsewhere, carrying on the work of government in the traditional manner of a justiciar.[1] The office may have been overshadowed by its greater self, the kingship, but it was still a useful one and it was not yet eclipsed.

I. THE JUSTICIAR AS REGENT

The rate of decline of the justiciarship was slowed down by the duty of regency in the months which King John spent abroad after 1203; Geoffrey fitz Peter ruled England in the king's absence for six months in 1206, for two in 1210. The first of these periods is relatively well documented; the second is not. As regent Geoffrey fitz Peter was directed to take a whole range of actions. Before the king actually sailed, while he was at Yarmouth waiting for a favourable wind, a series of orders were issued to Geoffrey fitz Peter, who, so far as the evidence goes, was not in the king's company. Two of these orders were to effect repayment of the king's debts, others for the purchase of wine, but Geoffrey was also ordered to ensure that the papal notary had his yearly pension, and another man was to have returned to him his lands and pools which were in the king's hand because he was now in service with the king.[2] Arrangements had been made for the justiciar to supply the king with treasure, and with the first consignment there was to go a prisoner of the king.[3] On 7 June the king sailed, and from

---

[1] For the activity of the justiciar when he was not with the king see the discussion below, pp. 151 ff.

[2] *Rot. Lit. Claus.* I, 72, 72 *b*. The last of these writs was issued *coram domino Wint'*, that is to say, before Peter des Roches bishop of Winchester. The purchase of wine was a frequent expense for the justiciar; *Pipe Roll 8 John*, p. 156; *Pipe Roll 9 John*, p. 112.

[3] *Rot. Lit. Pat.* p. 65. The prisoner was Ely de Pont, a knight, who was being kept at Norwich. This writ, too, was witnessed by the bishop of Winchester and noted *coram domino Wint'*. For other instances of the despatch of treasure by Geoffrey fitz Peter to the king: *Pipe Roll 8 John*, p. 54; *Pipe Roll 9 John*, p. 151. It seems likely that payments on the justiciar's writ on the pipe roll of Michaelmas 1207 belong to this period of the king's absence in 1206, as well as those on the roll of 1206.

the continent there came back to England similar instructions to the justiciar. Some of them were concerned with business arising on the continent; such were orders, for example, that the monks of St Jean d'Angély were to be put back in possession of their lands in England, and that the abbot and monks of Cluny should receive their lands which had been seized by the king with the lands of the Normans.[1] In the same way a layman, the count of Evreux, had a manor restored to him.[2] These duties arose as an immediate consequence of the king's presence on the continent, but by far the larger proportion of the orders which were sent related to purely English affairs. The justiciar was to receive a man's homage, to enforce a will, to make a gift of land from the royal escheats and to make various money allowances.[3] These duties concerned special acts of royal grace, not routine matters of administration, and some of them were important transactions. Thus Walter de Gray, the chancellor, had been granted by John a rent of 100 marks from the first which fell vacant in England, and the justiciar was to ensure that this was done.[4] As in a previous period of regency, the castle and county of Northampton changed hands. Geoffrey fitz Peter was not then sheriff of the county but he had been given land worth £15 at Thorpe to keep the castle.[5] Now he was ordered to hand it over to Walter of Preston, together with the land of William de Humeto and William de Lusors.[6] The justiciar's work was, however, by no means limited to carrying out royal orders. There was a range of activity which fell within his discretion. He maintained hostages of the king by giving them food and raiment, and he paid for the cost of transporting treasure to the king in Poitou as in the case of merchandise which had been collected at the fair of Winchester (where he held the castle), the value of which treasure was 2000 marks.[7] He kept an eye on the condition of royal castles and houses, for whose repairs he paid, and he supplied provisions to Philip of Oldcoates

---

[1] *Rot. Lit. Claus.* i, 73, 74.
[2] *Ibid.* p. 73 *b*.
[3] *Ibid.* pp. 74–5, where are printed a large number of writs to the justiciar commanding such actions.
[4] *Rot. Lit. Pat.* p. 66 *b*.   [5] *Rot. Lit. Pat.* p. 67.
[6] *Pipe Roll 8 John*, p. 170.   [7] *Pipe Roll 8 John*, p. 54.

for the island of Guernsey.[1] This work was not essentially different from that of Geoffrey fitz Peter himself in earlier years nor of any previous justiciar, although the loss of Normandy is plainly reflected in its nature. Concern with the lands of the Normans, with hostages, with prisoners, arose from the political and military situation; it is different, perhaps, in detail but not in degree from the regent's work in former years.

The justiciar, as regent, performed duties which were super-imposed on those which he would normally have carried out as head of the administrative system. He was regarded as the chief executive officer; the man who controlled sheriffs and bailiffs.[2] Thus he was instructed to put new sheriffs in possession of their counties, to protect the lands of those whom the king took into his special protection, to proclaim the pardon of an outlaw.[3] One reason for the justiciar's position at the head of the royal officers must have been administrative convenience. His was the authority which directed the government while the king was abroad; he was responsible for its working. The routine writs of law or finance might be directed by the king to the justices or the barons of the exchequer, but anything which required an extraordinary action, an act of royal grace, or which required an immediate and more detailed knowledge of a particular situation, or which involved some difficulty not determinable on the continent, was normally done through Geoffrey fitz Peter. Such a royal order might require many writs of the justiciar to put it into effect. The commission of the castle and county of Northampton to Walter of Preston must have involved the issue of letters of the justiciar to all who were affected by or interested in such an appointment; and, indeed, a matter involving prisoners kept in the castle men-tioned the part to be played by the justiciar's writ in giving effect

---

[1] *Pipe Roll 8 John*, pp. 57, 115, 150, 182, 228; *Pipe Roll 9 John*, pp. 31, 102, 130, 166. Some of the work was done on castles which the justiciar himself held: Winchester and Northampton, for example.

[2] As such he had earlier been sent writs from the continent addressed to the justiciar and the sheriffs, or the justiciar and the bailiffs of England; *Rot. Lit. Pat.* pp. 11 *b*, 21 *b*, 24, 30 *b*, 33, 34.

[3] *Rot. Lit. Pat.* pp. 6 *b*, 19, 21 *b*, 33, 67. The usual reason given for such protection of a man's lands was that he was serving the king.

to the king's wishes.[1] The seisin of land of a monastery, when it lay in several counties, must have demanded writs to the sheriffs of each of them; and the proclamation of pardon to an outlaw must similarly have required letters patent to a number of local courts. The task of producing the large number of documents necessary in some of these cases must certainly have been more conveniently dealt with by those chancery clerks left in England to write the writs and letters patent in Geoffrey fitz Peter's name than by the clerks who accompanied the king, whose time, when abroad, was well filled by all the continental business of government.[2] It was easier to send one order to the justiciar for transmission by copies in his name to the sheriffs or bailiffs, and to let the justiciar, named at the head of this group of royal ministers, take responsibility for its enforcement. The system which had been evolved to cope with the problem of government of two realms with but one king had been much used in the past. With the loss of Normandy and the relatively short periods of royal absence thereafter, it gradually fell into abeyance; and with it those functions of the justiciar which had been an integral part of it.

How far the system had declined by 1210 is difficult to assess. The political atmosphere was troubled by that time and King John suspicious even of those who had served him loyally.[3] The

---

[1] *Ibid.* p. 67 b.

[2] The question of the justiciar's chancery is discussed by Richardson, *Memoranda Roll 1 John*, pp. xi, xxxii–xxxiii. Richardson concludes that the clerks who served the justiciar were a branch of the chancery, not members of his own household. His chief reason for this belief is the fact that the diplomatic of royal and justiciar's writs is identical, therefore both types were drafted and written by clerks of the chancery. The logic of this belief seems somewhat defective, although the conclusion may well be substantially correct. There is no reason to assume that the justiciar's clerks were always chancery clerks or always members of his own household. Since the Geoffrey fitz Peter associates and messengers were men who had careers in the royal administration, Richardson's conclusion may be accepted in a general way without, however, ruling out the other possibility. Men described as clerks of the justiciar occasionally figure in the records; Joseph Aaron was justiciar's clerk (to Hubert Walter); Geoffrey fitz Peter had a clerk called Ralph; *Pipe Roll 6 Richard 1*, p. 141; *Pipe Roll 2 John*, p. 150.

[3] Painter, *King John*, pp. 255 ff.

administrative system, as will presently appear, showed signs of the tension which existed, but the absence of the chancery enrolments in that and the following two years draws a veil over it beyond which it is impossible to see anything with clarity. The length of John's visit to Ireland was not great; it was too short to have left much in the way of evidence. Geoffrey fitz Peter was engaged in a campaign against the Welsh and their ally William de Braiose.[1] The years 1209 to 1212 were years of continual military campaigns. The earliest of them saw John's own expedition against Llewellyn, and another against Scotland; in the second, the king invaded Ireland while the justiciar conducted another expedition against Wales; in 1211 John made yet another attack upon the Welsh and the following year witnessed more preparations for an invasion.[2] As regent in 1210 Geoffrey fitz Peter was a soldier, commander of the royal forces. He also, from the one document which is known certainly to belong to this period of his justiciarship, presided over a gathering of magnates and barons of the exchequer, to hear read the charters of Reading abbey which concerned its foreign hundred.[3] The gathering seems to have been something like a council (*consideratum fuit communi omnium consilio et assensu*), which met partly at least to sit in judgement upon charters of King John and his ancestors, a delicate enough proceeding to warrant some impressive group of ministers. Peter des Roches, bishop of Winchester, seems to have been the justiciar's chief colleague, and he attested the letters patent which Geoffrey fitz Peter despatched to the sheriff of Berkshire and the itinerant justices in the county on 3 August notifying them of the decision of this court. In default of other evidence, the implications of this document cannot be surely assessed. It may be that, by 1210, although the government operated in the justiciar's name—and he certainly sent out the autumnal justices[4]—the political situation was such that he acted in concert with a group of magnates and ministers of whom the outstanding one was the bishop of Winchester, later to

---

[1] Painter, *King John*, p. 264.   [2] *Ibid.*

[3] Egerton MS 3031, fo. 29; Richardson, *op. cit.* p. lxxv. Unlike Geoffrey's writs this letter bears a regnal year. Other of Geoffrey's writs may belong to this period but not certainly.

[4] *Pipe Roll 12 John*, pp. 120, 181.

become the next justiciar.[1] But the situation is obscure and complicated by the relations between John and the papacy. Peter des Roches was the only bishop left in England at the end of 1209. Geoffrey fitz Peter had urged John to negotiate with the pope in 1209, and he tried again in 1210.[2] The position in which the clergy who played a prominent part in royal administration found themselves, and the attitude of Geoffrey fitz Peter towards the quarrel, may account for the obscurity of the position generally and that of the justiciarship in particular. For by 1210 signs were not lacking that the traditional place of the justiciar was being affected by those factors which have been discussed; and the evidence is to be found in Geoffrey's administration.

2. THE JUSTICIAR AND THE COURT 'CORAM REGE'

When King John returned to England in December 1203 he had been abroad for more than two years; before the loss of Normandy he had, it will be recalled, spent about eleven months of his reign in England. Although, during this short time, there had been a court coram rege which accompanied him, as a constant or regular feature of judicial administration it belongs to the period after Normandy had fallen; and since this court now sat term by term, the situation which arose was novel. Hitherto the justiciar, presiding over the justices of the bench at Westminster, had been the pivot of the judicial system. He had issued writs calling or removing suits into the royal court, he had been approached by

[1] That the justiciar should have colleagues to whom he was required to listen was not unprecedented. Leaving aside the doubtful case of Richard I's provision for the regency of England in 1189–90, Hubert Walter was sent to Geoffrey fitz Peter and the justices of England in May 1202, the king ordering that they should trust what he said to them of the king's affairs, and that they should call him to be present at the treating of all royal business and take his counsel. This may mean no more than discussion of those aspects of administration in which Hubert was an expert; it does not necessarily imply a colleague in the regency (and the inclusion of the justices of England in the address suggests strongly that it does not); but this sort of administrative conference on technical points of law or finance is precisely what is involved in the case of the charters of Reading Abbey. See above, p. 97; and below, p. 170.

[2] Gervase of Canterbury, II, xcviii–cii; Rot. Lit. Pat. p. 89b; Rot. de Liberate, p. 123.

litigants who sought some favour or desired to appoint attorneys, he had notified the justices of the king's commands, of the postponement of a case, of the presence of parties to suits in the king's service.[1] The plea rolls are full of Geoffrey fitz Peter's activity. What, then, was the effect upon his position as chief justice when the king and the justices who accompanied him were a more or less permanent feature? What was the consequence of the king's own interest which has been indicated above?

The series of *coram rege* rolls begins with the Hilary term of 1204. The court sitting with the king heard pleas at York, at Clarendon and at London;[2] Geoffrey fitz Peter was in John's company at York, and he had been part of the royal retinue on its journey to that city by way of Newport, Northampton and Nottingham.[3] The justiciar was recorded in final concords as president of the bench at Westminster throughout the term,[4] and the presiding justice of the court *coram rege* when it sat in London was Joscelin of Wells who, with his brother Hugh, had been responsible for the royal chancery since July 1203.[5] In this Hilary term Geoffrey fitz Peter played no part in the proceedings of the court and the only reference to him was in a case in which one Thomas Blund was summoned before the king to show why he had disseised a minor of his land, and in his defence Thomas cited letters of Geoffrey fitz Peter which had given seisin.[6] In the first term of the year in which there were regular sessions of this court, Geoffrey fitz Peter, although in the king's company, took no part in its activity.

The following term, Easter 1204, found the justiciar in the

---

[1] See above, pp. 115–18.   [2] *Curia Regis Rolls*, II, 84–104.

[3] *Rot. Chart.* p. 133 b; *Rot. Lit. Pat.* p. 38 b. Geoffrey was at Newport 2 February, Northampton 4 February, Nottingham 10 February.

[4] Hunter, *Feet of Fines*, I, 230; CP 25(1) 127/6/6. The apparent contradiction between these two classes of evidence is to be explained by the formalism of the final concords and also, I believe, by the legal fiction of the justiciar's presence which had been asserted in 1201.

[5] *Curia Regis Rolls*, II, 99; from July 1203 to May 1206 the chancery was in the hands of these two brothers, and documents were given by their hands; *Rot. Chart.* pp. 73–135. On 28 May 1206 Joscelin was made bishop of Bath and Wells.

[6] *Curia Regis Rolls*, III, 99.

king's train for at least part of the time, and he played some part in the work of the court which travelled with him. Three cases were postponed by his order. Thomas of Erdington was in the king's service and this was sufficient to delay a case in which he and his wife were involved, first to three weeks after *Clausum Pasche* and eventually until the next term, by order of Geoffrey fitz Peter.[1] Another case concerned the church of Banstead, and a jury came to recognize whether or not it was in the king's gift; this jury remained without a day by order of Geoffrey fitz Peter.[2] Another jury summoned to decide between Alexander of Caldbeck and Robert de Courteney and his wife was appointed another day in the following Michaelmas term by the same authority because the jury was insufficient, some of its members not having appeared.[3] It was uncertain in the Easter term whether John would still be in England at the following Michaelmas, for the parties to this dispute were told to appear before him if he were and, if not, then to appear before the court at Westminster. None of these actions were said to have been performed on the justiciar's writ but by his order; *precepto* and *not per breve*. It would be dangerous to attach a very precise significance to the terms employed, but it is probable that the justiciar's commands in these cases were by word of mouth, and almost certainly so in the second postponement of Thomas of Erdington's case. Any writs required would usually run in the king's name since John was in England, but they might well be authorized by the justiciar. There is little evidence to point the truth of this distinction, but it may be significant that in 1208 a case in the bench was removed to the court *coram rege* by the king's writ by order of Geoffrey fitz Peter.[4] Whether or not such a precise distinction can be drawn, it

---

[1] *Curia Regis Rolls*, III, 104. The suit was then postponed until the following term on Geoffrey's order; *ibid.* p. 114. This second order of the justiciar's was apparently given personally, in view of the time factor involved. The case first appeared on the morrow of *Clausum Pasche* and was postponed until three weeks after the same feast on the justiciar's information; it was then postponed again, by another order of the justiciar, until the next Trinity term.

[2] *Ibid.* p. 117.   [3] *Ibid.* pp. 118–19.

[4] *Curia Regis Rolls*, V, 189. A day was given to the parties to hear judgement before the king within a month of Easter (the same term) and record of the suit was sent to the *curia*.

is evident that in the Easter term of 1204 the justiciar had some small part to play in the activities of the court which travelled with the king, and that his position in the king's entourage placed him in a situation in which he could take an interest in the work of the court.

Trinity term 1204 was the third consecutive term in which the court *coram rege* sat. As in the previous term Geoffrey fitz Peter played a small part in its proceedings. He informed the justices that a lady had appointed her attorney before him, and he ordered the justices to postpone a plea which was before the king between the abbot of York and the prior of Nocton *ad diem competentem in primo adventu domini regis*, that is to say, when the king came into Nottinghamshire; and in virtue of this order of the justiciar the plea was so postponed from the vigil of St Lawrence (9 August) until the day of the king's coming.[1] Clearly the justices *coram rege* took note of the justiciar's authority in matters of this kind. The relatively slight extent to which this authority was exercised, by contrast with Geoffrey fitz Peter's earlier activity in judicial affairs, may be gathered from a case which came up in this term. An assize came to recognize if Eva la Warre unjustly disseised Miles de St Maur and his wife.[2] Eva asserted that the assize should not be allowed because she had fined with Geoffrey fitz Peter in the sum of 15 marks to have seisin of the land and heir and upon this order of the justiciar the sheriff of Somerset had put her in possession. Miles replied that she had already disseised them before she had obtained the justiciar's order. To determine the question both parties relied upon a jury to be summoned before the king at Taunton on the following Wednesday. What had previously been done by order of Geoffrey fitz Peter was now to be done *coram rege*. It was inevitable that in many cases reference should be made to judicial proceedings which had taken place in the period before the king was so continuously in England and that therefore litigants should appeal to the justiciar to support their statements. In this term one Master Matthew, in his defence, referred to a plea before Geoffrey fitz Peter and Richard of

[1] *Curia Regis Rolls*, III, 139, 154.
[2] *Ibid.* p. 126.

Herriard at Oxford, and to a subsequent agreement made before Geoffrey at Aylesbury.[1] This case was given a day at the Nativity of Mary in the following September and Master Matthew was told to produce Geoffrey fitz Peter's warranty for his statement. The implication may well be that such warranty was not immediately available, for Geoffrey fitz Peter was not regularly present in the king's company in this term.[2] His intervention in proceedings before the court *coram rege* was spasmodic.

The justiciar's position as chief justice had been, and, so far as the bench was concerned, continued to be, such that it was inevitably reflected in the administration of justice; and since the relations between the bench and the court *coram rege* were close, the justiciar was drawn into contact with the latter. There is a continuous trickle of evidence for his judicial work to be found in its records until Geoffrey fitz Peter's death in 1213. Litigants appointed their attorneys before him and the justices had to be informed of the fact if the case came up before the king; writs of Geoffrey fitz Peter conveyed such information in the Easter term of 1206, the same term two years later, at Trinity 1208, Hilary 1210, and Michaelmas 1213.[3] Or, again, a sheriff might inform the justices that he had taken the land of a litigant into the king's hand, and the justiciar informed them that the party had sought to replevy it.[4] The justiciar's work in this way helped to ensure the smooth working of judicial administration; in some sense he correlated information required in cases before each of the

[1] *Ibid.* p. 147.

[2] On 20 June (Trinity Sunday) he was at Winchester, but thereafter he was not in the king's company again until 3 August when they were at Oxford. The justices *coram rege* heard pleas there on Tuesday after St Peter *ad vincula* (3 August), having previously been in the south-west, although their sittings had begun at Winchester on the Morrow of Trinity; *Curia Regis Rolls*, III, 123, 126, 137, 138, 144. Geoffrey was with the court when it moved to Northampton on 8 August and to Nottingham on 25 August; *Rot. Chart.* pp. 135b, 140b, 141; *Rot. Lit. Pat.* pp. 43b, 44b. The justices *coram rege* heard pleas at Northampton on 9 August; *Curia Regis Rolls*, III, 147. The justiciar was clearly with the king while the justices were holding pleas at times, but the great gap from 20 June to 3 August suggests that he was elsewhere for a considerable part of this term.

[3] *Ibid.* IV, 87; V, 158, 227, 252; VI, 5; VII, 4.

[4] *Ibid.* III, 322; IV, 78.

two courts, a necessary function when cases were so frequently transferred. In virtue of his own position as justiciar he would know details of this kind, either because litigants approached him personally, or because he presided over the bench. Some, at any rate, of the information with which Geoffrey fitz Peter supplied the court *coram rege* was conveyed by his writ or by his letters,[1] but it has sometimes been doubted whether the justiciar could issue writs in his own name while the king was in England. It is probably the case that a writ which initiated a suit in the royal court ran in the king's name if he was in England. In the Michaelmas term of 1210 the abbot of St Albans was summoned to be before the king to show wherefore and by what warrant he took the homage of Nicholas Bellesmains, uncle of Mabel daughter of Henry, for land of which Henry was in possession when he died.[2] The abbot appeared in court and sought its opinion whether he ought to answer, since the king was in England and the writ spoke in the name of Geoffrey fitz Peter. He was given a day late in the same term, the Wednesday after the feast of All Saints, to hear judgement. The justiciar's writ was probably issued during the king's absence in Ireland from June to August 1210, the Michaelmas term being the next after its issue, so that the abbot's plea may have been an ingenious way of holding up proceedings, but the court apparently paid some attention to it; it was a plausible argument which must be considered, although the result is not known. It is easy to understand the doubt raised by the plea, especially in the deteriorating political circumstances of the day when the king was suspicious of any independent administrative action, but it can hardly have been justified in the light of precedent, since many justiciar's writs must necessarily have been acted upon previously in similar circumstances if administration was not to be badly dislocated every time the king returned. The abbot's argument, however, does appear to assume that an original writ issued by the justiciar while the king was actually in the country would have been invalid; and in default of evidence

---

[1] Of the cases referred to in the last two footnotes, the majority were those in which specific reference was made to a writ or, on one occasion, to letters of Geoffrey fitz Peter.   [2] *Curia Regis Rolls*, VI, 80–1.

to the contrary this may be accepted. The judicial writs of Geoffrey fitz Peter which told the justices of the appointment of an attorney or of litigants seeking to replevy land taken into the king's hand, are in a different class; they did not begin pleading; they merely supplied information necessary for its continuance or completion. As such they were employed by the justiciar when the king was in England and were not apparently challenged.

On 24 May 1205 Geoffrey fitz Peter told the justices by a writ which he issued *teste meipso* and *per preceptum eius* that, since Geoffrey Lutterel was in the king's service, all the suits before the justices between him and other litigants should be postponed until the king should command otherwise; the writ was issued at Silverstone and it was cited in full on a membrane of pleadings before the court *coram rege* in the Easter term of 1205.[1] That it was issued by Geoffrey fitz Peter while King John was in England is hardly open to doubt, for he was there with the king's court on the previous and the following days in that year.[2] In any case, the last 24 May on which John was abroad was two years earlier than this,[3] and a time lag of two years is unlikely with a writ of this kind. Clearly it was issued by the justiciar while he was in King John's company. It was probably not exceptional, but unequivocal cases of this kind are difficult to establish because the date and place of issue was often omitted when writs were recorded in the plea rolls. Nevertheless, mention of Geoffrey fitz Peter's writs containing this kind of information cannot be assumed to be survivals from a period of royal absence, since it is certain that he issued one such writ at a time when he was actually in the king's company.[4]

Such, as they developed after the loss of Normandy, were the justiciar's duties in connexion with the court *coram rege*, and they flowed not from any official position *vis-à-vis* this court, nor any immediate duty of supervision over the work done there, but rather from Geoffrey fitz Peter's more general position as justiciar,

---

[1] *Ibid.* III, 346.
[2] *Rot. Lit. Claus.* I, 33 ff.; *Rot. Chart.* p. 150*b*. On the same day the court moved to Woodstock.
[3] *Handbook of British Chronology*, p. 36.
[4] See below, pp. 152–6.

as chief among the king's judges. And they were slight compared with those functions which he exercised in respect of the bench.

Geoffrey was frequently to be found in King John's company when he travelled about England, as a glance at his itinerary will show; in 1204, for example, they went north together, in October and November of 1207 they were in each other's company as the court moved from Lambeth to Winchester and thence to Silverstone and Tewkesbury; in June and July 1208 they were together.[1] The journeys of the royal court were marked, amongst other ways, by the series of final concords made before the justices who accompanied it, and in each one of these the king was said to preside. *Hec est finalis concordia facta in curia domini regis apud X coram ipso domino Rege.* In practice, however, it seems clear that the words 'before the king' did not mean in his actual presence. It may be true that the court *coram rege* could have no existence in the absence of the king from England, that it required his physical presence in the country,[2] yet it is nevertheless evident from the plea rolls that he did not sit regularly in court. Those adjournments to enable the justices to take his opinion, the annotations *loquendum cum rege*, if they denote the king's interest in the details of judicial work, are also evidence that his interest did not extend to sitting regularly by the side of his judges. Thus in the Michaelmas term 1207 a series of cases was postponed until they could be talked over with the king, and so, too, at Trinity 1208, Hilary 1210, Michaelmas 1210, and Trinity 1212.[3] Nor are such adjournments for discussion the only indication of the king's absence from the sessions of the court. In the first of the terms mentioned, for example, he despatched an order to the justices through the archdeacon of Wells, and similar instances can readily be found.[4] It would be unreasonable to suppose that the king, with all the many demands upon his attention, should take an interest in more than the most difficult or important cases or those which involved him personally. The fact, however, that a case was before the

---

[1] *Rot. Chart.* pp. 113*b*, 171, 171*b*, 172, 173*b*, 179*b*, 182; *Rot. Lit. Pat.* pp. 38*b*, 84, 85.

[2] Maitland, *Select Pleas of the Crown,* p. xv; Flower, *Introduction to the Curia Regis Rolls,* p. 19.

[3] *Curia Regis Rolls,* V, 53, 234; VI, 19, 54, 351.   [4] *Ibid.* III, 99.

justices *coram rege* meant that it was not difficult for the king to take such an interest if he chose, or to be appealed to by the judges. One explanation of the lack of any great interest of the justiciar in the proceedings before this court is that he was not in a position regularly to have such immediate access to the court, and even when he was in John's company it did not mean that *ipso facto* he attended any of its sessions. In fact, Geoffrey fitz Peter does not seem to have sat in this court, nor to have sat beside the king in judgement, on anything other than rare occasions.[1]

The king's name appeared at the head of final concords made before the court *coram rege*, the justiciar's at the head of those made before the bench. The judges who normally accompanied the king were Simon of Pattishall, whose career has been discussed, James of Potterne, Henry de Pontaudemer and, towards the end of the justiciarship of Geoffrey fitz Peter, Roger Huscarl or, a little earlier, Richard de Mucegros. This group of judges was distinct from those who normally sat in the bench at Westminster. James of Potterne was a judge of some small experience at the time when Normandy fell. At Michaelmas 1199 and at the exchequer session of the following year he accounted for York-shire as Geoffrey fitz Peter's deputy,[2] and this connexion with the northern county probably explains his standing as a pledge for Lawrence of Wilton who offered the king two palfreys to obtain confirmation of a stone house in Yorkshire.[3] It also explains his excommunication by Archbishop Geoffrey of York for activity in his lands.[4] Potterne is a village in Wiltshire, and it was with that county that James was most closely connected. At Michaelmas 1204 he was joint sheriff with Robert of Vipont, but they accounted by deputy.[5] In 1205 he was ordered to give Emma of Stanton full seisin of the farm of Itchen, held of the abbess and

---

[1] These instances will be dealt with in some detail below, pp. 150–1.

[2] *Pipe Roll 1 John*, p. 38; *Pipe Roll 2 John*, p. 101. Foss, *op. cit.* p. 529, was unaware that James was the justiciar's deputy in the earlier year.

[3] *Rot. de Finibus*, p. 355.

[4] Archbishop Geoffrey, who refused to pay the tallage demanded, had his lands despoiled by the king's officers in Yorkshire of whom, through his position, James was the chief. He was excommunicated by name in the archbishop's sentence on all those who entered his lands; Wendover, III, 154.

[5] *Pipe Roll 6 John*, p. 247. Their deputy was John Bonet.

convent of Winchester, which had been taken into the king's hand, for which Emma had offered to the king 40 marks and a palfrey, the same order being sent to the sheriffs of Wiltshire and Hampshire.[1] In the latter county, in 1204, King John gave him the manor of Wallop which had once been held by Matthew de Poteria and then by Baldwin of Wessington at a farm of 30 marks per year.[2] James's judicial career may have begun in the reign of Richard I,[3] but as one of the justices who accompanied the king, he sat regularly from 1204.[4] Two years earlier he had been with Geoffrey fitz Peter's eyre which travelled to Reading, Winchester and Chichester.[5] The fact that he was Geoffrey's deputy in Yorkshire suggests that he may have made his way into the royal service through the justiciar's good graces. In 1204 his judicial work was considerable. He began to sit regularly as a justice *coram rege*, and also to do a good deal of work in eyre. In that year he imposed amercements in his home county of Wiltshire with Stephen of Thornham; and in this and the year following he, with Joscelin of Wells, assessed the tallage in the four south-western counties of Dorset and Somerset, Devon and Cornwall, in the first two also imposing amercements. He revisited Wiltshire to assess the tallage, and carried out the same duty with Bishop John of Norwich in Norfolk and Suffolk. At the head of a party of justices he performed similar work in the *honor* of Gloucester, and in Hampshire joined with Eustace de Fauconberg for the same purpose.[6] This sudden outburst of judicial activity on James's part

[1] *Rot de Finibus*, p. 295.
[2] *Rot. Lit. Claus.* 1, 8. At Michaelmas 6 John Baldwin owed 20 marks of his oblation to have this, but the debt was noted as not payable since afterwards the king had given the land to James; *Pipe Roll 6 John*, p. 128. The account appeared under *Nova oblata* in Hampshire.
[3] Foss, *op. cit.* p. 529, asserts that he acted as a justice from 1197 citing *Abb. Plac.* p. 83. I can find no evidence of his continuous employment as such from this date.
[4] CP 25(1) 127/6/17, 26, 30, 41, 44. There are Lincolnshire concords which show him to have sat at the Old Temple at Easter 1205, and at Whitsuntide he was with the king at Northampton; in October he was at York. In the same Michaelmas term he was at St Bride's. In the same term, a year earlier, he had been sitting at Westminster; 261/8/6; *Feet of Fines, passim.*
[5] See above, p. 119.
[6] *Pipe Roll 6 John*, p. 255; *Pipe Roll 7 John*, pp. 3, 24, 92, 132, 142–3, 167, 252.

suggests that it was closely connected with his becoming a judge *coram rege* in the previous year, and that both were the result of an appointment demanded by John's presence in England; that James, in fact, was a man who must have had a judicial apprenticeship, possibly under the justiciar himself, possibly under Simon of Pattishall, as well as administrative experience, and who in 1204 was appointed a judge to accompany the king. Certainly from that date his work as a judge was continual, both in the court *coram rege* and locally. At Michaelmas 1206, accounts of his work rendered at the exchequer were considerable. He had been at the head of groups which assessed the tallage and imposed amercements in Buckinghamshire, Bedfordshire, Dorset, Somerset, Hampshire, Wiltshire and Huntingdonshire, in which last county one of his associates was Walter of Creeping, a justice of the bench. With Henry archdeacon of Stafford he had imposed amercements in Dorset and Somerset, Devon, Cornwall, and Hampshire. The following year, too, was filled with activity of the same sort, but it was the last to see such intensive work by James as a justice in eyre.[1] Thereafter his activity faded rapidly away.[2] He remained, however, prominent amongst the judges with the king and his name followed that of Simon of Pattishall in the lists of judges in the final concords.[3] He seems, indeed, to have been closely associated with that distinguished justice, for in 1204 Simon and he had recorded that Hugh de Balliol and not Ely of Aston ought to be distrained for the payment of 20 marks; and in 1207 each of them was fined 100 marks for giving Eustace de Vesci and Richard de Umfraville licence to agree about an appeal which lay between them without the king's licence.[4]

---

[1] *Pipe Roll 8 John*, pp. 40, 131, 136, 147, 158, 159, 162, 163, 187.

[2] *Pipe Roll 9 John*, pp. 62, 77, 147, 150, 155, 183, 208.

[3] In the accounts audited in 1208 there was no new activity of James of Potterne; and in 1209 only an account of amercements in Yorkshire; *Pipe Roll 11 John*, p. 139.

[4] *Pipe Roll 6 John*, p. 204. In 1204 the entry was made under *Nova oblata* in Essex and Hertfordshire. *Rot. de Finibus*, p. 386 recorded the debt *de dono* for this offence which ought to have been paid into the chamber. Under the Wiltshire account in 1207 it was recorded that James had paid 25 marks, but had then been pardoned the whole debt; therefore he had a surplus which was partly allowed to him in the following year in the account for Devizes; *Pipe*

The incident illustrates both the activity of the justices *coram rege* without the actual presence of the king in court and the degree of supervision which John exercised over them. James's career continued into the reign of Henry III with a possible break in the civil war period when his loyalty seems to have been suspected by John.[1] There is little evidence that his work was anything other than judicial after 1204, with the exception of the tallages he imposed, which was work done by every justice in the course of his eyres. And his career as a justice was bound up with the court *coram rege*, not with the bench at Westminster.

Another of the justices who sat in the king's court was Henry de Pontaudemer. Henry was a Norman who in 1195 and 1198 had been guardian of the escheats in the bailiwick of Evrecin, and bailiff of Caux in Normandy.[2] In 1199 he held a knight's fee of the *honor* of Gloucester, which was probably the fee in question in 1212 when he was required to find one knight for service in Poitou or wherever the king chose at his own cost for a whole year; and he actually paid 50 marks into the chamber of the fine which he had made with the king over this knight service on 28 January 1214.[3] The fine represented an agreement by which, if Henry found one knight for a whole year's service, he was to be quit of 46 marks of a fine of £100 made with the king for custody of the land and heir of Miles Neirnuit. Henry seems to have been

---

Roll 9 John, p. 207. His connexion with Simon and the justiciar is still further emphasized by the first term in which he sat regularly in the central court; at Michaelmas 1204 he was the third and last member of the court sitting at Westminster, CP 25(1) 261/8/6, of which the other two members were Geoffrey fitz Peter and Simon; in the next term and thereafter, he sat *coram rege* and Simon was the senior judge in the court.

[1] In 17 John the manor of Wallop was to be given by the sheriff to Roger Ely *si Jacobus de Poterna non sit ad servicium nostrum; Rot. Lit. Claus.* I, 232. He had recovered it in Henry III's reign; Foss, *op. cit.* p. 530.

[2] Foss, *op. cit.* p. 252, who wrongly gives the dates 1295 and 1298; see Stapleton, *Rot. Scacc. Norm.* I, clxix; II, cxxxiii.

[3] *Rot. de Finibus*, pp. 484, 521. He owed scutage on his fee throughout John's reign, although he was pardoned of the payment in 1199 and 1202, and in 1204 was acquitted because his name appeared in the roll which the king sent to the exchequer as *inbreviati sunt ad transfretandum* but whether Henry actually served in person or found a knight to do it does not appear; *Pipe Roll 1 John*, p. 37; *Pipe Roll 4 John*, p. 283; *Pipe Roll 6 John*, p. 123.

a man of some substance. He came later into the royal court than did James; he sat regularly as a justice *coram rege* from John's ninth year,[1] but, like James's, his previous judicial career was not extensive. He was usually last of the judges named, although he sat regularly until 15 John.[2] Apparently he performed no other administrative duties; he did not, for instance, act as a justice in eyre nor assess the tallage as did James of Potterne. Beyond his presence with the judges who accompanied the king, he seems to have done nothing. It was possibly as a reward for his judicial work that he was granted at the end of his career as a justice 60 shillings of the customs of salt upon the land which he held.[3] The third of the justices who accompanied King John was Roger Huscarl who came to the work later even than Henry, for he appeared among the justices only in John's twelfth year, and was then the last named justice.[4] He was then, as was natural, the junior member of the court, but his subsequent career was distinguished. In 16 John he was given the land of Roger de Tanton in Kent to sustain himself *quamdiu eidem . . . domino regi placuit*,[5] and in the reign of Henry III he was sent to Ireland to become the senior justice next to the justiciar, being granted the town of Dulscadam.[6] Other than his judicial function from the Easter term 12 John, he seems to have engaged in little other administrative

---

[1] From the Easter term of 1208 so far as I can discover; CP 25(1) 127/7/30. He was at Woodstock within 3 weeks of Easter and at Westminster within the month; 233/5/7; 261/7/56.

[2] *Ibid.* 127/9/37, 39; 261/12/31; in 15 John his name followed that of Roger Huscarl in the Easter term, although Roger was a newcomer to the group. The clerks' practice had then altered. At Easter 12 and 13 John, Henry was senior to Roger, and also in the Michaelmas term 15 John, 233/5/18, 20, 22; since the Easter term 15 John was the latest of these, it is reasonable to suppose that as Roger's seniority or experience grew Henry may well have receded into the background.

[3] *Rot. Lit. Claus.* I, 206.

[4] See the references quoted in note 2, above, and *Feet of Fines, passim.* Foss, *op. cit.* p. 358, says that his career began in 11 John; I can find no evidence for this.

[5] *Rot. Lit. Claus.* I, 204.

[6] *Ibid.* I, 526; II, 125. He is described by Foss as lord of the vill of Stepney, called Stebynhyth Huscarl, quoting *Gentleman's Magazine*, April 1855, p. 388; but I know of no other evidence to connect him with Middlesex than the name this place bore in 1290.

work. At Michaelmas 1210 he was deputy of William de Neville as custodian of Wiltshire for a quarter of the year, and he himself accounted for 25 shillings *de exitu* for a quarter of the year.[1] These duties and his judicial work began at the same time, and like James of Potterne he seems to have been engaged in them because he had been appointed to sit in the court *coram rege*, probably at the end of a judicial apprenticeship. These men made up the regular group of justices who travelled with the king, their careers starting at different times but showing substantial similarity. All of them were primarily judges who did little other administrative work, but not all of them could rival the volume of judicial work that Simon of Pattishall and James of Potterne transacted also in the counties. These two, indeed, seem to have been the really distinguished justices of the court, but since the careers of the others began rather late, they obviously still had their reputations to make; and Roger Huscarl succeeded in doing so. Both James of Potterne and Henry of Pontaudemer seem to have been in disgrace or at least under suspicion during the time of troubles.[2]

These justices did not, however, exhaust the personnel of the court. Two other men sat there in judgement from time to time, and one of them, for two years, was regularly present. Henry of London, archdeacon of Stafford, was the companion of James of Potterne in some of his itinerant work[3] and he was a justice *coram rege* in 5 John, thereafter making periodic appearances in court.[4]

[1] *Pipe Roll 12 John*, pp. 76, 82.

[2] James's position has been mentioned above. Henry's land he probably lost in the civil war, for it was restored to him in 1218; *Rot. Lit. Claus.* I, 339.

[3] *Pipe Roll 8 John*, pp. 131, 142, 147, 158. In the Dorset and Somerset accounts James's name preceded Henry's; in the other counties, Devon, Cornwall, and Hampshire, the archdeacon of Stafford was at the head of the party which imposed amercements, although James was the only other member of it mentioned by name.

[4] Foss, *op. cit.* p. 411. He had been one of the itinerant justices in Berkshire in John's first year, when he assessed the tallage and imposed amercements; Madox, *History of Exchequer*, I, 290, 722. Henry did not sit regularly in the court. He was there in the Michaelmas term 7 John; CP 25(1) 127/6/29–31; 233/4/19, 20; and at the following Easter term; 233/4/24. In 7 John he was with the king in the Hilary term at Worcester and at York; 261/8/14, 15, 16; he appeared again in the Michaelmas term 9 John; 261/8/56.

Henry was a distinguished man, an ecclesiastic whose work was never confined wholly or even largely to judicial administration. He may have been the Master Henry of London whom Richard de Luci, the justiciar of Henry II, sent to collect the rents of the vacant bishopric of Chichester.[1] By the beginning of John's reign Henry of London was archdeacon of Stafford.[2] He was a member of the embassy to the king of Navarre and of another to the king of Connaught.[3] In 1207 he was custodian of the vacant see of Exeter.[4] In 1209 he was one of the king's commissioners to meet the three bishops whom the pope had appointed to publish the sentence of excommunication against King John, and in the same year he was elected to the see of Exeter, an election declared void by Stephen Langton in 1211.[5] The archdeacon of Stafford was a trusted and important royal minister who shared his judicial and administrative work with diplomatic activity. His reward, in March 1213, was the archbishopric of Dublin,[6] and in the following May he was the first witness to the document by which King John surrendered England to the pope, being also one of those men sent to expedite the return of the exiled bishops.[7] He represented the king at the proposed Oxford meeting with the rebel barons on 16 July 1215, and he was one of the bishops who issued letters patent forbidding that necessary forest customs should be abolished. During the civil war John sent him with other trusted ministers to Rome to represent the king's position to the pope.[8] It is therefore hardly surprising that Henry's appearances in court should be intermittent, but his presence must have

[1] Foss, op. cit.

[2] The payment which he owed for King Richard's ransom at Michaelmas 1199 gives him this style; Pipe Roll 1 John, p. 248.

[3] Rot. Lit. Pat. p. 3; Rot. de Liberate, p. 83.

[4] Rot. Lit. Claus. I, 56. On 27 October 1207 the barons of the exchequer were told to allow Henry for money derived from the see of Exeter paid into the chamber.

[5] Gervase of Canterbury, II, c–ci; Annales Monastici, I, 31, 40, 59; IV, 54. He was one of four royal nominees for vacant bishoprics at the time, all of whom were royal ministers.

[6] Rot. Chart. p. 200.   [7] Wendover, II, 74–6; Rot. Lit. Claus. I, 164.

[8] Rot. Lit. Pat. p. 149; Richardson, 'The Morrow of the Great Charter', pp. 426–9, discusses the importance of this meeting at Oxford; Rymer, Foedera, I, 134; Rot. Lit. Pat. p. 182.

contributed to its prestige, and since he was an experienced minister, have helped its deliberations.

The other man who sat from time to time as a justice was Richard de Mucegros. He was probably the son of the sheriff of Gloucester of the same name in the early years of Richard I and he certainly belonged to the Gloucestershire family.[1] He had a brother, Ralph, for whom, in 1205, he paid 20 marks and a palfrey to be quit of a forest offence in Gloucestershire. Earlier, at Michaelmas 1200, he owed 3 marks for having royal confirmation of a gift of three hides of land in Gloucestershire to his son.[2] Richard was plainly a man of some substance, for he made considerable fines with the king for various purposes and stood as pledge of 40 shillings to William de Courteney.[3] At Michaelmas 1207 he was sheriff of Gloucester and accounted through Reginald Pancevolt who was his deputy. He had offered the king 250 marks to have the county and £100 increment each year,[4] it being noted that he ought to have the county so long as he served the king well,[5] but in the following year, on 5 January 1208, he was replaced by John's mercenary captain Gerard d'Athée, probably in preparation for an attack on William de Braiose.[6] As sheriff, Richard held the castle of Gloucester, but he was also given that of Chichester.[7] He was a faithful royal servant and his replacement by Gerard is no reflexion on his loyalty; it was probably simply a question of military expediency. In fact, Richard remained loyal to John in the struggles and was rewarded with land from the

[1] Foss, op. cit. p. 468.

[2] Rot. de Finibus, p. 294. The sheriff was ordered to take security for payment and to deliver Ralph quit. Richard paid 10 marks of the fine promptly; Pipe Roll 7 John, p. 98. For his fine for royal confirmation of three hides; Pipe Roll 2 John, p. 125 entered under Nova oblata in Gloucestershire.

[3] Rot. de Finibus, p. 445.

[4] Pipe Roll 9 John, pp. 210, 215. The pipe roll records the fine offered as 150 marks, differing from the fine roll.

[5] Rot. de Finibus, p. 385. John Lupus had custody of the county and he was ordered to account to Richard for expenses paid from the farm since Easter 8 John, that is, the preceding half-year.

[6] Painter, King John, p. 243. Gerard was given large supplies of money.

[7] Rot. Lit. Pat. pp. 71, 74, 79. The castle of Gloucester apparently contained prisoners and hostages of the king. The queen also stayed there for some time; Rot. Lit. Claus. I, 96.

king's enemies.[1] He was a member of a prosperous Gloucester-shire family, whose career as a judge began shortly after that of James of Potterne in 1205. In the next two years he sat regularly as a justice *coram rege*, thereafter making intermittent appearances in court until 12 John.[2] His name usually followed that of James, although towards the end of his judicial career Henry de Pontau-demer, who was sitting more regularly, preceded him.[3] Richard seems to have had little judicial experience before he came to the court, and his only other administrative work was the shrievalty of his home county of Gloucester.

Such then were the justices who accompanied the king in the later years of Geoffrey fitz Peter's justiciarship; such was the group which witnessed John's charters as a unit distinct from the barons. For example, on 2 December 1212 the king issued a charter to the prior of Lenton.[4] Those who witnessed the deed were Peter des Roches, bishop of Winchester, Geoffrey fitz Peter, William Brie-werre, William de Cantilupe, Adam de Port and William, arch-deacon of Huntingdon. They were barons and counsellors of the king. After their names there appeared Simon of Pattishall, James of Potterne, and Roger Huscarl in a group at the end of the list. Geoffrey fitz Peter was usually placed among the barons distinct from the justices on such occasions. And thus in 1211 a charter was heard before the king, Simon of Pattishall, James of Potterne, Henry de Pontaudemer, and Roger Huscarl, and a group of barons who were Geoffrey fitz Peter, earl of Essex, William Marshal, earl of Pembroke, and Saher, earl of Win-chester.[5] The distinction between the group of justices and the

---

[1] *Rot. Lit. Claus.* I, 237, 243. William Marshal was ordered to provide him with escheats of the lands of the king's enemies and also with the land of John son of Richard.

[2] CP 25(1) 127/6/26, 33. He was with the king at Northampton on Monday and Wednesday after Whitsunday. At Michaelmas 1205 he was with the court at Lincoln; *ibid.* 29; and later in the same term at St Bride's; *ibid.* 31; *Feet of Fines, passim.* He was with the king's court in the following Hilary and Easter terms; 233/4/24, 25. In the Trinity term 11 John he was at Lewes and Por-chester with the justices *coram rege;* 261/12/7, 12, 13; being the last named of the justices.

[3] E.g. *ibid.* 233/5/16 and the last reference of the preceding footnote.

[4] *Cartae Antiquae*, p. 112.   [5] *Curia Regis Rolls*, VI, 150.

magnates is apparent; and the justiciar was numbered with the barons. Nevertheless, there were times when the justiciar sat in the court *coram rege* as a judge, his name following that of the king. In one instance on the plea roll of Hilary 1209, Geoffrey fitz Peter was sitting as a judge beside the king, for a plea came before the pair of them at the Tower of London, and the agreement between the litigants was enrolled.[1] Such information is exceptional, but it is clear that the justiciar was sometimes in court. In John's seventh year, Geoffrey fitz Peter sat with the usual justices of the court *coram rege*, presided over by the king. He was with them at York in March 1205, and at Northampton at Whitsuntide; he sat with the justices *coram rege* when they were at Westminster in the Easter term 7 John and the Michaelmas term of the same regnal year. Two years later he was again in the court at Michaelmas. In 1209 he sat with these justices at Lewes and Porchester in the Trinity term, and in the last year of his life he was present at a session of the court at Westminster at Hilary.[2] These occasions of his appearance in this court fall into two categories. He was occasionally a justice when he was in the king's company and the court was sitting at the place where John was for the time being; he also joined it on occasion when, during term time, the king and his justices arrived in Westminster. There were also sessions of a court at Westminster which comprised the justices *coram rege* and the justices of the bench sitting together, when, naturally, Geoffrey fitz Peter as head of the bench was present; but these may be more conveniently considered later. Both plea rolls, chancery records, and final concords combine to suggest that Geoffrey fitz Peter's presence in the court *coram rege*

---

[1] *Curia Regis Rolls*, v, 324.

[2] CP 25(1) 261/8/5. The judges, besides the king and Geoffrey fitz Peter, were Simon, Ralph of Stoke, and James of Potterne, at York; at Northampton they were Simon, Eustace, James of Potterne and Richard de Mucegros; 127/6/26; at Westminster in 7 John, the judges who sat with king and justiciar were Simon, archdeacon Henry, James of Potterne and Richard of Mucegros in the Easter term; 233/4/24, 261/8/16; in 11 John his colleagues were Simon, Henry de Pontaudemer and Richard de Mucegros; 261/12/7, 12; in the last year of his life they were Simon, James of Potterne and Roger Huscarl; 146/4/57. These instances exclude those in which the justiciar sat in a court which was a combination of both the justices *coram rege* and the bench.

as a justice was exceptional rather than the rule, that in the king's retinue the justiciar was more likely to be associated with the barons and magnates. He was not, of course, rigidly confined to the bench so far as his judicial work was concerned; necessarily Geoffrey fitz Peter's position impinged upon all aspects of royal administration. If the lines between different types of government activity were fluid, so too were those between the different kinds of work performed by the justiciar. Yet Geoffrey fitz Peter's activity was conducted through some organizations rather than through others; and so it was that his judicial position was more intimately connected with the bench at Westminster.

3. THE JUSTICIAR AND THE BENCH

While the justices who sat *coram rege*, and sometimes the justiciar, accompanied King John on his journeys about his kingdom, there remained at Westminster another group of justices, occasionally called the justices of Westminster or London, more often *de banco*: of, or in, the bench; and in this description they were distinguished from the first group, who were justices *de curia*.[1] Over the court at Westminster there presided the justiciar; although his presence was not always actual, in theory he presided day by day, term by term, just as the king was said to be at the head of the justices in the court accompanying him. Geoffrey fitz Peter's concern with the bench is most obviously shown by the plea rolls in which his duties appear to be more extensive than those which he discharged in the court *coram rege*. The justiciar was peculiarly associated with the bench. In part, no doubt, this was a formal presidency demanded by the security sought by litigants as a consequence of their suits; the presence of the justiciar,

---

[1] These descriptions were not consistently used, but they were employed sufficiently frequently to lend point to the distinction. Thus in the Easter term 1204 a writ of the king came to the justices *de curia* that they postpone a plea until the morrow of Ascension day, and it was noted on the *coram rege* roll; *Curia Regis Rolls*, III, 113. For the address justices of Westminster or justices of the bench, *Curia Regis Rolls*, IV, 190, 215. Sir Cyril Flower, *op. cit.* p. 31, makes the point that the word bench could mean the physical boundary of the tribunal. It was not, however, applied to the justices *coram rege*.

real or nominal, was thought to lend greater security to any record of judgement which they obtained. Probably a more important factor was the place of Westminster in the administrative scheme of things; it was the centre of administration where the exchequer had its offices, where the records were kept, where the sedentary organizations of administration lived and worked. For the justiciar who was the chief administrative officer, there was an obvious advantage in his frequent presence there. Perhaps, too, there was some feeling that over the central court of justice the king should preside, or, failing the king (since this central court now had two branches), his *alter ego*. Whatever the reasons, the judicial position of the justiciar was closely linked with the bench at Westminster.

The effect of the king's return from Normandy upon Geoffrey fitz Peter's position *vis-à-vis* the bench is difficult to assess; and that largely for technical reasons. Original writs no longer ran in his name but in the king's, and therefore the apparent bulk of the justiciar's work diminished. The appearance, however, is probably misleading. The fact that a writ ran in the king's name did not mean that it was issued by the king; it might equally well have been authorized by Geoffrey fitz Peter.[1] And such a royal writ might bear either the royal seal or Geoffrey's as proof of its validity; if it lacked either seal it might be challenged.[2] In spite,

---

[1] The writs of the exchequer could, as is well known, be issued by the justiciar in the king's name under his own witness. Certainly legal writs at this time were issued in the king's name under Geoffrey's witness, and the possibility that he authorized their issue is strong; it was the practice of the exchequer; it must have been impossible for all litigants to obtain original writs from the king personally; if a writ of the king bore the justiciar's seal, it is reasonable to suppose that it was issued by him (see note f.).

[2] *Curia Regis Rolls*, v, 126. The writ in question was a writ of the justices which lacked either the seal of the king or the seal of lord Geoffrey (fitz Peter). This was offered as a reason why action had not been taken upon it, but the court considered that the writ of the justices had been held in contempt and the sheriff was amerced for not obeying it. In view of a later statement that the writ of the justices bore the seal of Bishop John of Norwich, it is clear that there was a third means of issuing writs: the justices themselves might do so. That their writ was challenged in 1207 suggests that the practice may have been new; but it was certainly one which might be expected in view of the large amount of litigation.

however, of the formal difficulty of the evidence, it is clear that Geoffrey fitz Peter's activity as chief justice continued, and that, so far as the bench was concerned, it was more extensive than anything which he did in the court before the king.

During the Michaelmas term 1204, Geoffrey fitz Peter carried out the same sort of judicial duties as he had previously done. He informed the justices that a party had replevied their land before him, that another had appointed his attorney, that a case should be given a day for hearing.[1] Because original writs ran in the king's name, the extent of this work is obscured. That it was considerable, even so, is suggested by a writ of King John to the justices which told them that Walter de Fauconberg was unable to appear before them because he was in the king's service, and therefore he was to lose nothing by his absence. The writ was attested by the justiciar, and it may well have been issued by him in the king's name.[2] There is no doubt, however, that Geoffrey fitz Peter's own writs were part of the necessary administration of justice in the bench. In the following Hilary term (1205), he told the justices that William of Studham had sought to replevy his land before him on the Saturday following the feast of the Epiphany.[3] The information was conveyed in a writ running in the name of Geoffrey fitz Peter and issued at Ruislip on 8 January. The year of its issue was not noted but it can only be 1205. In that year the first Saturday after Epiphany was 8 January, and in the preceding years the day was always later than that date.[4] Like the previous example, the justiciar's writ was issued while King John was in England, although in this instance there is no independent evidence for the justiciar's whereabouts at the time. Like the previous example, too, it was not an original writ but one incidental to the course of litigation. During the same term of the following year, another writ of Geoffrey fitz Peter was enrolled which addressed the king's justices of Westminster, and told them that the king had given Robert of Vipont guardianship of William de Gorneaco, in order

[1] *Curia Regis Rolls*, III, 175, 193, 222, 224, 236.
[2] *Ibid.* p. 178.
[3] *Ibid.* p. 264.
[4] *Handbook of Dates*, pp. 122, 123, table 20; pp. 114, 115, table 16; pp. 130, 131, table 24; pp. 152, 153, table 35.

that anyone wishing to plead against William should know who
was to stand to right on his behalf.[1] There is in this case no direct
check upon the year of issue, but since the last occasion when
King John was abroad on 28 December was 1202, it is reasonable
to suppose that this writ, too, was issued by the justiciar while
John was in England; and if the date of the writ was, as seems very
likely, 1205, then on 28 December Geoffrey fitz Peter was in the
king's company at Marlborough.[2] On yet a third occasion a writ
of Geoffrey fitz Peter was quoted in full which conveyed instructions to the justices of the bench. The term was also a Hilary term,
that of 1209, when, on 8 January, the justiciar who was at Berkhampstead ordered that the parties to a suit should be given
permission to reach agreement since their final concord *prolocuta
est*.[3] There is no other evidence for the justiciar's whereabouts, but
Berkhampstead was one of his own manors, and the king had not
been abroad in January since 1203. This, too, was a writ of
Geoffrey fitz Peter issued while the king was in England. None of
these documents was challenged, since they were not writs which
started litigation. They show that part of the duties of the justiciar
was to ensure the smooth working of judicial administration by
providing necessary information. They show, too, that litigants
who desired to take certain action, either to redeem land taken
into the king's hand or to be allowed to make an agreement with
an opponent, came to the justiciar; and probably when he was not
in the king's company. He was regarded as the king's *alter ego*
whose orders were as effective in achieving the ends they desired
as were those from the king himself. In the one instance in which
the writ was issued while Geoffrey was in the king's company, the
information given related not to any particular suit but to a condition necessary to be known in any prospective pleading; it was
probably issued by the justiciar because he was peculiarly the head
of the justices of the bench to whom it was sent. In each case, the
date at which the writ was issued was outside the legal term. The
octave of Hilary, the first return day of that term, was 20 January;

---

[1] *Curia Regis Rolls*, IV, 60.

[2] *Rot. Lit. Claus.* I, 60*b*; *Rot. Chart.* pp. 161, 161*b*.

[3] *Curia Regis Rolls*, V, 321.

and 28 December fell after the end of the Michaelmas term. This is probably the reason for their issue; in term Geoffrey fitz Peter was usually in a position to deliver his orders by word of mouth or by messenger. Out of term, when the justices were not sitting, or were on eyre, a written instruction was necessary as an *aide mémoire*, and when it was acted upon or noted in term time, the action was said to be taken on Geoffrey fitz Peter's writ. Thus days were given for parties to appear in court, notification was provided of the appointment of attorneys, or cases were adjourned or transferred.[1] These were the routine duties which the justiciar had always performed. The implication of them, while John was in England, and of those of Geoffrey's writs which were dated, is that Geoffrey personally was approached by litigants; that he was regarded as an authority whose wishes could cause the bench to take some particular action; that he was available at all times for such purposes; that the field of his judicial work was the bench

---

[1] *Curia Regis Rolls*, III, 224; IV, 61, 87, 125, 184. These are instances in which mention was made of Geoffrey fitz Peter's writ on which such action was taken. In many others, Geoffrey fitz Peter's order was referred to, but it was not specifically stated that it was a writ. A day was given to a suit *precepto* Geoffrey fitz Peter. At times this seems to imply a distinction. Thus an assize at Trinity 1206 was adjourned without a day by order (*precepto*) of the king and by writ of Geoffrey fitz Peter. Since John was then abroad, it is fairly certain that he must have sent a written order to the justiciar who issued his own writ; *Curia Regis Rolls*, IV, 204. Indeed, in a case in the same term an adjournment was made by the justiciar's writ quoted *per breve domini regis; ibid.* p. 152. Perhaps all that it implies is that the justices had not seen a written document. Other actions were taken *per dominum Gaufridum*. For example, in the Trinity term of 1205 a case was adjourned (because one of the parties was in the king's service in Dover castle) *per* Geoffrey fitz Peter; *ibid.* p. 13. On another occasion William prior of Norwich appointed his attorney against Geoffrey of Ash *per* lord Geoffrey and by his writ; *ibid.* 87. Again a distinction seems to be implied by the use of this terminology. But usage is not consistent, and it would be dangerous to build upon these distinctions. All that can safely be said is that sometimes the justiciar gave his orders by writ, sometimes by word of mouth; but any particular instance may have a dubious meaning. The writs, which usually have the date omitted, were probably issued outside term, unless the justiciar was absent from court in term, as he was for instance on 16 June 1206, when he was at Berkhampstead and thence issued a writ to the justices at Westminster that he had ordered the custodian of the Welsh Marches to return to his post because the truce had been broken; therefore he was not to be put in default and penalized; *Curia Regis Rolls*, III, 190.

and not the court *coram rege*, otherwise the king would have been approached. Both the justiciar and the bench were a convenience without which the administration of justice would have creaked along more slowly, with greater difficulty. The sedentary court at Westminster answered the needs of those who could not or did not care to follow the king's court wherever it might be in England. At Westminster there was always a court sitting during the legal terms, and even out of session the head of that court, the justiciar, could be sought out. The necessity of the arrangement for efficient administration and for the needs of would-be litigants was succinctly expressed in the demand in the Great Charter for this sedentary court. *Communia placita non sequantur curiam nostram sed teneantur in aliquo loco certo.*

The control which the justiciar exercised over the bench is undoubted. He was chief justice whose presence enhanced the prestige and competence of the court,[1] whose counsel solved its difficulties. When, as a consequence of his character, a man had to abjure the realm at Westminster, it was done before Geoffrey fitz Peter.[2] Or when a case was difficult and required further discussion, if the justiciar was in Westminster the case was adjourned for his advice. In the Trinity term of 1208 the abbot of Pipewell sought the advowson of a church against Hamo of Beedon who called Alice Clement to warrant him.[3] The abbot asserted that Alice was excommunicate (and therefore not capable of pleading in court) and that this had been proved before the lord Geoffrey (fitz Peter) and the bishop and justices. Alice denied this statement and called her judges to warrant it. *Loquendum cum justiciario.* The reason for the justiciar's advice being sought is explicable by the fact that he was one of the judges, and this fact presumably accounted for the presence of the case in the bench. For Hamo had appeared in the court *coram rege* at the octave of Trinity, and he was not to lose anything on account of this.[4] There was no such personal reason

[1] For example, at Trinity 1205 a day was given to Adam of Westminster and the prior of Merton who had a charter that he was not to plead unless before the king or his chief justice.
[2] *Curia Regis Rolls*, IV, 115.
[3] *Ibid.* v, 293.
[4] *Ibid.* p. 295. This fact was warranted to Hamo by the king.

for consultation with the justiciar in another case in the same term. Richard de Montacute appeared *versus* William son of Richard de Montacute and William father of Richard because they had not observed a final concord.[1] The defendants asserted that Richard had an elder brother and that they were, therefore, under no obligation to answer his plaint. Richard admitted the truth of the statement but asserted that his elder brother was a bastard, born before marriage. William replied that this brother was nevertheless the elder and had the rights of an heir, which Richard countered by denying that his brother had more than one virgate of the land in question and part of the land was held in villeinage (another legal disability). At this point in a difficult case the justices wished to talk matters over with the justiciar. In this Geoffrey fitz Peter's position was the same as it was when, from June to December 1206, King John was in Poitou. In two cases, one in the Trinity, the other in the Michaelmas term of that year, Geoffrey had an interest in being present. On the morrow of St John a suit concerned the court of William Marshal which had defaulted in justice and the sheriff was asked whether the matter had come into the county court on the same day on which the justiciar had ordered that it should be before him at Westminster.[2] At the morrow of All Souls in the following term, Robert de Aubeney was engaged in a dispute with Geoffrey de la Mare over the town of Didcot in Berkshire, and Geoffrey based his case on a charter of Henry II.[3] The justiciar ordered the justices of the bench to hear the charter and to give the parties a day so that he himself might be present at the hearing. In both cases persons or matters of importance were involved; in the former William Marshal, earl of Pembroke, who was a great magnate, in the latter a royal charter which would normally require the king's own attention. The equation made between the king's authority and Geoffrey fitz Peter's underlies each of these instances, and although the latter two occurred while the king was abroad, there is little evidence to suggest that the justiciar's authority over the justices of the bench was different when John was present; and some to suggest the contrary.

[1] *Ibid.* p. 299.   [2] *Curia Regis Rolls*, IV, 206.   [3] *Ibid.* p. 270.

The two rolls of pleas for the two terms in 1206 which fell during the royal absence were a reversion to an earlier and commoner situation before Normandy was lost. The justiciar's part in proceedings seems rather more extensive because during that time original writs ran in his name and there was no other court sitting. Yet the extent of his activity was not enormously increased, and its nature was the same as it had been in the immediately preceding term. He adjourned suits, he ratified the appointment of attorneys, and he gave parties days for hearing.[1] When Henry of Sopworth came to Geoffrey fitz Peter at Berkhampstead on the Wednesday following the octave of St John the Baptist to make his excuse for non-appearance in a suit at Westminster he was doing only what other litigants had done while the king was still in England, and were to continue to do after he had returned.[2] This instance is only remarkable because the justices of the bench by common consent (*commune consilium*) refused to accept Henry's excuse because he had not observed the day he had been given and therefore his land was taken into the king's hand. The explanation is not that the justiciar's authority was challenged, but probably that Henry should have been at Westminster on the morrow of St John (and his opponent, in fact, appeared for the required four days at that time) and that he had not cast his essoin until a day later than the Wednesday after the octave of St John when it was accepted by Geoffrey fitz Peter at his own manor. And in another respect these two rolls are similar to the others. The justiciar's authority over the bench was not merely exercised in person but by messenger. In the Michaelmas term of 1204 Geoffrey fitz Peter informed the justices that the plea between the abbot of Walden and Ralph de Cheneduit which

[1] E.g. *Curia Regis Rolls*, pp. 151, 168, 184, 204, 206, 214, 225, 226, 280. Two cases were adjourned in the Trinity term *loquendum*, but this need not necessarily imply discussion with the justiciar; it might mean that the justices wished to talk it over among themselves; *ibid.* p. 161. In the following term, however, an assize involved the abbot of St Valéry, which had been ordered by the king to appear before him in the quindene of Michaelmas. John was abroad, so that the justices gave a day in the octave of Hilary following and *consulendum est dominus G. super eo.* The incident arose directly out of the king's absence, and it was one of the few that did so; *ibid.* p. 280.

[2] *Ibid.* p. 206.

was to have been before the king within the quindene of the next Hilary term should instead be heard by them at Westminster within the octave of Hilary on account of the other suits which the abbot had *coram rege*.[1] The justiciar was apparently relieving some of the pressure on the latter court; and he was himself in the king's company at the time.[2] His order to the justices was transmitted through Richard Duket. He employed the same messenger to notify them of the appointment of an attorney in the Easter term 1206.[3] At Michaelmas of the same year his messengers were Roger of Norwich and Richard of Barking.[4]

Richard Duket has been mentioned earlier; he was on the threshold of his career at this time, being called a royal clerk.[5] He later became a sheriff of Henry III and an active itinerant justice. Richard of Barking was probably the religious of that name who was a baron of the exchequer in 1242.[6] He was plainly connected then with the royal administration, but he was also an important ecclesiastic; in September 1223 he was promoted from prior to abbot of Westminster. Roger of Norwich is probably misnamed; unless this was a scribal error for Ralph of Norwich he is otherwise unknown. Ralph was described as a royal clerk in letters of safe conduct granted to him by John at the end of his reign when he was sent to Ireland, there to serve at the exchequer.[7] His work in England, too, was of a financial character in the early year of Henry III's reign, until he became one of the justices of the Jews and, on 29 April 1230, a justice of the bench, in which he sat until 1234. He, too, was a cleric, who held the churches of Acle and Brehull. At the time of his appearance as Geoffrey fitz Peter's messenger, if it is the same man, he was simply, like Richard Duket, a royal clerk. It was through these men that the justiciar exercised his presidency of the bench, alike in King John's presence in England or in his absence. In the former situation, Geoffrey's whereabouts can be checked against other evidence than his writs

---

[1] *Ibid.* III, 22.
[2] *Rot. Lit. Pat.* pp. 46*b*, 47*b*; *Rot. Chart.* pp. 138, 139*b*.
[3] *Curia Regis Rolls*, IV, 141.
[4] *Ibid.* pp. 226, 299.   [5] See above, p. 123.
[6] Foss, *op. cit.* p. 55.   [7] *Ibid.* p. 487

or other indications in the plea rolls; thus he was certainly away from Westminster in the Michaelmas term of 1204, the Hilary and Easter terms of 1205, the Trinity term of 1208, but in other terms he appeared in the king's company only when the royal retinue was present at Westminster or Lambeth.[1] In the latter case, when the king was abroad, there is little or no evidence for the justiciar's whereabouts. On 29 August 1206 he was at the Tower and he there received the king's order from beyond the sea to command the justices to adjourn a case.[2] Earlier in the same summer he had been at Berkhampstead when Henry of Sopworth made his abortive excuse for non-appearance at Westminster. Whether the king was in England or not seems to have made no very great difference to the scope or nature of his judicial work in the bench, although, since there was in the king's absence but one court sitting, the amount of business done in the bench at Westminster must have increased.[3] Geoffrey fitz Peter's position as president of the bench involved routine duties which can have altered but little, whatever the effect of royal absence upon his political position. To judge from the plea rolls there was not even a vast increase in his judicial work in the latter event. The change which came over the justiciar's position at the head of this court was not so much a direct consequence of the king's presence in England after the loss of Normandy as of the current political situation in England itself.

The bench was a branch of the *curia regis* which was distinct from both the exchequer and the court *coram rege*; it was a separate group of justices presided over by Geoffrey fitz Peter. It was not a personal court of the justiciar, nor is there any evidence that there was such a court built up around his person.[4] The justices who sat

[1] The terms in which he appeared in the king's train only when it was in Westminster or London were Michaelmas 1208, Michaelmas 1212 (with the exception of 30 October at Southwark and 3 November when he was at Windsor), Easter 1213. The gaps in his itinerary and his appearance only at Westminster when the king was there argue for his presence there throughout the legal term.

[2] *Curia Regis Rolls*, IV, 214.

[3] Flower, *op. cit.* p. 33, comments on the lack of any marked increase in the business before the bench while the king was away.

[4] *Pace* Sayles, *op. cit.* p. xxx n. 19.

at Westminster under his presidency were a stable group whose personnel, like that of the court *coram rege*, was constant. At the time when Normandy was lost the judges were Richard of Herriard, Eustace de Fauconberg, John of Guestling, Osbert fitz Harvey, Walter of Creeping and Godfrey de Insula. Richard's career came to an end shortly after the loss of Normandy; it has been described earlier. He was succeeded as the senior judge in the bench by Eustace de Fauconberg who remained in that position, taking precedence immediately after the justiciar, until the sittings of the bench came to an end in 1210. The remaining four justices constituted the rest of the personnel of the bench, three of them sitting there until the end of the court; the fourth had previously died. This last was Osbert fitz Harvey who was a long-standing official of the court administration; he had been a judge of the central royal court since the reign of Henry II.[1] He has been given an implausible if imaginative pedigree which made him a descendant of Robert duke of Orleans' younger son who came over with William the Conqueror.[2] Whatever his remote ancestry the reality of the late twelfth century was a little more modest. He held land of the count of Perche which was worth £241. 10s. per annum.[3] This was a valuable estate, but not in the class of the greater baronies. It was worth an oblation of 200 marks and two palfreys on the part of William of Huntingfield (Suffolk) to have the wardship of Osbert's heir and the right of marriage with custody of the land at Michaelmas 1206.[4] The heir was presumably

---

[1] According to Foss, *op. cit.* p. 259, citing Hunter's preface, from 1182. The earliest date I have discovered, however, is 1183, when he sat at Westminster with Richard, bishop of Winchester, Glanville and others, his name being last.

[2] Foss, *op. cit.*, quotes this pedigree and its distinguished members in the peerage as earls and marquises of Bristol. He himself admits that the early history of the family is obscure, and he draws the pedigree from *Brydges' Collins Peerage*, IV, 140.

[3] *Pipe Roll 9 John*, p. 113. Under the account of Robert Peverel *de blado et catallis et redditibus de quarta parte anni antequam terre ille traderentur Willelmo de Huntingfeld* the value of Osbert's land was £60. 7s. 6d. This was paid into the chamber by the king's writ.

[4] *Pipe Roll 8 John*, p. 33. He was pardoned £59 by writ of the king at Michaelmas 1206; *ibid.* p. 35.

Osbert's son by Margaret of Rye whom he had married in 1198.[1] Osbert was a landowner of some importance in Norfolk and Suffolk. His judicial career had begun when Glanville was justiciar and he continued to sit as a justice of the central court at Westminster throughout that of Richard I, gradually becoming a judge of greater precedence in court as time went by. On one occasion, on 28 October 1192, he was second to Geoffrey fitz Peter who was then presiding over the court at Westminster,[2] but more usually he occupied a prominent position after the great magnates who sat in court.[3] At the beginning of John's reign, therefore, he had added to his social status considerable experience as a judge of the court at Westminster, but he now took second place to justices like Richard of Herriard and Simon of Pattishall.[4] By the time Normandy was lost his precedence in court had declined in favour of John of Guestling;[5] and in 1206 he died. His later years, although he was still an active member of the bench, were probably a period at which old age tended to reduce the part he played and to offer an opportunity to more junior men. He had had an honourable career. He had been closely associated with the royal *curia*. In 1194, for example, he had accompanied King Richard I during his brief visit to England and had crossed the Channel with him to Normandy;[6] and in the king's entourage

---

[1] *Pipe Roll 10 Richard I*, p. 94. Under *Nova Oblata* in Norfolk and Suffolk through the justiciar Hubert Walter offered £20 *pro ducenda in uxorem Margaretam de Ria per gratiam domini R.* He paid the amount in full by the same Michaelmas (1198) and was quit. Foss, *op. cit.*, asserts that he married Dionysia daughter of Geoffrey de Grey, and died in April 1206 leaving an only son Adam. He does not quote any authority save the *Peerage* mentioned.

[2] Cotton MS Faustina A iv, fo. 49. The judges were Geoffrey fitz Peter, Osbert, Michael Belet, William son of Richard. It was probably a group of itinerant justices continuing the work of their eyre after they had returned to Westminster.

[3] *Feet of Fines Henry II and Richard I*, pp. 9–19; Add. MS 33354, fo. 103 v; Harl. MS 2110, fo. 108 v.

[4] CP 25(1) 127/2/5–8; 146/2/1, 3; 73/1/2, 6; Cotton MS Claudius D xiii, fo. 125 v; Nero C iii, fo. 197.

[5] CP 25(1) 127/6/2/4, 6, 11; 233/4/1, 2, 6; Cotton App. 21, fo. 18; Harl. MS 2100, fo. 108 v, 109.

[6] *Itinerary of Richard I*, pp. 88–90, 91, 93; *Cartae Antiquae*, p. 97 no. 196. On 10 April 1194 he was at Westminster, 16 April at St Swithun's, 20 April Winchester, 24 April Portsmouth, 22 May Tuboeuf. In each of these charters,

he had taken precedence over men of the calibre of Simon of Pattishall and Reginald of Cornhill who were struggling into prominence at court.[1] His career as a justice in eyre had followed an active course too, and even towards the end of his life his work continued. In 1198 he had been head of a party of justices in Norfolk and Suffolk, his home counties, but by Michaelmas 1199 he was third in a group which consisted also of Richard, archdeacon of Ely, and William de Warenne who imposed amercements in Northamptonshire, Cambridge and Huntingdonshire, Norfolk and Suffolk, and, with archdeacon Richard alone, he carried out the same duties in Rutland.[2] In the following year, with the justiciar, he heard pleas in Warwickshire and Leicestershire; and the archdeacon may have been a member of this party too.[3] This seems to have been almost the last itinerant judicial work that Osbert undertook; he was a member of the justiciar's group in the great eyres of 1202; but thereafter nothing. He continued to sit in bench at Westminster until Michaelmas 1205, and he may either have died in office or very shortly after his retirement, since William of Huntingfield was to pay the first instalment of his fine for Osbert's land at the Hilary term, 1206.[4]

Towards the end of his long career Osbert was overtaken by another justice who had come into prominence at the royal court considerably later than he had himself. This was John of Guestling, who took his name from the Sussex village. He was, however, not a Sussex but a Kentish landowner, or at least Kent was the centre of his lands, for it was in that county that he offered the king two palfreys in 1201 that he might be taken into the king's protection and his land guarded from all injury as if it were the

although other witnesses varied, he was with William de Warenne, whom he followed in the witness lists. In each charter a group of great magnates and bishops was present.

[1] In the charter given at Tuboeuf, for example, for the burgesses of Doncaster, the witnesses were Hubert Walter, the archdeacon of Hereford, William de Warenne, Osbert, Simon of Pattishall, Richard Barre and Simon of Kyme.

[2] *Pipe Roll 10 Richard I*, p. 86; *Pipe Roll 1 John*, pp. 13, 20, 157, 275.

[3] *Pipe Roll 2 John*, p. 181; *Pipe Roll 3 John*, p. 242. The account at the exchequer in the following year added the archdeacon of Ely.

[4] *Pipe Roll 8 John*, p. 33.

king's demesne; he was to be quit of suit of shire and hundred and the duty of castle ward so long as he lived; and he was not to be impleaded unless before the king or his chief justice so long as he lived.[1] The result of his fine, which he did not pay off until Michaelmas 1209,[2] was a royal charter containing all these provisions, issued by King John at Chinon on 24 August 1201.[3] Such a grant seems to denote royal favour, and when it was made John was already a justice of some experience. He was sitting in the central royal court at Westminster in 1197 as a colleague of Geoffrey fitz Peter, Stephen of Thornham, Simon of Pattishall, and James of Potterne who had been sitting as an eyre court at Bedford earlier in the year.[4] At first he was the junior member of the court; in 1199, for example, he followed Osbert fitz Harvey who had himself conceded precedence to Richard of Herriard and Simon of Pattishall.[5] By 1200 he was no longer the junior member, and by 1203 he preceded Osbert.[6] John sat in the bench at Westminster so long as the court existed, and after the senior justice, Eustace de Fauconberg, he was the next in precedence.[7] Like his colleagues he did a good deal of work as an itinerant justice contemporaneously with his position in the central court. In 1198 he had, under the leadership of Stephen of Thornham, with Reginald of Cornhill amerced the men of the Cinque Ports

---

[1] The progress of John's desire for this protection can be presented in some detail; on the roll of oblates (*Rot. de Oblatis* p. 176) an offering in Kent in 1201 by John of Guestling of two palfreys for having protection; at Michaelmas 1202 in the Kentish account under *De Prestitis, Pipe Roll 4 John*, p. 216) John of Guestling owed two palfreys *pro quadam protectione habenda*.

[2] *Pipe Roll 11 John*, p. 12. John accounted for two palfreys on the Kent roll. He had paid the treasury 10 marks for them; and he was quit.

[3] *Cartae Antiquae*, p. 88, no. 174.

[4] *Feet of Fines 9 Richard I*, pp. 1 ff., 65. The eyre took place in September and October. They sat at Bedford until 21 September, at Hertford until 4 October. On 22 November the group sat in Westminster.

[5] CP 25(1) 73/1/2, 6; 146/2/1, 3; Cotton MSS Faustina A iv, fo. 50v; Claudius D xiii, fo. 125v; Nero C iii, fo. 197.

[6] CP 25(1) 127/2/12, 13, 14, 15; 6/2, 4, 6, 11; 261/2/11, 13, 16; 7/13/20; Cotton MSS Claudius D xiii, fo. 131v; Caligula A xii, fo. 159; Harl. MS 2110, fo. 108v, 109, 212v; Cotton App. 21, fo. 18.

[7] CP 25(1) 233/5/1, 2, 5, 6, 8, 12–14; 146/3/37, 38; Cotton MSS Vespasian E xx, fo. 49v; Claudius D xii, fo. 110; Julius D ii, fo. 129.

for sending goods into Flanders.[1] In the following year, as the last member of the group except on those occasions when Richard of Fleming joined it, he had imposed amercements in Gloucester-shire, Shropshire, Worcestershire, and Oxfordshire. In 1202, with Richard of Herriard and Reginald of Cornhill he amerced Kent, and he was one of the group under Bishop John of Norwich which went north in the summer; four years later, with Reginald and William de Wrotham, he was on eyre in Sussex.[2] This work in 1206 seems to have been the last of his work in the counties, although he sat in the bench until its closure in 1210.

The two junior members of the bench were Walter of Creeping and Godfrey de Insula. Of the two Godfrey seems to have taken precedence, sometimes indeed over John of Guestling.[3] Perhaps the reason for this was Godfrey's clerical rank or legal knowledge, for he was often accorded the title of *magister*,[4] and most of his colleagues were laymen. He, too, began his judicial career at the end of Richard I's reign, and then sat regularly in the bench at least until 1205.[5] Very little can be discovered about him other than his judicial work. He may have come from the same county as Osbert because in 1198 he was a pledge of William son of Gererammi who owed 5 marks for having right against Robert Russel over a knight's fee in Norfolk and Suffolk; and his work in eyre seems to have been confined to imposing amercements with

---

[1] *Pipe Roll 10 Richard I*, p. 209.

[2] *Pipe Roll 1 John*, pp. 29, 77, 84, 226; *Pipe Roll 4 John*, p. 216; *Pipe Roll 8 John*, p. 62. During the great eyre of 1202 he visited Nottingham, Doncaster, York, Carlisle, Newcastle, Appleby, Lancaster and Richmond between June and November. In 1206 they sat at London, Stratford, Colchester, Canterbury amongst other places.

[3] CP 25(1) 127/6/9; 233/4/7; 73/2/37; 261/8/2.

[4] In 1198, when he stood as pledge of a debt he was called Master Godfrey; *Pipe Roll 10 Richard I*, p. 94; and in 1203 when Richard of Herriard, Master Godfrey, Eustace de Fauconberg, and Walter of Creeping, justices, came before the barons of the exchequer to record a judgement of their court; *Pipe Roll 5 John*, p. 12.

[5] Foss, *op. cit.* p. 367, states that he sat as judge from 10 Richard I to 10 John and was also mentioned in 13 John. I have not found him among the judges at Westminster after Easter 1205; CP 25(1) 233/4/17; 261/8/2; but he, with Adam de Port and Simon of Pattishall, was on eyre at York at Michaelmas 1208; 261/9/34–6 and *passim*.

Reginald of Cornhill in the same counties in 1202.[1] This absence of any marked itinerant activity suggests that he may have been joined to the bench as an ecclesiastic whose knowledge of canon law was useful; but this is conjectural. His colleague Walter of Creeping took his name from the Essex village, and he seems to have had close connexions with that county; in 1198 he accounted for the farm of Colchester, and he had imposed the tallage there in 1196.[2] In 1209 he owed 100 shillings under *oblata* from Essex for having the king's goodwill.[3] He was a justice in the bench at least from 1200 and remained a member of the court to the end,[4] as did John of Guestling. As an itinerant justice he imposed the tallage on Southwark with Geoffrey fitz Peter in 1205. In the following year, at the head of a group including Henry de Vere, he imposed amercements in Gloucestershire and the *honor* of Gloucester, Herefordshire and Berkshire, in the latter county also assessing the tallage. He was head of a group which amerced and tallaged Worcestershire and was a member of another group headed by James of Potterne which imposed amercements in the shires of Cambridge and Huntingdon.[5] After this circuit in 1206, he did little more work in eyre.[6]

[1] *Pipe Roll 10 Richard I*, p. 94; *Pipe Roll 5 John*, p. 244. The account under Norfolk and Suffolk obscures the fact that they sat at Cambridge in June 1202, Chelmsford in September, as well as at Norwich (July) and Ipswich (August). Godfrey may have been head of the party which included Reginald Walter of Creeping and Reginald de Argentan.

[2] *Pipe Roll 10 Richard I*, p. 133; Foss, *op. cit.* p. 201, states that he imposed the tallage in 1186; this should be 1196.

[3] *Pipe Roll 11 John*, p. 194.

[4] CP25 (1) 127/2/12, 13; 73/1/37; and *passim*. Cotton MSS, Caligula A xii, fo. 159; Julius D ii, fo. 129. In 1209 on 24 June he was the last justice in court with the king at Tewkesbury.

[5] *Pipe Roll 7 John*, p. 154; *Pipe Roll 8 John*, pp. 14, 20, 67, 163, 212, 224.

[6] So far as the accounts of amercements go, he did none, but a copy of a final concord in a cartulary of the priory of Castle Acre made at Norwich on 18 January 1209 shows that he was a member of a group of justices headed by William of Huntingfield, Eustace de Fauconberg, James of Potterne, Walter of Creeping, Robert de Aumar and William de Furnell; Harl. MS 2110, fo. 109r. It may be, since there is a singular lack of corroborative evidence, that the monastic scribe has misdated the document; or more likely that Walter was not named in the account William and Eustace presented (for an example of a similar event see note 1, above).

Upon this staff of experienced justices the bench depended for its effectiveness. Whether Geoffrey fitz Peter presided over their work in person or not, they looked to him as their head, the source from which they drew their authority in difficult or politically important cases. A good many, perhaps most, of their consultations with the justiciar were on points of administration, technical details of procedure. Thus, for example, in the Michaelmas term 1206, the assize between Amalric Bataill and the abbot of St Valéry was placed in respite until the octave of St Hilary since the king had ordered that it should be before him in the quindene of Michaelmas. John was abroad at the time, and therefore the justices wished to consult Geoffrey fitz Peter about their procedure unless the king should meanwhile have come back to England.[1] The doubt arose not as to what the law was, but as to the proper procedure. Or, again, in the Trinity term of 1208 when the abbot of Pipewell sought the advowson of a church against Hamo of Beedon who called Alice Clement to warrant his statement,[2] the bench decided that she must produce warranty for her statement and they would consult the justiciar. The reason for discussion was not a rule of law but a factual point in dispute. Occasionally the difficulty was more concerned with legal precedents and a case in this same term shows the justices appealing to Geoffrey's knowledge of the law in the hard case of bastardy and villeinage that has been quoted earlier in which the justices wished to discuss the complications with Geoffrey fitz Peter, because bastardy and villeinage raised difficult points of law and precedent.[3] That consultation should more often concern administrative details rather than rules of law was perhaps inevitable in the context of contemporary society. The law was in theory unchanging because it was feudal custom: 'the good customs of our fathers' and our grandfathers' day'. This feature of society, which produced the later claim of the baronage that they did not wish the laws of England to change, set a premium on long judicial experience and knowledge of what had been done in the past, of what, in fact, the

---

[1] *Curia Regis Rolls*, IV, 280.
[2] *Ibid.* V, 293.
[3] *Ibid.* p. 299.

precedents were. In these circumstances much was certain, but where there was doubt the justiciar, having had longer experience at a higher level than his colleagues in the bench, was an obviously important source of knowledge to which they could turn. In his absence from the bench, the nearest equivalent to his experience, although not to his political and social importance, was that of Richard of Herriard. In the court *coram rege* the senior justice was Simon of Pattishall who occupied a place at the head of the justices which matched that of Geoffrey fitz Peter in the bench. The king himself could not be expected to have the detailed and increasingly professional knowledge of his ministers, although his interest in their work was obviously great. When the bench came to an end in 1210 the justiciar did not pass to a similar position in respect of the court *coram rege*; there could hardly, indeed, have been any necessity for such a transference, because his experience and knowledge could then have been little, if at all, greater than that of Simon of Pattishall, and his presence, real or fictitious, could not have enhanced the prestige or competence of a court over which the king himself presided.

From 1210 the bench at Westminster ceased to sit; its pleadings, as Sir Cyril Flower has said, came to an end with a jejune record of only three membranes on which most of the cases were reserved for the attention of the king. The pleas of the Crown should not be held at Westminster.[1] The reasons for the disappearance of the bench are obscure. Most probably political circumstances were largely responsible, and the personality of a king who was increasingly suspicious of independent action; it was, as it were, a general application of the principle which Simon of Pattishall had already been penalized for infringing, and the autumnal justices of 1210 also suffered. With the termination of the sittings of the bench at Westminster, Geoffrey fitz Peter's name vanished from final concords. In the Trinity term 11 John, he was sitting with the king, Simon, Henry de Pontaudemer, and Richard de Mucegros at Lewes and Porchester,[2] but even by that time the court over

---

[1] Flower, *op. cit.* p. 33.
[2] CP 25(1) 261/12/7, 12. Another concord at Lewes on the same day omitted the justiciar's name; *ibid.* 13.

which he had presided at Westminster in the previous term bore
an unfamiliar look, for, with the exception of John of Guestling,
the justices were all well-known financial officers: William de
Aubeney, William of Ely the treasurer, William archdeacon of
Taunton, William of Cornhill archdeacon of Huntingdon,
Robert Mauduit in whose family the chamberlainship of the
exchequer was hereditary, and Benedict of Ramsey.[1] When the
eyres went round in 1210, they too were composed of unfamiliar
men;[2] the bench had ceased to sit; and Geoffrey fitz Peter's name
had disappeared from the court records. The justiciar's work in
eyre had, in any case, been slight since the loss of Normandy.
With the exception of some final concords which may possibly
have been made before him at Clarendon in 1205,[3] he seems never
to have joined an *iter*. In the months of July, August, and September, when the eyres usually took place, Geoffrey fitz Peter was
often with the king, and since the latter was travelling round his
realm, the justiciar, in that sense, was on circuit. The limited
nature of his judicial work in respect of the king's court has been
pointed out; and his presence in final concords made before the
court *coram rege* was the exception, not the rule. The loss of
Normandy had already reduced the independent activity of the
justiciar so far as his direction of judicial work in eyre was concerned. Where formerly he had taken a prominent part in its
administration, sometimes at the head of a party of justices, since
1204 he had done little or nothing, and if the justices of 1210 were
sent out by his order, they were not carefully supervised by him.[4]
When he travelled about England it was in the king's company.
Thus it is peculiarly in respect of the bench that the break in his
judicial activity is apparent. When it ceased to sit, his judicial
work, to all appearances, came to an end until the last year of his
life. In the Michaelmas term 1212 Geoffrey fitz Peter presided
over a court at Westminster composed of Richard Marsh,
William Briewerre, Simon, James of Potterne, and Roger

---

[1] 261/9/27, 29.

[2] *Pipe Roll 13 John*, pp. xxxiv–xxxvi.

[3] Hunter, *op. cit.* I, liv. There is no evidence that the king was there at the
time.

[4] *Pipe Roll 13 John*, p. xxxv.

Huscarl.[1] The difference between this court and the earlier bench is obvious at a glance. Geoffrey was accompanied not by its former staff of justices, but by a chancery official and one of the king's intimate counsellors, and the justices of the court *coram rege*. Earlier in the same term King John himself had sat at Westminster with Simon, James, and Roger; in the following term the court at Westminster was also composed of the king sitting with these justices and Geoffrey fitz Peter.[2] It seems clear that with the cessation of activity in the bench at Westminster, Geoffrey fitz Peter's judicial position was considerably curtailed, and when he resumed his place at the head of a court in 1212, it was that normally presided over by the king; and associated with the justiciar were two of the king's confidential and intimate ministers who were to occupy a similar position of power in respect of Geoffrey fitz Peter's successor, Peter des Roches. In any normal judicial sense, Geoffrey's duties came to an end with those of the bench.

The facts, or such of them as can now be observed, are evident enough; interpretation and explanation of them is more difficult. It is unlikely that Matthew Paris was precisely right in the words which he put into John's mouth on his justiciar's death.[3] There is no evidence that Geoffrey fitz Peter served the king other than loyally, and no indication that he ever initiated, or attempted to initiate, a policy which fettered John's freedom of action if, indeed, such a concept was possible to a man of his day and tradition. This is not, however, to rule out the possibility that behind the story of Wendover there lies the fact that John's relations with Geoffrey may have been bad. The *Histoire des ducs de Normandie*, generally a reliable authority, describes a quarrel between John and his justiciar which must have taken place before the summer

---

[1] CP 25(1) 146/4/58, 62. The occasion was probably one on which the king had other claims upon his attention. Within the month of Michaelmas he sat with the justices *coram rege* without the justiciar, William Briewerre or Richard Marsh, *ibid.* 59; but later in the term, in the octave and quindene of St Martin, the court was composed of the justiciar and his colleagues.

[2] *Ibid.* 57.

[3] Matthew Paris, II, 559. For the reliability of Paris and his predecessor Wendover on details of this kind see Galbraith, *Roger of Wendover and Matthew Paris*.

of 1212 and probably earlier; it asserts that Geoffrey had to pay a large fine to regain the king's goodwill.[1] The story is given substance by the undoubted fact of John's bad relations with Robert fitz Walter, to whose daughters both of Geoffrey fitz Peter's sons were married, and his equally bad relations with Humphrey de Bohun, who had married Geoffrey fitz Peter's daughter.[2] In April 1212 King John supported his half-brother, William of Salisbury, in the latter's claim to Humphrey's chief fief of Trowbridge, and on the very same day as this plea was instituted, Geoffrey de Say claimed the Mandeville barony against the justiciar.[3] Whatever John's motives in allowing these claims to be pressed in his court, whether or not he was conducting a campaign of intimidation against Geoffrey fitz Peter and his relations, it is a reasonable assumption that their relationship must have been strained. It is possible that political motives and administrative development intersected and produced this reduction of the justiciar's field of activity. After his disappearance from judicial work in 1210, Geoffrey, when he was required to resume his position at the head of the court, was accompanied by two associates who were the king's trusted officials. To assume that politics alone lay behind these features would be rash. If the king really intended to curb or control the justiciar, one might suppose that after his judicial functions had slipped into abeyance they would not be revived at all unless there was a pressing need, for which there is little evidence. One might further suppose that if John elected to control the justiciar, whom necessity had recalled to his former position, by joining colleagues to him, he might have chosen his even more intimate counsellors: Peter des Roches, for example, whom he was to create justiciar on Geoffrey's death. When Peter did become justiciar, these same two men, Richard Marsh and William Briewerre, were associated with him, and since no suggestion of a breach with the king has ever been made in his case, it seems that the association of colleagues with the justiciar must have been primarily an administrative device.

[1] *Histoire des ducs de Normandie*, p. 116.
[2] For details of these squabbles see Painter, *King John*, pp. 260 ff.
[3] *Curia Regis Rolls*, VI, 270.

And if this is so, it is but one more indication that the growth of administrative machinery was rendering control by one man like the justiciar difficult or impossible. Geoffrey's disappearance from judicial duties after 1210 can be explained by the king's own presence in, or at least control of, the court that accompanied him; his resumption of them in 1212, in company with his two colleagues, may be a consequence of some other demand upon the king's attention. If the events of 1210 are taken to mark the eclipse of the justiciarship until necessity revived it, it would be necessary to show that Geoffrey fitz Peter's functions in other branches of government also lapsed; and this would be difficult to do, since his work went on at the exchequer.

4. THE JUSTICIAR AND THE EXCHEQUER

The loss of Normandy coincided with reform at the exchequer, for, like the courts of law, that organization was attempting to solve the problems created by the increased volume of business consequent upon the legal reforms of Henry II, and the king's urgent need for money. The reforms which took place under John were designed to relieve the congestion caused by the vast number of small debts owed by way of amercement or fine and accounted for individually with a separate tally for each.[1] The device evolved to cope with this difficulty was the *tallia dividenda*, the grouping of entries together and the employment of one tally for them all. This measure affected the lower exchequer of receipt rather than the upper, except in so far as the calculation on the chequered board was involved. It was a reform at a technical level, and has little bearing on the justiciarship. The other major attempt to alter exchequer tradition was, from this point of view, more important, for it involved Geoffrey fitz Peter and it had political overtones which affected the problems which the barons of the exchequer were called upon to decide and which ultimately played a part in the struggle between the king and his barons. For King John attempted to tap the considerable profits which a

[1] Mills, 'Experiments in Exchequer Procedure 1200–32', *TRHS*, 4th series, VIII, 153 ff.

sheriff might make after he had rendered account of the old fixed farm of his county. The idea was not new; it had occurred to Richard I or his ministers, but it was in John's reign that a systematic and determined attempt was made to reap for royal administration the benefits of increased land values and higher prices.

Geoffrey fitz Peter, as justiciar and president of the exchequer, was naturally caught up in this change. When Normandy fell, he held a group of shires under his control. When he relinquished them, he was succeeded by custodians, appointed, unlike the sheriff, to render account of all their profits and not merely of the farm of the shire. The reorganization therefore proceeded in something of the same manner as the reforms of 1232, when Peter des Rievaulx concentrated the shrievalties in his hands. Geoffrey fitz Peter's part was not so extensive in a reform which was itself only partial;[1] he held only a few shires; he was only one of the king's agents in the transference of counties; and after the reallocation of the shires he served neither as sheriff in those counties where the office remained nor as custodian in the others. Geoffrey's place in the reform may, in fact, have been only nominal; he had accounted for his counties by deputy, not in person. The limited part he played is probably a reflexion of the justiciar's changing position in financial administration; it is a marked contrast to the concentration of shires which Peter des Rievaulx held in 1232. Before Normandy fell, the justiciar had been represented at the exchequer session by Geoffrey of Buckland.[2] This may have been and probably was exceptional because of the burden of work falling on the justiciar during a royal absence. After the loss of Normandy and with the king's continual presence in England, these viceregal duties would, of course, be lighter or even non-existent. Relieved of them, Geoffrey could devote more time to the routine of administration, could resume something at least of the duties which traditionally fell to his office as president of the exchequer. Nevertheless, the increase of business in the bench and the time

---

[1] At Michaelmas 1204, sixteen shires were held by custodians. In ten of them there were two *custodes* jointly responsible. In four more shires the sheriffs accounted for their profits. By 1208 this attempt had broken down on this large scale, although it continued in attenuated form.

[2] See above, pp. 122–3.

taken up by his attendance upon the itinerant king must have offset the diminution of viceregal functions.

How constant Geoffrey fitz Peter's presidency of the exchequer was in these years it is difficult to know, since the pipe rolls wear the effective cloak of formality and the memoranda rolls do not survive in a series. In 1199 Geoffrey was not always present at the exchequer but, because he was regent, his authority was invoked and difficult cases waited upon his will. In 1208 King John was in England, and it was his authority which was cited by the barons of the exchequer. *Loquendum cum rege*; this was the annotation when the barons wished to know what they should do about 50 marks exacted from the abbot of St Edmund's for having an inquisition about the market held by the monks of Ely, or the debt owed by a man for having a writ of *mort d'ancestor* or the default in payment of the farm of certain mines; and they postponed a *loquela* between the Hospitallers of Jerusalem and Philip of Oldcoates until the quindene of St John the Baptist to be *coram Rege si venerit*.[1] Nevertheless, certain features of the justiciar's authority were exhibited. Geoffrey fitz Peter was to be consulted about £40 *qui locantur super Rob(ertum) fil (ium) Ernisi quas Eudon fil(ius) Patricii tenet in Meudon*. Eudo was given respite until the quindene of Easter. The king or the justiciar was to be consulted whether T. de Nevill was the farmer or the custodian of certain land in 3 John.[2] The implication behind the second of these entries is that the justiciar's authority to make a statement from his personal knowledge would be accepted in precisely the same way as the king's; and in the first the motive for consulting Geoffrey fitz Peter was plainly that he held the lands of Robert son of Ernis as his share in the lands of the Normans.[3] In neither case were the barons seeking direction as to procedure or a rule of the exchequer, but simply asking for information which the justiciar could conveniently supply. It is probable that the justiciar's authority still controlled the barons' actions; he had, for example, given terms to Solomon de Milcstret who owed tallage; and he recognized that he held the land of Henry de Mara in custody through

---

[1] *Memoranda Roll 10 John*, pp. 35, 58.   [2] *Ibid.* p. 52.
[3] See above, pp. 104-5.

the king.[1] More obvious expression of his authority appears from writs which still ran in his name although the king was in England. We have seen that this was so in judicial administration, and it appears to be true of exchequer procedure. Three writs of Geoffrey fitz Peter were quoted on the fragmentary roll of 1208.[2] He told the barons that 7 marks of a debt of 10 had been pardoned which Henry of the Weald owed for being in mercy; he asked the barons to place in respite 50 marks which were exacted from the vintners of London; he gave William the treasurer and the barons directions about the executors of the will of Peter of Stoke. The last two writs were issued *teste meipso* on 21 and 24 June respectively, and they might conceivably, although not probably, be relics from the last royal absence of 1206; it is unlikely, nevertheless, that in current matters of this kind there would be a time lag of two years. The third writ was almost certainly issued while the king was in England; its date was 27 February, and the last time the king was abroad on that day was 1203, five years before;[3] the business dealt with by the writ could hardly have waited five years for attention. The presumption must be that Geoffrey fitz Peter still issued writs in his own name in 1208 which guided the actions of the barons of the exchequer,[4] that his office was still, therefore, a great convenience for efficient administration.

He himself may not have presided regularly at the exchequer. That one of his writs greeted William, the treasurer, and the barons suggests that William was treated as their head and professional president.[1] There is no reliable evidence that the justiciar

---

[1] *Memoranda Roll 10 John*, pp. 28, 65.   [2] *Ibid.* pp. 38, 39.

[3] *Handbook of British Chronology*, p. 36.

[4] If this is so, then many of the writs of the justiciar cited in the Pipe Roll of 1208 may also have been issued while John was in England, and so, too, in the succeeding year. For example, the ship taking the king's treasure to Poitou which was conducted by the bishop of Winchester, or the expenses of the countess of Gloucester, John's divorced wife, or the repairs to the Tower; *Pipe Roll 10 John*, pp. 103, 166, 171. These writs are fewer in number than in years when John was abroad, naturally enough, but if once the assumption that they are relics from 1206 or earlier be abandoned, then they show the range of the justiciar's duties and authority while the king was in England; and this proves to have been narrower in scope, but not essentially different in kind. His writs authorized the expenses of royal servants and the upkeep of royal property.

was present at the barons' deliberations in 1208, and on the Wednesday before the feast of St Margaret the great ministers singled out by name were Peter des Roches and Williem Briewerre who had a special agreement with the king to make his services available at the exchequer.[2] In this year Geoffrey fitz Peter was in Westminster with the king in the late October, but by early November they had left for Clarendon.[3] In July, when Peter and William sat at the exchequer, the justiciar was with the king at Worcester and Bechel.[4] His connexion with the exchequer was still, however, close even if he did not sit there regularly. At Hilary 1208 he presided over a court at Westminster composed of prominent financial officials;[5] and when the king was in Ireland in 1210, the justiciar issued letters patent in favour of Reading Abbey stating that he, sitting with Peter des Roches and the barons of the exchequer, had heard read the charters of the abbey on 3 August.[6] And if the court of justices over which he presided was in abeyance, there was nothing in the pressure of administrative work to distract his attention from the exchequer and its deliberations. There is no evidence that the justiciar sat with the barons from 1210 to 1212, because of the disappearance of records for those years.[7] In 1213 he was sitting there when the king sent the messengers from Bishop John of Norwich, the justiciar of Ireland, to the justiciar, Earl Saher of Winchester, William Briewerre, and Richard Marsh, who were then sitting at the exchequer.[8] Moreover, criminal matters were there dealt with. William Moyn, an alleged murderer, was to appear before Geoffrey fitz Peter and the barons on the Sunday after St Luke; Robert the butler who had castrated his wife's lover had his lands seized into the king's hands, and the sheriff was to report the

---

[1] This is confirmed by the letters issued by William the treasurer, William, archdeacon of Huntingdon, and the barons to the justices itinerant in Berkshire, which gave the barons' opinions on the abbey's forinsec hundred. It suggests that William was the departmental head unless reinforced by those who sat there at the king's command, or on occasion; Egerton MS 3031, fo. 29.

[2] *Memoranda Roll 10 John*, p. 64. The Wednesday before St Margaret was either 2 or 16 July in 1208.

[3] *Rot. Lit. Pat.* p. 87.

[4] *Ibid.* p. 85.

[5] CP 25 (1) 73/3/60, 261/9/27.

[6] Egerton MS 3031, fo. 29.

[7] The chancery enrolment is missing.

[8] *Rot. Lit. Claus.* I, 132.

matter to the justiciar and the barons. The sheriff of Kent, similarly, was ordered to let the justiciar and the barons know on what occasion he had taken Adam of Westminster, Sybil his wife, and their son.[1] Plainly the exchequer was exercising a criminal jurisdiction; probably, as a consequence of political circumstances which seem to have inclined the king to reduce the areas of independent administrative activity, one omni-competent court had been established at Westminster. This view is borne out by the fact that at Martinmas 1212, after the king had left Westminster, the justices *coram rege* were afforced by the justiciar, William Briewerre, and Richard Marsh who were barons of the exchequer;[2] and it was recorded in the plea roll of the justices that Robert de Lake, who had cast an essoin *de malo veniendi* and who was now ready to appear, should come to court on the Sunday after the octave of Martinmas 1213 before the barons of the exchequer.[3] Geoffrey fitz Peter had just died when that case came into court, but it seems as if the wheel had come full circle, that in the last year of his life, for political reasons or administrative convenience, an omni-competent court had been revived at Westminster under his presidency. When the bench, the court *coram rege*, and the exchequer had seemed on the way to 'departmentalization', the disappearance of the former and the absence of the king from Westminster, leaving behind him his justices, had thrown the centre of administrative gravity temporarily back to the exchequer under its traditional president the justiciar.

[1] *Ibid.* I, 125, 126, 127. The Sunday after St Luke was 21 October. This writ was attested by Geoffrey fitz Peter at Westminster on 12 October.
[2] CP 25 (1) 146/4/58, 60, 62.
[3] *Curia Regis Rolls*, VII, 33.

CHAPTER VI

THE JUSTICIARSHIP IN
JOHN'S LAST YEARS

The death of Geoffrey fitz Peter in October 1213 marks another turning point in the reign of King John. Probably his death had little effect upon the king's relations with his barons. Geoffrey, it is true, was a great magnate, and it might have been expected that by holding the highest office within the royal administration he would have bridged the widening gulf between the king and other members of his own class and, that when he died, other magnates would have less confidence in royal government than they had while a great baron was at its head. Such a view is too superficial. The king's opponents among the baronage were only a section of it, and in many cases their relations with the king had been bad long before Geoffrey's death.[1] The barons were not united as a class, they were divided among themselves, and it is unlikely that the character of the justiciar could have reconciled them either to each other or to the king. If William Marshal and his son found themselves on different sides there is no reason to believe that Geoffrey fitz Peter could have persuaded men with whom he had no such ties of blood. The judgement that his death removed one of the last links between king and baronage really rests upon too high an assessment of the justiciar's influence, which in turn depends primarily upon Wendover's account of John's reaction to Geoffrey's death.[2] Wendover, however, is no reliable authority; there is no corroborative evidence that Geoffrey influenced or controlled policy against the king's will, and a good deal of information which shows that he was a loyal servant. Moreover, if relations between the justiciar and the king were

[1] For the relations of King John with his barons see Painter, *King John*, pp. 17-55.
[2] Wendover, II, 91; *per Pedes Domini nunc primo sum rex et dominus Anglie* was John's exclamation according to Matthew Paris. He was alleged to have made a similar remark upon the death of Hubert Walter. For the reliability of the St Albans account see Galbraith, *Roger Wendover and Matthew Paris*.

strained for two years or so before his death, then his influence must have been even less than it would normally have been. Royal administration, in fact, had passed the point where the influence of any one minister could dominate all its manifestations, and the branches which the justiciar actually controlled had already 'gone out of court' or were well advanced in that direction. The king's familiars were household officials or barons who were peculiarly intimate with him; and one of the chief of them was Peter des Roches, bishop of Winchester.

I. PETER DES ROCHES

Peter was a man whose training and experience in royal administration lay within the household. He was a familiar of King John as Geoffrey fitz Peter had never been. There is some *a priori* reason, therefore, for believing that if Geoffrey's death had little effect upon the political situation, it may have had considerable consequences for the justiciarship. Every justiciar, except during the first few years of Richard I, had been a trained judge and an experienced financial official; he had sat in the *curia regis* at Westminster; he had been a baron of the exchequer. Peter deviated from this pattern. He had not been trained as a judge, and he was not, as his immediate predecessors had been, in the tradition of Glanville. Although he was well acquainted with the exchequer, it was in fact the household financial department, the chamber, that had claimed most of his attention. Whatever Peter's considerable abilities, they had not been exercised in the same way as had those of Hubert Walter or Geoffrey fitz Peter.

Peter des Roches was probably a relative of William des Roches, the seneschal of Anjou, and he was apparently a knight learned in warlike matters before he took orders and became a royal clerk.[1] His military reputation survived, for he played a distinguished part in the Fair of Lincoln and was employed by the pope in his struggles with the Roman citizens. The path of service in the royal administration was a more certain way to distinction, for its

---

[1] Wendover, II, 9; *vir equestris ordinis et in rebus bellicosis eruditus.* In John's first year he was described as *clericus noster; Rot. Chart.* p. 10.

rewards were greater and more sure. William Marshal, the landless knight who fought his way to fame, is an exceptional figure in the ranks of the greater baronage, but there were many, like Becket or half a dozen other great curial bishops, who reached their eminence through faithful service as loyal clerks. The *cursus honorum* for Peter meant a steady advance. By 1199 he was prior of Loches in Touraine and treasurer of the famous church of Poitiers. In England he became precentor of Lincoln.[1] He was one of John's most trusted financial officers and he served under Hubert de Burgh, the household chamberlain, until, on the latter's disappearance, he discharged the duties of that office without its title.[2] It has been said that it is very likely that John did not want a permanent chamberlain because of the confidential business which was transacted through the chamber, but this seems to rest upon a confusion between the exchequer offices of that name and their counterpart in the household.[3] Since Hubert de Burgh, another familiar of John, held the latter office, and was succeeded by Peter des Roches in effect if not in name, it is unlikely that confidential business was the reason for the disappearance of the title; and the motive must remain obscure. The business which Peter transacted may have been largely confidential—with Alan Trenchmer he was responsible for ordering as many horses for the king to be shipped across the Channel as he thought fit[4]—but in as far as it appears in the rolls, it was mostly routine. Throughout 1200 he was one of those officials of the chamber who provided the warranty for money paid into the chamber and so diverted from the exchequer to the household. Thus when Henry del Pussac paid 30 silver marks into the chamber at Les Andelys in part payment of his fine of 200 marks which he had offered to the king in the course of the dispute he had with the bishop of Durham, the writ of *computate* which was sent to the barons of the exchequer to clear Henry of this payment was witnessed by the

---

[1] *Rot. Chart.* p. 34; *Rot. Lit. Pat.* p. 1; Foss, *op. cit.* p. 572; Painter, *op. cit.* p. 62.

[2] Painter, *op. cit.* p. 86.

[3] *Ibid.* p. 87; Tout, *Chapters*, I, 159, seems to make the same error.

[4] *Memoranda Roll I John*, p. 91. The order addressed to the bailiffs of Shoreham, is contained in a fragment of a liberate roll for 1200–1.

justiciar at Malmesbury *per Petrum de Rupibus.*[1] Peter travelled with the king round England as the court moved from place to place, taking care of similar transactions. In October and November 1200 he was at Malmesbury, Clipstone, and Stamford.[2] His responsibility for notifying payments made into the chamber to the barons of the exchequer was shared with other officials, for example Peter of Stoke,[3] but it did not exhaust his duties. When the king told the justiciar of Ireland that Geoffrey Marsh was to have 20 silver marks *ad firmandum domum suum de Katherain* the warranty for the issue of the order was Peter des Roches.[4] In 1201 a group of men complained to the king that fees they should have received at the exchequer were in arrears; John thereupon ordered the justiciar to ensure payment in each of these cases, and Peter des Roches, styled treasurer of Poitou, authorized the issue of the necessary writs.[5] The court was abroad, which perhaps explains the use of Peter's continental title, for he was at the time accompanying the court on its foreign travels. As a household official this was part of his normal duties. Orders for payment from the treasury of royal expenses, for the payment of royal servants and messengers, were also issued over Peter's warranty, and these duties continually devolved upon him.[6] His importance must have grown in these early years of the reign. In 1204 William Briewerre offered the king £800 for having the land and heir of Fulbert of Dover, the debt to be paid in instalments of £50 at each succeeding exchequer session. The fine was made before William, earl of Salisbury, the king's brother, William de Braiose, Roger de Toeny, Reginald of Cornhill, Hugh de Wells, and Peter, treasurer of Poitou.[7] His colleagues were all important people: three great barons, two prominent ministers of the king; and Peter's inclusion in the group is significant. In 1202 he had been one of those sent to negotiate a truce with the king of France.[8] Three years later he was custodian of the lands of the countess of Perche in England, and custodian of the vacant

[1] *Rot. de Liberate*, p. 7. [2] *Ibid.* pp. 7, 10, 11.
[3] *Ibid. passim.* [4] *Ibid.* p. 10.
[5] *Ibid.* pp. 16–17. [6] *Ibid.* 78, 79, 85, 87, 95, 97.
[7] *Rot. de Finibus*, p. 229. [8] *DNB*, under Peter.

bishoprics of Chichester and Winchester.[1] His importance and his relations with the king may be judged from his election, by an unwilling chapter under royal pressure, to the latter see in 1205. He was, wrote the Waverley annalist, a king's clerk and a familiar of John through whom he was elected.[2] The Winchester annals are discreetly silent.

Peter, however, was not the sole elected candidate. Richard, dean of Salisbury, had also been elected by the chapter, and the consequence was a journey to Rome. There Peter was consecrated by Pope Innocent himself through the influence of Bishop Savaric of Bath with senators and cardinals in one story, through the aid of much money collected from the church of Winchester in Wendover's account.[3] Both factors may have played their part, but it is at least as likely that Innocent III desired to be on good terms with John, and also that Peter was a skilful diplomat. The pope's confidence in him was demonstrated by his commission of the mandate to collect Peter's pence in England, and, perhaps more significant, by a papal letter exempting Bishop Peter from excommunication except by the pope himself.[4] The new bishop of Winchester returned to England in the spring of 1206, and on Palm Sunday he was solemnly received into the church of Winchester and enthroned.[5] By his elevation he had become a great baron and holder of one of the most important and wealthy bishoprics. He was to discover for himself the difficulties in his position as John's intimate and as churchman which other famous men had experienced.

Even while he was in Rome he had been caught up in the beginnings of the great controversy over the Canterbury election. In December 1205 there had arrived at the papal *curia* the agent of

---

[1] *DNB* under Peter.

[2] *Annales Monastici*, II, 257. According to Wendover Peter set out for Rome after his election, where with much money collected from the church of Winchester he was consecrated bishop; Wendover, II, 9.

[3] The supporters of the dean of Salisbury were treated harshly by John, suffering imprisonment and exile; Migne, *Patrologia*, CCXV, 562–3, 671–3, 792–3. Richard Poor, the dean, was illegitimate; Coggeshall, p. 162; Wendover, II, 9.

[4] Migne, *ibid.* 754–5; Lunt, *Papal Revenues in the Middle Ages*, II, 65.

[5] *Annales Monastici*, II, 79.

the bishops who were claiming a voice in the election of the archbishop against the claim of the monks of Christchurch to make the election. Unfortunately, the bishops' proctor had lost his credentials on the way, but Peter was able to confirm them.[1] As bishop of Winchester the struggle, as it developed, naturally affected him closely; as a churchman owing loyalty and obedience to the pope, as a baron and royal minister, a familiar and intimate of the king, his position could hardly fail to be at least as uncomfortable as that of the colleagues of Becket in an earlier time. Gilbert Foliot, for example, had been impaled on the horns of a dilemma, torn between his obligations to the king and his acceptance of Gregorian principles of church government.[2] Peter seems to have been made of sterner stuff, for he stood by King John, and with John de Grey, bishop of Norwich, received back from the king on 5 April 1208 the church lands which had been seized into the royal hand; and in Peter's case there was added a charter of the liberties of the bishopric confirmed by the king.[3] His position must, nevertheless, have been uncomfortable,[4] and it is therefore not surprising to find Peter among those who, led by the justiciar, urged upon John the necessity of making peace before he was excommunicated. John reopened negotiations, but they came to nothing. A new attempt was made in July 1209 when the king wrote to the papal agents that by the counsel of Geoffrey fitz Peter, the bishops of Winchester and Bath, and the elect of Lincoln, he had decided to satisfy the church, and a meeting took place at Dover.[5] When Stephen Langton himself arrived, the justiciar and Bishop Peter negotiated with him, but again no agreement was reached. And thus it was that at the end of 1209 Peter was the only bishop left in England, John of Norwich having been sent to Ireland as justiciar.

[1] Migne, *ibid.* pp. 740–2.
[2] Knowles, *The Episcopal Colleagues of Archbishop Becket*, p. 141.
[3] *Rot. Lit. Claus.* I, 108.
[4] *Rot. Lit. Pat.* p. 90; Painter, *King John*, p. 177. In January 1209 a papal mandate ordered Peter to do whatever the bishops of London, Ely and Worcester, the papal agents, ordered him to do in the matter of the church of Canterbury.
[5] Gervase of Canterbury, II, cii.

Peter remained in England throughout the interdict, and, indeed, the duty, never carried out, of releasing John's subjects from their allegiance was imposed upon him.[1] When peace was finally made, Peter was one of the guarantors of the payment which John promised to make.[2] The controversy necessarily involved Peter in high politics, and his loyalty towards the king is an extraordinary revelation of his character in a very difficult situation. There can be little doubt that it was a major factor in the reasons which led John to appoint him justiciar, and this appointment was foreshadowed in August 1213 when, at the side of Geoffrey fitz Peter, he presided over the council at St Albans which made vague promises of reform in the practices of government and planned an inquiry into the damage which the church had suffered.[3] No doubt Peter was assisting the justiciar primarily because of the latter proposal, but his position clearly shows the king's confidence; and with good reason. Peter had not allowed the interdict to interfere with his administrative work, and it is significant that a satirical attack upon his administrative position comes from this period.[4] He had never ceased since he became bishop of Winchester to perform his duties within the royal administration.

The satire on Bishop Peter mentioned a few lines previously

---

[1] *Annales Monastici*, ii, 215, 270.

[2] The settlement for the relaxation of the interdict was fixed at a meeting in London at 100,000 marks. Better terms were arranged for John, however, and he agreed to pay 40,000 marks before the interdict was relaxed, then 12,000 marks a year until he had restored the full amount determined by investigation. This was guaranteed by the bishops of Winchester and Norwich, the earls of Chester, Winchester and Pembroke, and William Briewerre; Wendover, ii, 100–2; *Rot. Chart.* pp. 208–9. John did not pay 40,000 marks; Nicholas of Tusculum, the legate, allowed him to postpone payment of 13,000 on the guarantee of the bishops of Winchester and Norwich; Wendover, ii, 102–3.

[3] Wendover, ii, 82.

[4] If we may believe the annals of Dunstable, he, with the justiciar and the earl of Chester, was one of the leaders of the royal army in Wales while King John himself was in Ireland; *Annales Monastici*, iii, 32, where the year is wrongly called 1209; it should be 1210. Peter's part illustrates both his military ability and his association with the justiciar as a leading minister. The earl of Chester, as a Marcher lord, would have his own interest in the progress of events.

described him as *praesidet ad scaccarium*,[1] and it is an accurate observation, as there is record evidence to show. When the memoranda roll of Michaelmas 1208 was put together, a case was referred to which had come up before the barons on Wednesday before the feast of St Margaret. Hugh de Neville, the forester, appeared before them to account for certain expenditure from the forest jurisdiction over the previous six years.[2] The barons were Peter des Roches, William Briewerre, and others unnamed. Now William Briewerre had an agreement with the king by which he was to put his experience to good use by sitting at the exchequer.[3] That Bishop Peter should have presided while Geoffrey fitz Peter was justiciar can be explained by reference to his trusted position, to his considerable experience in financial work, and to the development of royal government which had made it difficult for the justiciar to supervise the whole machinery of administration. Peter's presidency of the exchequer is the counterpart of the justiciar's having ceased regularly to sit there. Evidence for the position of president of the exchequer is difficult to come by from the pipe rolls themselves, and except for the survival of this memoranda roll of 1208 there would be little or no evidence of Peter's position, although it is clear from later evidence in the early years of Henry III that he was treated as an expert in exchequer procedure. The king and Geoffrey fitz Peter were still the authorities to whom appeal was made in difficult cases,[4] but if both were absent from the exchequer session, it is very likely that

---

[1] The satire was *Flacius Illyricus* (*Political Songs*, Camden Soc. pp. 10–11).

> Wintoniensis armiger
> Praesidet ad scaccarium
> Ad computandum impiger
> Piger ad evangelium.
>
> Regis revolvens rotulum
> Sic lucrum Lucam superat
> Marco marcam praeponderat
> Et librae librum subjicit.

[2] *Memoranda Roll 10 John*, p. 64.

[3] William's son was captured while fighting for John on the continent. On 21 June 1204 the king lent him 1000 marks to pay his son's ransom on condition that he sat at the exchequer for two weeks every year; *Rot. Lit. Pat.* p. 55.

[4] *Memoranda Roll 10 John*, pp. 25, 26, 27, 31, 39, 40–2, 49, 51, 52–8, 60.

Peter would act as president, and the satirist must have had some colourable justification for his wit.

Certainly Peter was very active within the financial department of the household, and probably the bulk of his duties were here. Many messengers and servants were paid on his authority; he seems especially to have been concerned with the followers of Henry, son of the duke of Saxony, and also the *balistarii* who were in the king's service in 1209 and 1210.[1] The fact that these household rolls are also isolated ones prevents a study of his work over a long period, and renders it impossible to state that this was his normal work, but it is reasonable to suppose that it was, because it is consistent with his earlier connexion with the chamber; and, like that work, it involved his regular attendance upon the king as he travelled. Payments were made by the bishop at many places where the court stayed.[2] Yet Peter was not always with the court; he was, after all, bishop of Winchester and probably gave a good deal of attention to the administration of his see.[3] The fact that messengers were paid from the household to go to him makes it clear that he was not always in the king's company, and that John found it necessary to correspond with Peter.[4] For this reason, if for no other, he was not alone in paying servants from household money, although he was perhaps the most active of the

---

[1] *Rot. Misae*, pp. 109–12, 117, 120, 121, 128–9.

[2] In 1209 at Bristol, Winchester, Havering, Wells, Tewkesbury, for example, and in 1210 at Dover.

[3] It may not be accidental that a pipe roll for the estates of the bishopric of Winchester survives from his pontificate, and a set of synodal statutes survives which Professor Cheney attributes to him. As against this, his episcopal *acta* do not seem to be very numerous, and he was not one of those bishops who were papal judges delegate. Most papal letters to him seem to be of a semi-political nature.

[4] *Rot. Misae*, p. 123, when a certain Alberic was paid 5s. for going with royal letters to Geoffrey fitz Peter, Peter bishop of Winchester, the bishop of Bath, the elect of Lincoln, the earl of Arundel and William Briewerre at Dover in 1209 on the Sunday next after the feast of St Mary Magdalen at York, i.e. 26 July; p. 131, when a messenger was paid for going to him at Bristol; p. 133, when William de Vendôme carried letters to the bishop, the justiciar, and William Briewerre from Havering; p. 142, when, at Bristol on the Saturday after the feast of the Conception of the Virgin Mary, a messenger was paid to carry letters to the bishop *de rumoribus Imperatoris Rom'*.

officers who did so. In 1213 a large number of offerings were made to the king for various favours, and their donors obtained, if the king was pleased to accept the fine, a writ to the sheriff, or some other local official, directing him to take the action desired by the donor, or at least to take security for payment of the offering. Such writs were almost invariably issued *teste meipso* but the warranty, the immediate authority for issue, was in many cases that of Peter des Roches.[1] For example, Thomas de Neville, a clerk of the archdeacon of Shrewsbury, offered 40 marks and two palfreys for having custody of all the lands and the heir of Henry de Montfort, together with the marriage of Henry's widow.[2] He offered security for payment through the bishop of Winchester and Earl Aubrey de Vere. The custodian of the *honor* of Gloucester and the sheriff of Dorset and Somerset were thereupon ordered to give Thomas seisin; witness the king *coram Petro episcopo Wint'*. This case, it is true, concerned Peter as guarantor of payment of the fine, but there were many similar which did not. Cecilia, widow of John Eshelling, gave the king 200 marks for custody of her eldest son and the sheriff of Dorset and Somerset was told to deliver seisin. The writ was attested by the king on 28 June 1213 *coram* Peter des Roches.[3] So, too, was a similar order in favour of the archdeacon of Huntingdon on the previous day.[4] It was often, however, the case that Peter's authority in the issue of like writs was shared by others; occasionally Brieuwerre, but more often Richard Marsh,[5] the archdeacon of Northumberland and an important and trusted official, formerly a clerk of the chamber, who, until 9 October 1213, bore the royal seal.[6]

Together Peter and Richard bore the responsibility for the issue of a large number of royal writs.[7] Probably this was an administrative device which ensured the king's control over the

[1] *Rot. de Finibus*, pp. 467, 468, 469, 470.
[2] *Ibid.* p. 467.
[3] *Ibid.* p. 469.
[4] *Ibid.* p. 468.
[5] *Ibid.* pp. 466, 470, 471, 491–3, 494, 502, 507–9.
[6] *Ibid.* p. 500. *Nono die Oct' anno regni domini Regis XV liberavit Magister Ricardus de Marisco domino Regi sigillum.* On whom see Foss, *op. cit.* p. 434. Richard Marsh had succeeded Philip de Luci who had succeeded Peter des Roches in the chamber.
[7] See references in note 5, above.

business of government carried on in his name. Both men were trusted royal servants, Peter the expert in financial matters, Richard the former chamber clerk and now bearer of the royal seal whose department, if one may use a slight anachronism, was the basis of government's effectiveness and whose loyalty had been amply demonstrated in the work of the chamber. Their association was to become even closer. At this time they were responsible for a great deal of the routine work of government, and Peter himself was concerned with some very important transactions. After Geoffrey fitz Peter's death, King John took the homage of his son, Geoffrey de Mandeville, for the *honor* of Earl William de Mandeville and all the lands which had been held hereditarily by the justiciar, together with all the wardships held on the same terms. Geoffrey was given seisin by a series of orders directed to the sheriffs of all the counties in which the lands lay; and these writs were, as usual, issued *teste meipso* at Woodstock on 4 November 1213, *per* the bishop of Winchester and William Briewerre *coram eodem episcopo.*[1] Throughout November more routine documents were similarly attested before the bishop of Winchester, Richard Marsh, and William Briewerre, the three men forming a close group round the king.[2] Whether this arrangement was a direct consequence of a worsening political situation in which John sought to control the administration more closely through his most trusted associates or whether it was dictated primarily by the administrative convenience of having three well-trained officials overlooking the work of government cannot be known; probably it owed something to both considerations. It was an arrangement which the king was to persist in.

2. THE JUSTICIAR AS REGENT

On 1 February 1214 royal letters patent were issued. *Sciatis quod constituimus justiciarium nostrum Anglie venerabilem patrem nostrum dominum P. Wintoniensem episcopum quamdiu nobis placuerit ad custodiendum loco nostro terram nostram Anglie et pacem regni nostri. Et ideo vobis mandamus quod ei tamquam justiciario nostro Anglie*

[1] *Rot. de Finibus*, p. 502.   [2] *Ibid.* pp. 507–9.

intendentes sitis et respondentes.[1] This is the date traditionally assigned to Peter's justiciarship. Yet it is open to doubt whether this document is really a commission of justiciarship. The words may mean that the office was, by these letters patent, committed to Peter des Roches, but they could equally well mean that Peter *already* justiciar was appointed *ad custodiendum . . . terram nostram*; and the former reading is the more unlikely in view of the verb *constituimus.* The text is ambiguous, but taken in conjunction with two earlier commissions, Longchamps's in 1190[2] and Geoffrey fitz Peter's in 1198,[3] it is probable that Peter des Roches was given on 1 February not the justiciarship but the regency of England.

There is some indication that he discharged the duties of the justiciarship before this date. On 15 January 1214 the king ordered Peter to give Miles of Ambian the first benefice of 20 marks' income to fall vacant *in England* (not merely in his own diocese as would have been the case had he not been justiciar), and on the very day the royal letters patent were issued, the abbots elect of Beaulieu, York, and Selby were to be given free administration of the lands and possessions of their respective churches when they came to the justiciar.[4] It is probable that Peter was already justiciar before 1 February 1214, that he had been appointed by word of mouth upon, or soon after, Geoffrey fitz Peter's death. While the king was in England the administration, of course, operated in his name; the justiciar's position was clear by reference to that of the king. When John proposed to go abroad, however, Bishop Peter's position was proclaimed over all England and general obedience to him was ordered. It is significant that Hubert de Burgh, his successor in the office, never obtained such a commission: there was no need, for he was justiciar but never

[1] *Rot. Lit. Pat.* p. 110.

[2] Diceto, II, 83. The title justiciar was not mentioned. Longchamps was appointed and general obedience to him enjoined; *sitis omnino intendentes . . . super omnibus quae ad nos spectant.*

[3] Cotton MS Vespasian C xiv, fo. 298; *. . . precipientes quatinus eidem gaufrido, tamquam justiciario nostro obedientes sitis . . . et intendentes.* The word justiciar was used in parentheses, as it were.

[4] *Rot. Lit. Pat.* pp. 108, 110; see also note 1, p. 188 above, for Peter's part in the seisin of Geoffrey fitz Peter's heir.

regent. The lack of a mass of evidence for Peter's position as justiciar before February is not remarkable; the period between Geoffrey fitz Peter's death and John's departure was not long; and it is difficult to acquire a very great amount of evidence for Geoffrey's own position during a much longer period while the king was in England.

Such indications as there are point to Peter's discharging the duties of the justiciarship before he was made regent on John's departure, but his position has been further obscured by evidence of doubtful interpretation. From 31 October 1213 royal charters were sealed by Peter des Roches.[1] He was not, however, chancellor, for this office was held by Walter de Grey who did not resign it until after his consecration as bishop of Worcester on 5 October 1214.[2] Walter was the king's ambassador to Flanders in October and therefore was not in England, but he had never discharged his chancery duties in person.[3] Since June 1209 the seal had been borne by Richard Marsh who returned it to the king at Ospreng on 9 October 1213.[4] On 22 December following it was handed to Ralph de Neville at Windsor to be borne under the bishop of Winchester.[5] Foss held that Peter was chancellor on the ground that he was not appointed justiciar until February 1214,[6] but if the argument above be accepted this is not a reliable foundation for his conclusion. It seems very likely that Peter had control of the seal in the chancellor's absence because he was already justiciar, and because, in view of the king's departure, he would control the seal of absence or employ his own seal for carrying on the government. Peter's control of the seal was not direct, except for the brief period between the return of the seal by Richard Marsh and its delivery to Ralph de Neville who became head of the chancery which accompanied the king abroad.[7] The accumulation of evi-

---

[1] *Rot. Chart.* pp. 195–6.
[2] *Handbook of British Chronology*, p. 67; *Rot. Lit. Claus.* I, 160.
[3] *DNB* under Grey; Foss, *op. cit.* p. 573.
[4] *Rot. de Finibus*, p. 500. The patent and close rolls have a similar note. *Rot. Lit. Pat.* p. 95; *Rot. Lit. Claus.* I, 118.
[5] *Rot. Lit. Claus.* I, 158 b.
[6] Foss, *op. cit.* p. 573, as against the opinion of Sir Thomas Duffus Hardy.
[7] *Rot. Chart.* pp. 196–201.

dence seems to indicate that Peter des Roches succeeded Geoffrey fitz Peter soon after the latter's death, but the manifestations of his authority largely come from the period of the king's absence, when his authority was proclaimed throughout England and the government ran in his name.

3. THE JUSTICIAR AND THE LAW COURTS

Peter des Roches, as justiciar, carried on the traditional duties of his office, although their exercise was perhaps influenced by his interests and previous training. He was not an experienced lawyer, and unlike Geoffrey fitz Peter he had served no judicial apprenticeship. His training was that of a financial officer, particularly in the chamber. He was not equipped to deal with difficult points of law or procedure: indeed as a cosmopolitan Poitevin he may have been indifferent to, or contemptuous of, English practice.[1] Nevertheless, he could not neglect the work which fell to the justiciar and, from the Hilary term 1214, his name appeared at the head of the justices sitting at Westminster.[2] His presence, like that of his predecessor, may occasionally have been fictitious. This is most obviously the case in the Trinity term of 1214 when Peter travelled to Chichester and Winchester just before Trinity, was at the Tower of London on 23 June, Chelmsford on 26 June, and Kingston in the quindene of St John Baptist.[3] He may well have been at Westminster for a large part of the term, but like his

[1] This is suggested by his contemptuous or perverse dismissal of the barons' argument about their peers under Henry III when Peter asserted, thinking of French society, that there were no peers in England; Powicke, *Henry III and the Lord Edward*, p. 76. There is a good deal of chronicle evidence, unreliable as it may be, for Peter's relations with English barons. The Waverley annals assert that he was made justiciar to subdue the mighty to the king's will and put down resistance, but, not using his power well, he turned the anger of the barons against the king into a fury; *Annales Monastici*, II, 281. Coggeshall relates that when Geoffrey fitz Peter died the bishop of Winchester succeeded him against the murmurs of all the English nobles that a man of foreign race should be over them; Coggeshall, p. 168. Quite obviously such generalizations are invalid, since William Marshal himself appointed Peter Henry III's tutor, but the baronial opposition may have used such arguments against him.

[2] CP 25(1) 127/10/37–40; 233/5/23, 24; 261/12/31, 32.
[3] *Rot. Lit. Claus.* I, 207.

predecessor he was certainly travelling elsewhere while pleadings went on. Again, in the following Michaelmas term he left Westminster to visit Chelmsford on 26 October, and if his itinerary were other than fragmentary, his travels might well appear to have been more extensive than this.

As in the case of Geoffrey fitz Peter, indications of Peter des Roches's absence from court appear in the plea rolls to confirm what the chancery rolls show of his movements.[1] During the Hilary term 1214, the king ordered by writ that the suit between Roger, prior of Dunholme, and Roger of St Martin over the advowson of Blyborough should be adjourned until the next term, and that the justices should then bring it before the bishop of Winchester since he wished it to be terminated before him. From the wording of the writ, it is plain that special action was required to ensure that a case appeared before the justiciar; it could not be counted upon in the normal course of proceedings. The implication is that Peter was not present in the court as a matter of course. In the Trinity term following, a day was given to Richard of Clare and one of his men to appear in a plea of false imprisonment brought by Philip son of John and his son against them, in order that it might proceed before the justiciar. The reason for both of these adjournments was not a matter of law or procedure, but, apparently, simply the importance of the litigants or, in the first case, the political desires of the king. Neither case involved a legal difficulty for the justices. The only case which implied some legal debate, although it was adjourned until the justiciar could be present, was not postponed so that his opinion could be sought. In the Hilary term 1214 the abbot of Chertsey replied upon a charter of exemption from pleading unless before the king or his chief justice.[2] The significance of this defence has been examined, and it seems likely that at this time the words of such a charter had acquired, in the eyes of the justices, a more precise significance than that which had originally attached to them. The abbot of Chertsey was an important baron, and his argument was upheld by the justices in a form usually employed for final judgement; he

[1] *Curia Regis Rolls*, VII, 58, 117.
[2] *Ibid.* p. 83.

need not answer the plaintiff Jordan son of Reginald.[1] The decision
was not made by the justiciar but by the justices; it did not imply
that Peter des Roches's legal knowledge was required, merely that
his presence would satisfy a formal need. The reasons for his
intervention in proceedings may therefore be described as political
and social rather than legal, and they were the reflexion of his
formal position as chief justice.

Peter des Roches's position rested upon an experienced staff of
justices presided over by Simon of Pattishall whose career has been
described.[2] His colleagues were James of Potterne, Roger Huscarl,
Henry de Pontaudemer, with the addition, in the sixteenth year of
King John, of Joscelin of Stukely.[3] Upon these men the justiciar
could rely for the administration of justice; they were skilled in its
mysteries while Peter's own experience knew little or nothing of
such matters; nor had he figured largely in the work of a papal
judge delegate or canon lawyer. There are a number of papal
mandates addressed to him, but they all required political or
administrative action, never the settlement of legal disputes.[4] No
doubt he had acquired some knowledge of English common law
and of canon law too, but in neither field was he treated as an
expert. The fact that writs ran in his name while King John was
abroad gives the appearance of continuity with the legal position
occupied by Geoffrey fitz Peter, when the reality may have been
simply the satisfaction of a formal need. The bishop of Winchester,
in the words of the plea rolls, appointed attorneys, told the justices
of litigants who were in the king's service beyond the seas, postponed suits, set down days for hearing,[5] but all this is, in a sense,
accidental; the accident of his being regent in the king's absence.

In as far as the chancery rolls reveal legal procedure, they

---

[1] The word used is *consideratum* which was employed for final judgements;
an interlocutory judgement would be *judicium;* C. Johnson, 'Notes on Thirteenth-century Judicial Procedure', *EHR*, LXII, 508 ff.

[2] See above, pp. 84-5.

[3] References as in pp. 141-6 *passim* above; 146/4/64, 65.

[4] *Calendar of Papal Letters*, pp. 21-4, 39; *Letters of Innocent III*, pp. 79-82. He
was not a papal judge delegate.

[5] *Curia Regis Rolls*, VII, 115, 125, 132, 133, 149, 161, 177, 186, 189, 195-6,
209, 244, 306.

confirm the formal nature of Peter des Roches's position. While King John was abroad in 1214, his orders treated Peter as the head of the legal administration. Thus the king told the justiciar to let a litigant have a writ of *mort d'ancestor*, to institute inquiries through lawful knights into a grant of seisin made by Geoffrey fitz Peter, or into the liberties which the ancestors of Robert de Mortimer had enjoyed in their lands.[1] All these instances were the result of Bishop Peter's formal position at the head of the judicial system; he was the motive force behind its operation. He was, in addition, an important figure within the system, and hence a man who had been found not guilty of murder was to stand to right before the justiciar in case anyone wished to speak against him, presumably because of his unsavoury reputation.[2] In another case, Peter des Roches had given 500 marks to James of Finglesham who was in the custody of William de Mores so that James might give safe pledges at the next meeting of the county of Kent for making peace with Thephanius de la Westland for a concord and judgement; and if James could not do this, William was to produce him at the Tower at the summons of the justiciar.[3] Again, the justiciar ordered the sheriff of Gloucester to permit the prior of Dorsington to have his riding service and all things quit, or be before the justiciar at Westminster to show why he detained the riding service against vow and pledge, and why he unjustly vexed the prior against the order of the justiciar.[4] In each of the cases, however, there was some exceptional feature which distinguished it from ordinary judicial cases. In all of them, a criminal element or at least a breach of the peace is implied; they were, in some sense, emergencies rather than common pleas between subject and subject. A normal civil dispute was summoned to Westminster to be before the justices, but if any urgency was involved the summons was to the Tower or before the justiciar, not necessarily in term time or while the court was sitting.[5]

---

[1] *Rot. Lit. Claus.* I, 169, 171, 201.   [2] *Ibid.* p. 204.
[3] *Ibid.* p. 213.   [4] *Ibid.*
[5] The Tower had been employed as a place where persons casting an essoin should appear within a year and a day, when the constable of the Tower would certify their appearance. It was used, in other words, as an administrative

The position of the justiciar was important in solving urgent cases of this kind, but what is lacking is any indication of his intervention in the normal judicial pleadings. That his authority was invoked, not on points of law, but to aid the maintenance of the king's peace suggests that his position was viceregal rather than that of an active chief justice. He was regent and justiciar, therefore the government operated in his name, on his authority, and the writs were issued accordingly. The fact implies no legal *expertise* or active personal interest, but merely administrative convenience. Even if Peter's training had inclined him towards active participation in the work of justice, pressure of other business while John was abroad and the going-out-of-court tendency at work within the royal administration would have combined to distract his attention to many other matters. As it was, his part in the formation of law was slight, and his mark upon the plea rolls less than that of his two immediate predecessors; it was not a difference of degree consequent upon his comparatively short tenure of office but a difference in kind. Hubert Walter and Geoffrey fitz Peter were sought out for their opinions, or intervened in cases because they were interested. Bishop Peter's control of the legal system was largely formal, or at most political or social, the consequence of his position, not of his interest. Technically this was possible because he had a staff of experienced justices. Hubert Walter and Geoffrey fitz Peter were themselves creating legal administration, and the system grew up with them. Only when justices like Simon of Pattishall knew as much as or more than the justiciar, when the courts of law were competent to go out of court, could the justiciarship cease to be the office of an active justice. While Geoffrey fitz Peter lived, his interests and knowledge could never be wholly withdrawn from the work of the justices. Under a man like Peter des Roches who was not a lawyer, the justices were the instrument of effective legal administration, and this both gave added impetus to the forces driving these branches of royal administration out of court, and created

convenience to assist the more efficient administration of justice. See Johnson, 'Notes on Thirteenth-century Judicial Procedure' (*EHR*, LXII, 510). Peter des Roches held the Tower as justiciar.

a position in which the office of chief justice could be largely formal.

Yet in one important respect Peter des Roches's justiciarship revived the legal tradition of the office. Since 1210 the bench of Westminster had ceased to sit, and pleadings thereafter were *coram rege*. John's absence in 1214 restored a court of justices to Westminster which, in all essentials, exhibited the features which earlier belonged to the bench, although with a difference: the personnel of the court was that of the court *coram rege*. Simon of Pattishall, James of Potterne, and their colleagues were men who had sat with the king, not in the bench. In the last year of his life Geoffrey fitz Peter had presided over a precisely similar court, but between his position and that of Peter des Roches there was one significant difference. Geoffrey in 1213 had been accompanied by Richard Marsh and William Briewerre when he sat in court, the men who were joined to Peter des Roches for the transaction of royal businesses.[1] They did not appear in court with Bishop Peter. No doubt the strained relations between John and Geoffrey fitz Peter were in part responsible for his association with two of the king's trusted ministers, but it has earlier been argued that probably effective administrative control was the chief motive for the arrangement. In 1213 the king was in England but if he was temporarily unable to preside over the court *coram rege*, it was convenient or reassuring that those ministers who controlled the exchequer should do so. In 1214 John was abroad and Peter des Roches was regent; thus while he headed the court at Westminster, his colleagues William and Richard acted with him at the exchequer. No doubt the trust which King John had in Peter des Roches strengthened his position in the administration; no doubt, also, the political and administrative importance which attached to the court over which the king himself presided passed to the

---

[1] *Rot. Lit. Pat.* p. 139. Letters patent to Peter des Roches justiciar of England and William Briewerre told them that the king sent to them Richard Marsh, archdeacon of Northumberland, whom he wished to be present *una vobiscum singulis* for the doing of *nostris tractatibus colloquiis et omnibus agend' nostris in Anglia tam de castris muniend' quam aliis;* therefore they were to admit him to their counsels. The letter was dated 12 May 1214. It is obvious that William Briewerre was already Peter's colleague, and Richard was sent to join them.

exchequer where his intimate counsellors deliberated when he was absent, while the justices were a body of legal experts whose sphere of work was detaching itself from the *curia regis*, the centre of royal power. Peter des Roches's lack of legal training may have hastened the process and with his two associates he may have exercised his powers from the financial centre of government with which he was so familiar, and with which William Briewerre was also closely connected. The concept of the bench of Westminster had probably vanished temporarily from royal administration, leaving a court intimately associated with the king, and, in his absence, with the justiciar. The one distinguished surviving member of the former bench was Eustace de Fauconberg, and he was now no longer a judge but an important financial official and Peter des Roches's right-hand man.

4. THE JUSTICIAR AND THE EXCHEQUER

If the man was more important than the office in the administrative organization of the time, and if the interests and training of a justiciar led to his operating through one instrument of government rather than another, it is to be expected that Peter des Roches would work through the financial organs, that his position should make itself felt through the exchequer rather than through the courts of law. His control over the machinery of government could be ensured by his lieutenants. Eustace de Fauconberg was competent to participate in the work of justice, but his activity seems in fact to have been largely non-judicial. The financial aspect of the justiciarship of Peter was further accentuated by his association with William Briewerre, a baron who had been specially required by the king to sit at the exchequer and who was left as Bishop Peter's associate in February 1214.[1] William had had long experience of local administration too, and had served many times as a royal sheriff. Richard Marsh, who was sent to join the

---

[1] William's career is discussed in some detail by Painter, *op. cit.* pp. 72 ff. He was a royal minister whose service was highly profitable to himself; like Geoffrey fitz Peter, although not to the same extent, he built up a barony.

justiciar and William, was then a chancery official, but he had been prominent in chamber finance and the more intimate parts of the royal administration.[1] Whereas, with Geoffrey fitz Peter, William and Richard sat in the court at Westminster, it seems very likely, since they did not sit there with Peter des Roches, that the exchequer was the centre of their deliberations, especially in view of their common experience of financial business.

The reality of Peter des Roches's position in respect of the exchequer is difficult to ascertain. The formality of the evidence available obscures the actual state of affairs. The fact, for example, that writs of Bishop Peter authorized payments from royal revenue need not imply personal interest in the exchequer or its proceedings. Thus, a tent was bought for the count of Boulogne on his writ, and supplies were paid for, horses bought, and *balistarii* were paid; many other such instances may be cited.[2] The right of the justiciar to disburse treasure was one of those which, for the author of *Dialogus*, made his office great, but it is evidence of a viceregal position rather than specifically the right attaching to the presidency of the exchequer; and if John had not been absent in this year, these indications of Peter's authority would not appear. To know the precise position of Peter des Roches at the exchequer, it would be necessary to have the memoranda rolls of these years, but these are missing. It is impossible, therefore, to know if his will and his decision entered into the deliberations of the barons, and how far William Briewerre was essential to their proceedings. There are indications that Peter must have taken part in exchequer procedure in no mere formal sense. The king treated him as one having a personal interest in financial affairs. John ordered Peter to cause Reginald of Cornhill to be allowed

[1] Foss, *op. cit.* p. 434. Richard held a subordinate office in the exchequer in 1197 and little more is known of him until he appears in the rolls as clerk of the chamber under John. In 1212 he was *residens ad scaccarium*, which fact links his association with the justiciar in 1214 more closely with the exchequer; *Rot. Lit. Claus.* I, 132. He is a contrast to justices like Simon of Pattishall in that his work was largely financial, and it was no doubt primarily as an official of the exchequer that he had custody of the Great Seal.

[2] PRO, Pipe Roll 16 John, under the farm of London and Middlesex £4. 4s. 3d. was paid for the count's tent; in Pipe Roll 17 John, the *balistarii* were paid their expenses from the farm of Knaresborough.

whatever he had spent in the king's affairs beyond the sea, over and above the income of the counties of Lancaster and Surrey of which he was custodian, according to the custom of the exchequer.[1] This betokens a control over proceedings beyond that of formality, and this impression is confirmed by a series of orders to inspect the rolls of the exchequer, or to make inquiries into them, so that it might be discovered if Roger Mortimer, for example, had served his terms for payment of a fine offered for the land of Watkin of Beauchamp; or what the sum total was of the debts of William of Canterbury, or the debts of Reginald de Valle.[2] The same assumption of Peter's personal interest in the details of the exchequer doubtless lies behind the orders he received to assign escheats or wardships to those to whom the king chose to give them. Land in the king's hand was accounted for at the exchequer and it was therefore of importance to the barons to know whether the king had given seisin to someone. When Ralph de Turville died, in addition to his own land he held in custody the land of Richard Abbot.[3] His own holdings were given to the earl of Chester, but Richard's land was to be taken into the king's hand and the king was to be informed of its value. All this implied action at the exchequer. The justiciar was required to deliver seisin of the land to the earl and also to determine its annual value. Significantly enough, William Briewerre was notified that this order had been sent to Peter des Roches, presumably because of his own position at the exchequer and the importance of a transaction involving the earl of Chester.[4] Rather more obviously Peter was treated as president of the exchequer in exactly the way described by the *Dialogus* when King John told him that he had committed the counties of Bedford and Buckingham to Hugh de Gournai; the justiciar was to receive Hugh's oath to deal with them faithfully, and also to arrange for Henry of Braybrook to account for these shires until the Michaelmas audit when Hugh and his bailiffs should assume office.[5]

---

[1] *Rot. Lit. Claus.* I, 142 b. The writ was dated 22 April.
[2] *Ibid.* pp. 168, 169.　　　　　　　[3] *Ibid.* p. 167.
[4] *Ibid.* The order was issued on 10 June.
[5] *Rot. Lit. Pat.* p. 121.

There is, however, a more striking example of Peter's duties in connexion with financial administration. On 26 May 1214 King John wrote to the justiciar that a scutage of 3 marks was to be taken on every knight's fee in England which was held in chief of the king in demesne, and in the bishoprics in the king's hands, and in the wardships and escheats.[1] The justiciar was to arrange for it to be taken, except from those knights who were with the king in Poitou. There followed upon this orders of quittance because knights were in the army in Poitou. Two knights' fees held in chief of the bishopric of Exeter were acquitted in this way. Perhaps a man had offered the king a fine to be quit of the scutage, like Thomas of Erdington, a royal sheriff, who was responsible for the land of William son of Alan. Again, the justiciar was ordered to cause to be collected the scutage of Watkin and to let the king know the amount since he had given the money to Watkin *ad militiam suam*.[2] The scutage once collected, it fell to the justiciar to arrange to supply the king with the money realized or use it as John directed; a fact which necessitated the justiciar's control over the exchequer. On 1 September the king, who was at Partenay, ordered Peter to send 2,000 marks to the emperor in whatever way seemed expedient to the justiciar.[3] It might be argued that this was a duty which became necessary when the king was abroad, that in so important a matter as the supply of money the power of the justiciar was deemed necessary, yet it is plain that Peter usually discharged the same duty when John was in England. The use of castles as depositaries for treasure to be supplied to the itinerant king to obviate the delays inherent in ordinary exchequer has been pointed out.[4] As justiciar Peter held the Tower of London, and on 22 April 1215 supplied the king with £500 from this source. Earlier in the same year at Windsor, by the hand of Peter Bacon clerk of the sheriff of London, the king received another £500, making £1,000 in all. In the previous March, the justiciar had been ordered to send another £1,000 to Oxford before Ash

[1] *Rot. Lit. Claus.* I, 166b. Issued at Partenay on 26 May.
[2] *Ibid.* pp. 167, 169, 170.
[3] *Rot. Lit. Pat.* p. 121.
[4] Jolliffe, 'The Chamber and the Castle Treasures under King John', *Studies in Medieval History presented to F. M. Powicke.*

Wednesday, and this royal order was despatched from Notting-ham.[1] Clearly, the justiciar was at all times an integral part of the system which kept the king adequately supplied with money.

For another reason, Peter's work as justiciar seems to have been closely linked with the exchequer and financial administration. This is the constant association with him of Eustace de Fauconberg who had been a justice of the bench earlier in John's reign and who was to become the treasurer of Henry III and bishop of London. Eustace's judicial career seems to have terminated some years before Peter became justiciar. In 1214 he was at the justiciar's side as his principal assistant, and his work was largely financial. The higher proportion of Peter des Roches's writs were issued *teste meipso* in the same way that royal writs were so witnessed; and the justiciar's orders covered the whole range of governmental activity; not merely financial business in the strict sense, but orders for seisin of land, orders to view land, ecclesiastical matters and so on.[2] Nevertheless, a considerable number of the justiciar's writs were attested by Eustace de Fauconberg, a fact which assumes greater significance when it is noted that only two other men ever witnessed a writ of the bishop of Winchester in 1214: William Marshal, earl of Pembroke, and William Briewerre, who witnessed only one each.[3] Eustace, on the other hand, witnessed orders to pay knights and servants, payments for passages across the Channel, for the cost of carrying the king's goods, for preparing ships and castles; in a word, the writs for which he took respon-ibility were all financial in that they directly involved payments from the royal treasure.[4] Now if all these writs had been issued at Westminster while the justiciar was travelling through England, there would be ground for some suspicion that Eustace acted as his deputy at the exchequer, and that the justiciar's control was

---

[1] *Rot. Lit. Pat.* p. 134; *Rot. Lit. Claus.* p. 192b. The cost of transporting this £1,000 to Oxford was 102 shillings and 5 pence; PRO Pipe Roll 17 John under the farm of London and Middlesex; *et in conductu mille librarum de thesauro a Lond' usque Oxoniam C et II s et v d. per breve domini Wint'.* The king's order being issued at Nottingham on 30 March 1215, it is quite apparent that Peter des Roches was issuing writs in his own name for the disbursement of treasure while John was in England.
[2] *Rot. Lit. Claus.* I, 204.   [3] *Ibid.* pp. 206, 211.   [4] *Ibid.* pp. 207–12.

exercised indirectly through him. Actually the writs witnessed by
Eustace came from places along the justiciar's route: from Chelmsford, Kingston, Westminster, St Albans, Berkhampstead,
Winchester, Guildford, Dover.[1] The area involved was the same
as that traversed by the justiciar's circle round London; and
Eustace was with him. The justiciar moved with his principal
financial assistant, and when Michaelmas came round they
returned together to Westminster for the audit.[2] Any assessment
of Peter des Roches's position in administration depends upon the
evidence which is available. His Close Roll is a document made
up of writs of a financial character and no collection of his legal
writs survives. From the indications of his authority in the plea
rolls, it seems probable, nevertheless, that his authority was more
immediately exercised through the exchequer than the courts of
law, and if this is so it must be largely a consequence of his own
interest and training which would undoubtedly have this effect
when government was not rigidly organized in departments nor
confined within the channels of administration of its own creation.

5. THE JUSTICIAR AS CHIEF EXECUTIVE

That personal interest or position could so colour the aspect of a
justiciar's office is borne out by the duties which fell to Peter des
Roches while John was abroad. Geoffrey fitz Peter, as we have
seen, had been the recipient of a whole range of royal orders
directing him to take action, and naturally as head of royal administration Peter des Roches occupied a similar position. To take
but a random selection of royal orders de ultra mare: he was to let
Ralph de Faya have the escheats to which he was entitled through
his marriage, he was to give William Briewerre seisin of the land
and heir of Lawrence the chamberlain. In this latter case the same
order was sent to Philip of Oldcoates, which suggests that the
justiciar received the instruction for his information and in order
that, if necessary, he could enforce the royal order if Philip failed
to obey. Or, again, Peter was ordered to provide William de la
Ferte with an income from the escheats equivalent to that he

[1] Rot. Lit. Claus. i, 207–12.   [2] Ibid. p. 212.

derived from the land of William Pipard to whom the king had now returned his land.[1] Orders for seisin, for the release of prisoners, for recompense to the merchants of Navarre may have arisen in part from a political situation, from the fact of the king's being at war or from incipient revolt against him, but they are not essentially different from the range of duties which Geoffrey fitz Peter performed. It is true that there are fewer orders to be found addressed to Bishop Peter and the justices of England, but this again is partly the consequence of the position of the law courts after 1210; and it may even be that royal writs *de ultra mare* to Peter had more financial implications. Nevertheless, his administrative position, at least in its formal aspects, was the same as that of Geoffrey fitz Peter. Possibly Peter des Roches's power was more extensive, or his position stronger, because of his closer and more intimate relations with the king. After John had returned to England, Peter was still exercising great authority. Thus he was required to give Philip de Aubeney seisin of the isle of Sark which John gave him in custody; and Peter was ordered to send one with his letters and in his confidence to deliver the royal castle of Winchester to Savaric de Mauléon, and to receive into it the king's Poitevins.[2] This betokens the confidence which existed between John and his justiciar, but here it is a difference of degree from Geoffrey fitz Peter's position, not one of kind.

Yet there is one important way in which Peter des Roches's justiciarship differed from Geoffrey fitz Peter's, which seems largely a consequence of his own career, and possibly the result of John's relations with the papacy. This was the marked concern with ecclesiastical affairs. A high proportion of writs which were sent to him from the continent in 1214 dealt with church matters. He was required, for example, to give to his nephew Bartholomew, archdeacon of Winchester, the deanery of York; and to assign to the bearer of the royal letters, one Paul, 100 gold shillings annually until a benefice became available.[3] The latter order plainly implies that the assignation of such a benefice was within the justiciar's power and discretion. Such benefices were used to

---

[1] *Rot. Lit. Claus.* I, 141 b, 142; *Rot. Lit. Pat.* p. 117 b.
[2] *Ibid.* pp. 125, 135.   [3] *Ibid.* pp. 113 b, 118 b.

cement the king's relations with the papacy. From the first vacancies which occurred, Bishop Peter was ordered to give rents to two Italians, Masters Gratian and Hugelin, who were clerks of the papal legate; and King John had made provision for the Cardinals Guala and John from benefices.[1] More strange, perhaps, was the gift of a benefice to Thomas de Argentoleo, a clerk of the king of France.[2] The reward of a royal clerk like Henry Abbot was normal; it was the practice of English administration of long standing, and in the case of Henry Abbot it was a necessity since the king urged speed upon the justiciar because the clerk was a pauper.[3] Peter des Roches's ecclesiastical position must have been helpful in such ecclesiastical affairs, but the position of the English church after the interdict may have been partly responsible for this great quantity of orders concerned with ecclesiastical matters; churches falling vacant were left unfilled, and a large number of benefices were in the king's hand. As a consequence of the vacancy of the archbishopric of York, for instance, the justiciar was directed to confer the church of Newbold on John of Walton, or, if it was already occupied, to find him some other equivalent benefice. Similarly, while the abbey of Burton was vacant, Bishop Peter was ordered to let Ralph de Neville have the church of Stapenhill since he had letters patent of presentation to the arch-deacon of Derby. The vacancy of the bishopric of Carlisle led to an order to the justiciar to give seisin of it in custody to the arch-deacon of Durham and Aimery the clerk.[4] Yet, allowing for the general situation, the fact that the justiciar was a bishop allowed him to work directly in matters of this kind and not through the medium of churchmen. After the king had returned to England, he employed the justiciar to secure the election of an important ecclesiastic. The convent of St Mary of Southwark was informed that Bishop Peter and William of St John were sent to them with power to provide their house with a suitable pastor.[5] The con-venience of a great ecclesiastic who was justiciar must, in cases of elections, have led to his employment in church affairs to a greater extent than his lay predecessor.

[1] *Rot. Lit. Pat.* p. 111; *Rot. Lit. Claus.* I, 168 *b*.   [2] *Rot. Lit. Pat.* p. 122.
[3] *Ibid.* p. 119.   [4] *Ibid.* pp. 117, 118.   [5] *Ibid.* p. 133.

The more important ecclesiastical duties of Peter des Roches most clearly reveal his association with William Briewerre and Richard Marsh. It hardly needs stressing that the election of a bishop or an abbot, because he became a great baron, was a matter of considerable moment to the king, and it is not surprising to find that the justiciar acted with the advice of his colleagues in such affairs. Provision for such joint action was made by the king before he left England. On 1 February 1214, at Portsmouth, he enjoined Peter des Roches that when the abbots of York, Beaulieu, and Selby, elected to vacant churches with royal assent and with the assent of the king's faithful men William Briewerre and William de Cantilupe whom he had assigned to deal with these matters, came to the justiciar, they were to be given free administration of their lands and possessions.[1] This seems to have been a commission assigned to cope with the problems arising out of the interdict, and it was through this group of ministers that the papal legates worked. The king announced that Nicholas, bishop of Tusculum, had told him that the prior of Coventry who was elect of Selby had declined election, therefore Peter des Roches, when a pastor useful to his house and faithful to the king had been elected by the monks with the legate's counsel, should *vice nostra* give his approval and assent.[2] The same order was sent to William Briewerre and Richard Marsh. The three men plainly had limits set to their authority, for it sometimes required a special mandate from the king to act in his place. A few days after the king issued the above letter, he was again directing his three ministers to promote the brother of Walter Mauclerc who was prior of Reading to the abbey of St Albans.[3] A more routine affair, however, shows that the justiciar might act with other counsellors. On 12 July John ordered the justiciar to determine the amount of money given to the Cardinals Guala and John, and with the

---

[1] *Ibid.* p. 110. William de Cantilupe was steward of the royal household, having likewise served John when he was count of Mortain. He had been sheriff of Worcestershire and Herefordshire, and in 1215 of Warwickshire and Leicestershire and constable of Kenilworth. He was a trusted and intimate royal servant.

[2] *Ibid.* p. 121. Issued at Partenay, 30 August 1214.

[3] *Ibid.* p. 140. Issued at St Maxent, 5 September 1214.

counsel of the bishop of Norwich, the abbot of Beaulieu Regis, and Thomas of Erdington, to search the rolls to discover what rent each of them had and to assign them equivalent benefices.[1] The matter involved an action which could be carried out at the exchequer with the help of the men who sat there and who were familiar with its rolls and proceedings; it did not necessitate political action at a high level, such as the election of a bishop or an abbot.

The place of the justiciar seems to have been qualified by his association with these counsellors in important matters. No doubt this had always been customary, but in a political situation such as that of 1214 it became much more explicit. Peter's independent sphere of action was the execution of the consequences of decisions taken at a high level; he conveyed seisin of the lands of ecclesiastics, or delivered their goods to them.[2] This is not to say that his was not the most important single voice in the deliberations of those whom the king assigned to these matters. Where John himself made a decision he worked directly through the justiciar. He sent, for example, letters patent to Peter addressed to the archbishop of Canterbury for William, archdeacon of Huntingdon, who, as the king had heard, had been elected to the see of Coventry; the justiciar was to direct these letters to the archbishop inducing him to confirm the election.[3] Apart from the immediate pressure which the justiciar could exercise in a case like this, the king worked through him apparently because he was not altogether sure that William had actually been elected. Where

[1] *Rot. Lit. Claus.* I, 168 *b*. The bishop of Norwich was John de Grey who was a trusted minister and familiar of John and justiciar of Ireland. The abbot of Beaulieu Regis was a favourite ecclesiastic of John and head of his own royal foundation, having been one of John's agents in the negotiations over Stephen Langton's election, bearing John's offer to the pope in 1208 and going again to Rome in November 1212 to conclude peace. Thomas of Erdington started his career in 1198 as Geoffrey fitz Peter's under-sheriff in Staffordshire. In 1205 he was sheriff of Staffordshire and Shropshire and he held these counties till 1216. In May 1206 he accompanied the abbot of Beaulieu to Rome as one of the king's proctors and on the final mission in 1212 he was captured by John's enemies. He visited John in Poitou in late July or early August, because on 16 August he was despatched to England to give secret instructions to many royal officials; *ibid.* p. 202.

[2] *Ibid.* p. 204.   [3] *Ibid.* p. 169 *b*.

benefices were to be conferred, a good deal, as we have seen, was left to the justiciar's discretion.

Ecclesiastical affairs were not, however, the only ones to be transacted by the justiciar in consultation with other ministers. When, on 22 May 1214, the king told Peter des Roches and William Briewerre that he was sending Richard Marsh to join them, it was in order that he could be present at *tractatibus colloquiis et omnibus agend' nostris in Anglia tam de castris muniend' quam aliis.*[1] He was associated for the general business of government but especially for castles since they were singled out for mention, and by inference for military and political affairs. Before his arrival, the same general arrangement for counsel was in existence. The affairs of the widow of King Richard I engaged the attention of the legate and the justiciar; and Peter des Roches, having heard the messenger of Berengaria, was, through the counsel of William Briewerre and other faithful men, to do as the king had commanded him before leaving England.[2] After Richard joined them his counsel was added in important matters. Such, for example, was the question which has cropped up several times in the history of the justiciars, the Mandeville barony. Geoffrey de Say brought King John 15,000 marks to obtain seisin of the lands of Earl William de Mandeville; and therefore the king ordered the justiciar to take counsel with the bishop of Norwich, Richard Marsh, and William Briewerre, and to do as seemed best.[3] The royal order was dated 11 July. In August writs were issued to the sheriff of Kent and the sheriffs of other counties to give Geoffrey de Say seisin because he had arranged this fine with the king.[4] The

---

[1] *Rot. Lit. Pat.* p. 139.   [2] *Rot. Lit. Claus.* I, 141.

[3] *Ibid.* p. 168 *b*; Painter, *op. cit.* p. 289, states that the suits which Geoffrey de Say brought were dismissed; *Curia Regis Rolls*, VII, 110–11. It is true that a suit was dismissed in the Hilary term 1214, but this was some months before this present series of writs. Painter seems to have confused the evidence. Geoffrey de Say's fine of 15,000 marks and the king's order of 11 July 1214 were some months later than his suit against Geoffrey de Mandeville; and Painter nowhere explains the orders for seisin issued in August 1214. The king made no reference to such a writ in his suit of July, and possibly intended to proceed without the judgement of his court. Geoffrey de Say was, in any case, told at Hilary 1214 that he could have another writ if he wished.

[4] *Rot. Lit. Claus.* I, 209.

decision and its execution had been left to the discretion of the justiciar and his counsellors, who may, in view of the large profit to the king, have treated his letter as an order. The political consequences may have been offset, in their opinion, by the grant to Geoffrey de Mandeville, the son of the old justiciar, of the heiress and barony of Gloucester, and orders were issued, shortly after those for Geoffrey de Say, ordering sheriffs to give Geoffrey de Mandeville seisin.[1] Decisions on such important matters did not imply political authority, for there can have been little doubt in the ministers' minds of the king's desire in any of these cases.[2] The association of these counsellors no doubt had political overtones, but it is equally clear that the arrangement was also one of administrative convenience; and, perhaps, primarily so, since political counsel in feudal society meant the baronage, and these men were royal ministers. As a group, Peter des Roches, William, and Richard were ordered to inspect the rolls of the exchequer to discover the fees held by royal prisoners, to pay the expenses of men who had given presents to the emperor, to give a messenger, Reginald de Regula, some Gascon wine.[3] The first of these three orders concerned the exchequer where they sat, the two last were payments to the bearer of messages to them who would no doubt come into their presence. As a group they deliberated together, but the justiciar, from the evidence which has been reviewed, was the source of executive action. Writs ran in his name, he carried out the king's orders. The advice and counsel which he took, like the counsel of the king himself, can only have strengthened his position rather than placed limitations upon it. The more or less continuous presence of John in England after 1204 is probably the reason no such formal evidence of counsel emerges from the

[1] *Rot. Lit. Pat.* p. 109; *Rot. Lit. Claus,* I, 162, 209.

[2] Painter, *op. cit.* pp. 282 ff., discusses John's relations with Geoffrey de Mandeville and Geoffrey de Say at this time. Perhaps John had the idea of giving Geoffrey de Mandeville the *honor* of Gloucester, Geoffrey de Say the Mandeville barony and collecting 35,000 marks in fines and gaining the goodwill of two barons. If this was so, the king was clumsy, for both men were baronial supporters.

[3] *Rot. Lit. Claus.* I, 179. These orders were issued after the king's return to England, which supports the thesis of their administrative importance as distinct from their viceregal position.

justiciarship of Geoffrey fitz Peter, for the same ministers, William Briewerre and Peter des Roches, served the king in those earlier years and it can hardly be doubted that if John desired the advantage of their expert administrative advice he availed himself of it; and also of less formally constituted counsel like that of John de Grey, bishop of Norwich and justiciar of Ireland. It is quite clear that these men did not decide policy. What they were called upon to do was to advise upon its efficient execution in important matters under the presidency of the justiciar, who then took action himself.

There remains one other point on which the justiciarship of Peter des Roches provides valuable information. The system of writs *de ultra mare* had a long history behind it. The first examples of writs specifically grounded upon this authority come from the reign of Henry I, but until the justiciarship of Bishop Peter it is impossible to discover how efficient it was in detail, or how much it left to the justiciar's discretion. On 19 August at Cognac, King John ordered Peter des Roches to take the remainder of Thomas of Erdington's fine for the land of William son of Alan, and a second order was issued that if the scutage had been taken in William son of Alan's land, allowance was to be made for the fact in Thomas's fine.[1] On 7 September, nearly three weeks later, the justiciar issued a series of writs.[2] To the sheriffs of Norfolk, Wiltshire, Warwickshire, Leicestershire, Shropshire, and Staffordshire he sent orders that Thomas was to have the aid of the knights of the *honor* of William son of Alan and quittance of the fine made with the king for the heir of William. The sheriffs of Staffordshire and Shropshire were further told that Thomas had given pledges for his fine and therefore he was to be given full seisin. In the case of the first series of orders it was noted that the justiciar had the king's order for his action, in the second that he acted *per breve regis de ultra mare*. If the notations were made on the roll in every case of the receipt of a royal order from beyond the sea, there would be a yardstick by which to measure the amount of work performed on the orders of the justiciar within his discretion. The amount of this activity must have been great. Certainly payments

[1] *Ibid.* p. 170. [2] *Ibid.* p. 212.

were necessary to keep the government working; for example, payments to messengers like the archdeacon of Taunton going to the king in Poitou, or an order to Reginald of Cornhill to send all the shields in his possession to Portsmouth,[1] must have been made on the justiciar's initiative. The delay of three weeks between the king's order and the justiciar's obviously implies that any urgent action must have been within the justiciar's discretion; and Thomas of Erdington was an important person who may have secured speedier action than many men. The correlation between the king's roll and the justiciar's close roll would probably be higher if the latter were not fragmentary, but it is impossible not to be struck by the large range of royal orders addressed to the justiciar from the continent which are strictly comparable with the number issued by Peter himself. The king intervened frequently in English affairs, and his interventions required the justiciar to take action and very often action which resulted in the production of several writs for every single order *de ultra mare*, as, for example, in the case of the numerous orders required to give Thomas of Erdington seisin of William son of Alan's land. The chancery staff with the justiciar were kept busy, and if every writ issued *teste meipso* by Peter des Roches was a personal order, his time must have been well filled.[2] A good deal of business may have been taken off his shoulders by Eustace de Fauconberg. Thus while the justiciar gave orders for the delivery of seisin, or ecclesiastical elections, or similar actions, Eustace was concerned with the routine payments which kept government working.[3]

The justiciarship of Bishop Peter revived the predominantly viceregal character the office had had before the loss of Normandy. It was a short period of regency, and the last in which a justiciar ruled England in the king's absence. When John returned, the political situation was already far deteriorated and normal administration was slipping into abeyance.[4] Peter, as justiciar, still

---

[1] *Rot. Lit. Claus.* I, pp. 204–5.   [2] *Ibid.* pp. 204–13.   [3] *Ibid.*
[4] When John returned to England in late 1214, there had been widespread opposition to the collection of the scutage. None had been paid in Lancashire, Essex and Hertfordshire, little in Norfolk and Suffolk; Mitchell, *Studies in Taxation*, pp. 112–13. Three northern barons had been distrained for non-payment; among them was Eustace de Vesci. Shortly after his arrival the

supplied the king with money from the Tower store and was ordered to give Philip de Aubeney seisin of the isle of Sark, but there is little other evidence of his administrative activity, although one order to Peter of an ordinary administrative character suggests that he carried out something like a normal justiciar's duty until March 1215; he was then required to deliver Stephen Blund of Rye, taken because he removed chattels and merchandise of the Danes, to William de Wrotham who had undertaken to produce him if anyone wished to speak against him.[1] This looks like an order to the chief justice but Peter's main pre-occupation was with the political situation. In April 1215 John sent the justiciar north and issued letters ordering his ministers there to obey the bishop's orders,[2] and probably this visit was part of the king's preparation to attack the land of the northern rebel barons should need arise. The overt act of rebellion came when the barons laid siege to Northampton castle, and thereafter the justiciar's part in normal administration was at an end. With Magna Carta Peter's tenure of office ended, probably as a condition of agreement between the king and his barons, for on the day agreement was reached Hubert de Burgh was appointed justiciar.

dissident barons met at Bury St Edmunds (Wendover, II, 111–12; *Histoire des ducs de Normandie*, pp. 145–6) and swore to make war upon the king if their just demands were not granted.

[1] *Rot. Lit. Claus.* I, 190. Again, as an ordinary administrative action, on 10 December he was ordered to give William Malet seisin of two manors which Isaac the Jew of Norwich held, until Twelfth Night, so that the king could speak to the justiciar. On 18 January 1215 he was to find supplies for the custodian of Winchester castle, but this seems to have been an order to Peter as bishop and local magnate in a dubious political situation with open fighting imminent; *ibid.* I, 181b.

[2] *Rot. Lit. Pat.* p. 134.

CHAPTER VII

THE JUSTICIARSHIP UNDER HENRY III

When King John sealed Magna Carta at Runnymede, one of his supporters was the seneschal of Poitou, Hubert de Burgh, who was also one of the thirty-eight *obsecutores et observatores*, taking his place beside great magnates like William Marshal, earl of Pembroke, and the earls of Arundel and Warenne.[1] The baronial host lingered at Runnymede until 25 June, by which date Hubert was styled justiciar;[2] and twenty-four years later Lawrence of St Albans was to assert in his defence that Hubert was given the office there, in the presence of Stephen Langton, the earls of Warenne and Derby, and other magnates.[3] The Great Charter mentioned the justiciar in several of its clauses and always as the king's deputy who would redress wrongs or take action if the king should be abroad. In a more general way it declared that justiciars, constables, sheriffs, and bailiffs should be men who knew the law of the kingdom and would observe it.[4] Whoever was appointed justiciar would have to be a man trusted by the king to act as his *alter ego*, and competent as an administrator to do so, but he must also be a person whom the barons could trust, or, at the lowest estimate, tolerate.

[1] Matthew Paris, II, 605.
[2] *Rot. Lit. Pat.* I, 144 b; in July Hubert, styled justiciar, was ordered to deliver seisin of certain houses in Canterbury, plainly in his capacity as custodian of Kent with Dover and Canterbury; *Rot. Lit. Claus.* I, 220.
[3] Matthew Paris, VI, 65.
[4] Magna Carta caps. 18 (the justiciar, if the king was abroad, was to send two justices through each county four times a year, to hold assizes); 41 (the king or his chief justice was to discover how English merchants had been treated in a land at war with England); 45; 61 (if any of the articles were transgressed, the complaint to be notified to four barons of the Twenty-five, who would notify the king, or if he were abroad the justiciar).

I. HUBERT DE BURGH

Among the household officials of John when he was count of Mortain, Hubert, at least from 1198, was chamberlain.[1] After John's accession Hubert's continued in office as chamberlain to the king of England. The new justiciar was peculiarly John's man in a sense in which Hubert Walter or Geoffrey fitz Peter was not. His parentage is unknown, but in an early charter which he issued as chamberlain the witnesses included Geoffrey, archdeacon of Norwich, and Thomas de Burgh, who were his brothers.[2] Hubert's inheritance consisted of the manors of Burgh, Beeston, Newton and Sotherton, the first three in Norfolk, the last in Suffolk.[3] These he augmented by the purchase of two knights' fees in Beeston and Runton, and two carucates of land in Hindringham.[4] The king gave him Cawston and Aylsham and, as count of Mortain, Croxton, during King Richard's captivity, but this Hubert lost on the king's return, recovering it after he had become justiciar.[5] Hubert's estates thus lay in Norfolk and

[1] A charter of Count John of 12 June 1198 includes the chamberlain Hubert de Burgh among the witnesses; *Ancient Charters*, p. 110. It is likely that Hubert had been chamberlain for some years previously; Johnston, 'The Lands of Hubert de Burgh', *EHR*, L, 421 nn. 3, 4; Painter, *King John*, p. 84.

[2] Harl. MS 2110, fo. 29v. Geoffrey, in 1200, held the living of Orford in Suffolk, and on 14 August 1200 he became archdeacon of Norwich; *Rot. Chart.* pp. 60, 74. On 2 June 1225 he was elected to the see of Ely; *CPR 1216–25*, p. 532. Thomas was castellan of Norwich when the castle was taken by Prince Louis, and he was used to try to induce Hubert to surrender Dover, in 1216; Matthew Paris, III, 3–4. There was a third brother, William, older than Hubert, who was chief lord in the Limerick region in Ireland; Painter, *op. cit.* pp. 44–5, and Johnston, *loc. cit.* p. 418 n. 2. All that is known of their parents is that their mother's name was Alice; Cotton MS Nero E vii, fo. 91.

[3] *CClR 1231–4*, p. 443; *de hereditate sua*. Hubert's lands, or some of them, are discussed by Johnston, *loc. cit.* See also *Complete Peerage*, VII, 133 ff. Ellis, *Hubert de Burgh*, appendix II, pp. 203 ff., has a not altogether accurate list of his lands. Johnston identifies (*loc. cit.* p. 419) Newton in South Greenhoe hundred, Burgh in South Erpingham hundred, Beeston Regis in North Erpingham hundred.

[4] *Pedes Finium, or Fines Relating to Norfolk*, nos. 355, 357–91, 479. Hubert bought the land at Hindringham in 1208 and the others in 9 and 11 John; Johnston, *loc. cit.* pp. 419–20.

[5] *Book of Fees*, p. 127; *Rot. Hundr.* I, 525; *Monasticon*, VI, 877; *Rot. de Liberate*, p. 18.

Suffolk, but King John also gave him Corfe Mullen in Dorset, and
he held Babcary and Stoke of the *honor* of Mortain; by 1213, in
addition, he had Camel of the king's gift.[1] When inquisition was
made in this year Hubert held more than fifty knights' fees stretch-
ing through the counties of Norfolk and Suffolk, Buckingham,
Surrey, Hampshire, Dorset, Somerset, Wiltshire, Essex and
Cambridge.[2] Apart from royal gifts Hubert had built up part of
this complex of lands by his own efforts. In 1202 he obtained the
land of Emma, wife of Gilbert of Norfolk at Creake, and also
Ludham in Nottinghamshire.[3] The most effective way, however,
in which to increase estates was a successful marriage, like those of
Geoffrey fitz Peter and William Marshal. Hubert's first attempt
was an agreement towards the end of April 1200 to marry Joan,
youngest daughter of William, earl of Devon, with whom he
would obtain the Isle of Wight and the manor of Christchurch,
Hampshire. The proposal came to nothing, presumably for the
reason that the countess of Devon bore a son and, provision having
been made for this possibility in the agreement, Hubert would
then have received not these lands but £60 a year and the service
of ten knights.[4] The birth of this young brother must have
reduced Joan's attractions. About 1209 Hubert married his first
wife, Beatrice, daughter of William de Warenne lord of the
honor of Wormegay, the greatest of Hubert's neighbours in his
ancestral manors.[5] Possibly Hamelin, earl of Warenne, head of
the senior branch of this family, used his influence to instal
Hubert in John's household, but this is conjectural. Beatrice was
widow of Doon Bardolf by whom she had a son called William.
Hubert obtained some lands with the lady, namely Stowe and
North Runcton in Norfolk and Finborough in Suffolk, but he

---

[1] *Book of Fees*, pp. 79, 80, 85, 90. In 1210–12 Hubert had 17 knights' fees in
Somerset and Dorset; *Red Book*, II, 545. The possession of these lands explains
Hubert's interest in Cleeve Abbey. The Roumar lands were usually known as
the *honor* of Camel; *Pipe Roll 3 John*, p. 200.
[2] *Red Book*, p. 142; *Complete Peerage*, VII, 135.   [3] *CChR*, I, 44.
[4] *Rot. Chart.* p. 52; *Rot. de Oblatis*, p. 67. On Hubert's alleged marriages see
Johnston, *loc. cit.* p. 427.
[5] *CChR 1231–4*, p. 166. The precise date of the marriage is not known but
Hubert's son by Beatrice, John de Burgh, was knighted in 1229; Matthew
Paris, III, 190.

also became guardian of William and the lands of his father which included the *honor* of Wormegay; and in fact William never obtained the *honor* until Hubert was dead.[1]

When Hubert de Burgh became justiciar he was already a considerable landowner. In office his wealth and power grew rapidly. In August following the grant of the Great Charter he was given an *honor*, Rayleigh in Essex, of the lands of Henry of Essex, and perhaps he obtained the other *honor* of Haughley in Suffolk at the same time.[2] He was already custodian of the *honor* of Peverel.[3] In October of the same year he was given the lordship and hundred of Hoo in Kent.[4] All these lands and possessions were taken into royal protection by King John ten days before his death; none of them was to be subject to taxes or interference, to loss or damage.[5]

The death of King John did nothing to stay the steady acquisition of lands by Hubert. He contracted a second, and more spectacular, marriage. His new, though scarcely young, wife was Isabella, divorced wife of King John, widow of Geoffrey de Mandeville, son of Geoffrey fitz Peter, who was countess of Gloucester in her own right.[6] On 13 August 1217 the sheriffs of nine counties were ordered to give Hubert custody of all her lands.[7] Isabella died childless shortly after the marriage and the earldom passed to her nephew Gilbert of Clare, but Hubert obtained custody not indeed of the immediate heir but of his son

[1] *CClR 1231–4, ibid.* From the land of Beatrice's son by Doon Hubert gave the advowson of the church of Portslade to the Premonstratensian abbey of Bradsole in 1221; Bodl. MS Rawlinson B 336, pp. 170–1; *Monasticon*, VI, 942; in 1229 he gave the manor to his daughter Meggotta; PRO Curia Regis Roll, no. 85 m 23 v. William had already given Hubert the manor and ten knights' fees; Salzmann, *Abstract of Feet of Fines* (Sussex Record Soc. 1902), no. 200; Johnston, *loc. cit.* p. 427.

[2] *Rot. Lit. Pat.* p. 153; *Book of Fees*, p. 282. In a return of 1219 Haughley was said to be held by Hubert *per regem Iohannem*.

[3] *Rot. Lit. Pat.* p. 145.   [4] *Rot. Lit. Claus.* I, 233.   [5] *Ibid.* p. 199.

[6] Johnston, *loc. cit.* p. 429, wrongly states that Isabella was the widow of Geoffrey fitz Peter, but she was actually given by King John to the former justiciar's son with the major part of the *honor* of Gloucester; *Rot. Lit. Pat.* p. 109; *Rot. Lit. Claus.* I, 162, 209.

[7] *Rot. Lit. Claus.* I, 319b. Fawkes de Bréauté was ordered on the same day to give Hubert seisin of Walden *ut de libera dote* of the countess.

Richard on his father's death.[1] Such a wardship was not a permanent source of profit, but possession of one gave its holder considerable power and wealth and the opportunity to reap some lasting benefit; in this particular case the opportunity to unite his own family with the Clares. For in 1221 Hubert had wed yet a third time and his wife was Margaret, eldest sister of the king of Scotland, and by this marriage he had a daughter, Margaret or Meggotta, who was secretly married to Richard of Clare.[2] None of his marriages brought him any permanent gain of importance, but he held a succession of other great baronies in his hands. Thus in 1224 he became guardian of the lands of the earl of Arundel and two years later of the lands and heir of Hugh Bigod, earl of Norfolk.[3] There was no successor to the former until 1235.[4] But if these estates could not be used to build up a great family, Hubert nevertheless could hope to found one, for in February 1227 he was created earl of Kent and the succession was conferred on his descendants by Margaret.[5] At the same time he was given £50 per year in lieu of the third penny of the county, which made his income considerable since he was paid, from December 1222, £300 per annum to sustain himself in the justiciarship and another £1,000 a year for custody of Dover castle.[6] To this fortune were added the manor, castle, and *honor* of Knaresborough in October 1229, and the *honor* of Eye in Suffolk a few days later.[7]

When Hubert fell from power in 1232, there was drawn up by the chancery an enormous list of his lands.[8] This was divided into two sections: those which Hubert had by inheritance or purchase, which the king allowed him to keep, and those held in chief of the

[1] *Complete Peerage*, v, 692; vii, 138.
[2] Powicke, *Henry III and the Lord Edward*, pp. 760 ff.
[3] *Complete Peerage*, vii, 137.
[4] *Ibid.*; *Handbook of British Chronology*, p. 415.
[5] *Rot. Lit. Claus.* ii, 173; CChR, i, 13. The peculiarity of this limitation of succession has often been noticed. It seems likely that Henry III insisted on this provision because Hubert was a *novus homo*, and his descendants by Margaret would have the blood of kings of Scotland in their veins; Johnston, *loc. cit.* p. 430; *Complete Peerage*, vii, 137; Powicke, *op. cit.* p. 767.
[6] *Rot. Lit. Claus.* i, 495, 526.
[7] CChR, i, 101; CClR 1227–31, p. 215.
[8] CClR 1231–4, p. 166.

king, which Henry III took away. Both are considerable and the former very long. There is, however, little evidence to suggest corruption on Hubert's part, although it is a possibility. Only one charge of abusing his position to obtain land was made against him, and that can be disproved.[1] Hubert held the lands of several rebels who had suffered confiscation in the civil war, but the circumstances are not clear and in the face of his enemies' silence nothing can be asserted. Hubert's lands consisted of scattered manors which never possessed the unity of an *honor* although he may have administered them as a single whole.[2] Hubert had built up no great barony but simply a large collection of scattered manors,[3] many of which, under the terms of Henry III's grants, were held jointly with the Countess Margaret.[4] John de Burgh, Hubert's son and heir by Beatrice de Warenne, only succeeded to these in 1259 when his stepmother died. The title of earl had been limited to the issue of this third marriage, and it died with Hubert.

[1] Johnston, *loc. cit.* pp. 424, 429, where the charge against Hubert that he had sent messengers to the pope to have the king declared of age in order to obtain the lands of Henry of Essex is discussed. From the foregoing account it is clear that Hubert held these lands in King John's reign. Johnston discusses the rebels' land and finds the evidence of corruption insufficient. His acquisition of Banstead, Surrey, from William de Mowbray is suspicious, but the circumstances are far from clear; CChR, I, 83.

[2] Johnston, *loc. cit.* p. 431. Lawrence of St Albans was steward of all his lands; Matthew Paris, III, 233. A roll in the PRO gives the accounts of a number of Hubert's manors while they were in the king's hands; Ministers Accounts bundle 1117, no. 13. These manors were acquired in different ways, and belonged to different honours. The fact that they were lumped together suggests to Johnston that Hubert treated them as a whole, but within these manors were some of the *honor* of Arundel, and various other baronies which were unities in themselves with their own honorial administrations; they can never, therefore, have been organically part of Hubert's own lands even if convenience set one steward over the whole complex.

[3] 'We have been watching the growth of a barony, a growth that is suddenly cut short by Hubert's fall'; Johnston, *loc. cit.* p. 431.

[4] This condition in Henry III's grants was a necessary corollary to the limitation of the earldom to their descendants in order to maintain an earl's dignity. Hubert and Margaret were regarded as joint tenants, each having a life interest; CChR, I, 248. The king had frequently granted lands to husband and wife jointly, so that such an arrangement was not peculiar to Margaret and Hubert; Powicke, *op. cit.* p. 766.

Apart from the earldom and the lands in Norfolk and Suffolk and other English counties, Hubert had made a determined attempt to create a powerful marcher lordship. In May 1201 King John made him warden of the Welsh marches, and he received the three castles of the justiciar, as they came to be called, Grosmont, Skenfrith, and Llantilio, a triangular group of fortresses in Upper Gwent dominating the approach to South Wales.[1] He lost these fortresses in 1205 but recovered them by a suit against Reginald de Braiose in 1219.[2] Four years later he acquired the new castle and *honor* of Montgomery, and six years later still, by gaining the castles and honours of Carmarthen and Cardigan, he had created a powerful marcher lordship. On the death of John de Braiose he added the lordship of Gower.[3] Hubert's power was considerable. His lands in the Welsh marches, added to the *honor* of Henry of Essex and that of Peverel of London, made Meggotta a great heiress, and the only one in line of succession. If the marriage with Richard of Clare had been successful these lands and earldoms would have been united. The loss of the estates held in chief of the Crown in 1232 destroyed the inheritance, and John de Burgh eventually obtained nothing like the lands which would have come to Meggotta. The *coup d'état* of 1232 not only reduced the justiciarship; it spelled the ruin of Hubert's hopes of a great family.

The household of a great magnate like Count John of Mortain would be a highly organized one, a repetition in a minor key of the royal household. The chamberlain of Count John must have been an official of some importance, perhaps one of the three most important officers in the household, and his duties can have differed only in degree from those of the royal chamberlainship.[4]

[1] Howden, IV, 163; *Rot. de Liberate*, p. 19.

[2] *Rot. Lit. Claus.* I, 386, 398 b.

[3] *CChR*, I, 74, 100, 127; *CPR 1225–32*, p. 417. Professor Powicke states (*op. cit.* p. 126) that in the first months of 1233 John de Braiose was killed at Bramber by a fall from his horse, and that the beneficiaries of his death in the southern march were first Hubert de Burgh and then Peter des Rievaulx. I do not know his authority for this statement. Hubert had the *honor* of Gower on 20 November 1230.

[4] Johnston, *loc. cit.* pp. 421–2, describes the household of Count John as highly organized. It has recently been the subject of a study for an M.A. degree

Hubert de Burgh, who held the former position and succeeded to the latter when John became king, must have had considerable experience in the work of administering a great *honor* when, in 1199, he was suddenly transferred to the greatest *honor* of all. Yet, in view of the other offices which he came quickly to occupy, he can have had little time to devote to the chamberlainship, although he continued to hold it until 1205.[1] In the three years after 1200 he was sheriff of Hereford, Somerset, and Dorset; from 1202 he had Cornwall and Berkshire too; and as sheriff he held the castles to which the counties were appended.[2] During these years his power and fortune were increased by his becoming custodian of three baronies, Beauchamp of Somerset, Dunster, and that of William of Windsor.[3] These shires and baronies account for many of the castles Hubert held; Windsor, for instance, and Launceston and Dunster; but these do not exhaust the list. By 1202 he also held Wallingford and, more important, in March 1201 he became constable of Dover and warden of the Cinque ports.[4] In May of the same year he became warden of the Welsh marches and his position was buttressed by possession of the three castles of the justiciar in Upper Gwent. As sheriff of Hereford and warden of the marches Hubert may have been the means King John sought to employ in order to keep the Braiose family in check, but if so his object was soon abandoned.[5]

Hubert had been described as the most important official in the country in the early years of King John, but his position, like his function as a check on the Braioses, was temporary. In 1202 he was summoned to Normandy where he became castellan of Falaise

of Manchester University. I am indebted to Professor Cheney for allowing me to read this. On honorial administration and the precedence of the chamberlain see F. M. Stenton, *First Century of English Feudalism*, pp. 69–70.

[1] *Rot. Lit. Claus.* I, 33.
[2] *Complete Peerage*, VII, 134.
[3] *Rot. de Liberate*, p. 23; *Pipe Roll 3 John*, pp. 38, 126; *Pipe Roll 4 John*, p. 96.
[4] *Rot. Lit. Pat.* pp. 7, 9.
[5] Painter, *King John*, p. 85. Hubert may also have been sent to deal with Fulk fitz Warin who was the chief source of trouble in the marches in 1201, and the legend of Fulk, curiously enough, mentions 100 knights sent to hunt him down; *ibid.* p. 50. In view of John's Norman commitments at the time it seems doubtful if this was the sole purpose.

and subsequently joint castellan of Chinon in Touraine.[1] This translation to the continent need not have affected Hubert's English position but in the latter fortress he was besieged by the French king while Normandy and the continental lands were falling. Hubert made a considerable reputation as a soldier; for, while King John returned to England in December 1203 and Rouen fell little more than six months later, Hubert held out in Chinon until the summer of 1205; and the castle was only taken when it had been virtually levelled to the ground and Hubert himself wounded and captured.[2] He probably remained in captivity for two years, during which time he lost all of his English offices and some of his lands.[3] Probably in the interests of administrative efficiency it could not be otherwise; there is no real evidence of royal displeasure with him and some assistance was given with his ransom. When he returned to England it was not long before he received another office, that of sheriff of Lincolnshire, with custody of Sleaford castle.[4] Lacunae in the evidence prevent any description of his work for the next few years and speculation, although interesting, is idle. Perhaps his

[1] *Rot. Lit. Pat.* pp. 16, 17. It was at Falaise, after the battle of Mirabeau, that Hubert, traditionally, refused to mutilate Arthur; Coggeshall, pp. 139–41; Ellis, *Hubert de Burgh*, p. 15; Painter, *King John*, p. 85. Both writers seem to accept this story and offer it as a reason for the king's loss of confidence in Hubert which led to the loss of his English lands and offices; they believe that he fell out of favour. Perhaps, but it seems unnecessary to adduce this rather melodramatic evidence when the fact was that Hubert, wounded and a prisoner, could not administer his offices; administrative efficiency or military security demanded some other provision for them. In any case, if the story be accepted, the king's displeasure must have been delayed until 1205. As castellan of Chinon he was addressed jointly with Philip of Oldcoates; *Rot. Lit. Pat.* p. 40 (a letter of 21 April 1204). It is improbable that John should so trust a man who had disobeyed previously and whom he was to punish for this same disobedience a year later.

[2] Coggeshall, pp. 154–5.

[3] *Rot. Lit. Claus.* I, 51 b, 55 b, 58; *Rot. Lit. Pat.* p. 57. On 6 February 1207 the exchequer was ordered to pay 300 marks to a pledge of Hubert de Burgh (*Rot. Lit. Claus.* I, 64), possibly part of his ransom; and also in 1207 the sum of £100 was advanced to Hubert; of which half was to be refunded in September of that year and half after Christmas. If the first payment was part of the ransom, Hubert must have returned to England in the latter half of 1207.

[4] *Complete Peerage*, VII, 134–5. Sleaford castle belonged to the bishop of Lincoln; Lincoln castle itself had an hereditary constable.

wound prevented the activity of the early years, perhaps his marriage to Beatrice occupied his attention, or perhaps behind the curtain of silence his career continued as before. It was again interrupted by his removal to the continent.

On 23 August 1213 Hubert was made seneschal of Poitou in the place of Ivo de Jallia, possibly in association with Philip de Aubeney and Geoffrey de Neville; he was also called mayor of Niort.[1] It is axiomatic that such an appointment showed the king's trust in Hubert, but his experiences as castellan of Falaise and Chinon, and perhaps his military reputation and his administrative background, were likely factors in his being given the post. That his reputation as a soldier was involved may be gathered from his accompanying John when in the next year the king made his attempt to recover the lost possessions. This continental connexion of Hubert's had a number of important consequences in his career. He had already gained early administrative training in England and he was familiar with the work involved in caring for a great *honor*; as sheriff he would be familiar with exchequer procedure and, to a lesser extent, with judicial processes. Yet from 1205 his part in royal activity, so far as the evidence goes, was insignificant and he accounted for Lincolnshire from 1208 to 1212 by deputy. Thus he had taken little part in those royal proceedings which bore heavily on the baronage, providing the irritations which came to a head in the demand for the Great Charter. He was abroad, too, in the years immediately preceding its grant. On the continent he had gained a military reputation; he had shown himself a loyal minister of the king, faithful almost unto death. And so, at Runny-mede, he must have been one of the few men, perhaps the only man, who was acceptable to both parties; an obvious candidate for the justiciarship in the situation created by Magna Carta.

Upon Hubert's appointment as justiciar, his collection of offices and castles started to grow rapidly. In 1215 he was made sheriff of Hereford, Surrey, Kent, Norfolk, and Suffolk, of which counties he held the first pair until 1226 and the second, with a break of two years to 1217, until 1225.[2] In Surrey and Kent he displaced

---

[1] *Rot. Lit. Pat.* pp. 106, 126 *b*; *Rot. Lit. Claus.* I, 142 *b*.
[2] *Complete Peerage*, VII, 134.

Reginald of Cornhill, an active supporter of the barons, but in Hereford he succeeded Engelard de Cigogné, one of the foreign mercenaries whose removal, the barons protested, King John had promised. Another baronial supporter, John fitz Robert, held the counties of Norfolk and Suffolk although John Marshal had been appointed to succeed him; as a compromise Hubert was given these counties also.[1] He held them until the general change in sheriffs and the new appointments under Henry III, although in 1228 he became sheriff of Westmorland as guardian of the Vesci heir.[2] At the same time as he received these counties he retrieved the castle of Dover, to which, with Kent, were added Canterbury and the Norfolk and Suffolk castles of Norwich and Orford as well as that of Hereford. These, except the last, he held, with the acquisition of Rochester and the three Welsh castles, until the general surrender of castles in December 1223.[3] As justiciar he also had the Tower of London, and, presumably as the successor of Reginald of Cornhill, the chamberlainship and exchange of London.[4] None of these shires or castles was held beyond the early years of Henry III, but in the uncertain political situation which existed at that time they gave the justiciar a powerful position until, with the king's coming of age and the elimination of colleagues in or rivals for power, Hubert became justiciar without rival.

Hubert's rise to social and political significance invites comparison with Geoffrey fitz Peter, his predecessor in the justiciarship, and William Marshal who as *rector regis et regni* overshadowed Hubert for the first two years of the new reign. Geoffrey's career has been described in some detail in previous chapters, and William Marshal has been the subject of a learned monograph.[5] Both Geoffrey and William started from scratch, as it were, in the social world. Both were knights, and William a landless one. The

---

[1] *Rot. Lit. Pat.* pp. 144, 149–50; Painter, *op. cit.* pp. 329, 337; Richardson, 'The Morrow of the Great Charter', pp. 441–2.

[2] Powicke, *op. cit.* pp. 95–8; Mills, 'Experiments in Exchequer Procedure', *TRHS*, 4th series, VIII, 166–7; Mills, 'Reforms at the Exchequer', *TRHS*, 4th series, X, 132; *Complete Peerage*, VII, 134.

[3] *Complete Peerage*, VII, 136–7; Powicke, *op. cit.* pp. 55, 60.

[4] *Rot. Lit. Pat.* I, 129 b.   [5] Painter, *William Marshal.*

way in which they rose to eminence differs. Geoffrey made his way in the royal administration; William fought his way into favour by knightly prowess. But their careers were only the means by which they gained royal attention, and the acquisition of large estates came by marriage. Both were given royal wards, in Geoffrey's case Beatrice de Say, in William's the heiress of Pembroke, and in the right of these ladies, whom they married, both entered the magnate class; and both subsequently achieved the highest office. Hubert's career superficially looks very similar. In terms of his inheritance he was probably better off than either of the other two. He served an administrative apprenticeship in John's early years, and he made a military reputation. At first sight he combines something of the merit which secured the fortunes of both Geoffrey and William. Like them, he thought to improve his position by marriage, but in this he failed. His early proposed match with the daughter of the earl of Devon never took place; his two succeeding marriages brought him little permanent gain. Nevertheless, by 1212 he held more knights' fees than, for example, Richard de Luci, one of his predecessors.[1] The part he played in events at the time of Magna Carta shows that he was then acceptable to the baronage and was probably actively supported by the earl of Warenne.[2] How is it, then, that against Hubert should be raised the cry of *novus homo*, an upstart of whom no gossip was too bad to be believed, when Geoffrey and William, at roughly the same time, were socially acceptable and seem to have been honourably regarded?

No answer can be given with certainty. 'It is', says Professor Powicke, 'a pity that we know so little about these people. As we stir these cold ashes, a tongue of flame seems to dart out and flicker and die. We cannot feel sure of very much.'[3] Hubert's birth and inheritance cannot in themselves have justified the cry that he was

---

[1] Richard de Luci, the justiciar of Henry II, might have been introduced as another example of a man of the knightly class who was not a great magnate, but who became justiciar and built up a barony of thirty knights' fees with its *caput* at Ongar which was treated as a barony and therefore as a unity; see above, pp. 38–9.

[2] Painter, *King John*, p. 328.

[3] Powicke, *op. cit.* p. 767.

a 'new man'; so, too, were Geoffrey fitz Peter and William
Marshal. The speed with which Hubert accumulated lands was no
doubt responsible in part. Geoffrey and William were already
possessors of a great *honor* before they reached highest office; and
Hubert was not. Envy must certainly have been one factor. As
justiciar he must have seemed to monopolize the good things
which the king had in his gift. Not having a great *honor* when he
became justiciar it must have seemed that through his office he had
an unfair advantage in aggrandizement. But perhaps the easiest
explanation is the right one; there was something in his character
that promoted bitter enmity.[1] For whatever the reason or reasons,
Hubert had many enemies, although the gossip and extravagant
charges brought against him were produced after his fall, and
many of them may have been specious reasons brought up from
the past to justify his persecution. It is quite certain that in 1232
Hubert had little or no support—except protection from the
extremest measures proposed against him by Henry III—among
the baronage, and political antagonism was the necessary condition of his downfall without which personal dislikes would have
beat against his position in vain.

For, with the death of King John, the political situation was
quite different from that which had confronted any other justiciar.
The new king was a minor and England was in the throes of civil
war. On 28 October 1216 Henry was made king at Gloucester,
but Hubert was not present; he was instead defending Dover
against Louis of France.[2] After the coronation the Earl Marshal,
William of Pembroke, was persuaded by the papal legate Guala
to be regent, Henry's person being committed to Peter des Roches
as tutor, an arrangement which was seen as a triumvirate of legate,
earl, and bishop.[3] A fortnight later royal counsellors, bishops, and
magnates met at Bristol. Oaths of fealty were taken to Henry and
the Great Charter reissued under the seals of the legate and the
marshal. Hubert de Burgh attended this council as justiciar, the

---

[1] Powicke, *op. cit.* p. 69.
[2] The fact that he was there besieged explains his absence as an executor of
John's will which Turner, 'The Minority of Henry III', *TRHS*, new series,
XVIII, 247, interpreted as a sign of lack of trust in Hubert.
[3] Powicke, *op. cit.* pp. 4–5.

earl of Pembroke being *rector regis et regni*.[1] Thus in the first years of the reign the justiciar, after he had been relieved by victory of the defence of Dover and other purely military activity, was overshadowed by the council in which the dominant figure was William Marshal. The latter died in May 1219, committing the kingdom to the new papal legate Pandulf, with whom Hubert de Burgh co-operated and shared power, the king being still under the control of his tutors Peter des Roches and, for knightly purposes, Philip de Aubeney.[2] There was considerable doubt about the age when the king reached legal manhood, but his tutelage came to an end in the summer of 1221 when Peter des Roches and Philip de Aubeney ceased to be his tutors.[3] Pandulf left England in this same year and then Hubert de Burgh came into his own as justiciar; he held the realm of England in his hand.[4]

He was not, however, free from the restraints imposed by the authority or influence of others. In the first place there was the young king himself, and secondly the archbishop of Canterbury, Stephen Langton, with whom Hubert co-operated and who, with his great prestige, had the dominant voice in times of crisis; he and the bishops were an influence which outweighed that of Peter des Roches.[5] And so, in 1223, when the pope declared Henry III of age for certain purposes, Hubert was, in the normal course of events, in control. The figure of the archbishop emerged in times of crisis, the council was in the background, and Peter des Roches still on the scene until 1228, but, in the practical affairs of government and in the control of the king, Hubert was dominant. He was free, within the scope envisaged by the Great Charter in its reissued form, to exercise the functions of the justiciarship. His term of office falls into three parts. In the first, Hubert was a member of, but not the dominant figure in, the council; a phase

---

[1] William Marshal had previously been given the title of justiciar by the chancery clerks in documents which they issued; *Rot. Lit. Pat.* pp. 1, 2; *Rot. Lit. Claus.* I, 293.

[2] Turner, *loc. cit.* pp. 294–5. The legate delegated his administrative duties to Hubert, but he himself certainly acted as regent; Shirley, *Royal Letters*, I, xx.

[3] Powicke, *op. cit.* p. 43; a note in the *Curia Regis Rolls*, VIII, 236, implies that the king's thirteenth birthday was considered a few months after his second coronation. [4] *Bracton's Note Book*, p. 1221. [5] Powicke, *op. cit.* p. 43.

which ends with the marshal's death. In the second, under the supervision of the legate, he and Peter des Roches were, if not two firm friends like David and Jonathan, at least the two outstanding personalities, a not unnatural situation in view of Peter's own justiciarship and his present guardianship of the king. This phase ended with the papal declaration in 1223 and also, if we may believe the annalist of Dunstaple, with an ugly scene in which Hubert called Peter a traitor to the king and the kingdom.[1] The third was the period in which Hubert, having shed his competitors for power, stood alone as justiciar and chief minister of the king. His authority was never seriously challenged until the return of Bishop Peter, and it is, perhaps, useful to distinguish yet a fourth period in Hubert's justiciarship: from 1232 onwards, when, slowly but surely, his ruin was accomplished. His fall in 1232 marked the end of the Angevin justiciarship.

Hubert de Burgh had been appointed justiciar under the shadow of Magna Carta. He attained the office because he was acceptable to both king and baronage, although he lacked much of the training of his predecessors. Peter des Roches, too, was no lawyer. Both he and Hubert were household officials of the king, and it may have seemed to John that by appointing such men his use of administrative machinery would achieve greater flexibility than it would in the hands of one bred in the tradition of stricter formality in the exchequer or the courts. All administration was the king's, his will prevailed, but, if the mentality shown by Richard fitz Nigel in the *Dialogus* is any indication, the rules which government procedures had evolved might start to be held to be binding even on the activity of the king who created them. There was one attempt, at least, in John's reign, for the exchequer to insist on its rules against the less rigid practice of the wardrobe.[2]

---

[1] *Annales Monastici*, vii, 84; Matthew Paris, iii, 79; in connexion with a conspiracy headed by the earl of Chester. The occasion was the resumption of royal castles in 1223. According to the story, Hubert blamed Peter des Roches for the trouble.

[2] At Lambeth in 1207 the treasurer and chamberlains refused to pay money over to Philip de Lucy on two occasions and each writ was noted *quia breve redditum fuit*; *Rot. Lit. Claus.* i, 75–6. Eight days later the king ordered the iusticiar to see on his own authority that the payments were made; *ibid.* p. 76.

The whole tendency towards 'departmentalization' is an expression of the evolution of rules which make for rigidity. Whatever the truth of this, it is at least true that both of the appointments John made to the justiciarship were household officials, men whom he had raised up, who were peculiarly his servants. The nature of his appointments may have changed the character of the justiciarship. If the office depended for its power and direction upon the man who held it, the sort of training which its holder had received was plainly important, although it is clear from the work of both Peter des Roches and Hubert de Burgh that the traditional functions of the office commanded their attention. The pace at which the machinery of government was developing placed it beyond the effective control of one man; it depended more and more upon the specialized skills of different classes of officials. The final authority, other than the king or the council in Henry III's minority, might be the justiciar's, but his routine supervision of the work of royal administration could only be exceptional in any given sphere. There remained, however, the viceregal tradition of the justiciar's office and it was this conception which was present in the baron's minds when they drew up the Great Charter; in every instance the justiciar is conceived not as an administrator or the greatest of the king's ministers, but as the king's *alter ego*, his regent. Yet the effective basis of this concept of the justiciarship had gone with the loss of Normandy. It lingered only because the loss was not regarded as permanent, and as hope of recovery died so the *raison d'être* of the justiciarship faded. Hubert's tenure of office saw both a change in its nature from the original justiciarship as it was created by Henry II and carried on by his sons, and its abolition with his own fall in 1232.

2. THE JUSTICIAR AND THE COUNCIL

When King John died in the midst of a civil war, Hubert de Burgh was besieged in Dover castle. He was not, for this reason, named

The incident also caused the removal of Philip de Lucy and his work was done first by Peter des Roches and afterwards by his confidential clerk, William de St Maxence; Jolliffe, 'The Chamber and the Castle Treasures under King John', *Studies in Medieval History presented to F. M. Powicke*, p. 129.

as an executor of John's will which, if it were to be given effect, needed as executors people who were accessible, men without whose counsel, as the king said, even in good health he would do nothing. There is no reason to suppose that Hubert's loyalty was in doubt, simply his availability.[1] The fact that he was entrusted with Dover castle, one of the keys of England, is sufficient to dispel any such suggestion. It was therefore without the justiciar that the magnates assembled at Gloucester to crown the young Henry, that the legate prevailed upon William Marshal, earl of Pembroke, to become regent, that the person of the king was entrusted to Peter des Roches. Contemporaries asserted that there was a triumvirate of legate, bishop and marshal. Hubert's position as justiciar may, indeed, have been forgotten by chancery clerks who described the earl marshal as justiciar and gave him the title in letters that were issued;[2] and this forgetfulness may have been helped by Hubert's position in the last months of John's reign when orders were sent to him as a local royal officer, but very few as justiciar. When the magnates reassembled at Bristol on 11 November 1216 Hubert was freed by his truce with Louis of France to attend, and a new title for the marshal was devised; he became *rector noster et regni nostri*.[3] Hubert, styled justiciar, headed the list of barons who witnessed the reissue of the Great Charter, but his was not the seal attached to the document which was authenticated by those of the marshal and the legate.[4] The fact is significant of the justiciar's status. He was not to be the king's *alter ego*, for the king was a minor and the council acted for him. His viceregal character was in abeyance and his work was to be executive and administrative.

The justiciar's position was complicated by the facts of political life. His primary duty while the war against Louis lasted was the defence of Dover. He was not the dominant figure in the council, nor did he have control of the king, for this belonged to Peter des Roches, an important figure, an able administrator, and a former

---

[1] Hubert's loyalty was doubted by Turner, 'The Minority of Henry III', *TRHS*, new series, XVIII, 247.

[2] *Rot. Lit. Pat.* pp. 1–2; *Rot. Lit. Claus.* p. 293.

[3] Turner, *loc. cit.* p. 246.   [4] *Ibid.* p. 248.

justiciar. Hubert could hardly have hoped, even if he had been available, for the position filled by William Marshal. He was not yet among the greatest magnates, he was a *novus homo*, and he had been a compromise candidate, as it were, for the justiciarship since, in the nature of things, he could not have been first favourite with either party. The council, too, was an active force in English government, and above all there was the papal legate representing Henry III's feudal suzerain; in the background there moved the figure of Stephen Langton, archbishop of Canterbury and a cardinal. If Hubert had had the same training and antecedents as most of his predecessors in office, the political situation would still have robbed him of their traditional dominance in government. The part which he played can only be assessed against the position of the council and in relation to the three most important figures, the legate, William Marshal, and Bishop Peter.

The minority of Henry III was a unique situation in Anglo-Norman history. When the king had been abroad in the past the justiciar had been regent, although the idea of reinforcing his authority with that of other prominent figures of royal counsellors was not new. Hubert Walter had been joined to Geoffrey fitz Peter; Richard Marsh and William Briewerre were joined to Peter des Roches; the justiciar's strength, like the king's, was reflected in the quantity of counsel which he had. These expedients were limited to specific circumstances and occasions; they were primarily an administrative device, and the determination of policy always lay with the king. Now, however, there was a boy king, a minor who could not make decisions, and the council took his place within certain limits. It had no precedents to guide it and no authority to which it could turn for direction, for it was itself the final authority until the king should come of age. The authority of the council manifested itself in every field of government: in the chancery, in the exchequer, in the courts of law, the marks of its guiding hand may be seen. Until the beginning of Henry's third year letters were sealed with the seal of the earl marshal, but then a royal seal was introduced. It was provided by common counsel that no charter or letter of confirmation, alienation, sale or gift should be sealed with the Great Seal until the king came of age, and this restriction upon its use was witnessed by the legate, the two archbishops, the marshal, and the justiciar before most of the bishops of England.[1] This was counsel in its widest sense, embracing any magnate who could be present, and on matters of great importance, for example the truce with France, the greater the counsel the greater the king's strength and dignity.[2]

Letters patent were issued by the council's authority. When the seneschalship of Poitou and Gascony was committed to Hugh de Vivon the appointment was decided upon by the council before which Hugh swore good faith to the king.[3] Or, again, when his lands in England were returned to the count of la Marche, Richard de Ripariis, to whom the notice was addressed, was requested to come before the council to hear its instructions.[4] These were affairs of moment, but it was detail, too, which interested the council. It required to know of Robert Lupus what warrant he had for an action, and its authority was noted on the roll of letters close for the issue of writs of seisin or payments from the treasury.[5] Similarly its authority was invoked at the exchequer. On occasion it sat there with the barons;[6] more often writs addressed to the barons of the exchequer, a gift of alms for

[1] *CPR 1216–25*, p. 173.
[2] Baldwin, *The King's Council*, p. 22. The conversations held at Shrewsbury with the prince of North Wales were conducted by the legate, Langton, Peter and Hubert de Burgh; *CPR 1216–25*, p. 260.
[3] *CPR 1216–25*, pp. 306, 308.
[4] *Ibid.* p. 330.
[5] *Rot. Lit. Claus.* I, 395, 406–10, 495, 501.
[6] Pipe Roll 2 Henry III, m. 4v. A judgement was recorded there by William Marshal, Peter des Roches, Hubert de Burgh, and the king's council by which Nicholas de Verdun was acquitted of £551 of the aid of the knights of the honor of Leicester; *provisum est per concilium domini regis ad scaccarium in crastino S. Valentini quod David' Lardinarius recipiet liberationem suam de civitate Ebor';* LTR, i, m. 1v, *amerciamenta c marcarum pro foresta abbatis Sancti Edmundi cancellatur in originali per libertatem carte sue per justiciarium et consilium Regis;* LTR 5, m. 12r. Similarly a convention was enrolled before the council and the barons of the exchequer; *Rot. Lit. Claus.* I, 361. The barons also sought to consult the council in difficulties; KR 2, m. 18v; and the marshal and the council postponed cases; KR 1, m. 4r. The exchequer session consisted of the treasurer, the bishops of Winchester and Coventry, the *rector*, the justiciar, William Briewerre, William de Cantilupe, Thomas of Erdington, Geoffrey of Buckland, Robert de Neville.

instance, were issued on the authority of the council.[1] It intervened actively in the work of justice. Thus in the Michaelmas term 1219 the bench at Westminster was probably reinforced by the council, for it was recorded in one case that the justices and especially the magnates doubted if a litigant was of age and therefore required him to produce the proof of twelve lawful men.[2] This reinforcement of the court by at least some magnates of the council is reflected in final concords, although a court of judges presided over by Martin of Pattishall was more usual.[3] The council occupied a definite place in legal administration. When it was at Hereford it ordered a day to be given to Hugh Mortimer and his brother to hear their judgement through the clerk of William Briewerre.[4]

Direct intervention may have been the exception rather than the rule but the supervision of the council was continuous. In the Hilary term of 1220 the suit between the archbishop of York and Richard de Percy was adjourned *sine die* at the prayer of the parties and with the consent of the king's council.[5] In the following Easter term two suits were postponed by its order.[6] The reason for the council's intervention was probably the quality of the persons involved. The Mortimers were important magnates, and so was Stephen Langton, who was a party to one of the other suits. Another consideration which might draw the council into legal proceedings was the question of royal charters. At Hilary 1220 it had ordered a day to be given to Matilda de Say and Earl William de Mandeville because it dared not do judgement on charters of the king; and for the same motive it adjourned a suit which came up at Easter 1220 without a day because the prioress of Amesbury had a royal charter.[7] Its interest in legal affairs flowed from the

[1] KR 5, m. 7v; KR 3, m. 7v.

[2] Curia Regis Roll no. 71, m. 2r. For other instances of the council's intervention see the references collected by Sayles, *Select Cases in the Court of King's Bench*, I, xxxiii.

[3] CP 25(1) 233/6/2, 233/7/27; 128/11/1–7; 128/15/1–24.

[4] *Curia Regis Rolls*, VIII, 74.   [5] *Ibid.* p. 183.   [6] *Ibid.* p. 295.

[7] *Ibid.* p. 236. The attorney of Matilda had been appointed before Peter, William Marshal, the earl of Chester, the earl of Warenne, Earl Ferrers, Walter de Lacy, Fawkes de Bréauté and other magnates of the council at Oxford on the feast of St Lawrence 1217; *CPR 1216–25*, p. 113.

limitation upon its power and from the quality of the litigants involved, and it was exceptional, not routine. Government rested upon the authority of the council as the final arbiter, but its task was to preserve political tranquillity and the king's rights, and to determine policy, not to supervise the details of administration in its normal course.

The council was not an abstraction, a clearly defined institution of government; it was an indefinite group of men, the personnel of which fluctuated. 'It is unlikely that any baron was ever excluded except for grave political reasons.'[1] Men were rather counsellors than councillors; de consilio nostro. In such a vague, unstable group, the power and influence of those men who attended the king constantly, those who had some office or special relationship with him, would be the greater. This was the permanent element, the nucleus round which the larger council gathered, and this quality of permanence is expressed in the evidence for the council's activity. It is more usual to find that action was taken by William Marshal and the council, or Peter des Roches or William Briewerre or the justiciar and the council, than it is to find the council acting as an abstract title.[2] The quality of permanence which is involved in those who held executive positions is shown in the singling out by name of members of the council, but the association demonstrates the overriding authority of the council; those mentioned by name were acting as members of it and on its behalf. The papal legate who was the representative of Henry's feudal suzerain issued orders, but he was careful to take the advice of the council by writing to the prominent members of it whom he regarded as its representatives.[3] This tendency towards greater influence on the part of those more frequently in the king's company was reinforced by the professional element in the curia regis. The council might meet at the same time and place as the barons of the exchequer although the barons were usually dis-

---

[1] Baldwin, The King's Council, p. 21.

[2] CPR 1216–25, pp. 258, 308, 330, 532; Rot. Lit. Claus. I, 495, 501; II, 17; LTR 4, m. 5r; KR 5, m. 7v; KR 2, m. 18v.

[3] Royal Letters, I, 76. Si enim super his vestrum et aliorum qui sunt in scaccario expressissetis consilium, processissemus forsitan adhibeto consilio vestro. He would consult them at Worcester and request the justiciar to be there.

tinguished from the rest of the council.[1] (The council of the exchequer was rather a later development.) Between them there can have been no hard and fast division. Peter des Roches and William Briewerre had been barons of the exchequer themselves, and Hubert de Burgh as justiciar was in theory still president. Since the council was drawn from a wide variety of men, magnates and bishops who had to deliberate on matters of policy and administration, it would have to depend for its efficiency in securing the execution of its decisions upon the professional element in it, and upon a class of exchequer officials and judges. Thus a meeting of the exchequer would be, administratively speaking, a convenient place for their deliberations, since they must be translated into executive action. The same holds true of the bench of justices. The council decided policy; it was left to the judges to carry it out, with, if necessary, the authority of the council to back them up not so much on points of law as on political difficulties.

The idea that a group of men could be responsible for government was asserted in the conception of a baronial committee in the Great Charter. The novelty of the situation for the justiciar lay in the fact that his was not the dominant voice in the council, nor was he at first even among those ministers who were singled out by name from the generality of councillors and those who carried out executive functions. William Marshal's seal was used at the beginning of the minority for authenticating royal letters, and he bore the responsibility for their issue by witnessing them, with very few exceptions, as he moved about England.[2] The letters and writs spoke in the king's name but the authority for them was William Marshal's, and the few exceptions were issued by Peter des Roches and William Briewerre.[3] The legate, too, issued orders

---

[1] Rot. Lit. Claus. I, 361, 410; Excerpta e Rotulis Finium, I, 67, 88. There is one reference to the 'council' of the exchequer per consilium scaccarii et M. de Pateshull, Rot. Lit. Claus. I, 406, but this probably means 'advice' or 'counsel' rather than the council of the exchequer. Baldwin, op. cit. p. 42, quotes much later references, for example the memoranda rolls of 45 and 55 Henry III, to support his point.   [2] CPR 1216–25, passim; Rot. Lit. Claus. I, 294 ff.

[3] CPR 1216–25, p. 158; Turner, loc. cit. p. 291, who describes Peter des Roches as acting for the marshal on occasion.

of his own, but usually he worked through the prominent members of the council.[1] From the beginning of the third year of the reign the king had his own seal, but the orders which it authorized were still attested by William Marshal, although an increasing number were issued by the warranty of Peter des Roches.[2] The marshal also issued writs and conveyed orders by documents in his own name. On the memoranda roll of 2 Henry III it was noted that the chamberlain of London ought to account for 100 marks which he received at the exchequer *ad negotia domini regis facienda Per breve Willelmi Marescalli.*[3] This is a rare instance of an administrative writ, as distinct from a personal letter, in the marshal's name; usually, since he authorized writs in the king's name, his order would be described as *breve regis.*

There is other evidence for the *rector*'s personal interest in the exchequer at the time, for he appointed days for accounts to be taken, and he was consulted by the barons about an exaction from the count of Aumale.[4] This was natural. The marshal took his responsibilities seriously, and the financial problem was one of the most acute of those that faced him when he assumed office. His own interests did not run in the direction of administration; he was a knight and a warrior by experience and inclination. As a magnate he must have been aware of the necessities for administering large estates and familiar with the work of doing so. It is likely, nevertheless, that he left the supervision of routine largely to those who knew about it, while he remained the dominant figure in the council. Petitions from suitors or requests for favour were addressed to him and the council, and he and the council issued instructions. When the itinerant justices made their dignified reply to instructions from the council which they thought

---

[1] *Royal Letters*, I, 58, 75, 77, 100, 136.

[2] *CPR 1216–25*, pp. 173–85; *Rot. Lit. Claus* I, 384–5.

[3] LTR 1, m. 6r. An instance of a letter of the Marshal may be found upon the same roll. *W(illelmus) Marescallus comes Penbroc' Karissimis amicis suis baronibus de scaccario salutem. Sciatis quod recepi per manum meam de abbate de Teokesberi xx marcas per quas finem fecit cum domino rege pro habenda seisina de manerio de Godrinton cum pertinenciis unde vos rogo quatinus eum inde quietum esse ᶠaciatis quoniam vobis inde respondebo. Valete;* LTR 1, m. 7v.

[4] LTR 1, m. 1r, 1v, 6r; KR 2, m. 18v.

would lower their prestige, the remonstrance was addressed to the earl marshal, the bishop of Winchester, and Hubert de Burgh.[1] But William Marshal was an old man, and soon after Pandulf became legate in succession to Guala his health began to fail. The responsibility which he had borne for the issue of royal letters passed to others. From November 1218 other men witnessed letters occasionally, probably under some degree of urgency,[2] but from December Peter des Roches took his place by the side of the marshal as the authority for issuing the commands of government.[3] On 9 April the marshal attested his last letter; in May 1219 he died; but from 20 April Hubert de Burgh had begun to witness royal letters in a steady stream.[4]

Hubert had not succeeded to the position of the marshal. The dying *rector* had decided to entrust the king to God and the pope, and to the legate as their representative.[5] The decision is indicative of the position which the marshal had held and it was sufficient even now to prevent Peter des Roches asserting his right to keep the king. Pandulf thus succeeded William Marshal at his desire with the consent of the magnates, but he knew less of English administration than the marshal, and although he issued orders 'as the haughtiest of the Plantagenets might have written to his humblest minister',[6] of necessity Pandulf had to work through the council and, in order to make the council an effective instrument, through its leading figures Peter des Roches and Hubert de Burgh. To Peter was again delegated the care of the king,[7] but Hubert was responsible for a large range of administrative duties, as previous justiciars had been. He was not head of the administration, because he was subordinate to Pandulf who had taken immediate steps in 1219 to control the administration,[8] and

[1] *Royal Letters*, I, 20.
[2] *Rot. Lit. Claus.* I, 382, 388. Eustace de Fauconberg, Walter of Cornhill, bishop of Coventry and Lichfield, and even the king. All were writs of *computabitur* and possibly urgent; Turner, *loc. cit.* p. 291.
[3] *Rot. Lit. Pat.* p. 179, and *Rot. Lit. Claus. passim.*
[4] *CPR 1216–25, passim.*   [5] *Histoire de Guillaume le maréchal*, III, 283–6.
[6] *Royal Letters*, I, xx.   [7] Turner, *loc. cit.* pp. 293–4.
[8] There is a series of letters of Pandulf of May 1219 of which the correct dates were established by Powicke, 'The Chancery during the Minority of Henry III', *EHR*, XXIII, 229–30. Pandulf, who had put himself in touch with

another check upon his authority was Peter des Roches whose knowledge of administrative routine was as great as or greater than Hubert's. If the arrangement made at Bristol was a triumvirate of legate, bishop, and marshal, the situation on the latter's death was a triumvirate of legate, bishop, and justiciar. With the marshal's death, Hubert may have had additional duties since the legate was less inclined to be active regent than the earl, and his share in the determination of policy must also have been the greater because as justiciar he was not now overshadowed by the great reputation of the *rector*, which title perished with William.

3. THE JUSTICIAR AND PETER DES ROCHES

Henry III's minority lasted until December 1223 when for certain purposes he was declared of age.[1] The papal legate had departed in 1221[2] and, although he was succeeded in prestige by Stephen Langton,[3] executive control passed more and more to Hubert de Burgh. This control was secured in 1223 by the declaration which obviated the need for the king to have a guardian and so removed Peter des Roches from his position of influence. Until that date, however, Peter was on the scene and his position was of considerable importance since he shared in the justiciar's executive control. It could hardly be otherwise. Peter had been justiciar, he was loyal to John and therefore important in the king's party at John's death, and care of the king had been given to him by William Marshal after the council at Bristol. He, and not Hubert, had acted in the

Hubert de Burgh to arrange their co-operation, looked towards the vice-chancellor who held the great seal and the treasurer as persons in command of the situation and it was to them that his letters directing the operations of government through the seal and the treasury were addressed; *Royal Letters*, I, 28, 112–21.

[1] *Annales Monastici*, II, 83. The papal letters making this declaration were acted upon in a council at London; *Royal Letters*, I, 430.

[2] *Flores Historiarum*, II, 172–3. The date of his withdrawal was 19 July. He was last mentioned in chancery documents as legate on 20 July; *Rot. Lit. Claus.* I, 464.

[3] Powicke, *Henry III and the Lord Edward*, pp. 57–60. Sir Maurice believes that the representations for the papal letters declaring Henry III of age came from Langton and his suffragans.

marshal's place when there had been need for other responsibilities in the issue of royal letters. When Hubert, after the earl's death, began to attest royal letters as had the *rector* before him, Peter's influence was more apparent than it had been. Before the marshal was dead orders had been issued, like that to Peter de Mauley, to perambulate the forests and let the council know the result, attested by Hubert *per eundem* and the bishop of Winchester.[1] After his death, the same situation prevailed, and Peter's position is indicated by letters patent to all knights and free tenants of the Channel Isles notifying them that the nephew of Philip de Aubeney had been appointed as his deputy; this document was witnessed by Hubert de Burgh at Westminster on 7 June *per litteras suas factas auctoritate domini Wintoniensi episcopi*, the plain meaning of the warranty being that Hubert had authorized the issue of royal letters by his letters which the bishop had authorized.[2] This association of the two men persisted. Together they authorized the sheriff of Gloucester to let the executors of William Marshal's will have corn from his lands, and to let the justiciar know if the earl had sown corn at Burton and if he had had the corn of the previous year. The mayor and reeve of Lincoln were to pay servants as Peter and Hubert should tell them.[3] Peter was no judge, but on one occasion a litigant came before him to replevy his land which had been taken into the king's hand. The fact was notified to the justices of the bench presumably by a royal order authorized by Peter.[4]

To find Peter concerned with judicial affairs is perhaps more surprising than to find that he occupied a position of importance at the exchequer. In 2 Henry III he had given orders there that, for example, Margaret, the nurse of Isabella the king's sister, should have payment of 2d.[5] No doubt this was a consequence of Peter's position as Henry's guardian. If so, his order probably took the form of a royal writ authorized by his own witness, such

---

[1] CPR 1216-25, p. 190. There is a similar order on p. 197.
[2] CPR 1216-25, p. 194.   [3] Rot. Lit. Claus. I, 399.
[4] Ibid. p. 406.
[5] KR 1, m. 2r. Similarly Reginald Tortus had 2d. per diem but he was dead and Hamo cook of King John was assigned it through the bishop of Winchester; LTR 1, m. 5r.

as a *computate* addressed to the barons for Fawkes de Bréauté.[1] The bishop also ordered payment to John Bataill of 1½*d.* which had formerly been assigned to Ferrant the clerk, and a payment of 2*d.* to Geoffrey le Sauvage.[2] These were small sums which look like payments to lesser members of the household or for some domestic purpose, and they are the kind of payments which the king's guardian might easily make on his own authority. If this is the correct interpretation of them, then Peter's guardianship of the king and control of his household was an effective one. But Peter's position at the exchequer involved more than this, for his control of the disbursement of royal treasure was not confined to minor domestic purposes. He and the legate by their letters had assigned in the third year of the reign £52 of the tallage of the citizens of Gloucester for the king's expenses, so that as guardian he had considerable sums of money under his control.[3] His concern with the exchequer was yet closer than possession of the power to spend money and direct the barons accordingly. He sat there when the council was at the exchequer, as it was when the men of Hereford complained about the doings of the abbot of Battle who had shown his royal charters before the bishop of Winchester, William Marshal *tunc rector regis*, and other barons of the king's council at the exchequer.[4] He also sat there in his own right, for he gave days to accountants and postponed the account of the nephew by marriage of the bishop of Salisbury at the latter's request.[5] The barons, too, wished to consult him about the scutage payable by Robert de Courtenay and Henry de Tracy.[6]

Peter des Roches exercised authority at the exchequer in a way

---

[1] LTR 1, m. 7v.

[2] *Ibid.* m. 5r. Geoffrey le Sauvage seems to have been a recipient of Peter's favours. William Marshal junior was ordered to postpone his demand upon him for 15 marks for the escape of two robbers until another order was issued by writ attested by Peter des Roches; KR 3, m. 1r.

[3] KR 2, m. 18v. He had also, for example, spent £426. 17s. 4d. *in pluribus misis*, £471. 15s. *in liberationibus servientum*, £212. 18s. 4d. *in liberationibus per duos annos videlicet Albini et sociorum suorum;* LTR 2, m. 13r.

[4] LTR 1, m. 2v.

[5] KR 2, m. 8r, 10r, 21r.

[6] KR 2, m. 20v; and also about the scutage of Peter son of Herbert (LTR 1, m. 1v) who had sworn to pay his debt and had not done so, and other men.

which was analogous to the expression of the justiciar's authority in time past. The right to order the disbursement in his own name of money had been, under Henry II and his successors, reserved to the justiciar; the setting aside of days for an account to be taken, the swearing before him of oaths by the deputies of accountants, and the resolution of difficulties had been work done by the justiciars because they were presidents of the exchequer. It is, however, significant that the author of the *Dialogus* uses the term president rather than the title justiciar. The latter could not always be present, and then the president discharged his duties. If, as seems likely, Peter des Roches presided over the exchequer at some of its sessions in these early years of Henry III, then his work there was done in virtue of this position. But Peter's position was rather more than that. The *Dialogus* had implied a president other than the justiciar, but said nothing of his right to issue orders in his own name; he would have, instead, control of the exchequer seal, that duplicate of the Great Seal of England which was kept there for the purpose of sealing writs in the king's name. Such a seal was kept at the exchequer at this time;[1] possibly it was made at the same time as the king's seal which began to run at the beginning of 3 Henry III. No doubt many of the orders which bear the warranty of Peter des Roches were sealed with this instrument. Thus, for example, on 13 October 1219 the sheriff of Essex was ordered to distrain John of Cornerthe to be before the barons of the exchequer at Westminster to account for the abbey of St Edmunds during the time he was custodian, and the sheriff of Northumberland was told that if Peter de Vallibus gave security for prosecuting his claim, he was to summon John, son and heir of Robert son of Reginald, to be before the barons at the exchequer at Westminster within three weeks of Easter to answer for the time during which his father was sheriff of Northumberland and the land in question was in the king's hand.[2] Both writs were

---

[1] At the time Pandulf took over the administration on the marshal's death there is some suggestion that an exchequer seal did not then exist; *Royal Letters*, I, 112; *mandamus ne a scaccario pro alicuius mandato cum sigillo aliqua ratione redeas: quoniam sic et scaccario processus et regis impediretur utilitas;* but it was more likely that Pandulf addressed Neville in his capacity as keeper of the exchequer as well as of the great seal.   [2] LTR 3, m. 3.

witnessed by Peter des Roches at Westminster. Earlier, while William Marshal was still alive, Peter had warranted the issue of similar writs.[1] It seems probable that even then, in the interests of administrative efficiency, there must have been an exchequer seal or at least some seal other than the marshal's.

Even with the exchequer seal in existence, there may well have been difficulties about sealing, for Peter himself issued orders in his own name. His authority was thus greater than that of a president of the exchequer, and it rivalled that of the justiciar. In 1220 the memoranda roll recorded that at the advent of the sheriffs at Easter it was ordered *per litteras domini Wint'* that the sheriff of Berkshire was in the king's service and should not therefore suffer for his non-attendance at the exchequer.[2] A year later a writ of Peter's was enrolled to the sheriff of Northumberland that he had inspected the royal charter of Robert son of Reginald for the manor of Newburn and the service belonging to it, and that therefore it was not to be tallaged.[3] Since these two orders are not quoted *in extenso*, they may well have been letters cast in the form of personal communications rather than in the strict writ form, although the content of the latter which was quoted at length in the roll suggests that it may have been a normal writ; it has none of the elaboration of personal letters.[4] There are two likely explanations of the issue of these writs in the name of the bishop of Winchester. The first has been mentioned; the exchequer seal may, for some reason, have been unavailable and Peter des Roches, as an important figure, acted in his own name; the second is that Peter may have been away from the exchequer when he was approached by the sheriff of Berkshire and Robert son of Reginald to direct the action they required, for there is no inherent

---

[1] LTR 1, m. 7v, 8r. [2] KR 3, m. 6r. [3] KR 4, m. 2v.

[4] *Ibid.* The address, for example, is *Dominus Wint' vicecomiti Northumb'*, not the elaborate *P. permissione divina episcopus dilecto et sincero amico,* etc. of Peter's letters. The text of the writ reads like a royal order. *Scias quod inspecsimus cartam quam Robertus filius Reginaldi habuit de domino rege de manerio de Neuburn' et de servicio Roberti de Trokelawe quod tenet in pertinenciis eiusdem manerii per servicium xl solidorum et quoniam ex tenore predicte carte nobis testatum est quod predictum servicium est de feodo militis quod idem Robertus tenuit in eodem manerio tibi precipimus quod nulli super eum assideas vel assideri facias tallagium.*

reason in either order to suppose that the writs were issued at the exchequer; they would come to the barons' notice only when the sheriff was required to appear or the tallage to be levied on Robert's manor. Whichever is the true explanation the authority which Peter had over the exchequer is not in doubt. It was of the same kind as previous justiciars' and greater than that of the president with the more limited rights set out in the *Dialogus*. It is clear that Peter des Roches was, with Hubert de Burgh, one of the executive arms of the council, and this was a part that he was well equipped to play. An experienced administrator who was yet one of the great ones of the council and the king's guardian, his influence and authority were reflected throughout the work of government.

The bishop of Winchester's position established him beside Hubert de Burgh in the council and in the conduct of government. Reasons for his prominence have previously been suggested, but another reason which may have been important can only be referred to, not discussed: his personality. As in the case of Hubert and the bitter enmity which he aroused, so we can only speculate on the qualities which helped Peter des Roches to power and to his downfall. Peter had been associated with Hubert, perhaps to secure executive control to the council, before William Marshal's death. The old man's interest could hardly have extended to a sustained one in the details of administration and the execution of policy, however keen he may have been or however seriously he took his duties. He and the magnates of the council might determine policy, for example seisin of land after the civil war,[1] but it was to Peter and Hubert that the sheriff of Sussex sent his complaint about those who prevented him from delivering seisin of some land to one man.[2] To them the mayor and men of Southampton sent the report of a jury about the horse of a

---

[1] *Rot. Lit. Claus.* I, 602. The sheriffs were directed to inquire in their counties and inform a council which was to meet at London on 20 October, what demesne belonged to the king and who held it. Escheats similarly attracted attention; *Rot. Lit. Pat.* pp. 66, 70, 101, 118 and *passim*.

[2] *Royal Letters*, I, 13. The date was about April 1218. Gilbert Basset who was sheriff of Sussex addressed his letter to Bishop Peter, Hubert de Burgh and others of the council (a general term for unnamed individuals).

knight; and Pandulf informed them of his decision to join Walter Mauclerc to the sheriffs for the collection of revenue on 16 May 1219.[1] Theirs was not the ultimate authority; the regent and the council decided policy, but as experienced administrators they were the men who could overlook the routine required to give that policy, which they also had some share in deciding, effect; and as such they were singled out by those on whom the operations of government bore; they were the eyes and ears and the arms of the council.

William Marshal's death can only have caused their position to become more prominent and important. Hubert de Burgh was still not regent, for that place was occupied by the legate in fact if not in title; the justiciar could not stand alone, and Peter des Roches, who had been justiciar and who was now the king's guardian, was an almost inevitable partner. Pandulf wrote to them, jointly: that they should not permit Nicholas, to whom the legate had committed the chamberlainship of London, to be molested in his office; that they should restrain the activities of the constable and men of a castle; about the exactions of Isaac the Jew of Norwich upon the abbot and convent of Westminster which the latter had complained of to the legate; that they should order the bailiffs of the bishopric of Ely to assign the *regalia* of the bishopric to the abbot of Fountains whom Pandulf, Langton, and the bishop of Salisbury had elected as papal commissioners.[2] Pandulf's position has been described, and it is clear that he exercised his regency through Peter and Hubert. One of the reasons for this is evident enough from the legate's correspondence. He moved about England—he was particularly fond of the south-west—and showed reluctance to come to London.[3] To carry out his decisions royal writs were required to be issued, and for administrative convenience a royal seal was in London and another usually, although not always, with the king under the control of Peter and Hubert. It was therefore necessary before

---

[1] *Royal Letters*, I, 8, 27. The former letter is probably 1217.

[2] *Ibid.* 137; Ancient Correspondence, Sc 1/39, 43, 45.

[3] The letters quoted in note 1, p. 234, above, for example, came from Wenlock, Doncaster, Wells. Turner, *loc. cit.* (*TRHS*, 3rd series, I, 260-1), observed that Pandulf's letters were written mostly from the south-west.

Pandulf could secure execution of his decisions to have them embodied in royal writs for which the intermediary of the bishop and justiciar was required. As the legate said in one of his letters, *mandamus ut ballivis Episcopatus Elien' per sigillum Regium demandetis ut universa regalia sine dilatione ac difficultate assignent eidem* (i.e. John, the abbot of Fountains). *Datum apud Well' xvii Kal' Febr.*[1] This is precisely the reason for Henry III's own correspondence with Peter and Hubert. *Et quoniam sigillum nostrum nobiscum non fuit fecimus aponi sigillum Dilecte et fidelis nostri Willelmi de Cantilup'. Valete.*[2] A technical reason of this kind was obviously important in maintaining the position which the two ministers held. Their experience as administrators was another. The king was young and inexperienced; Pandulf, earnest though he was, was a foreigner not altogether at ease with English practice.

The recognition that effective action came through the bishop and the justiciar is the assumption underlying the letters addressed to them jointly by all sorts and conditions of men. It is common alike to the archbishop of York, who related how he had been unable to accompany the legate because he had been dangerously ill but promised compliance with their instructions, and to Fawkes de Bréauté, who stated that the countess of Huntingdon complained of ejectment from some of her lands and that he wanted instructions as to what he should do.[3] It underlies the story Stephen Langton told them by letter of his meeting and conversation near Staines with people who were going to hold a tournament.[4] On such information or requests, or, from the legate, orders, Peter and Hubert would take action. Much of this is hidden behind the formality of the rolls, which record business done in the king's name, but, behind this façade, the structure of government depended upon the will of Peter and Hubert. They would despatch a letter to Ralph de Neville keeper of the seal and dean of Lichfield; they had heard the complaint of a certain Roger and it seemed to them that he ought to have a writ of the king directed to Henry, son of the earl of Cornwall, that he cause the

---

[1] Sc 1/45. [2] *Royal Letters*, I, 105.
[3] *Royal Letters*, I, 39, 47. Both letters written, probably, in the latter half of 1219. [4] Sc 1/35.

judgement and record of the county, through four knights of the
county of Cornwall, to come before the justices of the bench, and
meanwhile a duel which was waged between them was to be
postponed.[1] Further, it seemed to them that the sheriff of Devon
should be ordered to take security of Roger for the prosecution of
his plea since it was alleged that the sheriff of Cornwall did not
wish to obey the king's mandate as he ought. Ralph de Neville
was also to let the sheriff of Cornwall know what they had decided
after taking counsel with Martin of Pattishall and other discreet
men as to what was right and just on the basis of Roger's complaint. The letter reveals much of the way in which government
worked at this time. The plaintiff came to Peter and Hubert to
relate his story, and they took the advice of the professional
justices, notably the most distinguished of them all, Martin of
Pattishall. As a consequence they directed the keeper of the seal
to issue three royal writs, one to Henry, son of the earl of Cornwall, one each to the sheriffs of Devon and Cornwall. There can
be little doubt that this was a typical procedure; such a letter to the
keeper of the seal is implied by most of the letters to Peter and
Hubert which have been mentioned and it was through this
procedure that Pandulf made his position effective. The document
shows the operation of government through the co-operation of
the bishop and the justiciar taking expert advice and ruling
through their control over the chancery. This was the reality
behind government in the name of young Henry III.

There was perhaps some idea that the justiciar, with the great
traditions of his office behind him, was the senior partner in this
relationship with Peter des Roches. The bishop certainly acted on
instructions from the justiciar. In September 1220 the former
wrote to the legate that he had been waiting for Hubert near
Winchester but now, on the latter's instructions, he was coming
to join the legate.[2] The justiciarship was an important office which
must certainly have overshadowed guardianship of the king, but
this is to ignore both the peculiar political conditions which
existed and also that intangible factor, the personalities of those
who held these offices. No doubt Peter deferred to the justiciar's

[1] Sc 1/26.   [2] *Royal Letters*, I, 154.

traditional position, buttressed as it was by Hubert's growing social importance, but the latter must have recognized in these early years the need for co-operation and consultation with so important a colleague; Peter's authority and advice were probably necessary to the doing of a good deal of business. Something of the relationship between them can be gauged from a letter which Peter wrote to Hubert. He had received the justiciar's letters to the effect that the land which had belonged to Walter de Hauvill was to be committed to Geoffrey and Gilbert de Hauvill who kept the king's falcons.[1] Their promotion pleased him and was for the king's honour but he thought that the justiciar should know that the king had written to the legate about this matter on the vigil of the feast of the Circumcision when they were at Salisbury and had committed custody of the land to Henry de Hauvill. Peter believed that the legate had written to the justiciar about this and therefore he advised (*consulimus*) that the justiciar should talk it over with the legate. He was, however, grateful to Geoffrey and Gilbert for their faithful service to the king, and about their promotion and that of others similarly he wished Hubert to write to him. *Scientes quod multum desideramus loqui vobiscum. Valeat semper in domino.* The position which Peter held in relation to the king, and his advice to the justiciar upon a matter in which the latter seemed to have forgotten what had been decided, were clearly a limitation of the justiciar's authority; Peter's advice might restrain his action upon such occasions. In at least one case the legate's orders were transmitted to the justiciar through Bishop Peter, with a covering letter asking (*rogantes*) that Hubert should act upon them.[2] Of Pandulf's relations with Peter personally it is impossible to write; perhaps they were closer than with Hubert because Peter was a churchman and the king's guardian. The association of bishop and justiciar is undoubted and they were treated as colleagues not merely by the legate but by a large number of men who sought executive action from the government. There is no indication as yet of a struggle for power. And, indeed, it could hardly be so. Neither Peter nor Hubert could hope to attain the dominant voice in government while the legate

[1] Sc 1/198.   [2] *Ibid.* 200.

was on the scene. While Pandulf remained, the justiciar was one, perhaps the most important but still only one, of a group of councillors, and he shared executive power with Bishop Peter. Until the legate withdrew in 1221 they were effective colleagues.

Government by the council, the position occupied in administration by prominent members of it, should not, nevertheless, obscure the fact of Hubert de Burgh's own work. On 29 July 1217 Fawkes de Bréauté complained to him that the servants of the earl marshal had taken possession of one of his manors and nothing but the justiciar's presence could settle the matter.[1] The fact that the *rector* was involved was reason enough for Fawkes to seek the justiciar's intervention, but it is plain that he made his request to Hubert in virtue as much of the latter's position in the council as of his traditional place in the administration; *et quoniam,* wrote Fawkes, *in praesentia domini legati et superni concilii domini regis estis et justiciarius Angliae, pro quo unicuique tenemini justitiam exhibere, haec vobis tam frequenter significo rogans quod tale consilium habeatis....* William, earl of Salisbury, informed the justiciar that after he had left him at the exchequer he had received a letter from the earl of Aumale that the projected marriage between his son and the latter's daughter had been called off, therefore he would not be responsible for any misdeeds which the earl might commit.[2] The earl of Salisbury carried out administrative duties— he had, as he said, been at the exchequer with the justiciar—and was himself a prominent member of the council. His letter seems to recognize the executive position held by Hubert. It may be that the justiciar's authority was confined to details—a manor or a marriage or the like—and that in more serious matters he could not stand alone. When, early in 1218, Philip of Oldcoates wrote to the justiciar a letter informing him that Hugh de Balliol had threatened to withdraw from the king's service if his manor of Mere were not restored and had also threatened the writer of the letter, the situation was more serious; Philip advised Hubert to comply with Hugh's wishes, and suggested that, together with Peter des Roches, the justiciar should tell him what to do as he had

[1] *Royal Letters,* i, 4.   [2] *Ibid.* p. 19.

promised.[1] The implication seems to be that Hubert attended to details, but complications which arose and which threatened the king's peace required counsel. Hubert's position was politically more important and more complicated than his predecessors', because of the king's minority, but what of the routine of government which traditionally fell under the justiciar's control?

4. THE JUSTICIAR AND THE CHANCERY

He who controlled the seal controlled the government in an age when the validity of any document depended upon its authentication with a seal. One of the difficulties which faced the regent and the council in 1216 was the absence of a royal seal. Not until 1218 did such an instrument come into use, when the patent roll bore a heading that a new seal had begun to run. Nevertheless, its use was circumscribed, and no permanent grant could be made until the king came of age; the authority of the regent and the council had its limits and they refused to judge upon royal charters. Before the introduction of the new seal that of William Marshal had been used and, where the occasion seemed to demand more, that of the legate. Yet even after 1218 the royal seal was by no means always employed to authenticate the orders of the government.

After William Marshal's death, and even while Peter des Roches was associated with him, Hubert de Burgh controlled the seal; and the chancellor himself, although he drew the revenues of his office, wrote to the justiciar when he wished for royal letters. He besought the justiciar to issue royal writs to the sheriffs of Lancaster and Westmorland to allow the lands of William Lancaster to remain in peace;[2] he requested that R. de Ros, who accompanied him to the north of England to meet the king of the Scots and who had a day appointed to him in the bench, should be given respite by the justiciar's issuing a royal writ to the justices.[3] Equally evident is the fact that the king did not have his seal with him, for he ordered the justiciar and Peter des Roches to do justice to the bishop of Fernes according to the tenor of letters of

[1] Ibid. p. 11.   [2] Sc 1/135.   [3] Ibid. 138.

King John, and since Henry III was without his seal, he employed that of William de Cantilupe, the steward of his household, to seal his letters,[1] and he employed the same device on at least one other occasion in favour of the abbot of Fountains.[2] More usual was the employment of the justiciar's seal in lieu of the royal one, and the two previous letters may be explicable on the assumption that neither the justiciar nor Bishop Peter nor the seal was in the king's company. A considerable number of royal letters bore Hubert's seal after the king came of age, and previously the justiciar had used his writ and seal as a mandate to the great seal. In June 1219 two letters close were issued *per litteras Huberti de Burgo justiciarii Angliae*; the first of them being attested by the bishop of Coventry.[3] In Henry's semi-majority after 1223, Hubert's seal was again used as a mandate to the chancery for the issue of royal letters, although such mandates probably ran in the king's name. The document which the clerks enrolled in response to the order was attested by the bishop of Bath at Westminster.[4] Even more specific was the annotation made after the king had finally come of age, which described the authority for the issue of letters patent as *sub sigillo justiciarii transmissis ad sigillum regis*.[5] For the last time the method was employed in 1230[6] but the control of government by Hubert was slipping and the king had already employed the seal of his steward Geoffrey de Crowcombe and the privy seal for purposes similar to those for which the justiciar's had previously been employed.[7]

The attestation of the bishop of Bath to the document which the chancery issued in response to a royal mandate was not unusual. Both he and the bishop of Salisbury had played their part with Hubert in the administration before and after 1223. The bishop of Bath was Joscelin of Wells. Not a figure of outstanding

---

[1] Sc 1/34.   [2] *Ibid.* 106.   [3] *Rot. Lit. Claus.* I, 392 b.
[4] *Rot. Lit. Claus.* II, 173 b, 174, 174 b.   [5] *CClR 1227–31*, p. 60.
[6] *Ibid.* p. 463.
[7] *Ibid.* pp. 285, 458, 460. See Tout, *Chapters*, I, 210. There is reference to the use of the justiciar's seal as a privy seal and those of the bishop of Bath and Wells; *ibid.* p. 207. Hubert's privy seal was to be left in England in 1230 to transact exchequer business, and, *ibid.* note 1, one of the acts consequent upon Hubert's fall was the breaking of his small seal.

political importance, he had had a career closely bound up with administration, at first in the chamber and the exchequer, then as vice-chancellor. He had been named as one of the council in Magna Carta, and he was one of the bishops who attested the first letters patent given under the new royal seal in 1218. Granted that the justiciar could not sustain the whole responsibility for the functioning of government, Joscelin was a suitable colleague: an experienced administrator devoid of political ambition. Richard Poore, bishop of Salisbury, was quite a different type. His career had been one of scholastic and ecclesiastical achievement and he was not a *curialis*. He was probably not well disposed towards Peter des Roches, for when Richard had gone to Rome seeking election to the see of Winchester Peter had obtained it. The two bishops were a balance to Peter des Roches, and one may suspect that this motive was not far from the justiciar's mind. Both men carried out administrative duties beside Hubert de Burgh. The court was at Southampton on 7 June 1224 when royal letters patent declared that the king had received sealed chests containing treasure, in witness whereof the letters were issued sealed with the seals of the bishop of Bath and the justiciar before whom the coffers had been formally received.[1] Many letters were issued before Joscelin and the bishop of Salisbury, and many times they were the warranty for issue. The former, indeed, bore witness to letters which followed the receipt of a mandate to the great seal.

In spite of the position of the bishops, Hubert de Burgh had the effective control of the administration once the bishop of Winchester was in eclipse, and Joscelin of Wells and Richard Poore were administrators rather than constitutional checks and balances. When Hubert was at Westminster, and the king elsewhere in the country, he commanded the use of the seal in response to royal orders or the requests of suitors; the implication of that chancellor's letter mentioned previously is that Hubert could issue writs on his own authority in the king's name and sealed with the royal seal. When the justiciar accompanied the king on a progress the seal apparently remained in Westminster, for mandates to the great seal all belong to periods of such a royal progress; the heading on

[1] *CPR 1216–25*, p. 444.

the patent roll, *De licencia sub sigillo justiciarii*, belongs to May 1225 when the court was at Winchester,[1] and in the previous year the king's travels in June to Southampton, Andover, and Winchester produced a similar crop of mandates for the issue of royal letters.[2] It was in 1226 and 1227 that such orders to the chancery resulted in letters patent given at Westminster and under the witness of the bishop of Bath who, it seems, was responsible for their issue,[3] since the normal witness of documents after 1223 was *teste meipso*, and the practice had not yet achieved that uniformity which makes chancery practice so uninformative at a later date.

The chancellor had quite clearly ceased to be much more than a dignified official, and the survival of Ralph de Neville in the crisis of 1232 emphasizes his relative unimportance in the scheme of things. It was the king's will and the king's seal which set the chancery in motion, and the real control of government lay in the hands of the man or men who controlled the privy seal, or the seal the king used in its stead. Until 1230 such a man was Hubert de Burgh, but even he was amenable to the king's will when Henry III ordered the application of the seal. When the king's confidence was withdrawn and the privy seal or its equivalent no longer the justiciar's or under his control, Hubert fell from power. His authority had been great, and different in kind from that of his predecessors. Whatever the justiciar's power and influence, the government ran in the king's name, not the justiciar's. Whereas his predecessors in the office had issued their own writs, Hubert had to use the instruments of government in the royal name. Potentially it was a limitation on his power, but his authority while the king was in England and not of age was probably greater than that of his predecessors, although he never exercised viceregal authority in the king's absence.

5. THE JUSTICIAR AND THE LAW COURTS

Hubert de Burgh differed from most of his predecessors in his lack of judicial training. Glanville, Hubert Walter, and Geoffrey fitz Peter had all had considerable experience, and the latter's career

---

[1] *CPR 1216–25*, p. 517.   [2] *Rot. Lit. Claus.* I, 604 b–605.   [3] *Ibid.* II, 158 b.

had been predominantly that of a royal justice. Even Peter des
Roches who was no judge had devoted himself to judicial work
after his appointment as justiciar. As sheriff Hubert would have
had at least a minimum of judicial experience, and as a landowner
he would have held his manorial courts, but the scope of his
activity as chief justice seems to have been limited; it was certainly
not so extensive as that of his predecessors. Professor Sayles
observed that Hubert's mark upon the plea rolls was slight and
held that there was a change in the nature of the justiciarship or, at
least, its duties.[1] The conclusion may be accepted, but not for that
reason. The usual form of a legal writ in Henry III's time was for
it to be couched in the royal name. A typical example of an
original writ, one of the few that survive for the early years of
the reign, is this:

Henricus dei gratia Rex Ang*lorum* Dominus Hiber*nie*. Dux Norman-
norum Aquita*nnorum* et Comes Andeg*avorum* Ballivis Widonis de
Lapontener' in Haffeld' Salutem. Precipimus vobis quod sine dilacione
plenum rectum teneatis Hug*oni* de Nevill' de una caruc*ata* terre cum
pertinenciis in Haffeld' quam clamat tenere de predicto Widone per
Tiberum servicium . . . per annum pro omni servicio. Quod idem
Wido ei deforciat. Et nisi feceritis vice*comes* Essex*ie* faciat Ne amplius
inde Clam*orem* inde [*sic*] audiamus pro defectu recti. *Teste Huberto* de
Burgo Justiciario nostro apud Wintoniam xiii die Decem*bris*.[2]

The probable date of this writ is 1219 when Peter des Roches
entertained the king at Winchester.[3] The witness of the justiciar
and the fact that the title was given to him in the writ suggest that
he was responsible for its issue but the citation of it in the court
roll would describe it as a royal writ. The responsibility of the
justiciar for the issue of such routine judicial writs may be gauged
from the requests suitors addressed to him to obtain them. One
has already been quoted: the request of the chancellor in favour of
R. de Ros; but there are others. John Marshal, who had been
given a certain manor by King John, asked the justiciar to postpone any pleading which might arise about it until he could come

[1] *Select Cases in the Court of King's Bench*, I, xxxiv.
[2] PRO Chancery Files, A 1/445 (in a bundle).
[3] Wendover, II, 237.

in person.[1] The earl of Pembroke wrote that his servant who bore
the letter had been unjustly disseised by royal letters of some land
in Hampshire, and asked the justiciar to give justice in the matter,
in the meanwhile allowing the land to be replevied.[2] There is no
reason to suppose that such requests as have survived are exceptional, and the business they concern was routine judicial procedure. Application to the justiciar was made for a writ to originate
a suit, like the writ of right transcribed above, or for a writ to
control the course of litigation. Such a document would run in
the royal name and it is not surprising, since Hubert issued few
writs in his own name, that the court rolls bear little mark of his
influence.

Occasionally the clerk noted that an order was the justiciar's.
In the Trinity term 1220 a royal writ informed the justices that
Ralph son of William appointed an attorney before Hubert de
Burgh, and warranted that he sent William of Flamborough and
Serlo son of Amfrid to answer Arnold de Marton and Walter de
Marton.[3] The attorneys were probably appointed before the
justiciar during his progress through the north in that year, and he
despatched a writ in the king's name to inform the bench.
Judicial, as distinct from original, writs of the justiciar had been
common in John's reign, but only occasionally did Hubert's name
appear in connexion with such an order. A plea between Henry de
Vere and his men concerning services owed was adjourned without a day by the justiciar's order transmitted to the court through
Richard Duket and Osbert Giffard.[4] Possibly the order was an
oral one to which these two bore witness. Because a litigant was
in the king's service in Poitou, a day was set down for judgement
whether the case in which he was involved should proceed, at the
justiciar's order.[5] Failure of the recognitors of an assize to appear
was the reason for another postponement which Hubert commanded.[6] But the sum total of orders which we know to have
been issued by the justiciar was small. The information that the
king orders something to be done covers many occasions when

[1] Sc 1/140.
[2] Ibid. 148.
[3] Curia Regis Rolls, IX, 88.
[4] Ibid. VIII, 7.
[5] Ibid.
[6] Ibid. pp. 30–1.

the command originated with the justiciar, but royal intervention was not so frequent as in former times, and since legal writs were not usually enrolled by the chancery, it is difficult to obtain evidence of their source or authorization. The rolls themselves do not prove that the justiciar's legal activity diminished: all they establish is the fact that it was unusual for legal writs to run in the name of Hubert de Burgh.

Nevertheless, it seems reasonable to suppose, from other evidence, that the justiciar did not take so large a part in judicial affairs in Henry III's reign. The characteristic attestation of documents has been commented upon. Until 1218 almost all were issued under the witness of William Marshal: after that date, most frequently under the witness of Hubert de Burgh but occasionally under that of Peter des Roches, and, more exceptionally still, under the witness of the bishop of Bath. Then, in 1223, the usual attestation was *teste meipso*, which became so regular that it was common form later in the reign. Hence, it seems a reasonable supposition that he who witnessed the writs had assumed responsibility for the aspect of administration with which they dealt, with the proviso that the warranty for the writs was provided by administrative officers. The practice of the chancery was becoming so regular that any deviation from the norm must excite interest. Such a departure from normality appeared in the few legal writs which found their way on to the chancery rolls, probably on the dorse which was used for miscellaneous notes. From these it appears that the witness of many legal writs was Martin of Pattsihall, the senior professional justice in England.[1] There is good cause, therefore, for the belief that the justiciar, albeit he retained a final authority over the legal system, had relinquished the routine administration of justice in favour of a professional judge, and the time was not far distant when the senior judge was to become justiciar in the person of Stephen of Seagrave.

The final concords of the court at Westminster reveal the identity of the judges sitting in the *curia regis*. Until 1215, with the exception of some years from 1210 to 1212, the justiciar presided

[1] E.g. *CPR 1216–25*, p. 497; *Rot. Lit. Claus.* I, 569, 655.

over the judges, or the legal fiction of his presence was maintained
in almost all the concords levied at Westminster. Even Peter des
Roches sat regularly in court. But a cursory glance at the final
concords for the minority of Henry III shows the change which
had taken place. In the Michaelmas term of 2 Henry III, the
justices were William, earl of Arundel, Martin of Pattishall, Alan
Basset, Ralph de Hareng, Stephen of Seagrave, John of Guestling,
and Simon de *Insula*.[1] At the feast of the Purification of the
Blessed Virgin, the justices were the same group, but the earl was
absent and Martin presided.[2] On occasion, the earl of Oxford
took the earl of Arundel's place; this was the case in the Trinity
and Easter terms of Henry's fourth year, and in the Easter and
Michaelmas terms of the year following.[3] When a magnate
presided, however, Martin headed the names of the professional
justices present who, with slight variations which included Robert
of Lexington and Thomas of Haydon, both well-known judges,
were much the same group of men. There can be little doubt that
the bench was a body of professional justices whose sessions were
occasionally graced by the presence of a magnate who was a
member of the council, and on occasion by the full session of the
council when the king, the *rector regni*, the justiciar, and others
were present.[4] The justiciar was infrequently in court, but sometimes he replaced the earl as president; he did so in the Michaelmas term 3 Henry III, in the Hilary term three years later, and in
the Easter term of the following year.[5] In this he may have been
fulfilling a duty of supervision which fell equally upon other
magnates, but the frequency of the justiciar's absence is evidence
enough that he no longer devoted the greater part of his time to
judicial work as had Geoffrey fitz Peter.

---

[1] CP 25 (1)/128/11/1–3.
[2] *Ibid.* 11/5.
[3] *Ibid.* 128/15/2–5, 9, 10, 11, 12, 15; Harl. MS 2110, fo. 109.
[4] CP 25(1) 233/6/2; 7/27; Harl. MS 4714, fo. 26v; Harl. MS 3697, fo. 115v.
These concords of the quindene of Easter, 4 Henry III, and octave of Michaelmas 7 Henry III, give Martin, Ralph Hareng, Stephen of Seagrave as the first
three justices, and in the latter add Thomas of Haydon, Robert of Lexington,
and Geoffrey le Sauvage.
[5] CP 25(1) 128/12/3; 15/19, 20; 15/25, 32, 36.

One good reason for the interest of earlier justiciars in the proceedings of the royal courts was a factor no longer operative when Hubert de Burgh held office. The limitation upon the council's use of the seal meant that few grants contained the clause, frequent a few years earlier, which forbade anyone to implead the grantee unless before the king or his chief justice. Such a charter or letter of protection could be pleaded as a legal defence to halt proceedings. One such grant was made to the prior and canons of Bradenstock on 24 January 1220, but it was specifically provided that the letter was valid only for the succeeding six years.[1] Moreover, a strict interpretation of such an immunity was insisted upon. In 1226 the abbot of Byland, against whom Stephen de Mesnil brought an assize of *mort d'ancestor*, tried to plead such a charter to bar the progress of the suit.[2] A mandate, attested by the king, instructed Martin of Pattishall that, notwithstanding the charter, the case should proceed, because the clause granting judicial exemption, which was apparently granted by King John, made no mention of the latter's heirs and it could not therefore be held to bind Henry III. Few of John's charters of which copies have survived made such a specific statement, and it was more usual to seek for confirmation of such a grant from the new king. Until Henry came of age this could obviously not be done. Success attended Pandulf, as bishop elect of Norwich, when he produced in court, by his attorney, a charter which Bishop John, his predecessor, had from the king containing the provision that he was not to plead unless before the king or the justiciar and which had been enrolled at the exchequer.[3] No reply was recorded on the roll, but a day was given to hear judgement in the quindene of the Hilary term following, so that the court presumably adjourned to take counsel since neither the king nor the justiciar was then present. But the occasion was unique, and possibly the fact that Pandulf was the papal legate impressed the court unduly.

Turning from the central court at Westminster to the relations of Hubert de Burgh with the itinerant justices, the evidence is a

---

[1] *CPR 1216–25*, p. 225. For a similar confirmation to the bishop of Exeter in 1218, *Rot. Lit. Claus.* I, 377.
[2] *Ibid.* II, 162. [3] *Curia Regis Rolls*, IX, 382.

little more plentiful. Hubert himself made progresses through the country, and his presence must have been necessary to solve many of the problems which the civil war had left in its wake. There were parties of justices at work in the country in 1218. Eight groups of justices visited thirty shires, partly to do justice but, equally important, to replenish the coffers of an exchequer which had been idle since 1215.[1] Again in 1220 there was a general eyre.[2] But the journeys of the justiciar do not seem to have been part of the normal judicial circuits. In 1220 he made a progress through Yorkshire, of which the results are apparent on both the court rolls and the chancery enrolments. An entry for the Michaelmas term of that year was headed *De Itinere* and contained the information that the *iter* was one of the justiciar and the justices.[3] Their work was not completed, because in the following year letters patent appointed judges to take the assizes of novel disseisin which had been summoned before the justiciar at York.[4] That his tour of the north was not confined to the group of counties which normally constituted the circuit is evident from the fact that he had also heard inquisitions at Nottingham and Blye.[5] The letter quoted previously, including the remark that only the justiciar's presence could settle a dispute, was probably typical, and the justiciar's presence in the north must have been urgently required, for again in 1221 he took his way via Huntingdon to Newcastle on Tyne, and spent some time in Yorkshire visiting Pontefract and Stamford.[6] Probably in the autumn of 1219 he had toured Suffolk, but there is no evidence that he was one of the group of justices in that area.[7]

But if the justiciar's activity in eyre was exceptional rather than the rule, his authority was nevertheless involved in matters arising out of the justices' visitations. A suitor might implore Hubert's protection against the itinerant justices, and a letter of 1220 informing the justiciar that the owner's castle was not adulterine was probably stimulated by the attention the justices were to give

---

[1] Powicke, *Henry III and the Lord Edward*, p. 29.
[2] *Flores Historiarum*, II, 172.   [3] *Curia Regis Rolls*, IX, 318.
[4] *CPR 1216–25*, p. 261.   [5] *Rot. Lit. Claus.* I, 421 b, 451 b, 452 b.
[6] *Ibid.*   [7] CP 25 (1)/288/12/3.

to unlicensed fortifications.[1] Or a litigant might ask that a case be transferred from the justices to the king.[2] A charter containing the grant of judicial immunity was produced by the attorney of the master of the Temple at Shrewsbury in 1221, and a day was set down for the parties in the octave of Hilary for that reason, presumably to enable the justiciar to deal with the matter at Westminster.[3] Two years previously the justices who were sitting at Lincoln on the morrow of St John the Baptist placed a suit in respite until three weeks after the feast, when it was to be at Westminster by order of the chief justice.[4] The case was one of novel disseisin and there is no obvious reason for the justiciar's intervention. Such a command was highly exceptional, and contrasts with the abundant evidence of assize rolls in the reign of King John for the part played by the justiciar. Again, one must bear in mind the fact that writs ran in the royal name, and the requests addressed to the justiciar connected with itinerant justices suggest that to some extent the silence of the rolls is deceptive as to the extent of his duties.

Nevertheless, allowing for the fact that Hubert's judicial activity may have been greater than one would believe at first sight, it is clear that the council was equally concerned with judicial affairs, and it is probable that where Hubert intervened he did so as a member of the council. His was an authority to which the justices might refer, and to which suitors might apply, but the council had achieved a recognized status, and even though the justiciar might be the dominant figure in the body, there were limits to his authority; and his judicial duties were those of exception rather than routine.

6. THE JUSTICIAR AND THE EXCHEQUER

The nature of Hubert de Burgh's control over the exchequer and its deliberations is rather clearer than are his legal duties, since the

[1] Powicke, *Henry III and the Lord Edward*, I, 30; *Royal Letters*, I, 140.
[2] Sc 1/115.
[3] *Rolls of the Justices in Eyre for Gloucestershire, Warwickshire, and Staffordshire*, no. 642.
[4] *Rolls of the Justices in Eyre for Lincolnshire and Worcestershire*, no. 732.

memoranda rolls, which supply a good deal of the detail which lies behind the formality of the pipe rolls, survive in a series. It is even possible to make some reasonably trustworthy generalizations about the character of Hubert's influence. It was in general conservative. Most obviously this appears from the reforming tendencies which had been at work in exchequer administration.[1] In the early years of Henry III there had been several noticeable changes in exchequer practice: the increased use of the *tallia dividenda*, and the grouping of entries of debts which depended upon it. In 1223, when Hubert de Burgh's power was strengthened by the king's being declared for certain purposes of age,[2] there was a reversion to older forms and a marked tendency to enter debts again under individual names. By 10 Henry III the group entries of debt had been replaced in the pipe roll by individual amercements on a large scale.[3] This reaction began to end in 1228 when the king was fully of age; and it coincides with the appointment of Seagrave to three shrievalties, thus anticipating the position of Peter des Rievaulx in the *coup d'état* of 1232.[4] In 1224 the profits of the shire, which had been forbidden by Magna Carta (although not by the reissue of the charter by Henry III), were suddenly restored, and this coincides with the large-scale appointment of new sheriffs, in which Hubert de Burgh seems to have been the moving spirit, and the disappearance from the wardrobe administration of Peter des Rievaulx.[5] The coincidence is remarkable, and it suggests that with the strengthening of Hubert de Burgh's power there was a change in exchequer policy,

---

[1] Mills, 'Experiments in Exchequer Procedure 1200-32', *TRHS*, 4th series, VIII, 166 ff.

[2] Powicke, *Henry III and the Lord Edward*, pp. 57 ff.

[3] Pipe Roll 10 Henry III m. 4r; Mills, *loc. cit.*

[4] Mills, *loc. cit.* Seagrave acquired two more shrievalties in the following year.

[5] Pipe Rolls, *passim*, under the farm of the county; Mills, *loc. cit.* The profits of the shires had increased in the quarter of a century before 1215 from £14 to over £2,500. From 5-7 Henry III Buckinghamshire paid the old increment and seven other counties made similar payments, the total being £220. In 8 Henry III the profits were suddenly restored to their old place, their total value being £650 for three quarters of the year; ten other counties were liable but no values were given. For the appointment of sheriffs, see *CPR 1216-25*, pp. 417-21; Tout, *op. cit.* I, 191.

or at least not so much a change as a reaction towards the old system against the reforming movement of Peter des Roches and his nephew Peter des Rievaulx. The change in exchequer policy from 1223 to 1228 argues for the very considerable influence which Hubert de Burgh exercised upon it while the Poitevins were in eclipse as a factor in politics and the king was not yet possessed of the legal or technical means to assert his own will. The change, however, seems to have had little effect upon the position occupied by the justiciar in respect of the everyday work of the exchequer and the deliberations of the barons. The policy determined the direction of the detailed operation of the system, but it could hardly affect the personal intervention of the justiciar which was necessary to solve points of doubt or difficulty, and which would have been necessary whatever the general direction had been.

The growth of Hubert's control of the exchequer and of administration generally is quite clear from the composition of the court which sat at the exchequer. The place of the council and of Peter des Roches has been described. It need only be noted, therefore, that in 1218 William Marshal, Peter des Roches, Hubert, and the king's council sat at the exchequer where they reversed a payment assessed *sine judicio* in the time of King John; and that when the sheriffs came to the exchequer on the morrow of St Martin in that same year, the bishops of London and Coventry, William Briewerre, Eustace the treasurer, William de Cantilupe, Thomas of Erdington, Geoffrey of Buckland, and Robert de Neville were also present.[1] Under these circumstances it is fairly apparent that Hubert could have had little decisive influence upon policy. Clearly, however, such an impressive session can hardly have been normal. A matter of some importance might warrant their attention or the attention of some of them; such, for example, seems to have been the case with a gift to the archbishop of York: the bishop of Durham, William Briewerre, and Alan Martel testified before the archbishop of Canterbury, the bishop of London, the justiciar, and Fawkes de Bréauté, on the feast of St Luke the Evangelist, that when they had asked King John how the

[1] Pipe Roll 2 Henry III m. 4v; LTR 1, m. 4r; KR 1, m. 3r.

gift should be enrolled the latter replied *Vel de prestito vel de dono* as the archbishop might opt. A more usual gathering of barons of the exchequer seems to have been the justiciar, the treasurer, and the barons unnamed.[1] It was the less distinguished group of professional officials who were the usual baronage of the exchequer until the justiciarship vanished, for the Poitevins chose to work through the household organization. In February 1223 it called for a special order from the king to the barons of the exchequer, witnessed by Hubert de Burgh, that William de Cantilupe, steward of the royal household, who had in 1218 been present at the exchequer session, should sit with them and be admitted to their deliberations.[2] It is quite clear that the barons were sometimes afforced by distinguished persons. In 1225 when a debt owed from the time of King John's second scutage came up, a payment made through Geoffrey fitz Peter in the pre-civil-war period was allowed by the justiciar before the bishop of Chichester, the chancellor, the bishops of Salisbury and Bath, who were frequently associated with Hubert, the bishop of Rochester, and other barons of the exchequer.[3] In 1230 the king himself, the justiciar, the earls of Chester, Cornwall, Gloucester, Warenne, Aumale, Hertford, and Huntingdon, and other barons who were present at the exchequer on the Wednesday after the feast of the Purification decided an important matter of policy, namely that tallies made before the civil war which were recognized to be exchequer tallies and which had not yet been accepted, should be accepted.[4] This was before Henry's departure for France. Such great assemblies serve only to throw into relief the usual composition of the upper exchequer, which was the justiciar, the treasurer, and those professional men who were described beneath the anonymous label

[1] Madox, *op. cit.* II, 27; KR 3, m. 3 v; Pipe Roll 11 Henry III under Wiltshire; Pipe Roll 12 Henry III under Gloucester.

[2] LTR 5, m. 13 (1)v. *Communia de Sancto Hilario.*

[3] Pipe Roll 9 Henry III m. 12v. *Willelmus de Abrincis r.c. de xxix li(bris) et i marca de duobus scutagiis de temporis Regis J(ohannis). In thesauro xvii li(bras) et i marcam per ii taleas ante guerram pacatas per G. filium Petri et allocatas per H. de Burgo Justiciarium coram R. Cicestr' Episcopo Regis cancellario R. Sar' J. Bath'. B. Roff' episcopis et aliis baronibus de scaccario Et Q. e.*

[4] *Memoranda Roll 14 Henry III,* p. 30.

barones de scaccario. Obviously it was customary for the justiciar still to take an active interest in the exchequer, and to be regarded as its president. The distinction of the treasurer by name may suggest that this official was the permanent head of the barons.[1] The justiciar might preside, and certainly he controlled or guided the deliberations of the barons in person or by writ, but the treasurer's power was increasing.

Hubert de Burgh evidently spent a good deal of time actually sitting with the barons, not merely to decide difficult or important points which arose during the sessions, but to take part in their day-to-day work. In 1220 the bishop of Bath was given respite from accounting for 32 marks of certain farms until the Easter session by the justiciar and the barons, and the justiciar appointed a day within the octave of Hilary for the sheriff of Hereford to make his account.[2] In the year following, the demand made upon John son of Hugh for 100 shillings was postponed by the justiciar, and the account of the scutage of a pilgrim was also postponed until he had returned from his journey; this latter decision was embodied in a writ which was sent to the sheriff of Hereford in Wales.[2] In 1222 Hubert de Burgh was present at the exchequer on the morrow of Martinmas, and also in the Hilary term when he appointed a day for Hugh de Neville to account for cattle which he had handled in 15 John.[3] Even if he were in West-minster, however, other business might attract his attention and thus it was that William of Harlow, coming with a Norwegian hawk offered for the land of Brian *Aquarius*, was sent to the justiciar *qui tunc fuit in turri Lond'*.[4] That the justiciar was regularly present on these occasions, and throughout the reign, to deliver his commands or decisions to the barons can hardly be doubted;

---

[1] Madox, *op. cit.* II, 26. 'In the beginning of this second Period, and for a short Time after, the King's Chief Justiciar continued to preside and act at the Exchequer, as he had before used to do. Afterwards, when he ceased to preside there, the Power of the Treasurer increased. Then, the Affairs of the Exchequer were guided and ordered by the Treasurer and Barons of the Exchequer.'

[2] KR 3, m. 2r, m. 3v.

[3] KR 4, m. 8r, m. 10r. The justiciar's verbal order led to the issue of a *breve de scaccario*. For other examples of this procedure, see LTR 4, m. 2r; KR 5, m. 4v.

[4] LTR 4, m. 3r.   [5] *Ibid.* m. 5(2)r.

he assigned days to accountants, he received offerings at the exchequer. It is equally clear that his authority was not necessarily expressed by enshrining his orders in a writ; his word of mouth alone was sufficient. In 1223, for example, William son of Osmund owed an amercement of 10 marks; he was quit by order of the justiciar through Thomas of Blundevill *sine brevi*.[1] So, too, Walter de Godarvill' owed an amercement for a forest offence which was cancelled *in originali per preceptum justiciarii sine brevi*.[2] Commands by word of mouth imply the justiciar's presence, and their acceptance as sufficient authority for an action suggests that they were a fairly common phenomenon. Since the administration operated in the king's name, writs or letters of the justiciar were not frequent. A private letter of the justiciar would, of course, be a normal enough means of communicating with his colleagues, and certainly Hubert de Burgh conveyed information to the barons in this way.[3] A document cast in the strict writ form was not so usual, but there were at least two cases on which Hubert despatched a writ to the barons. In 1219 Hubert told the treasurer and the barons that the earl of Gloucester was by the king's order at Gloucester with the council; in 1220 he informed the treasurer and other barons of the exchequer that he had detained the sheriff of Kent on the king's business; in both cases neither accountant was to suffer for his non-appearance, but was to be examined on another day appointed by the justiciar.[4] At a time when business was done in the king's name, these are striking indications of the authority exercised by the justiciar over the exchequer, even when he acted on behalf of the council. Hubert's training, like Peter des Roches's, had been financial rather than

[1] LTR 5, m. 12(1)r. *Willelmus fil' Osmund' de misericordia x marcas pro duabus bassis captis inter Use de Derewente propter quas amerciatus fuit per Brianum de Insula est quietus de mandato justiciarii per Th' de Blundvill' sine brevi.* Thomas was described by Matthew Paris as *clericus de scaccario regis* when he was promoted to the see of Norwich on the death of Pandulf, the former papal legate; Paris, III, 121.

[2] *Ibid.*

[3] KR 3, m. 11r. The men of Dunwich owed £168. 15s. for two years for which Hubert de Burgh ought to answer for 100 marks as he recognized by his letters.

[4] KR 2, m. 2r; KR 3, m. 3r.

judicial, and in respect of the exchequer his authority seems to spring more from his professional interests than do his interventions in judicial procedure. And this, no doubt, is how his position appeared to contemporaries. Walter de Casey informed Hubert that he was sending T. his clerk to the exchequer to offer his account for the county of Hereford.[1] Similarly Geoffrey de Neville wrote to Hubert that his sheriff of Yorkshire was engaged on the king's business on the morrow of Michaelmas when he should have appeared before the justiciar and the barons; his clerk would, however, be present and he asked that the sheriff be excused.[2] Hubert de Burgh, as justiciar, not only took a personal interest in exchequer proceedings, but it seems to have been assumed that he would frequently be present at the exchequer sessions, presiding over the treasurer and the other barons.

His absence from the session caused matters to be deferred until he could be consulted. In 1219 the barons wished to consult him about the fine of Robert Mantel for his relief for two fees of the *honor* of Peverel of London;[3] but this was a matter which concerned the justiciar personally since the fine had been negotiated with him. Other difficulties were discussed with the justiciar not because of his personal involvement but for other reasons. He was to be consulted about 10 marks which the abbot of Ramsey promised in order to extend his fair of St Ives beyond its usual duration; the sheriff, however, asserted that such extension was contrary to the liberty of the king's men of Huntingdon.[4] The view of accounts on the morrow of the octave of the Nativity 1221 was taken before Bishop John of Bath, one of the justiciar's important colleagues, but when a sheriff asserted *quod ipse non potest apponeri manum nisi per justiciarium* for the hundreds of Rochford, and also that he had no seneschal who could satisfactorily account for the hundred, the matter was referred to the justiciar.[5] Land which was taken into the king's hand, too, caused consultations with the justiciar over the account.[6] These were

[1] Sc 1/100.
[2] *Ibid.* 162. The *Dialogus* explains that if a sheriff wished to account by deputy, the appointment of his deputy should be made before the justiciar.
[3] KR 2, m. 12v.
[4] LTR 2, m. 12r.
[5] LTR 3, m. 5v; KR 4, m. 20v.
[6] LTR 3, m. 8v.

technical matters which the exchequer needed to know in order to proceed with its work, and the justiciar, like his predecessors, was expected to solve the difficulties which arose, not so much because his opinion of the correct procedure was needed, but because he might be expected to know the king's will and the way in which it was desired that business should be disposed. This position of authority Hubert occupied, whether the general tendency of exchequer practice was towards reform or reaction.

The reforming movement began to set in again in 1228, but in 1230 Hubert's control of exchequer proceedings was still the same. Thus, among the *communia* of the Hilary term, it was recorded that Roger Gernet was given respite for the remaining farm of his bailiwick by the justiciar's order; at Easter, W. de Vesci's account of many debts was postponed by the justiciar, as was the account of Walter de Godarville for having the lady Johanna.[1] Again, the justiciar ordered that if any sheriff, or servant of any sheriff, shall have taken anything from anyone by summons of the exchequer and not have paid it into the lower exchequer, and through witnesses or recognition can be convicted, he shall be sent to prison and punished with a large amercement.[2] This seems to be a general direction of the justiciar's about the policy to be pursued by the barons in respect of a particular problem. As evidence of the justiciar's control of the exchequer, it suggests that it endured even after Stephen of Seagrave's collection of shrievalties heralded the return of the Poitevins and the grouping of shires under Peter des Rievaulx. Hubert's control of the exchequer was removed by his absence with the king in France in 1230. His place at the exchequer was taken by Seagrave and the bishop of Chichester, the chancellor, who were left as the regents. When the justiciar returned from the continent his days were numbered. In 1232 the Poitevin reforming party triumphed. They did not directly assault Hubert's position in the administration. Indeed, the grant to him of the justiciarship for life suggests that his office was unimportant in their scheme of things; it could be ignored because it could be circumvented by the household administration; it could be isolated in a formal position while the effective power was with-

---

[1] *Memoranda Roll 14 Henry III*, pp. 44, 55, 61.   [2] *Ibid.* p. 61.

drawn from those branches of government which had 'gone out of court'. Potentially, the office was still important; no doubt Peter des Roches could have used it to control the administration, but this danger was eliminated by the appointment of Stephen of Seagrave, a professional lawyer of no political importance, and after two years the office was abolished. The king's government could operate effectively without it.

7. STEPHEN OF SEAGRAVE

Hubert de Burgh was succeeded by Stephen of Seagrave, the last, least, if not quite the briefest, tenant of the justiciarship. The tenure of Stephen does not fall within the scope of his study,[1] but something must be said of his rise and his position while Hubert was still in office, since he was partly instrumental in the justiciar's fall and by his character and training gave to the office a purely judicial character devoid of political importance.

The family of Stephen of Seagrave was settled in Warwickshire before 1166, and held a quarter of a knight's fee of William, earl of Warwick, not at Seagrave but in Brailes.[2] The lands at Seagrave were bought by Stephen's father, Gilbert, and confirmed to him by Herbert son of Roger of Seagrave. Gilbert, son of this Herbert, gave Stephen of Seagrave himself a virgate of land which he held of the earl of Chester of the soke of Barrow.[3] Gilbert of Seagrave, Stephen's father, was a royal official. In 1187 he was joint accountant for the revenues of the abbey of St Mary of Leicester; in 1192 he was one of the deputies of Hugh, bishop of Coventry, who held the counties of Warwickshire and Leicestershire; in 1196 he was one of the justices in eyre in Lincolnshire.[4] His career was not very distinguished and he died presumably before Michaelmas

[1] A thesis has been written upon the office under Stephen of Seagrave by K. Williams-Jones for the degree of M.A. in the University of Wales.

[2] An account of these lands, from which I have taken the information presented in the text, may be found in *Complete Peerage*, XI, 597; *Monasticon*, VI, 464.

[3] Harl. MS 4748 quoted in *Complete Peerage;* in 1295 Nichola de Seagrave held one-third of the manor of Seagrave *in capite* and two-thirds of the abbot of Leicester; *Cal. Inquisitions Post Mortem*, III, no. 297.

[4] *Complete Peerage, ibid.*

1201. Stephen of Seagrave was Gilbert's son and heir, and his own career was both busier and more distinguished than his father's. In 1206 he was *custos* with William Picot of the pleas of the Crown in Leicestershire and in 1208 he was an attorney of the prior of the Hospital of Jerusalem.[1] His work thus began as judicial. In 1215 he was sent by the king with others to the earls and barons of Worcestershire to expound royal business, and from this time his fortune began to rise steadily. In January 1216 he held the land which had been Stephen de Gant's in his home county; by July he had been granted the manor of Kineton in Warwickshire, and four years later was given a weekly market there; in 1228 he also obtained there a yearly fair. The manor of Alconbury in Huntingdonshire was granted to him in 1220. In 1228 he obtained land at Cotes, Derbyshire; in 1229 the wapentake of Goscote (Leicestershire); and a little later the manor of Finedon and land in the town of Northampton.[2] Apart from land granted to him, Stephen held two important custodies: all the fees of Earl Simon de Montfort of the *honor* of Leicester and the bailiwick of William de Cantilupe were committed to him in 1218, and in 1221 the *honor* of Boulogne, apart from lesser custodies.[3] It is worth noting, however, that the real increase in his wealth came after 1228 and most of all after he had become justiciar in 1232.[4] He had started from the relatively humble origin of a knight, and when he attained the justiciarship his wealth was in no way comparable with that of Hubert de Burgh nor of Geoffrey fitz Peter when they entered upon the office. Stephen was never a great baron or magnate. His importance is not political or social, but it is to be sought in his long career of service in the royal administration, service which was primarily judicial in character.

[1] *Complete Peerage* XI, 597.

[2] The picture of Stephen's accumulation of land may be gathered from the following references: *Rot. Lit. Claus.* I, 246, 278, 415, 428, 471; *CClR 1227–31*, pp. 125, 140, 170, 282, 317; *CClR 1231–4*, pp. 163, 395; *CChR*, I, 3, 81, 84, 95, 109, 116.

[3] *Rot. Lit. Claus.* I, 366, 465.

[4] The yearly fair at Kineton was given to him 30 November 1228; the land of Cotes in Derbyshire ten days earlier; the wapentake of Goscote in April 1229; the manor of Finedon 1229–30; the manor and soke of Kirton, Lincolnshire, 3 November 1232; the manor of Melbourne, Derbyshire, 1233/4.

From 1217 Stephen played a prominent part in judicial work. In 1220 he delivered the gaols in Warwickshire, Leicestershire, and Herefordshire. From 1226 his work in eyre was very considerable, and in successive years he visited the counties of Leicester, Worcester, Nottingham, Derby, Hereford, Stafford, Shropshire, Oxfordshire, Northampton, and Warwickshire.[1] On these eyres he was head of the party of justices, in this respect rivalling the distinguished judge Martin of Pattishall who headed a similar group of justices. Stephen's itinerant judicial work seems to have been concentrated in the midland counties and one or two of those in the west towards the Welsh border. Since Hubert de Burgh's judicial work, particularly in eyre, seems to have been slight, the effective administration of justice depended upon Martin and Stephen and their colleagues. Possibly Stephen was helped on his way in royal administration by the justiciar himself. From 1221 to 1223 Stephen was constable of the Tower of London which was held by the justiciar; and in 1221, when Stephen received 40 marks to sustain himself in the king's service, the payment was made under Hubert's witness and by his warranty.[2] Stephen's position is reflected in his seniority among the justices in the bench at Westminster. At the beginning of the reign he occupied a junior place in court. For example, in the quindene of Michaelmas 2 Henry III, the justices were the earl of Arundel, no doubt as a representative of the council, Martin of Pattishall, Ralph Hareng, Stephen of Seagrave, and Simon de Insula.[3] In the absence of great magnates and when professional justices alone sat at Westminster, as in the Easter term following, the order was Martin of Pattishall, Ralph Hareng, Stephen, and Simon de Insula.[4] Stephen was last but one of the justices named. By Henry III's fifth year he was senior to two justices who had joined the court, Thomas of Haydon and Robert of Lexington, but it was still usual

---

[1] This list has been compiled from mandates addressed to him; *Rot. Lit. Claus.* II, 140, 142, 151, 154, 156, 160, 165, 169, 170, 171, 185, 194, 197, 202, 205, 208, 213, 413, 474.

[2] He received £50 p.a. as constable of the Tower; *Rot. Lit. Claus.* I, 459, 472, 496, 512, 545; in addition to money for repairs; *ibid.* pp. 466, 471, 472; £25 was paid at each exchequer session of Easter and Michaelmas.

[3] CP 25 (1) 128/11/1-3.   [4] *Ibid.* 6, 7.

for him to follow Martin and Ralph in the lists of justices.[1] His rise in precedence was gradual; from 1229 onwards he was the second senior justice to Thomas of Milton, and at times he presided over the bench.[2] At Easter 1229 the pleas at Westminster in the quindene were heard by Stephen presiding over a court composed of William Ralegh, Robert of Lexington, William of London, and Thomas of Milton.[3] In 1230, when he and the chancellor were left as regents, Stephen, curiously, took second place in final concords to Thomas, and in the Hilary, Easter, and Trinity terms of the following year was not named in court as a justice at Westminster, although he headed an eyre which visited Lincoln.[4] In 1232 Stephen presided over the justices at Westminster in the Hilary term, but was not in court thereafter, nor in the following year. The lack of any clear precedence among the justices suggests that Stephen's career, although it led him to some prominence, was not that of the most distinguished justice of his day; he was never senior to Martin of Pattishall, and had no clear superiority over Thomas of Milton.[5] He was an important justice, but not, obviously, without his competitors. His stature may, however, have been enhanced by the absence of the justiciar from judicial proceedings at Westminster and there were occasions when Stephen presided over the bench; but part at least of his importance must have come from his intensive local activity, both as a justice in eyre and as a sheriff, and probably, although this is speculation, from his connexion with the Poitevins. His collection of shrievalties, for example, was the herald of the strengthening of the reforming party in exchequer proceedings.[6]

---

[1] CP 25 (1) 128/15/10–24.   [2] Ibid. passim.

[3] PRO KB 26/102; Placita Apud Westmonasterium in xv dies anno regis Regni H. fil. J. xiii Coram S. de Segrave, W. de Ralegh, R. de Lexington, W. de London et T. de Muleton et Sociis eorum.

[4] CP 25 (1)/129/21 passim; 129/22 passim; 129/23 passim.

[5] Thomas of Milton was a sheriff, under John, of Lincolnshire, and accompanied him to Ireland in 1210. He joined the baronial party, but his lands were restored to him by Henry III when he returned to his allegiance. His second marriage to Ada widow of Richard de Luci of Egremont and daughter of Hugh de Morville brought him the office of forester of Cumberland. He was an itinerant justice in 3 Henry III and in 1224 sat in the bench. In January 1227 he headed a circuit; Foss, op. cit. p. 468.   [6] Mills, loc. cit. p. 166.

Of Stephen's own interest in the exchequer it is difficult to speak before 1230. As a sheriff it cannot have been strange to him and in 1230 he displayed an active and expert interest in the barons' deliberations; he gave terms to an accountant; he attested exchequer writs; he and the chancellor were to be consulted about a debt of an heir whose mother had paid it to two of the king's stewards, one of whom acknowledged receiving it.[1] His interest in and knowledge of exchequer proceedings is borne out by the compilation of a statement in 1241 of profits which may have provided the basis for a new and additional farm of the shires.[2] All the evidence seems to point to a man who was an experienced administrator, more particularly perhaps in judicial matters but also in exchequer affairs, whose administrative career was not the most distinguished. The clue to his importance to the Poitevins probably lies partly in his long administrative experience, but as much in his character. He was, said Matthew Paris, *vir flexibilis*; and it was probably his pliability which led to his usefulness in the 1230s, and to his promotion to the justiciarship.[3] He was a capable administrator, but a man who, socially and politically, was not of the highest importance; useful, in short, in the *coup d'état* of 1232 for these reasons, and not, therefore, of the calibre of his predecessors in the justiciarship.

One last point remains to be mentioned. The year 1230 saw the end of one of the traditional duties of the justiciar. When the king sailed for Poitou in April of that year, he left behind as his regents not the justiciar but Stephen of Seagrave and Ralph de Neville, bishop of Chichester. The king announced the arrangement by letters patent.[4] By common counsel of the earls, barons, and all his faithful men, he had provided that, since Hubert de Burgh was to accompany him, these two were left that they might govern the kingdom of England; and so long as the justiciar was with the king, Stephen, *loco predicti justiciarii*, by the counsel of the chancellor should dispose of all the king's business and that of the kingdom. The letter goes on to make provision for the exchequer seal

---

[1] *Memoranda Roll 14 Henry III*, pp. 18, 73, 87, 89.
[2] Powicke, *op. cit.* p. 98.
[3] Matthew Paris, III, 240. [4] *CPR 1225-32*, p. 399.

to be employed as the seal of absence, and to provide that, if Stephen made a journey through England, the seal in custody of the chancellor should go with him, the private seal of the justiciar remaining at the exchequer in the custody of the chancellor. The king went on to enjoin general obedience to their orders in his name thus sealed and also to those issued by the barons of the exchequer under the justiciar's privy seal. The corollary to this letter was an order to William of Carlisle, the treasurer, to deliver the exchequer seal to the chancellor and to admit the justiciar's privy seal.[1]

These documents are interesting as a comment both on contemporary administration and on the traditions of the justiciarship. In appointing Stephen *loco predicti justiciarii*, the king seemed to recognize the assumption that the justiciar had, in the past, become regent in the royal absence. He assumed, too, that it would be necessary for the justiciar to make a tour of England while he was away to facilitate the work of government, and that in the justiciar's absence from Westminster the exchequer and a seal would carry on the administration at the centre. Also the position of the chancellor, theoretically controlling all the seals of government, necessitated his being taken into counsel. All this represents, and states specifically, what must have been the position of every justiciar; it is a succinct comment upon the office and its duties. This was the machinery of government which administered England, which served the regent and which handled royal writs *de ultra mare*; it was to handle a large number of writs from Poitou in 1230, addressed to Stephen and the bishop, which set this machinery in motion.[2] Yet the arrangement also betrays the growth of 'departmentalism' which was working against the concept of the justiciarship. The treasurer was treated as head of the exchequer, having practical control of his departmental seal, and a special order was necessary to assign the seal to the chancellor who nominally controlled it and to replace it with another. In 1230 administration and regency could both dispense with the

---

[1] The Patent Roll was annotated 'Claus' and the mandate to the treasurer summarized thereon; *ibid.*

[2] *CClR 1227–31*, pp. 327 ff.

justiciar, and the political (and in Poitou the military) failure of Hubert de Burgh, which had been shown up by a series of incidents throughout the reign, revealed how difficult or impossible it was to use royal administrative machinery to achieve the maximum efficiency and advantage for royal government and yet remain within the situation represented by the Great Charter. This was the factor which sealed the doom of the justiciarship, already undermined by administrative development and deprived by the loss of Normandy of its viceregal *raison d'être*.

BIBLIOGRAPHY

A. PRIMARY SOURCES

Unpublished sources

British Museum

Additional MSS 15350; 24521; 29436; 30311; 33354; 46487
Cotton Charters
Cotton MSS
  Appendix 21
  Caligula A xii
  Claudius A iv; D xii, D xiii
  Cleopatra C viii; D iii
  Domitian A iii; A x
  Faustina A iv
  Galba E ii
  Julius D ii
  Nero C iii; E vii
  Tiberius A xiii, C ix
  Titus A i
  Vespasian A xxii; B xxiv; C xv; E v; E xvii; E xx; E xxiv; F xv
  Vitellus A i
Egerton MSS 2823; 3031
Harleian MSS 61; 391; 436; 1499; 1708; 1881; 2110; 3660; 3697; 3891; 3911; 4660; 4714; 6964
Lansdowne MSS 415; 417; 830; 939
Royal MS 11 B ix

Public Record Office

Ancient Correspondence
Ancient Deeds
Cartae Antiquae Rolls
Chancery Files
Chancery Master Exhibits
Chancery Miscellanea
Curia Regis Rolls
Duchy of Lancaster Records
Feet of Fines
Memoranda Rolls
Ministers' Accounts
Pipe Rolls
PRO Transcripts

Cathedral and college libraries
Balliol College, Oxford
Canterbury, Library of the Dean and Chapter
Corpus Christi College, Cambridge
Ely, Muniment Room of the Dean and Chapter
Wells, Library of the Dean and Chapter

Published sources

(1) *Collections of charters and documents*

(a) Cartularies (in alphabetical order of place)

Two Cartularies of the Priory of St Peter of Bath, ed. W. Hunt, Somerset Record Society, London, 1893.

Cartulary of Chester, ed. J. Tait, Chetham Society, 2 vols., Manchester, 1920–3.

Early Charters to Chicksand, Bedford Historical Society, 1913.

Cartularium Monasterii S. Johannis de Colecestriae, ed. S. A. Moore, 2 vols., Roxburgh Club, London, 1897.

Liber Eliensis, ed. D. J. Stewart, Anglia Christiana Society, London, 1848.

Cartulary of the Abbey of Fynshoom, od. H. E. Saltei, Oxford Historical Society, 2 vols., 1907–8.

Cartulary of the Monastery of St Frideswide, ed. S. R. Wigram, Oxford Historical Society, 2 vols., 1895.

Historia et Cartularium S. Petri Gloucestriae, ed. W. H. Hart, Rolls Series, 3 vols., London, 1863–7.

Cartulary of St Benet of Holme, ed. J. R. West, Norfolk Record Society, 1932.

Registrum Antiquissimum, vols. I–III, ed. C. W. Foster; vols. IV–V, ed. K. Major, Lincoln Record Society, 1931–40.

Registrum Malmesburiense, ed. J. S. Brewer, Rolls Series, 2 vols., London, 1879–84.

Cartulary of Oseney Abbey, ed. H. E. Salter, 6 vols., Oxford Historical Society, 1929–31.

Cartulary of St John of Pontefract, ed. R. Holmes, 2 vols., Leeds, 1889, 1902.

Cartularium Monasterii de Rameseia, ed. W. Hart and P. A. Lyons, Rolls Series, 3 vols., London, 1884–93.

Cartularium de abbathie de Rievalle, ed. J. C. Atkinson, Surtees Society, Durham, 1889.

Cartulaire de la Ste Trinité du Mont de Rouen, ed. A. Deville, Paris, 1861.
Vetus Registrum Sareberiense, ed. W. H. R. Jones, Rolls Series, 2 vols., London, 1883–4.
Sarum Charters, ed. W. D. Macray, Rolls Series, London, 1891.
Heming's Cartulary of Worcester, ed. T. Hearne, 2 vols., Oxford, 1723.

(*b*) Miscellaneous collections (in alphabetical order of editors)

Armitage-Robinson, J., *Gilbert Crispin, Abbot of Westminster*, Cambridge, 1911.
Bigelow, M. M., *Placita Anglo-Normannica*, Boston, 1879.
Davis, H. W. C., *Regesta Regum Anglo-Normannorum 1066–1100*, vol. I, Oxford, 1913; *Regesta Regum Anglo-Normannorum 1100–35*, vol. II (ed. C. Johnson and H. A. Cronne), Oxford, 1956.
Delisle, L., *Recueil des Actes de Henry II* (ed. E. Berger), Paris, 1909–27.
Douglas, D. C., *Feudal Documents from the Abbey of Bury St Edmunds*, British Academy, Records of Social and Economic History, London, 1931.
Dugdale, W., *Monasticon Anglicanum* (2nd ed. J. Caley, H. Ellis, B. Bandinel), 6 vols., London, 1817–30.
Eyton, R. W., *Court, Household and Itinerary of Henry II*, London, 1878.
Farrer, W., *Early Yorkshire Charters*, 3 vols., Edinburgh, 1914–16.
——*Honours and Knights' Fees*, 3 vols., London, Manchester, 1923–5.
Hamilton, N. E. S. A., *Inquisitio Comitatus Cantabrigiensis*, London, 1876.
Sir Christopher Hatton's Book of Seals, ed. L. C. Lloyd and D. M. Stenton, Northamptonshire Record Society, Oxford, 1950.
Landon, L., *Itinerary of Richard I*, Pipe Roll Society New Series, London, 1935.
Madox, T., *Formulare Anglicanum*, London, 1702.
Migne, J. P., *Patrologiae Cursus Completus*, Series Latina, 161 vols., Paris, 1844–64.
Oliver, G., *Monasticon Diocesis Exoniensis*, Exeter, 1846.
Reports of the Royal Commission on Historical MSS, London, 1870 *et seq*.
Round, J. H., *Ancient Charters*, Pipe Roll Society, London, 1888.
——*Calendar of Documents Preserved in France*, Rolls Series, London, 1889.
Rymer, T., *Foedera, Conventiones, Litterae* (ed. A. Clarke, F. Holbrooke and J. Caley), Record Commission, London, 1816–69.
Stubbs, W., *Select Charters* (9th edn., ed. H. W. C. Davies), Oxford, 1913.
Wharton, H., *Anglia Sacra*, London, 1691.

(2) *Financial and Chancery Records*

Book of Fees (Calendars of State Papers), London, 1920.

Cartae Antiquae, Rolls 1–10, ed. L. Landon, Pipe Roll Society New Series, London, 1939.

Calendar of Close Rolls, London, 1902.

Calendar of Charter Rolls, London, 1903–27.

Calendar of Patent Rolls, London, 1891–1916.

Chancellor's Roll 8 Richard I, Pipe Roll Society New Series, London, 1930.

Liber Rubeus de Scaccario, ed. H. Hall, Rolls Series, 3 vols., London, 1896.

Magnus Rotulus Pipae Anno Primo Regni Ricardi Primi, ed. J. Hunter, Record Commission, London, 1844.

Magni Rotuli Scaccarii Normanniae, ed. T. Stapleton, Society of Antiquaries, 2 vols., London, 1840, 1844.

Memoranda Roll 1 John, ed. H. G. Richardson, Pipe Roll Society New Series, London, 1943.

Memoranda Roll 10 John, ed. R. A. Brown, Pipe Roll Society New Series, London, 1957.

Memoranda Roll 14 Henry III, ed. C. Robinson, Pipe Roll Society New Series, London, 1927.

Pipe Rolls 2, 3 and *4 Henry II*, ed. J. Hunter, Record Commission, London, 1844.

Pipe Rolls 5 Henry II to *34 Henry II*, Pipe Roll Society, London, 1884–1925.

Pipe Roll 2 Richard I and onwards, Pipe Roll Society New Series, London, 1925 onwards.

Rotuli Chartarum 1199–1216, ed. T. D. Hardy, Record Commission, London, 1837.

Rotulus de Dominabus et Pueris et Puellis, ed. J. H. Round, Pipe Roll Society, London, 1913.

Rotuli de Liberate ac Misis ac Prestitis, ed. T. D. Hardy, Record Commission, London, 1844.

Rotuli Litterarum Clausarum 1204–27, ed. T. D. Hardy, Record Commission, London, 1833.

Rotuli Litterarum Patentium 1201–16, ed. T. D. Hardy, Record Commission, London, 1835.

Rotuli de Oblatis et Finibus, ed. T. D. Hardy, Record Commission, London, 1835.

(3) *Judicial records*

Bedfordshire Assize Roll 1202, ed. G. H. Fowler, Bedford Historical Society, 1913.

Curia Regis Rolls (Richard I–Henry III), ed. C. T. Flower, London, 1922 onwards.

Feet of Fines Henry II and Richard I, Pipe Roll Society, London, 1894.

Feet of Fines 7 and 8 Richard I, Pipe Roll Society, London, 1896.

Feet of Fines 9 Richard I, Pipe Roll Society, London, 1898.

Feet of Fines 10 Richard I, Pipe Roll Society, London, 1900.

Feet of Fines Norfolk 1202, Pipe Roll Society, London, 1950.

Feet of Fines Lincolnshire 1199–1215, Pipe Roll Society, London, 1953.

Feet of Fines Norfolk, 1201–15, Suffolk 1199–1214, Pipe Roll Society, London, 1956.

Fines sive pedes Finium 1195–1214, ed. J. Hunter, Record Commission, London, 1835–44.

Five Membranes for a Hilary Term Richard I, ed. F. W. Maitland, Pipe Roll Society, London, 1900.

The Earliest Lincolnshire Assize Rolls, 1202–9, ed. D. M. Stenton, Lincoln Record Society, 1926.

Northampton Assize Rolls, ed. D. M. Stenton, Northamptonshire Record Society, 1926.

Pleas Before the King or His Justices, 1198–1202, 2 vols., ed. D. M. Stenton, Selden Society, London, 1949, 1953.

Rolls of the King's Court Richard I, ed. F. W. Maitland, Pipe Roll Society, London, 1891.

Rotuli Curiae Regis, ed. F. Palgrave, Record Commission, 2 vols., London, 1835.

Royal Writs in England from the Conquest to Glanville, ed. R. C. Van Caenegem, Selden Society, London, 1959.

Rolls of the Justices in Eyre, Lincolnshire 1218–19 and Worcestershire 1221, ed. D. M. Stenton, Lincoln Record Society, 1934.

Rolls of the Justices in Eyre, Yorkshire 1218–19, ed. D. M. Stenton, Selden Society, London, 1937.

Rolls of the Justices in Eyre, Gloucestershire, Warwickshire, Staffordshire, 1221, 1222, ed. D. M. Stenton, Selden Society, London, 1940.

Select Cases in the Court of King's Bench, vol. I, ed. G. O. Sayles, Selden Society, London, 1936.

Select Cases in the Exchequer of Pleas, ed. H. Jenkinson and B. E. R. Formoy, Selden Society, London, 1931.

Select Civil Pleas 1200–3, ed. W. P. Baildon, Selden Society, London, 1890.

Select Pleas of the Crown, ed. F. W. Maitland, Selden Society, London, 1888.

Select Pleas of the Forest, ed. G. J. Turner, Selden Society, London, 1901.

Select Cases of Procedure without Writ, ed. H. G. Richardson and G. O. Sayles, Selden Society, London, 1941.

Staffordshire Assize Roll, ed. G. Wrottesley, Salt Society, London, 1882.

(4) *Narratives and Letters* (in alphabetical order of author or place of authorship)

Chronicon Monasterii de Abingdon, ed. J. Stevenson, Rolls Series, 2 vols., London, 1858.

Anglo-Saxon Chronicle, Two Chronicles Parallel, ed. J. Earle and C. Plummer, 2 vols., Oxford, 1892–9.

Annales Monastici, ed. H. R. Luard, Rolls Series, 5 vols., London, 1864–9.

Historia Monasterii de S. Augustino, ed. C. Hardwick, Rolls Series, London, 1858.

Chronicon Monasterii de Bello, ed. J. S. Brewer, Anglia Christiana Society, London, 1846.

Materials for the History of Thomas Becket, ed. J. C. Robertson, Rolls Series, 7 vols., London, 1875–85.

Brakelond, Joscelin of, *Chronica Joscelini de Brakelond*, ed. J. G. Rokewoode, Camden Society, London, 1879–80.

Epistolae Cantuarienses, ed. W. Stubbs, in *Chronicles and Memorials of the Reign of Richard I*, Rolls Series, London, 1865.

Canterbury, Gervase of, *Historical Works of Gervase of Canterbury*, ed. W. Stubbs, Rolls Series, 2 vols., London, 1879–80.

Coggeshall, Ralph of, *Radulphi de Coggeshall Chronicon Anglicanum*, ed. J. Stevenson, Rolls Series, London, 1875.

Coventry, Walter of, *Memoriale Fratris Walteri de Coventria*, ed. W. Stubbs, 2 vols., London, 1872–3.

Devizes, Richard of, in *Chronicles of the Reigns of Stephen, Henry II, and Richard I*, ed. R. Howlett, Rolls Series, 4 vols., London, 1884–90.

Diceto, Ralph of, *Radulphi de Diceto Opera Historica*, ed. W. Stubbs, Rolls Series, 2 vols., London, 1876.

Durham, Simeon of, *Opera Omnia*, ed. T. Arnold, Rolls Series, London, 1882–5.

Eadmer, *Historia Novorum*, ed. M. Rule, Rolls Series, London, 1884.

Chronicon Abbatie de Evesham, ed. W. D. Macray, Rolls Series, London, 1863.

Fantosme, Jordan, *see* Devizes.

Histoire de Guillaume de Maréchal, ed. P. Meyer, Société de l'Histoire de France, 3 vols., Paris, 1891–1901.

Histoire des ducs de Normandie et des rois d'Angleterre, ed. F. Michel, Paris, 1840.

Howden, Roger of, *Chronica Magistri Rogeri de Hovedene*, ed. W. Stubbs, Rolls Series, 4 vols., London, 1868–71.

Huntingdon, Henry of, *Historia Anglorum*, ed. T. Arnold, Rolls Series, London, 1879.

Innocent III, *Selected Letters of Pope Innocent III Concerning England*, ed. C. R. Cheney and W. H. Semple, London, 1953.

Malmesbury, William of, *De Gestis Pontificum Anglorum*, ed. N. E. S. A. Hamilton, Rolls Series, London, 1870; *De Gestis Regum Anglorum*, ed. W. Stubbs, Rolls Series, 2 vols., London, 1887–9.

Newburgh, William of, *Historia Rerum Anglicarum*, *see* Devizes.

Calendar of Papal Letters (Calendar of State Papers, vol. 1), London, 1893.

Paris, Matthew, *Chronica Majora*, ed. H. R. Luard, Rolls Series, London, 1872–84.

Peterborough, Benedict of, *Gesta Regis Henrici Secundi*, ed. W. Stubbs, Rolls Series, London, 1867.

Poitiers, William of, *Gesta Guillelmi Ducis*, ed. A. Duchesne, Paris, 1619.

Royal and other Historical Letters Illustrative of the reign of Henry III, ed. W. W. Shirley, Rolls Series, 2 vols., London, 1862–6.

Wales, Gerald of, *Opera Giraldi Cambrensis*, ed. J. S. Brewer, J. F. Dimock, G. F. Warner, Rolls Series, 8 vols., London, 1861–91.

Wendover, Roger, of, *Flores Historiarum*, ed. H. G. Howlett, Rolls Series, London, 1886–9.

Worcester, Florence of, *Chronica ex Chronicis*, ed. B. Thorpe, English Historical Society, 2 vols., London, 1848–9.

Map, Walter, *De Nugis Curialium*, ed. M. R. James, Oxford, 1914.

Vitalis, Orderic, *Historia Ecclesiastica*, ed. A. Le Prévost, 5 vols., Paris, 1838–55.

Salisbury, John of, *Johannis Saresberiensis opera omnia*, ed. J. A. Giles, 5 vols., Oxford, 1848.

(5) *Treatises*

Dialogus de Scaccario, ed. C. Johnson, London, 1950.

Tractatus de Legibus et Consuetudinibus Angliae, ed. G. E. Woodbine, Yale, 1932.

B. SELECT SECONDARY SOURCES

The immense learning contained in the introductions to publications of the Selden and Pipe Roll Societies has not been listed again; reference should be made to the previous section.

Adams, G. B. *Council and Courts in Anglo-Norman England*, New Haven, 1926.

Baldwin, J. F. 'Council and Exchequer in Henry III's Minority', *Transactions of the Royal Historical Society*, new series, XIX, 1905.

—— *The King's Council*, Oxford, 1913.

Barlow, F. 'Roger of Howden', *English Historical Review*, LXV, 1950.

Beautemps-Beaupré, C. J. *Coutumes et Institutions de l'Anjou et du Maine*, Paris, 1890.

Boussard, J. *Histoire du Comté d'Anjou sous Henri Plantagenet et ses fils 1151–1204*, Paris, 1938.

Cam, H. *Studies in the Hundred Rolls*, Oxford, 1921.

Cheney, C. R. *English Bishops' Chanceries 1100–1250*, Manchester, 1950.

Chrimes, S. B. *An Introduction to the Administrative History of Mediaeval England*, Oxford, 1952.

Complete Peerage of England, Scotland, Ireland, Great Britain and the United Kingdom, new edn. by V. Gibbs and others, London, 1910.

Corbett, W. J. 'England 1087–1154', *Cambridge Medieval History*, vol. v, Cambridge, 1926.

Darlington, R. R. 'Aethelwig of Evesham', *English Historical Review*, XLVIII, 1933.

Dibben, L. B. 'Chancellor and Keeper of the Seal under Henry III', *English Historical Review*, XXVII, 1912.

Dictionary of National Biography, 1st edn. London, 1885–1900.

Ellis, Clarence. *Hubert de Burgh*, London, 1953.

Freeman, E. A. *The Norman Conquest*, Oxford, 1867–79.

Farrer, W. 'Itinerary of Henry I', *English Historical Review*, XXXIV, 1919.

Flower, C. T. *Introduction to the Curia Regis Rolls*, Selden Society London, 1943.

Foss, E. *A Biographical Dictionary of the Judges of England*, London, 1870.

Galbraith, V. H. *Studies in the Public Records*, London, 1948.

Halphen, L. *Le Comté d'Anjou au xiime siècle*, Paris, 1906.

Harcourt, V. *His Grace the Steward and the Trial of the Peers*, London, 1907.

Haskins, C. H. *Norman Institutions*, Cambridge, Mass., 1918.

Holdsworth, W. S. *History of English Law*, 3rd edn., London, 1922.

Hoyt, R. S. *The Royal Demesne in English Constitutional History 1066–1272*, New York, 1950.

Hurnard, N. D. 'Magna Carta, Clause 34', *Studies in Medieval History presented to Frederick Maurice Powicke*, Oxford, 1948.

Jacob, E. F. 'The Reign of Henry III', *Transactions of Royal Historical Society*, 4th series, X, 1927.

——'England: Henry III', *Cambridge Medieval History*, vol. VI, Cambridge, 1929.

Jenkins, C. *The Monastic Chronicle and the Early School of St Albans*, London, 1923.

Johnson, C. 'Notes on Thirteenth Century Judicial Procedure', *English Historical Review*, LXII, 1947.

Johnston, S. H. F. 'The Lands of Hubert de Burgh', *English Historical Review*, L, 1935.

Jolliffe, J. E. A. *Constitutional History of Mediaeval England*, London, 1937.

——*Angevin Kingship*, London, 1955.

——'The Camera Regis under Henry II', *English Historical Review*, LXVIII, 1953.

——'The Chamber and the Castle Treasuries under King John', in *Studies in Medieval History presented to Frederick Maurice Powicke*, Oxford, 1948.

Knowles, M. D. *The Episcopal Colleagues of Archbishop Thomas Becket*, Cambridge, 1951.

Le Patourel, J. H. 'Geoffrey of Montbray, Bishop of Coutances', *English Historical Review*, LXIX, 1944.

Lloyd, J. E. *History of Wales*, 2 vols., 3rd edn., London, 1939.

Lunt, W. E. *Papal Revenues in the Middle Ages*, New York, 1934.

Macdonald, A. *Lanfranc*, Oxford, 1926.

Mackenzie, H. 'The Anti Foreign Movement in England 1231–2', *Anniversary Essays in Mediaeval History by Students of Charles Homer Haskins*, Cambridge, Mass., 1929.

Madox, T. *The History and Antiquities of the Exchequer of England, 1066–1327*, London, 1711.

Maitland, F. W. *Constitutional History of England*, Cambridge, 1908; (with Pollock, F.) *History of English Law*, 2nd edn., Cambridge, 1898. *Forms of Action at Common Law*, ed. H. H. Chayter and W. J. Whittaker, Cambridge, 1948.

Maxwell-Lyte, H. C. *Historical Notes on the Use of the Great Seal of England*, London, 1926.

Miller, E. 'Ely Land Pleas in the Reign of William I', *English Historical Review*, LXII, 1947.

McKechnie, W. S. *Magna Carta*, 2nd edn., Glasgow, 1915.

Mills, M. 'Experiments in Exchequer Procedure 1200–32', *Transactions of the Royal Historical Society*, 4th series, VIII, 1925.

——'The Reforms at the Exchequer', *ibid*. X, 1927.

Mitchell, S. K. *Studies in Taxation under John and Henry III*, New Haven, 1914.

——*Taxation in Medieval England*, New Haven, 1951.

Morey, S. A. *Bartholomew of Exeter, Bishop and Canonist*, Cambridge, 1937.

Morris, W. A. *The Mediaeval English Sheriff to 1300*, Manchester, 1927.

Norgate, K. *John Lackland*, London, 1902.

——*The Minority of Henry III*, London, 1912.

Painter, S. *William Marshal*, Baltimore, 1933.

——*The Reign of King John*, Baltimore, 1949.

Palgrave, F. *The Rise and Progress of the English Commonwealth*, London, 1832.

Poole, A. L. *From Domesday Book to Magna Carta*, Oxford, 1951.

Poole, R. L. *The Exchequer in the Twelfth Century*, London, 1912.

Powicke, F. M. 'Roger of Wendover and the Coggeshall Chronicle', *English Historical Review*, XXI, 1906.

——'The Angevin Administration of Normandy', *ibid*. XXI–XXII, 1906–7.

——'The Chancery in the Minority of Henry III', *ibid*. XXIII, 1908.

——*The Loss of Normandy*, Manchester, 1913.

——*Stephen Langton*, Oxford, 1928.

——*King Henry III and the Lord Edward*, Oxford, 1947.

——'England: Richard I and John', *Cambridge Medieval History*, vol. VI, Cambridge, 1929.

Richardson, H. G. 'William of Ely, the King's Treasurer', *Transactions of the Royal Historical Society*, 4th series, XV, 1932.

——'The Morrow of the Great Charter', *Bulletin of the John Rylands Library*, XXIX, 1944.

——'The Chamber under Henry II', *English Historical Review*, LXIX, 1954.

——(with G. O. Sayles), *The Governance of Mediaeval England*, Edinburgh, 1963.

Round, J. H. *Feudal England*, London, 1895.
——*Commune of London*, Westminster, 1899.
——*Geoffrey de Mandeville*, London, 1892.
——'King John and Robert fitz Walter', *English Historical Review*, XIX, 1904.
Russell, G. 'The Attestation of John's Charters', *Speculum*, XV, 1940.
Sayles, G. O. *See under* Richardson, H. G. and *Judicial Records* above.
Southern, R. W. 'Ranulf Flambard and the Anglo-Norman Administration', *Transactions of the Royal Historical Society*, 4th series, XVI, 1933.
——'Note on the Text of Glanville', *English Historical Review*, LXV, 1950.
Stenton, D. M. 'England: Henry II', *Cambridge Medieval History*, vol. V, Cambridge, 1926.
——'Roger of Salisbury, Angliae Regni Procurator', *English Historical Review*, XXXIX, 1924.
——'Roger of Howden and Benedict', *English Historical Review*, LXVIII, 1953.
——'King John and the Courts of Justice', *Proceedings of the British Academy*, XLIV, 1958.
Stenton, F. M. *Anglo-Saxon England*, Oxford, 1947.
——*The First Century of English Feudalism 1066–1166*, Oxford, 1932.
Stubbs, W. *Constitutional History of England*, Oxford, 1874–8.
——*Historical Introductions to the Rolls Series*, London, 1902.
Stamp, A. E. 'Some Notes on the Court and Chancery of Henry III', *Historical Essays in Honour of James Tait*, 1933.
Tout, T. F. *Chapters in the Administrative History of Mediaeval England*, Manchester, 1920–3.
Turner, G. J. 'The Minority of Henry III', *Transactions of the Royal Historical Society*, new series, XVIII; 3rd series, I, 1904, 1907.

Victoria History of the Counties of England, ed. various, London, 1900 onwards.

West, F. J. 'The Curia Regis in the Late Twelfth and Early Thirteenth Centuries', *Historical Studies*, VI, no. 2, 1954.
——'An Early Justiciar's Writ', *Speculum*, XXXIV, 1959.
White, G. H. 'The Household of the Norman Kings', *Transactions of the Royal Historical Society*, 4th series, XXX, 1948.

Wilkinson, B. *The Chancery under Edward III*, Manchester, 1929.
—— 'The Government of England during King Richard's Absence on the Third Crusade', *Bulletin of the John Rylands Library*, Manchester, 1944.

Works of reference

The Concise Oxford Dictionary of English Place-Names, 3rd edn., ed. E. Ekwall, Oxford, 1947.
Handbook of British Chronology, ed. F. M. Powicke, London, 1939.

INDEX

Clerks (*cont.*)
the, 204; Ferrant the, 238; Richard
the, 34 n. 2; *see also* Chancery
Clinton, Geoffrey de, 23
Clipstone, 114, 191
Cluny, abbot and monks of, 54, 129
Coggeshall, Ralph of, 191 n. 1
Cognac, 209
Colchester: 39, 40; farm of, 166; eyre
in, 165 n. 2; tallaged, 166
Colebrook, 16 n. 1
Cologne, Reginald archbishop of, 41
Colwell, Gilbert of, 62
Comes palatii, 28
Connaught, king of, 147
Constable, the, 25
Corbeil, William of, 17
Corfe (Mullen, Dorset), 214
Cornerthe, John of, 239
Cornhill: Gervase of, 44, 47; Reginald
of, 123, 163–6 *passim*, 181, 198, 210,
222; William of, 235 n. 2
Cornwall: 11, 74; Earl Reginald of, 38;
earl of, 260; Henry son of the earl
of, 244, eyre in, 143, 146 n. 3;
sheriff of, 219, 244; tallaged, 142
Coroner, the, 91
Costock (Northants), 106 n.
Cotes (Derby), 266 and n. 4
Council: royal, 65, 67, 68, 80, 249,
262; of regency, 69; in administration, 225, 227–35 *passim*, 237,
241, 242, 246, 247, 254, 255; in
judicial procedure, 231–2, 257; at
the exchequer, 132, 238; composition of, 232–4; professional element in, 233
Court:
curia regis: 8, 9 n. 1, 15, 41, 52,
53 n. 2, 61 n. 4, 69, 74, 124, 139;
in Normandy, 2, 12, 28; presided over by the queen, 14; of
Henry II, 66, 108; of Richard I, 66,
72, 77, 78, 86; of King John, 110,
114, 226; of Henry III, 229, 232;
capitalis, 22 n. 7, 51, 58, 66, 88 and
n. 3, 91, 92, 144 n., 152, 162, 164;
at Westminster, 60, 62, 72, 77, 83,
84, 85, 87, 88 n. 3, 90, 92, 107 n. 6,
19

108 n. 2, 114, 115 and n. 6, 122,
162, 176, 198, 225; at exchequer,
21, 23, 46, 61, 67, 78, 82, 83, 176–
7; 'differentiation' of, 50, 53, 58,
61 and n. 3, 82, 160; justiciar pre-
sides over, 177; neither king nor
justiciar present, 255; rush of business into, 48, 95; composition of,
68, 83, 90; rolls of, 89, 90, 256;
oblata de curia, 60; *scriptor curie*, 50
coram rege: 114–15, 117, 125 n. 2, 133,
136, 143, 144–7 *passim*, 149, 156,
160, 168, 170, 196; composition of,
115, 141–61; after the loss of Normandy, 125, 133; rolls of, 115,
117 n. 1, 127, 134, 139, 140, 150,
151 n. 1; justiciar and, 133–9 *passim*, 141, 150, 168–70 *passim*;
travels with king, 134–6; actual
presence of king, 140, 144; pressure of business, 159; relations with
bench, 137
de banco: at Westminster, 84, 88, 114,
117, 118, 121–3, 133, 134, 144,
150 n. 2, 151 n. 1, 161–3, 165–97
passim, 231, 233, 237, 244, 247, 254;
distinct from exchequer, 85–7, 118;
relations with court *coram rege*,
114–15, 137; rolls of, 117 n. 1,
125 n. 2, 127, 134, 151; justiciar
and, 114–18, 133–4, 140, 151, 153–
5, 159–60; justices consult justiciar,
118, 156–8, 167–8; fiction of
justiciar's presence, 134 n. 4, 151–
2; cases removed *coram rege* by
order of the justiciar, 135 and n. 4;
justiciar's authority in, 158, 167–8;
justiciar absent from, 168, 252;
case reserved for king, 168; writs
of justiciar to, 153–5; composition
of, 143, 159, 161–5 *passim*, 201;
distinct from court *coram rege*, 141,
160; combines with, 150; prestige
of, 117, 156; pressure of business,
116; disappears under King John,
125 and n. 2, 161, 168–70 *passim*;
rolls of, 97, 117 n. 1, 125 n. 2, 127,
134, 151; *see also* Justices; Justiciar;
Writs

Leicester (*cont*).
35, 36, 265; eyre in, 22, 108 n. 2,
n. 3, 118, 163, 266–7; justiciar in,
94; sheriff of, 54, 71, 205 n. 1,
209; St Mary of, 265; abbot of,
117, 265 n. 3
Lenton, prior of, 149
Le Pré, 33
Les Andelys, 180
Le Sire, Geoffrey, 104 n. 3
Lessay, 8 n. 1
Letters patent: of the council, 230; of
Geoffrey fitz Peter, 131, 132 and
n. 3, 176; of King John, 248; of
the king, 188, 189, 196, 204, 206,
269; roll of, 247, 250, 270 n. 1;
see also Chancery, rolls of
Lewes, 149 n. 2, 168 n. 2
Lewisham, 44
Lewknor, 14
Lexington, Robert of, 254 and n. 4,
267, 268 and n. 3
Lichfield, dean of, 243
Lillebonne, 12
Limerick, 213 n. 2
Lincis, Urse de, 71
Lincoln: 71, 115, 183, 186 n. 4, 220 n. 4;
bishop of, 7; bishops: Robert, 15,
16; Alexander, 24; Walter, 74;
bishopric of, 51; castle of, 220 n. 4;
Fair of, 179; mayor and reeve of,
237; precentor of, 180; shire: 36;
eyre in, 62, 119, 149 n. 2, 257, 265,
268; final concords from, 142 n.
4; sheriff of, 49 and n. 1, 104 n. 2,
220, 221, 268 n. 5
Lisieux: Bishop Arnulf of, 28; Bishop
John of, 28
Little Barton (Essex), 101 n. 3
Little Nutley (Essex), 101 n. 3
Little Stamford (Essex), 101 n. 3
Llanthony, canons of, 32
Llantilio, castle of, 218
Llewellyn, prince of Wales, 132
Loches (Touraine), 124 n. 2, 180
London: 38 n. 3, 118, 123 n., 134, 184
n. 2; bishop of, 16, 21, 183 n. 4,
201, 259; Bishop Eustace of, 201;
chamberlain of, 234, 242; constable of Tower of, 267 and n. 2;
citizens of, 25; council at, 236 n. 1,
241 n. 1; justiciar at, 76; and at
Tower of, 150, 160 n. 1, 191, 194
n. 5, 195 n., 261; justices in, 165 n.
2; pleas at, 150, 160; royal justice
of, 32; sheriff of (and Middlesex),
25, 32, 200; Tower of, 26, 38, 40,
67, 95, 175 n. 4, 211, 222; vintners
of, 175; William of, 268 and n. 3;
see also Fitz Nigel; Westminster
Longchamps, Osbert de, 72; *see also*
Ely, bishop of
Long Compton (Warks), 100
Louis, prince of France, 213 n. 2, 224,
228
Luci: Godfrey de, 59; Philip de, 187 n.
6, 226 n. 2, 227 n.; Richard de,
justiciar of Henry II: 25, 26, 35, 70,
100, 101 and n. 3, 102, 147, 223 n.
1; barony of, 38–9; early career,
39; justiciarship of, 45–58 *passim*;
and the exchequer, 40–1, 45–6;
and justice, 42, 44 and n. 1, 46–9
passim; retirement of, 49–50, 53,
55; of Egremont, 268 n. 5
Ludgershall, 106
Ludham (Notts), 214
Lullingstone (Kent), 105 n. 3
Lupus, John, 148 n. 5; Robert, 230
Lusors, William de, 14, 129

Madox, T., 38 n. 3, 43 and n. 2
Magna Carta, 156, 211, 212, 215, 221,
223, 226, 227, 249, 258, 270; re-
issued, 224, 225, 228, 233, 258
Maitland, F. W., 86 n. 1
Maldon (Essex), 104 n. 1
Malet, Robert, 8, 54; William, 211 n. 1
Malherbe, Adam, 38
Malmesbury: 181; William of, 17;
castle of, 17
Mandeville: Geoffrey de, baron of King
Stephen, 46, 99–100; Geoffrey de
(II), 100; Geoffrey de (III), 106 n.,
188, 189 n. 4, 207 n. 3, 208 and n. 2,
215; Robert de, 43; Earl William
de, regent of Richard I, 65–7, 87,
100, 188, 207; William de, son of